FAMILY DRIVEN FAITH

FAMILY DRIVEN FAITH

DOING WHAT IT TAKES TO RAISE SONS
AND DAUGHTERS WHO WALK WITH GOD

VODDIE BAUCHAM JR.

CROSSWAY BOOKS

A PUBLISHING MINISTRY OF
GOOD NEWS PUBLISHERS
WHEATON, ILLINOIS

Library of Congress Cataloging-in-Publication Data
Baucham, Voddie
    Family driven faith : doing what it takes to raise sons and daughters
who walk with God / Voddie T. Baucham, Jr.
        p. cm.
    ISBN 13: 978-1-58134-929-0 (hc : alk. paper)
    ISBN 10: 1-58134-929-7
    1. Parenting—Religious aspects—Christianity. 2. Child rearing—
Religious aspects—Christianity. 3. Christian education—Home training.
I. Title.
BV4529.B378   2007
248.8'45—dc22   2007000388

LB		17	16	15	14	13	12	11	10	09	08	07
15	14	13	12	11	10	9	8	7	6	5	4	3	2	1

To Jasmine, Trey, Elijah, Asher, and
other "arrows" yet to come

Soli Deo Gloria!

CONTENTS

1

THE LAY OF THE LAND

It's 10 o'clock. Do you know where your children are?" If you are part of my mom's generation, you recognize that saying. You probably heard it each evening before you watched the nightly news. The idea was simple enough: parents ought to make sure their children are in the house at a decent hour. Who would argue with that (other than a teenager wanting to stay out late)?

Today the question should be asked this way: "Do you know where your children are *spiritually*?" Is little Johnny biblically literate? Does Sally know the difference between virginity and purity? Are your children on the road to responsible Christian adulthood, or are they part of an alarming new trend that has seen the overwhelming majority of so-called Christian children walk away from the faith?

As I was writing this book I had the privilege of preaching a series of sermons at Palm Beach Atlantic University. In the Thursday morning chapel service I preached a message on biblical manhood. I basically walked through Ephesians 5:25ff. and issued a challenge to the young men and women to live up to and expect nothing less than the biblical standard when considering marriage. It was a powerful experience. I knew I had hit a nerve.

After the message I had an opportunity to talk to a number of students who had never heard such a challenge. Even faculty and staff members walked up to me and said, "I wish my father had shared that with me twenty years ago." Several young ladies asked if they could speak with me privately. A number of young men remarked, "You really raised the bar." The campus was buzzing.

One young woman who was obviously wrestling with what she had heard sat down next to me during lunch, took a deep breath, and began to share her heartbreaking story. She was a twenty-one-year-old junior who was wrestling with a serious relationship. She said that she loved a young man very much, but he was none of the things that the Bible clearly taught a prospective husband must be. She began to fight back tears as she asked, "What am I going to do?"

As I probed, I discovered that she had been seeing the young man for over two years. The two of them were "very serious," and although she did not say so, I would be very surprised if they did not have a sexual relationship. She had obviously been agonizing over the future of this relationship long before my sermon, but what she heard that morning pushed her over the edge. However, the relationship was so serious and had lasted so long that she wondered if she needed a support group to help her get over it. I asked her if she knew any mature Christian women who could help her through this difficult time; she did not. I asked her if she was part of a Bible study or a small group; she was not. I asked if she was attending a church; she was not.

I spent half an hour with this young woman. At the end of that half hour I tried to think about her situation from the perspective of a father whose daughter is just a few years younger than this young lady. Immediately my heart began to break. This young woman to whom I was speaking had grown up in the church. She came from a good family. In fact, her family was so committed to her and to her future that they sent her off to an expensive, private, Christian university. However, just a few years after leaving home she was not attending church, had invested two years in a relationship with a young man who had also abandoned the church, and had developed a worldview that was anything but biblical.

Unfortunately, this is not an isolated incident. According to researchers, between 70 and 88 percent of Christian teens are leaving the church by their second year in college.[1] That's right, modern American Christianity has a failure rate somewhere around eight (almost nine) out of ten when it comes to raising children who continue in the faith. Imagine the alarm if nearly 90 percent of our children couldn't read when they left high school. There wouldn't be room enough at school board meetings to hold all of the irate parents.

While these numbers are astonishing, they should not be surprising. Over the past several years a number of researchers have discovered that the overwhelming majority of our teenagers who still attend church and identify themselves as Christians have belief systems that mitigate their claims. Researcher George Barna, for example, discovered that 85 percent of "born again teens" do not believe in the existence of absolute truth.[2] Over 60 percent agreed with the statement, "nothing can be known for sure except the things you experience in your own life."[3] More than half of those surveyed believed that Jesus sinned during His earthly life!

Christian Smith and his research team at the University of North Carolina, Chapel Hill conducted the largest study of teen religion to date. Their research was published in a book called *Soul Searching*. The National Study of Youth and Religion discovered that while U.S. teens are very religious, their religion is largely ambiguous. This ambiguity is due in large part to the lack of time and attention devoted to spiritual matters compared to other activities. Smith notes:

> Our research suggests that religious congregations *are* losing out to school and the media for the time and attention of youth. When it comes to the *formation* of the lives of youth, viewed sociologically, faith communities typically get a very small seat at the end of the table for a very limited period of time. The youth-formation table is dominated structurally by more powerful and vocal actors. Hence . . . most teens know details about television characters and pop stars, but many are quite vague about Moses and Jesus. Most youth are well versed about the dangers of drunk driving, AIDS, and drugs, but many haven't a clue about their own tradition's core ideas. Many parents also clearly prioritize homework and sports over church or youth group attendance.[4]

As a result, Smith and his research team found that "The majority of American teenagers appear to espouse rather inclusive, pluralistic, and individualistic views about religious truth, identity boundaries, and the need for religious congregation."[5] In other words, the culture of secular humanism appears to have co-opted America's Christian teens.

Thus we should not be surprised that young people are fleeing the church in droves. Why would anyone remain faithful to an organization with which they largely disagree? How could anyone remain faithful to a belief system that is relegated to the outskirts of their lives? The problem is not that these children are leaving Christianity. The problem is that most of them, by their own admission, are not Christian! Hence their leaving makes complete sense. The apostle John put it best when he wrote:

> *They went out from us, but they were not really of us; for if they had been of us, they would have remained with us; but they went out, so that it would be shown that they all are not of us. (1 John 2:19)*

I realize that I just opened a can of worms, but this can needs to be opened. What if Christian parents are going through life convinced that their children are regenerate when in fact they are not? What if our sons and daughters are merely going through the motions as they walk through life as goats among the sheep or tares among the wheat? What if that four- or five-year-old we baptized because he or she was able to look out at the congregation and parrot the words, "Jesus is in my heart" was just saying what he or she had been conditioned to say?

Unfortunately, this is far from unusual among Christians in our culture. Thom Rainer's research among Southern Baptists (arguably the most "evangelistic" denomination in America) indicates that "nearly one-half of all church members may not be Christians."[6] This is not just disturbing for SBC churches—it is indicative of a much larger problem. Thousands, if not millions, of people have been manipulated into "repeat after me" prayers and "if you ever want to see that dearly departed loved one again . . ." altar calls without a trace of the Spirit's regenerating power.

My goal here is not to get parents to doubt their children's salvation. I am simply trying to sound a desperately needed alarm. It is as though Christian parents in America have been lulled to sleep while the thief has come in to steal, kill, and destroy our children right under our noses (see John 10:10). I didn't write this book as an expert with all of the answers. I am just a minister who has seen this alarming trend over the past decade and a father with a desire to see his family characterized by multigenerational faithfulness.

Two Sides of Life

There are two sides to my life. One is personal, the other professional. On the one hand I am a preacher, a writer, an elder in a local church, and a professor. This side of my life is rich, full, and rewarding. This is the place where people call me doctor and reverend. It is this side of my life that has taken me all over the country preaching, teaching, and lecturing. This is the side of my life that puts food on the table and brings me before thousands. It would be easy for me to get caught up in the professional side of my life. However, there is another side of me, a far more important side.

The most important side of my life is the one where I bear my most cherished titles—husband and father. There is nothing in this world that means more to me than the fact that I am Bridget's husband and Asher, Jasmine, Trey, and Elijah's father. Whenever I say that, I can almost hear people thinking, "Shouldn't your relationship with Christ mean more to you than your family life?" I guess in an ultimate sense that is the case. However, my family is the primary place where my walk with Christ takes on flesh. It is one thing for me to have a personal relationship with Jesus. However, if I spend hours reading the Bible and praying and invest the lion's share of my time ministering to others while neglecting my role as husband and father, my relationship with Christ is out of balance or, worse, inauthentic.

It is my relationship with my wife and children that gives my walk with Christ legitimacy. Jesus made this point clear in Matthew's Gospel:

> *But when the Pharisees heard that Jesus had silenced the Sadducees, they gathered themselves together. One of them, a lawyer, asked Him a question, testing Him, "Teacher, which is the great commandment in the Law?" And He said to him, "'YOU SHALL LOVE THE LORD YOUR GOD WITH ALL YOUR HEART, AND WITH ALL YOUR SOUL, AND WITH ALL YOUR MIND.' This is the great and*

foremost commandment. The second is like it, 'YOU SHALL LOVE YOUR NEIGHBOR AS YOURSELF.' On these two commandments depend the whole Law and the Prophets." (22:34-40)

If my wife doesn't qualify as my neighbor, who does? How could I possibly make an argument for the integrity of my walk with Christ if I can't love my closest neighbors?

John puts an even finer point on it when he writes:

The one who says he is in the Light and yet hates his brother is in the darkness until now. The one who loves his brother abides in the Light and there is no cause for stumbling in him. But the one who hates his brother is in the darkness and walks in the darkness, and does not know where he is going because the darkness has blinded his eyes. (1 John 2:9-11)

Here again the Bible makes it clear that my earthly relationships are the proving ground for my heavenly one. If I love God, it will be evident in my love for my brothers and sisters (especially those who live under my roof).

In fact, my very status as a minister of the gospel is contingent upon how well I conduct myself as a husband and father. While there are many qualities a minister must possess, there are but two *skills* required of those who would serve in positions of pastoral leadership. First, one must be able to teach. Second, he must manage his household well (see 1 Timothy 3, Titus 1, and 1 Peter 5). In other words, if I am not a good husband, I am not qualified to lead God's people. Moreover, if I have not performed in an exemplary fashion as I strive to raise my children in the nurture and admonition of the Lord, I have no business shepherding God's flock. "If a man does not know how to manage his own household, how will he take care of the church of God?" (1 Timothy 3:5).

Unfortunately, this is a foreign concept to most Christians in our culture. Most pastoral search committees never even bother to meet a man's wife and children, let alone observe him at home or question those close enough to know how he teaches the Word to his family, leads them in family worship, disciplines, instructs, and encourages his children, or loves his wife.

This may seem like a separate issue, but I assure you it is right on point. The fact that we no longer require exemplary family life from those who lead us is indicative of the fact that we have dropped the ball on this issue from the top down. In fact the term *preacher's kid* has become a euphemism for the poorly behaved, rebellious, oft-neglected sons and daughters of our leaders. If our leaders are failing as husbands and fathers, what hope is there for the rest of our families?

One Man's Journey

My wife, Bridget, and I were married my sophomore year in college. I had just turned twenty years old. In fact, I didn't even have a driver's license. I remember that because I had to go get one in order to apply for a marriage license. We were two youngsters setting out on an incredible journey. We had no idea how difficult things would be, nor did we realize how soon our difficulties would begin.

When the two of us set out on this journey, we knew we wouldn't have much help. Neither Bridget nor I come from ideal family backgrounds. In fact, over the past two generations on both sides of our family there have been twenty-five marriages and twenty-two divorces, a fact that is even more astonishing when you realize that our marriage is one of the three that hasn't ended in divorce. It didn't take long for us to realize that we were going to have to look elsewhere for role models.

Ultimately this book is about our journey. I have gone from a clueless twenty-year-old kid trying to figure out how to stay married, to a semi-clueless, battle-hardened thirty-eight-year-old veteran father of two teenagers, a toddler, and another one coming soon, and our family has been richly blessed in the process. I have seen the difference that observing the biblical model can make. I have watched God bring other young couples to our door seeking advice because of the evidence they see in our lives.

More importantly, I have seen God use us in our family as those around us have watched Him work. One of the greatest compliments I have ever received (twice) came from two of my younger female cousins. In two separate discussions about marriage and family they both said to me, "I don't just want to get married—I want what you and Bridget have." I was floored! When I look at our family, all I tend to see are the flaws, those places where we fall short and need to do better. However, God sometimes uses those around me to remind me how far He has brought us.

Bridget and I have spent years trying to figure out how to keep three commitments. First, we are committed to staying together and thriving as a couple. Second, we are committed to investing in our children with a view toward multigenerational faithfulness. Finally, we are committed to doing whatever we can to reproduce the first two commitments in the lives of others. This book is just a feeble effort to keep the third commitment.

A Wide-screen Family in a Full-screen World

My family and I love movies. We mark our calendars when a new family film is scheduled to be released and do our best to get to the theater on the day the movie comes out. We also love to watch movies at home. Our DVD library is quite extensive. In fact, we sometimes have friends come by to borrow movies from us instead of running down to the local video store. We also have several friends and family members who come by from time to time for a Movie Night.

Sometimes, however, we have a bit of a problem with our less media-savvy visitors. There are times when Movie Night turns into Fight Night as debates break out. I'm not talking about debates over whether to watch a comedy or a drama; our disagreements are far more fundamental than that. I'm talking about the dreaded wide-screen versus full-screen debate. You see, we are strictly a wide-screen family. In fact, we have taken movies back to the store after discovering that we mistakenly picked up the full-screen version. However, some of our friends and family are convinced that the black edges on the top and bottom of the screen are indications that they must be missing something.

The most intense and longest running wide-screen versus full-screen debate was the one between my brother-in-law and me. This debate went on for years! Moreover, the debate persisted even after I had more than proven my point.

One day he and I were out with all of our children, and we decided to stop by our favorite electronics store. As usual, we went in for one thing and came out with twelve. However, while the kids and I were walking around the store, we lost track of Uncle Kevin. Eventually we found him standing in front of the big-screen plasma TVs watching the end of one of his favorite movies. We all stood there watching the marching band scene in the movie *Drumline*, and Kevin said two things that should have ended our debate forever.

First, he said, "I never knew what the formation was." As he watched the band on the field during their climactic performance, he could finally see that their formation made the number 2001. Second, he said, "Now I see what you mean when you say I've been missing a third of the movie." Finally! After all these years I had finally convinced my brother-in-law that wide-screen movies only appear to cut off part of the film, when in reality it is the full-screen version that cheats viewers. It was then that he said the words that continue to resonate in my mind. In a moment of complete honesty, he looked at me and said, "I still can't stand those black bars."

In other words, even though he was now completely aware of the benefits of wide-screen movies, he was not willing to leave the full-screen world. At that point all I could do was shake my head and walk away. Eventually he gave in, and I am proud to say that he now enjoys wide-screen films. While this was a rather silly argument between two very opinionated men, it illustrates the power of perception and the danger of failing to question the status quo.

In June 2004 Bill O'Reilly interviewed the author of a new book, *Home Invasion*. The author, Rebecca Hagelin, was a mother of three who had very strict views on her children's consumption of media and entertainment. Mr. O'Reilly asked the woman if her seventeen-year-old son watched MTV. To his astonishment, the woman said no. Furthermore, she explained that as a result of the moral foundation she and her husband laid in their children's lives, her son had no desire to consume such things. At this point O'Reilly was completely taken aback. He made several tongue-in-cheek statements, but his basic message was, "You're lucky to have children who are willing to stand for such nonsense." At one point he said, "I would have run away."

I am not arguing that Bill O'Reilly is the standard-bearer for parenting. However, his view is very consistent with the views I have heard expressed by many Christian parents. I can't tell you how many times my wife and I have been told that we are stifling our children because they are only allowed to watch four hours of television per week (the national average has been stated as four and a half to five hours per day) or because my fifteen-year-old daughter is not allowed to date. Inevitably we hear the standard cop-out argument, "When they get to college, they're going to go crazy!" Interestingly, though, none of the "wild ones" I remember from my college days were rookies. None of them went off the deep end into immorality after leading chaste lives at home. Most of them simply walked farther into the debauchery with which they were allowed to experiment earlier on.

There is a larger issue at stake here. The question is not whether or not our children sin later in life. The question is, *do we have a biblical obligation to train them before they leave home?* Is there any biblical validity to the idea that Christian parents should allow their children to experiment with ungodliness?

Many families have been lulled into what I like to call a full-screen view of parenting. We look at the biblical mandate and compare it to societal norms, and there appears to be something missing. We believe that somehow we are depriving our children of experiences that will make them more liked, more respected, more normal. Hence we trade in the biblical standard for a cultural norm that hovers just below mediocrity. All of a sudden our desires for our children change. Now all we want for our kids is what "every other parent" wants for their children.

The result is a generation about whom Christian Smith has written, "Religion seems to become rather compartmentalized and backgrounded in the lives and experiences of most U.S. teenagers."[7] This compartmentalization is completely understandable in light of the minimal weight given to spiritual matters. Smith explains:

This is not surprising. It simply reflects the fact that there is very little built-in religious content or connection in the structure of most U.S. adolescents' daily schedules and routines. Most U.S. teenagers' lives are dominated by school and homework.[8]

He continues:

Many are involved in sports and other clubs besides. Most teens also spend lots of time with their friends just hanging out or doing things like going to the mall or bowling. In addition, most teens devote a great deal of life to watching television and movies, e-mailing or instant messaging friends, listening to music, and consuming other electronic media. Boyfriends and girlfriends sometimes consume a lot of teenage time and attention as well.[9]

It seems there are a few things that we deem more important for our children than growing in grace. Let's consider three of them.

Making the Grade

Ask parents what they want most for their children, and you will likely get the same answer whether they are Christians or garden-variety unbelievers. They will likely say, "I want my children to get a good education." In fact, that's exactly what George Barna found when he interviewed Christian and non-Christian parents. The number one goal they had for their children was that they would get a good education.[10]

I'm not suggesting there is anything wrong with emphasizing education for our children. On the contrary, my wife and I are fanatics when it comes to our children's education. However, our children's education is not our primary goal. Our primary goal for our children is that they walk with the Lord. Unfortunately, the aforementioned study found that only half as many parents (whether Christian or not) considered their children's having a relationship with Christ as important as their child's education.[11]

This is a prime example of a full-screen view of parenting. The world's limited view of life says that the most important thing we can do is get good grades, go to a good (read: reputable, high-profile) college, get out of school, and get a good job so we can make more money than our mom and dad did. What a limited view of what's really important! There is more to life than making the grade.

Making the Team

Another full-screen issue is found in the ever-so-popular arena of sports. Not long ago I had the privilege of sharing my views on biblical parenting with several classes at one of the world's largest seminaries. One of the things the students found most intriguing was the fact that my wife and I homeschool our children (more about that later). Several students asked me the same question: "What about sports?" Their curiosity was piqued even more when I responded, "Who cares?" They didn't know if I was being provocative or if I had simply taken leave of my senses. Inevitably they would follow up with something like, "How do your kids learn teamwork and sportsmanship?" Or "How do your children learn to be competitive?" At this point I answered their question with another question. "How did Thomas Jefferson, Benjamin Franklin, or George Washington learn those things?" Better yet, since Jesus is our ultimate model of Christian manhood, how did He learn those things? Was Jesus in Little League?

I'm not trying to say that it is necessarily wrong for children to play organized sports. My point is simply this: Being a member of an organized traveling baseball squad at age ten doesn't add a single day to one's life. In fact, many of these activities get in the way of much loftier pursuits. People turned boys into men and girls into women for most of recorded history without dragging them around town with their tongues hanging out in an effort to keep up with their overachieving, undereducated, theologically illiterate peers as they try to win trophies that will eventually gather dust in a basement somewhere.

If I teach my son to keep his eye on the ball but fail to teach him to keep his eyes on Christ, I have failed as a father. We must refuse to allow trivial, temporal pursuits to interfere with the main thing. Making the team is a tremendous achievement; however, it must be put in its proper perspective. No sports endeavor will ever be as important as becoming a man or woman of God.

Making Time

One Monday evening several years ago I was scheduled to meet at a large gathering at a prominent Houston church. I had preached at this church several times before, so I was no stranger to the members of the congregation. As I entered the building, a gentleman walked up behind me and asked if I needed any help carrying some books and tapes I had brought with me. I was grateful for his kindness and gladly accepted his offer.

As the man grabbed a box under my arms, he handed it to a strapping young lad who he introduced as his "future son-in-law." I was immediately struck by this young man's boyish appearance. As it turned out, the young man was fifteen years old. Moments later a thirteen-year-old girl walked up, and he introduced her as his daughter and the young man's "girlfriend." It took every ounce of restraint I had not to shout, "What are you thinking?" I wanted to ask this man if he had any idea what it meant for a father to protect his daughter's purity. I wanted to ask him if he had any idea how much pressure he was putting on these two teenagers by going around talking about their impending marriage. Moreover, I wanted to put him in a head-lock and . . . but I digress.

Modern American dating is no more than glorified divorce practice. Young people are learning how to give themselves away in exclusive, romantic, highly committed (at times sexual) relationships, only to break up and do it all over again. God never intended for His kids to live like this. And instead of stepping in and doing something, many Christian parents simply view these types of relationships as a normal and necessary part of growing up. Unless your child is wiser than Solomon, stronger than Samson, and more godly than David (all of whom sinned sexually), they are susceptible to sexual sin, and these premature relationships serve as open invitations.

I want my children to grow up and find mates. I can't wait to walk my daughter down the aisle. I can't wait to see my sons go out and buy rings for that special someone. However, at this point there are more important things in life. Besides, being involved in such exclusive relationships before you are ready to be married is like going shopping without any money; either you will leave frustrated, or you will take something that doesn't belong to you.

Making the team, making the grade, making time—all of these are fine in their proper context. The problem is, they have replaced more important pursuits. Instead of striving for godliness and multigenerational faithfulness, many Christians have settled for just getting by. Unfortunately, our children are paying the price. There is, however, a better way. God's Word has given us a road map to follow.

The Anti-Marriage Culture

Another area where we tend to have a full-screen attitude is marriage. The January 2005 issue of *Time* magazine featured an article on the extension of adolescence in our culture. Young adults in America are acting more and more like children every day. They leave home for college only to return after graduation, and often without jobs. They are also getting married later in life.

R. Albert Mohler, president of the Southern Baptist Theological Seminary in Louisville, set off a firestorm in August 2005 when he told a radio audience: "The sin that I think besets this generation . . . is the sin of delaying marriage as a lifestyle option among those who intend some day to get married but they just haven't yet."[12] Numerous media outlets picked up on Mohler's comments, which apparently enraged many Christians. However, I believe Mohler is on to something.

As I travel across the country, I am amazed at the number of intelligent, Jesus-loving, Bible-toting, ministry-minded young men who absolutely refuse to grow up and take a wife! It is as though there was a new book of the Bible discovered (I call it 2 Hesitations) that reads, "Thou shalt not marry prior to graduate school, or at least until you have a middle-class income and a 401(k)." The only thing worse is looking into the eyes of the scores of young women who ask me what they have to do to get these guys to man up and marry them.

Perhaps it's the skyrocketing divorce rate that has young men and women backing away from marriage. Or maybe it is the bad marriages they witnessed growing up. Then again it could be that the cost of living has soared so high that one needs significantly more income to support a wife. However, if you ask me I believe the answer is none of the above. The young men and women I meet actually believe there is something out there that they need to experience before they dive into the deep, dark, oppressive world of marriage. For some it is traveling to Europe or Africa. Others want to spend time on the mission field first. Still others believe there is some magic age at which one automatically becomes "ready" for marriage. Whatever the case may be, it is a far cry from the biblical admonition, "He who finds a wife finds a good thing and obtains favor from the LORD" (Proverbs 18:22).

The Anti-Child Culture

I often have the privilege of preaching to college students. I say privilege because I absolutely love the challenge and potential inherent in every one of these encounters. I am excited by the potential of God using me to speak into the life of a young man or woman whose situation in life affords him or her the freedom to say, "Sure, Lord, why not?" Where else can a preacher give a message on missions and have someone walk up at the end and say, "I needed to hear that" or "I have been wondering whether or not I should go to Eastern Europe next year, and I think I have my answer"? However, I have discovered one challenge that today's Christian college students are often unwilling to embrace—the challenge of parenting.

One passage I love to share with college students is Acts 1:6-8. The outline of my message is simple: God has a purpose that is larger than you—God has a plan that includes you—God has a place that suits you. The response is usually very positive. That is, until I begin to apply the last point.

I direct the students' attention to verse 8 where Jesus says, "You will receive power when the Holy Spirit has come upon you; and you shall be My witnesses both in Jerusalem, in all Judea and Samaria, and even to the remotest part of the earth." I point out that not everyone who heard Jesus made it to the remotest parts of the earth. In fact, many of them never made it to Samaria. The point, of course, is that not every person is called to the same type or place of ministry. I go on to apply this truth to the lives of the students by suggesting that each of them has a place of ministry that fits them to a T and that finding that place should be the passionate pursuit of their lives. Sounds harmless enough, right?

Several months ago I was teaching this at a retreat for a church tucked away securely in the Bible Belt. During that retreat I suggested that for some of those college students the application of this biblical principle might mean earning a linguistics degree and translating the Bible into the languages of unreached people groups. As I looked across the room at the approving wide eyes and nodding heads, I added, "Others of you, however, may be called to have large families and train your five or six kids in righteousness so that they will in turn impact the world for Christ." You could have cut the tension with a proverbial knife. This room full of approving, eager young men and women turned into a convention of Martians hearing English spoken for the first time. They looked at me as if to say, "That was a good one. When are you going to say, 'Just kidding'?"

I took that opportunity to make an important observation. I pointed out the obvious discomfort in the room and asked, "When did we begin to hate children?" Suddenly the attitude in the room changed. These young people were being forced to examine a cultural assumption that has been allowed to trump biblical truth for far too long in our culture. Again Mohler places his finger firmly on the pulse of the culture when he writes, "Christians must recognize that this rebellion against parenthood represents nothing less than an absolute revolt against God's design."[13]

The idea that motherhood, fatherhood, and family are not as honorable as high-income careers or highly visible ministry positions is biblically uninformed at best and grossly heretical at worst. This attitude has been manifested in numerous ways in recent years both inside and outside the church. In fact, it was this attitude that led me and my wife to the most painful decision of our lives.

Bridget and I had our first baby ten months after we got married. Our next child came along three years later. During those three years we heard from every person in our life at the time that having our first child so soon was a mistake (thus the three-year gap). We were also informed that if our second child was a boy (our firstborn is a girl), we would have "the perfect *little* family."

After Bridget became pregnant with our son, the pressure was on. Countless well-meaning people were whispering in Bridget's ear. Some warned, "Girl, you'd better not get stuck with a bunch of kids." Others tried to be more diplomatic and simply pointed out how much the cost of college tuition had risen, or the price of groceries. Unfortunately, the voices in our ear trumped the voice of God. When Trey was born, we hired a doctor to speak to God on our behalf. He took his scalpel and sutures and told God, "The Bauchams hereby declare that they no longer trust, nor welcome you in this area of their lives."

Several years later my wife knelt before me with tears in her eyes and asked me two things. First, she asked if I would forgive her for closing her womb. Second, she asked me if it would be all right if she got the procedure reversed. I was floored. I couldn't hold back the tears as I told her how wrong I was to sit back and let it happen and how happy I would be to make it right.

We went to a specialist the next week. Unfortunately, we discovered that what the doctors had done could not be reversed. I wanted to crawl under a rock. I wanted to go back in time and grab my twenty-three-year-old self by the collar and say, "Don't you dare let this happen!" It was at that moment that we decided to extend our family through adoption. As I write, we have one adopted child and are on call for baby number four at any moment. We cannot go back and undo what we did. However, we can shout from the rooftops until all who hear us know that children are a blessing and that God opens and closes the womb. We must receive children with joy instead of bemoaning their birth.

You Have How Many Children?

The Johnsons are a loving, committed Christian couple in their thirties. They are active in their church and community. They are also very serious about their responsibility as parents. Their children are among the most thoughtful and well-behaved you will ever meet. However, one day the Johnsons found themselves embroiled in a church controversy. What had this godly Christian couple done? They got pregnant . . . *again!*

The Johnsons had five small children when they joined the young marrieds Sunday school class. At first they paid little attention to their fellow class members' snide remarks. Like any couple with five small children, they were used to the typical, "Don't you guys have a TV?" and "Haven't you figured out how to stop that?" In fact, they just chalked it up to innocent fun. However, when they announced that they were pregnant again—and this time with twins—the comments turned ugly.

Suddenly people in their Sunday school class began to question their wisdom, their responsibility, and their sanity. The problem got so far out of hand that one of the pastors had to be brought in to address the situation. When pressed for a biblical basis for their outrage over the size of the Johnsons' family, the offended members of the class could only say, "If God wanted us to have that many children, he wouldn't have given us birth control." Another gentleman in the class asked, "How are they going to afford to send that many kids to college?" A young lady in the class, looking at the situation through the eyes of a busy mother of two, added, "I know how much work motherhood is, and I just think it's inconsiderate of him to pile that much on her plate."

The size of our families has become a matter of income and convenience. Our attitude toward children is, "A boy for me and a girl for you, then praise the Lord, we're finally through!" I am amazed at the number of people I meet who live in two-thousand-square-foot homes with two cars parked outside and argue that they can only "afford" to have one or two children. Amazing! Our forebears successfully raised houses full of children in homes that we would now consider meager at best, but we can't afford it.

Before you throw this book down (or have a heart attack), I am not suggesting that everyone has to have seven children. I think there are legitimate reasons to limit family size. However, I have only met a handful of people whose family size was limited for any of those legitimate reasons. I usually meet people who stopped having kids because they got their boy and their girl, so they're "the perfect 'little' family."

Or I meet people who have calculated (and extrapolated) the cost of their children's college education, their annual vacation, and their early retirement and determined that 1.9 children is their break-even point. I also meet people whose children are undisciplined, untrained, and out of control, so they find it too stressful to have more kids. Rare is the couple who left the doctor's office with a legitimate warning against further pregnancies.

A New Lesson from an Old Source

God has not left us to wander aimlessly in the wilderness as we raise our children. He has given us a blueprint for multigenerational faithfulness. That blueprint is expressed throughout the Bible, but there is one place where it reads like a how-to manual. That place is Deuteronomy 6.

I must admit that I haven't always liked the book of Deuteronomy. In fact, the first time I read it, I didn't like it at all. It seemed as though the God whom I had come to know and love in the Gospels and epistles of the New Testament was absent in the book of Deuteronomy. I remember my astonishment the first time I realized that the Mosaic Law unapologetically called for stoning in cases of disobedience and lawbreaking. I was also put off by what I considered archaic laws and regulations.

That all changed when I learned how pivotal the book of Deuteronomy is in the overall structure of the Bible. Moreover, I was amazed at the frequency with which Jesus quoted from Deuteronomy and its companion, Leviticus. Eventually I came to love this book of the Law. I have also grown to appreciate its relevance in my everyday life. That's right, I said Deuteronomy is relevant today! Much of its relevance, however, is lost on those of us who have been unwilling to press forward in our attempts to read, understand, and appreciate the Old Testament.

Think about it—Moses sits down and examines the situation. Israel is on the threshold of a monumental occasion. They are about to possess "the Promised Land." They had an opportunity forty years earlier but were unwilling to trust God to defeat the inhabitants of Canaan. Two lone voices, Joshua and Caleb, stood out in the crowd as

Caleb said, "We should by all means go up and take possession of it, for we will surely overcome it" (Numbers 13:30). However, the people sided with the naysayers and did not go forward.

Now, forty years later, Israel once again stands on the verge of possessing the Promised Land, and Moses, the great leader that he was, decided to give them a few final instructions. Thus he stood before the people to give the law again. Thus the book bears the name Deuteronomy (*deutero* = repeat; *nomos* = law), a restating of the Law.

What would you say to a group of believers about to enter a land occupied by pagans? What would you say to the faithful if you knew their faith would be challenged at every turn? What would you say to a group of people upon whom the burden of carrying and representing the covenant message of God rested? Moses knew exactly what to say. He gave them God's word. That word echoes through the halls of history and still resonates today.

You and I desperately need the words of Moses' challenge. You and I are living in an age and in a culture that is tearing at the very fabric of the Christian community. How many of us look at our teen-aged sons and daughters and know they are not with us? How many of us lay our heads on the pillow at night and know that as soon as our kids leave the house they are probably going to leave the faith as well? All of the statistics point to children leaving when they get to college, but my experience and my conversations with Christian parents leads me to believe that the problem manifests itself much earlier.

I am often stopped after a sermon by a mother fighting back tears as she asks, "What can I do?" These women want to know what they can do to intervene in the life of their teenagers who are on the way out. I am often stopped by fathers who shake their heads as they say, "I wish I had heard this twenty years ago." I try to offer comfort as I encourage them to try to make an investment in their grandchildren.

Not long ago a father stopped me after I shared a message on multigenerational faithfulness and said, "Wait right here." He gathered up his whole family, admitted his failure to live according to the biblical mandate, and asked me to pray for him right then and there. Another gentleman came up to me after a message, grabbed my shoulders, and sobbed as he pleaded, "Tell me it's not too late." On another occasion the mother of a rebellious teenaged daughter who had grown up in the church grabbed my hands and said, "Please pray for my daughter; she has left home, and I don't know where she is." Over and over I am reminded of how high the stakes are in this battle. We are not talking about children getting bad grades or even getting in trouble with the law. We are talking about young men and women turning their backs on the faith of their fathers, and worse, on God Himself.

I don't know that this book will answer all of your questions or address all of your issues, but I will promise you this: I am going to show you how to get into the fight. Something simply must be done. We cannot stand idly by while our children leave the faith in droves. We cannot simply shake our heads and accept defeat. We must fight for our sons and daughters.

The other day I looked at my teenaged daughter while we were walking through the mall. Suddenly I found myself choked up as I thought about how much time was behind us compared to the amount of time ahead. I just cried out to God and prayed, *Lord, help me make the most of the time.*

There are many worthwhile pursuits in this world, but few of them rise to the level of training our children to follow the Lord and keep His commandments. I desperately want my sons and daughters to walk with God, and I am willing to do whatever it takes, whatever the Bible says I must do in order to be used by God as a means to that end. My prayer for you is that God would awaken in you that same passion. Something tells me He already has.

2

A GOD WITH NO RIVALS

Hear, O Israel! The LORD is our God, the LORD is one!
DEUTERONOMY 6:4

When I got married, I knew that my "Big Man on Campus" days were over. I was not under the illusion that I could maintain relationships with other women and expect to foster the bond between my wife and me. By the way, if you are one of those men who believes that God made men and women with the ability to "just be friends" and that your wife should be more understanding of your platonic relationships with other women, I have a newsflash: Plato is about to ruin your marriage!

I thought I had it all under control. My little black book was gone; my phone number was changed; I had taken care of *almost* everything. Then it happened! My wife decided to go through a locked chest where I kept some old papers. Bridget and I looked through the chest together as I told her the story behind every item. There were recruiting letters, newspaper clippings, and medals from my days as a high school athlete. There were media guides from more recent college football games. Then there, beneath the memorabilia, tucked away at the bottom of the chest, were several letters from old girlfriends. Who is Tracy? What about Jill? My life flashed before my eyes. All I could say was, "You know this trunk hasn't been opened since *long* before we got married!"

We have often looked back on that night and laughed. But at the time it wasn't very funny. It was as though unwanted, unwelcome strangers had invaded our home. In a way my wife's turf had been trampled. I can't imagine what it would have been like if it had been more than old letters. What if I had an old girlfriend calling the house? What if I had an affair?

An Affair of the Soul

While we can all understand the serious nature of an extramarital affair, we often fail to realize that allegiance to God's spiritual rivals is no different. A chef on a recent cooking show illustrated the carelessness of which many of us are guilty. She had baked some Bundt cakes and was about to remove them from the pan. She loosened the cakes, turned over the pan, tapped the bottom to further loosen the cakes, and then offered a brief prayer. "Lord, please don't let 'em stick," she said as she looked up toward the sky. She then successfully removed the pan, revealing perfect (unstuck) Bundt cakes. She wiped the back of her hand across her brow and said, "Alright, a little good karma."

This woman wasn't trying to declare allegiance to both the Lord of the Bible and the Hindu/Buddhist deities of the New Age Movement. However, that is exactly what she did. Imagine if she had done the same thing to her husband. I can just see it. "Bill, please get those Bundt cakes out." Bill accomplishes the task without a single cake sticking, and then she looks at a picture of her ex-boyfriend Tom and says, "Praise Tom, they came out right!" If you think this is an exaggeration, you may need to reconsider what the Bible says about God's jealousy concerning His name and His glory:

> [F]or you shall not worship any other god, for the LORD, whose name is Jealous, is a jealous God—otherwise you might make a covenant with the inhabitants of the land and they would play the harlot with their gods and sacrifice to their gods, and someone might invite you to eat of his sacrifice, and you might take some of his daughters for your sons, and his daughters might play the harlot with their gods and cause your sons also to play the harlot with their gods. (Exodus 34:14-16, emphasis added)

You shall have no other gods before Me. You shall not make for your-self an idol, or any likeness of what is in heaven above or on the earth beneath or in the water under the earth. You shall not worship them or serve them; for I, the LORD *your God, am* a jealous God, *visiting the iniquity of the fathers on the children, on the third and the fourth generations of those who hate Me. (Exodus 20:3-5, emphasis added)*

I am the LORD, *that is My name; I will not give My glory to another, nor My praise to graven images. (Isaiah 42:8)*

For My own sake, for My own sake, I will act; for how can My name be profaned? And My glory I will not give to another. (Isaiah 48:11)

You cannot read these verses and come away with a flippant attitude about God's glory. The Lord is jealous about His name and His glory. He is not satisfied being *E Pluribus Unum*. God is God. He's not running for God, and He doesn't need your vote (or mine). He was the only one around when the votes were cast, and there will never be a recount. God is God.

A family without a commitment to the God of the Bible has no hope of stemming the tide of cultural onslaught. If we mix a little biblical truth, a little secular psychology, a little romance novel ideology, and a little eastern mysticism, we will get a deadly mixture of lies. Unfortunately, this is exactly what many Christian families do. We do marriage according to Dr. Phil, raise our children according to Dr. Spock, govern our sex lives according to Dr. Ruth, and only run to Dr. Jesus when things have gotten so bad we can't find another doctor to help us.

Thomas's Story[1]

Not long ago I sat down with a grieving father. He wasn't grieving because his child had died, but over something potentially far worse. His son, Thomas, had grown up in church. He was a good kid. He was a fixture in the youth group, he dated a girl from the church, he went to Disciple Now weekends, Youth Camp, and YEC (a Baptist youth outreach), and even participated in a mission trip his sophomore year in high school.

However, when he went off to college, things changed. His parents had heard of the dangers of "secular" schools, so they guided him toward a Christian university. He was an outstanding athlete and had won a baseball scholarship. Thomas's story was not just typical—it was exceptional. He had done all of the things Christian parents desire for their children—good grades, great friends, active in church, popular, and off to college on an athletic scholarship. So why was his father grieving?

As it turns out, there was a darker side of Thomas's life. Things were lurking beneath the surface that his mom, dad, youth pastor, and Sunday school teacher never saw. Once he was away at "All-American Christian University," this darker side began to surface.

First, Thomas stopped attending church. He occasionally attended the large weekly Bible study on campus or the area-wide college service hosted by a large church in town, but he was not plugged into a local body of believers. Moreover, there was no sense of personal holiness, no pursuit of Christian disciplines.

Next Thomas began to struggle a bit in class. He had always been an A/B student, but now he was struggling just to pass his midterms in some of his classes. Upon closer examination of his academic struggles, they found that Thomas was staying out late and drinking heavily and often missed classes.

Finally, Thomas was suspended from his baseball team when a random drug test revealed that he had taken anabolic steroids. The father was so distraught that he did not allow Thomas to return for his second year. He opted instead to place him in a local community college until the young man could "get his head on straight."

Upon hearing Thomas's story, I tried to console this grieving father as best I could. He cried for a while and then asked me a question that I don't think he wanted answered. "Where could I have gone wrong?" he asked as he shook his head in disgust. Over the next several days he and I unpacked the situation and dealt with some very tough issues. I am not suggesting that this case is cut-and-dry, but we did find some very familiar patterns.

First, Thomas's lack of commitment in spiritual matters was not as strange as it seemed. As I talked with this father, I learned that Thomas was more than just a naturally gifted ballplayer. This kid had been playing baseball since he was six and started taking private instruction at nine! He had been part of a traveling squad at age twelve and was an all-star at every level. This man and his wife had gone to great lengths to see to it that their son became the best baseball player he could be.

This also meant that during the summer and fall their church attendance was sporadic at best. Like many parents, they found themselves traveling to tournament after tournament and praying for the opportunity to be out on Sunday since that meant they were playing for a title somewhere. What they didn't realize is that they were teaching Thomas to prioritize baseball above the Fourth Commandment. They were teaching Thomas that he should honor the Sabbath and keep it holy *unless it's baseball season.*

Thus when Thomas got to college and had to choose between going to church and hanging out with his teammates, the foundation for his decision had already been laid. When he had to choose between extra time in chemistry lab and extra time in the batting cage, he knew intuitively which choice to make. And when he had a choice between sitting on the bench for the first time in his life or taking a shortcut to a bigger body and a faster bat, he struggled for a while but eventually made his decision based on the one thing that had directed his path since he was six years old.

In other words, Thomas's lack of commitment to spiritual matters laid the groundwork for his moral compromise. Christianity was never the center of Thomas's universe. It was always something on the periphery. Church, and more importantly Jesus Christ, always orbited around baseball, the bright, shining star at the center of his universe. Does this mean that every young ballplayer will experience moral compromise? Certainly not; nor am I arguing that we should abolish all sports. I am simply arguing that anything that causes us to compromise our beliefs can (and probably will) become an idol. Some people will only worship that idol halfheartedly, but some will sacrifice all on its altar.

Thomas's father had never missed one of his son's games. Moreover, it was his father who taught him how to throw a curve ball, how to put his body in front of a grounder, and how to turn a double play. In fact, Thomas's father was the coach of his first T-ball team. However, when I asked whether or not he led his son (and his family) in worship, his only response was, "I never even thought about it."

In other words, this man had spent countless hours and immeasurable amounts of energy teaching his son how to be a ballplayer but hadn't done a thing to teach him how to be a Christian. When I pressed him on this issue, he said, "I thought the youth pastor was doing a good job of that." The point here is so obvious that I hesitate to state it. When it came to baseball, he had coaches and leagues, but *he* was the one providing private instruction in the backyard. However, when it came to spiritual matters, he passed the buck.

When it came to game time, he was not willing to miss (and wore that fact as a badge of honor), but when it came to church, they thought nothing of being absent for weeks and at one point months at a time. This family was worshiping a rival, and their son's life was the fruit of their idolatry. There were certain things for which they were willing to sacrifice all. Unfortunately, their son's walk with the Lord was not one of those things. Is there any wonder that a young man in his situation would miss church? Is there any doubt that a young man in Thomas's situation would be hard-pressed to find the courage to resist having a few drinks with the guys on the squad?

Sadly, this story is very familiar to those of us who have been around the church for a while. In fact, many of us see ourselves as we read between the lines. We live in an age where many gods vie for our allegiance. What's worse, these gods try to convince us that if we bow down and worship them, they will give our children what the God of the Bible cannot give—success by worldly standards.

The idol we had to crush in our family was the god of academics. My wife and I both come from families with a relatively short history of college attendance and graduation. We both spent our lives chasing a dream of academic success. For me, growing up in a single-parent home in south-central Los Angeles, academics served as "a way out." My mother worked hard to instill a sense of urgency in me in regard to education. And for that I thank her. However, like anything else, the pursuit of academic success can be taken too far.

Not long ago Bridget and I sat up until well after midnight talking, praying, and weeping over the state of our family. Our children were working like slaves every day to try to keep up the pace we had set. They were in school from 9 in the morning until as late as 6 or 7 some nights. Much of our effort was geared toward preparing them to do well on the SAT and get into a good college. They were doing work at levels far beyond anything most children their age could imagine. However, our home was tense all the time, and we had very little time for anything but school.

We brought our kids into our bedroom the next morning and told them there would be no school that day. We spent the day talking, laughing, praying, and playing. We told the children how sorry we were for the way things had gotten and how far out of line our goals had become. We were still committed to the stewardship of their minds, and we still work hard. However, we start school at 9:30 and are done by 2:30. We get up in the mornings, take our time at breakfast, go for walks, have family worship, and soak in the day.

Bridget and I simply had to admit that much of what we were doing was geared toward achieving the American dream at the expense of weightier matters. After all, what good would it be for our children to go to the best colleges in the world if we neglected to take advantage of the time we have with them? How much Latin, logic, philosophy, theology, history, algebra, biology, etc. did my twelve-year-old son really need at this point in his life?

Ironically, the new schedule has allowed us to focus more attention on fewer subjects and achieve much more than we ever have before, and the spirit of our home was completely transformed in the process. The idol we were worshiping was actually robbing us of the very thing it promised.

How can we avoid worshiping idols in a culture filled with them? How do we rise above the culture and walk with God? It can be challenging, but I believe it can be done. We simply need to follow Paul's admonition in Ephesians 5:

> [B]e careful how you walk, not as unwise men but as wise, making the
> most of your time, because the days are evil. So then do not be fool-
> ish, but understand what the will of the Lord is. And do not get drunk

with wine, for that is dissipation, but be filled with the Spirit, speaking to one another in psalms and hymns and spiritual songs, singing and making melody with your heart to the Lord; always giving thanks for all things in the name of our Lord Jesus Christ to God, even the Father; and be subject to one another in the fear of Christ. (vv. 15-21)

These words give us a pattern that will set our lives on a Godward trajectory. Interestingly enough, this passage is connected to Paul's passionate statement about parents' responsibility to teach their children in Ephesians 6:1-4. As we will see, this text closely parallels Moses' teaching in Deuteronomy. In fact, Paul quotes Deuteronomy 6 in his teaching.

Paul offers a blueprint for those seeking to live lives that honor God in the midst of a culture rife with paganism. From this text we learn that we must watch our walk, be good stewards of our time, understand God's will, constantly yield to God's Spirit, and order our relationships by the Book.

Watch Your Walk (vv. 15-16)

It has been said that when it comes to our children, much more is caught than taught. I believe that; and if your kids aren't Martian test-tube babies, you believe that too. We have all seen things in our kids that we wish we could punish them for, but we can't because they are just doing what we modeled for them. One day my son had clothes strewn all over his floor, and my wife sent him down to our room to talk to me. When he came into our bedroom, he said, "Mom wanted me to come talk to you about not putting my dirty clothes away." Immediately his eyes glanced around the room at my clothes from the previous night, strewn all around my bedroom floor. All I could do was look at him and say, "I guess we've got to do better, son."

We cannot expect our children to rise above our example. If my kids don't see me spending time in God's Word, they probably won't. If they see me using inappropriate language or involved in "coarse jesting" (Ephesians 5:4), they will probably follow suit. If they see me scream at their mother and treat her with contempt, they will probably disrespect her as well. We can try to teach them to do as we say, not as we do, but our words can only go so far when they are contradicted by our actions.

Be Good Stewards of the Time (v. 17)

When Joe Gibbs retired from coaching (he later returned to the profession), a reporter asked him why he was calling it quits when he seemed to be on top of his game. Gibbs's response is legendary. He said he went home one evening after one of his legendary twelve- or fourteen-hour days and decided to go kiss his boys good night. He went into their rooms only to discover that they had become men, and he had missed it!

Joe Gibbs learned a lesson that far too many parents learn way too late. Time is precious, and you only get one chance to raise your children. They are only young once, and they are only in your home for a short while. Once they are born the clock starts ticking, and there is nothing you can do to stop it or slow it down. Your only hope is to make the most of the time you have. I'm sure Joe Gibbs would tell you that none of the trophies, money, or accolades he earned as an NFL head coach was worth the price he, and especially his children, paid.

I look at my daughter sometimes, and I just want to weep. As I write this, she is fifteen years old. She has gone from a precious little bundle of joy to a beautiful young woman right before my eyes. In a few short years she will be gone. My oldest son is only a few years behind her. I constantly pray that God will give me ways to cheat the clock and multiply our time together. I want to savor every moment. That means I have to make the effort.

Be There When You Can

I have several good friends who are committed golfers. These guys love to go out and strike the ball. In fact, they are such avid golfers that they cannot comprehend why anyone would be otherwise inclined. I, on the other hand, do not play the game. It's not that I don't think I would like it. I'm sure I would. Nor is it the amount of money involved. We have a golf course in our neighborhood that is very affordable for residents. I don't play golf because it takes too much time. I spend ten days per month traveling around the country doing conferences. The last thing I need when I get home is a hobby that takes half a day to enjoy!

I am not saying that every man who plays golf is sinning. I am just saying that with my schedule I have a hard enough time maximizing my family life without having such a time-consuming hobby that would take me away from home. Perhaps if my whole family played I would feel differently. Or maybe if I did not have to be away as often as I do, I wouldn't feel such pressure to guard my time. However, as things stand I have to be here when I can.

Every one of us needs to evaluate the way we spend our time. Are you involved in things that take you away from your duties as a husband or wife? Are those things necessary, or are they merely convenient and enjoyable? Can you do something to make up for the time? If not, is this an area that needs to be brought into submission to your biblical duties and roles? These are questions we simply cannot avoid if we are serious about family-driven faith.

Schedule Your Time or Lose It

If you fail to plan, you are planning to fail. If we've heard this once, we've heard this a thousand times. Why? Because it is absolutely true, especially when it comes to family. If we don't plan that family vacation, the summer will come and go and we will wonder what happened. If we don't put that piano recital on the calendar, something else will fill the space. And if we don't carve out time to disciple our children, it simply will not get done.

Start with a few non-negotiable dates and put them on the calendar. For me those dates include everyone's birthday, our annual family vacation, at least one short getaway with Bridget (preferably two), and any special events that I know about far enough in advance to schedule them. Once these things are on the calendar, I cannot book any events that will interfere with them. The only exception is the occasional ministry opportunity in Hawaii that allows me to take Bridget and/or the kids along to "suffer" with me while I minister in the Aloha State.

You will be amazed by how much excitement this will bring to your children. It will let them know how important they are, how important your marriage is, and how precious you consider your time with them. It will also send a clear message that they will remember when the culture tries to pry them away. It is much easier to tell Junior that he has to miss a band practice here and there if he knows there are certain events in the family that relegate even Dad's job to the backseat.

Understand God's Will (v. 17)

We serve a sovereign God. Say that to the average Christian, and you will get a hearty amen. However, delve a little deeper, and you will discover there is a wide chasm between orthodoxy and orthopraxy on this one. What we say simply does not match the way we live.

Take, for example, a young man named Rick whom I knew in college. Rick and I had a class together my senior year. He was a sophomore at the time. Rick was going through a crisis that is all too common. He sensed that God had called him to preach, but he couldn't convince his parents that he needed to use his college years to prepare.

Rick's dad had told him that he would cut him off financially if he changed his major from business administration and accounting to Christianity and philosophy. This young man was miserable. He wanted to honor his father and mother, but he also wanted to obey God. What was he to do?

Similarly, Elizabeth (not her real name) was a beautiful, intelligent, twenty-year-old college student whose parents were irate over the idea of their little girl getting married before graduation. They, like most Christians I meet, believed that marriage should be put off until after college. They came to me thinking I would back them up, but I almost had to pick them up off the floor when I told them I disagreed.

I believe that marriage is far more important than college. Moreover, I think we lead our children to compromise when we ask them to endure two-year engagements while remaining true to their Christian convictions. If they weren't ready to be married, we shouldn't have allowed the relationship to blossom.

Both Rick and Elizabeth represent what I have seen as a pattern among modern American Christian parents. There seems to be an increasing emphasis on our children achieving the "American Dream" at the expense of any sort of costly Christian commitment. It is as though we have forgotten that this is not our home, that the best this world has to offer pales in comparison to what God has in store for us.

Rick's dad wanted his son to be a successful businessman. Elizabeth's parents just wanted to protect their daughter from harm and to see her get married after she had gained the "stability" that comes with a college degree. Is any of that so wrong? Is it wrong to want good things for your children? Not necessarily. Unless in our effort to attain "the best for our children" we ignore their God-given gifts, talents, abilities, and passions.

The key is to understand that *our children don't belong to us—they belong to God.* Our goal as parents must not be limited by our own vision. I am a finite, sinful, selfish man. Why would I want to plan out my children's future when I can entrust them to the infinite, omnipotent, immutable, sovereign Lord of the universe? I don't want to tell God what to do with my children—I want Him to tell me! When I allow my will to take precedence over God's will, I have not only given way to a rival—I have become one.

Constantly Yield to God's Spirit (v. 18)

This morning as my family and I sat at the breakfast table, my wife and children watched in bemusement as I fussed over a box of raisins. The problem wasn't that I was devoting an inordinate amount of time to this. The problem was that I had not yet prayed over our food. My wife looked at me, cleared her throat, and gave me that, "If it's not too much trouble, the kids and I would like for you to pray so we can eat" look. I looked around the table, and all eyes were on me. I quickly bowed my head, apologized to my drooling children, and offered thanks to God for our meal and a brand-new day. After my prayer we all had a good laugh as we began to eat.

I don't think God would have struck us down (or given us indigestion) had we failed to pray before the meal. Nor do I believe my family and I gained any special merit from God by doing so. I do, however, believe that it is important for us as a family to acknowledge God whenever we can. It is important that my wife and I remind our children that every meal we eat is a gift from the hand of the Almighty. It is also important that we instill habits of holiness that will have lasting influence on our children. I believe there are several instances each of us can use to remind ourselves and our children of God's provision and place in our lives.

Mealtime

I don't think that anything bad will happen to my food or to me if I don't pray before my meals. Moreover, I don't believe that the fact that I pray before I eat necessarily makes me more spiritual than anyone else. I know several people who incorporate a ritualistic prayer into each of their meals, and they would have to try hard to be less spiritual than they are right now. That being said, I think mealtime prayer can be a powerful parenting tool if employed properly.

I travel about ten days per month. That means I spend about twenty or twenty-one days a month at home. While much of my time at home is spent working in my home office, it is also spent enjoying the benefits of working out of my home. One of those benefits is eating meals with my family. That's right, I have the privilege of sitting down to breakfast and dinner with my wife and children about twenty days a month.

Perhaps the most precious benefit of this is the time we spend around the table just talking. And God is usually at the center of our discussions. We acknowledge God at the beginning of each meal as we pray and give thanks, and we acknowledge Him as we talk about the lessons of the day and how they apply to our walk, as well as situations in our life and family where we see God's hand.

Times of Crisis

It has been said, "Trials enable people to rise above religion to God." Truer words were never spoken. A crisis is a tremendous opportunity to demonstrate true biblical faith. In fact, one could argue that moments of crisis say more about our walk with God than any other occasion or circumstance. It is crisis that brings out the best and the worst of who and what we are. Moments of crisis also say a great deal about the nature and content of our faith.

I am amazed at how many Christians confess to me that their family does not pray together in times of crisis. In fact, I am amazed how many times it has happened in my own life. A crisis comes, we are all tense, and although each of us prays, we sometimes fail to gather together for prayer. I think every true crisis, no matter how small, should serve as a call to family prayer.

God made this principle abundantly clear to us during Hurricane Rita. We were directly in the line of fire of a Category Five hurricane with two days to make a decision. I was scheduled to preach in Atlanta that weekend, but my flight was not leaving until Friday. By Wednesday everything going out of town was booked, and the highways were starting to back up. This was a time of crisis.

As we watched the news nonstop that Thursday morning, I had already called the people in Atlanta and told them I wouldn't be there. I was not leaving my family, my flight would surely be canceled Friday morning, and we had to get out immediately. When I looked at the terrified countenance of my wife and children, it dawned on me that it was 11 o'clock, and we had not had family worship that day (or the day before). I called the family together, and we had one of the sweetest times of singing, prayer, and study that we had ever experienced.

As soon as we were done I went to my cell phone and discovered a message from my travel agent. She had found three tickets leaving Thursday evening and put my wife and children on the flight. However, there was not a seat for me. Immediately, I called the Frequent Flier Elite desk and asked if there was anything that could be done. "Can I go on standby?" I asked. "No," the woman replied. "There are no seats available, and they won't even let you in without a confirmed seat." Just then the woman gasped and said, "You must be praying." "Why?" I asked. "Because a seat just opened up on that plane!"

We gathered our things, left the house, and traveled down an empty highway the whole way because everyone was headed north and west to get out of town and we had to go south and east to get to the airport. We got to the airport, went through a back entrance that only savvy frequent fliers know about, and were through security in twenty minutes on a day when the average wait was several hours. Moreover, we all ended up in first class on our trip to Atlanta.

I'm not saying that happened because we had family worship. However, I can say with confidence that God used the events of that day to show Himself as real and powerful in our lives. I can also say that we will never look at family worship the same way we did before the storm. Over the next few days we told our story to countless people who were blessed by the faithfulness of our God. Never again do I intend to allow crisis to keep me from the prayerful acknowledgment of God.

Special Occasions

In 1996 Bridget and I had the privilege of hosting several of our family members for Christmas dinner. We had been married about seven years at the time, and it was our first opportunity to spend Christmas with the family on "home turf." Previous years had found us traveling to visit my relatives or hers. However, that year was different. That year we finally had a house big enough to host everyone and a kitchen big enough for all the cooks!

I don't remember much about that Christmas, but what I do remember is the moment the food was ready and it was time to eat. We gathered around the table and instinctively joined hands as all eyes glanced toward me. Nobody said a word, but we all knew exactly what was supposed to happen next. I smiled at the faces around my table, bowed my head, and offered a prayer to our Lord. It was incredible. The moment lasted but a short while, but the impact lingers even today. I will never forget the first time I had the privilege of offering that prayer.

My children were six and three at the time, but I remember thinking, *What a blessing!* Maybe it meant so much to me because I never saw my father do it. Maybe it was the joy of our first Christmas as hosts instead of visitors. Or maybe it was the fact that I realized the pivotal role that acknowledging God had come to play in our family. Regardless of what the reason was, it felt good.

It may sound simplistic to say we should acknowledge God as a family during special occasions, but we all need to be reminded of this. How many times have we allowed a birthday, graduation, or some other milestone go by without huddling our family together for a special moment of prayer? We must take advantage of every opportunity we have to mark special occasions and milestones by acknowledging God.

Special Trips

Before we started homeschooling, my son went to preschool at our church. He would get up in the morning raring to go. I remember the days that I had the privilege of driving him. We would get into the car, get all buckled up, and drive off. When we got to a specific intersection a block or so away from the school, we would bow our heads and pray. I would pray for my son, and then he would pray.

One Saturday morning we were on a family outing that happened to take us past our preschool prayer intersection. My son, not quite old enough to know what day of the week it was, bowed his head and began to pray, "Dear Jesus, please help me to be a big boy at school today . . ." Then, as though someone had tapped him on the shoulder and reminded him that we were on our way to someplace other than school, he looked up and said, "Well, Jesus, just help me be good wherever we're going."

I would love to be able to tell you that my family and I pray every time we get in the car to go somewhere together, but we do not. There are, however, occasions when we are embarking on a long journey or just a very special one and we pause to pray for traveling mercies. However, as I write this chapter I am reminded that we don't do it nearly as often as we should.

Order Your Relationships by the Book (v. 21)

"We're going to have mommy and daddy time; we'll be out in a bit." That's Bridget's famous phrase. The kids know that if she sticks her head out the door and announces "mommy and daddy time," anyone who comes near had better be bleeding profusely! We're not talking, I scraped my toe—that puppy had better be hanging off! Sometimes "mommy and daddy time" means we need a nap; sometimes it means we need to discuss the children behind their backs; other times it means things that I wouldn't dare write in this book. Whatever the reason, our children know that we are not to be disturbed.

One of the most important things mommy and daddy time does is to establish the priority of our marriage in the home. Our children get a very clear message: "When the two of us are together, our time is more important to us than even you." This may sound harsh to some who have bought into the "children above everything" culture. However, this is a lesson that both you and your children must learn. Mom and Dad's marriage takes precedence over everything else.

There are at least three reasons this priority must be established. First, our job as parents is to get our children grown and gone. There is going to come a day when the children leave. When that day comes, marriages that make the kids top priority will be hard-pressed to refocus and carry on. In fact, this is at least part of the reason for the new trend of twenty-five- and thirty-year marriages breaking up out of thin air. I have had numerous conversations with people who said, "Once the children were gone, we didn't have any reason to stay together."

Second, our marriage is the foundation upon which all other aspects of family life must be built. Our children need to be led by a united front. Bridget and I must function as a team, like a well-oiled machine. This will not happen unless we invest significant time in our relationship. Our marriage serves as a strategic command where we plan and oversee the discipleship of each of our children; it functions as a counseling center where our children come to feel safe in the midst of a frightening world; and it functions as a laboratory where our children watch and learn what marriage is all about.

Our marriage also sets the tone for discipline in the home. Verse 21 says that we are to be subject to one another in the fear of Christ. Verse 21 is an umbrella under which the next twenty-one verses fall. The submission in verse 21 is demonstrated in three relationships: wife/husband, child/parent, and servant/master. In other words, obedience to verse 21 (which is connected to verse 18 and the command to be filled with the Spirit) requires not only that children submit to parents, but that wives submit to husbands. You show me a wife who is not in submission to her husband, and I'll show you a household in disarray. Can you imagine an army where sergeants openly disrespect generals, yet expect privates to respect them?

Finally, our children will likely marry someday, and they need to realize they are going to establish a relationship that takes precedence over all other relationships (including their relationship with Mom and Dad). Many a marriage has suffered due to the failure or unwillingness of a spouse to cut the apron strings. Oftentimes this is the result of children who have not heard a clear message from their parents about the priority of the marriage relationship. With all of this at stake, we can't afford not to prioritize our marriage. This is especially true if we desire to experience multigenerational faithfulness.

Take Action

1. Make a list of potential idols in your life. Are there things in your life that require of you things that are only due to our God? If so, identify them. Ask your children to participate in the process.
2. Get your family together, and decide how you are going to crush the idols in your life. There may be things that you need to get out of your house. More than likely, there are also things you need to get off your schedule.
3. Have a special time of family prayer and repentance. Confess the sin of idolatry before God, receive His forgiveness, and celebrate the renewed freedom you now enjoy.

3

LEARN TO LOVE

You shall love the LORD your God with all your heart and with all your soul and with all your might.

DEUTERONOMY 6:5

If you want to be a godly head of a family, you must ensure that there is Christian harmony among those under you, appropriate for a house where the leader fears God.

JOHN BUNYAN

Initially I was going to title this chapter "Learn to Love God." However, after closer observation I realized there was more to it than that. Moses' exhortation to "love the LORD" encompasses much more than a vertical, worshipful relationship. This exhortation involves more than our relationship with God.

Love Is Love

One thing evident in this passage is that the love God expects from His followers is not foreign to other relationships. Think about it. Is there one kind of love that is religious and another that is irreligious? Is there one definition of love that governs my prayer life and another that governs my family life? Of course not. Love is love. Sure, there are a variety of words for love in the Old and New Testaments, but they usually distinguish the relational or directional aspects of our love, not its essence.

For example, many view the New Testament terms *agape* and *phileo* as two different kinds of love. Perhaps you have heard it said, "*Agape* is God's kind of love." While it is true that *phileo* literally means "brotherly love," whereas *agape* refers to a selfless, sacrificial love, it is not true that *agape* is God's love and *phileo* is man's love. In fact, there are several instances where *phileo* is attributed to God.

For the Father loves [phileo] the Son, and shows Him all things that He Himself is doing; and the Father will show Him greater works than these, so that you will marvel. (John 5:20)

[F]or the Father Himself loves [phileo] you, because you have loved Me and have believed that I came forth from the Father. (John 16:27)

So she ran and came to Simon Peter and to the other disciple whom Jesus loved [phileo], and said to them, "They have taken away the Lord out of the tomb, and we do not know where they have laid Him." (John 20:2)

Those whom I love [phileo], I reprove and discipline; therefore be zealous and repent. (Revelation 3:19)

The Bible also makes it clear that both *phileo* and *agape* are acceptable in terms of man's love for God. Paul warns those who do not *phileo* God when he states, "If anyone does not love [*phileo*] the Lord, he is to be accursed" (1 Corinthians 16:22). If *agape* is the standard for man's love toward God, then Paul would not have used *phileo* to make such a strong statement. Note also that he did not say, "If anyone does not at least *phileo* God . . ." He clearly states that *phileo* is sufficient.

Even Jesus showed His acceptance of *phileo* as a sufficient expression of man's love toward God when He restored Peter based on the proclamation, "Lord, You know all things; You know that I love [*phileo*] You" (John 21:15-17). Jesus did not rebuke Peter for his inferior form or level of love. On the contrary, He commissioned Peter to feed His sheep.

Both the Greek and Hebrew language are at times more precise than common English. Whereas you or I would say to a friend, a spouse, or a child, "I love you," these languages would afford us the option of using different words to communicate the same idea in different contexts. In other words, *phileo* is not a cheap or watered-down form of *agape*; it is merely an alternative that carries different nuances. In other words, *love is love*.

Love God; Love Your Brother

The second issue that changed my direction in titling this chapter struck me during a personal study of the epistle of 1 John. As I studied this short letter, I came across a familiar verse that took on new meaning in light of my work on this book. John raises a question in chapter 4 that cannot be overlooked: "If someone says, 'I love God,' and hates his brother, he is a liar; for the one who does not love his brother whom he has seen, cannot love God whom he has not seen" (v. 20).

There it was! I was able to see Moses' admonition in an entirely new light. This was about more than just our vertical relationship. If we learn to love God, we will inevitably learn to love, period. Lest you think this is a stretch, listen to the words of Jesus as He answers that all-important question, "Which is the great [greatest] commandment in the Law?" Jesus said, "'YOU SHALL LOVE THE LORD YOUR GOD WITH ALL YOUR HEART, AND WITH ALL YOUR SOUL, AND WITH ALL YOUR MIND'" (Matthew 22:37). But He went on to say, "This is the great and foremost commandment. The second is like it, 'YOU SHALL LOVE YOUR NEIGHBOR AS YOURSELF'" (Matthew 22:38-39).

Thus Jesus, referencing Moses, comments on the essential nature of loving people as well as loving God. Therefore, to limit this chapter to learning to love God would have been insufficient. If our homes are to reflect our position as the people of God in the midst of the opposition of a pagan culture, we, like the Israelites, must learn to love.

Our homes must be rife with the aroma of love. Those who visit us should notice immediately that they have left the world of self-serving, egocentric narcissism and have entered a safe harbor where people value and esteem others above themselves. Outsiders should enter our homes and never want to leave. Our neighbors should find excuses to visit us just to get another whiff of the fragrant aroma of love. The brokenhearted should long to be near us. The downtrodden and the abused should seek us out. Families on the brink of disaster should point to us and say, "Why can't our home be like that?"

Unfortunately, this is rarely the case. Far too often professing Christians in our culture don't love better, more deeply, or longer than the pagans who surround us. At times we bear more of the stench of this world than the fragrant aroma of the people of God. That's the bad news. The good news is that things don't have to remain as they are. We can learn to love. The first step is to rid ourselves of the ineffective methods and ideologies that have led us down the current path.

The Dilemma

"I love you with all my heart." These are familiar words. Mothers and fathers say them to their children. Husbands and wives say them to one another. Star-crossed lovers are often overheard whispering this familiar phrase as they gaze deeply into each other's eyes. Unfortunately, these words seem to have lost their luster. Nowadays "I love you with all my heart" eventually gives way to "I never want to see you again."

I have stood at the altar with many couples as they stare longingly into one another's eyes while they carefully and nervously repeat their vows and publicly pledge their unending, undying love. I have also sat in many a room as a man looks at his wife (or a wife at her husband) with that longing, loving gaze nowhere to be found as he or she recants every vow with a single phrase—"I'm just not in love anymore."

What happens between "'til death do us part" and "I want half"? How do two starry-eyed kids turn into a couple of angry, bitter adversaries racing one another to the back door? I believe one of the main causes of the current epidemic of "falling out of love" is ignorance. That's right, people just don't know any better. We think love is a random, overwhelming, uncontrollable, sensual force that comes and goes on a whim. In short, we have fallen for the Greco-Roman myth of romantic love hook, line, and sinker.

Cupid and the Greco-Roman Love Myth

You see him on Valentine's Day greeting cards. He stars in cartoons and comic strips. He is the little arrow-wielding cherub known as Cupid. While this myth has its roots in the story of Cupid and Psyche, the story has evolved. Now Cupid is said to roam the earth shooting his arrows of love at unsuspecting saps who then "fall in love" with whomever happens to be nearby. If you think this myth is harmless, think again. The idea of love as a random, overwhelming, and uncontrollable force has tremendous consequences.

Myth #1: Love Is a Random Force

"We don't choose who we fall in love with." Most of us have heard this axiom before. It is usually code for, "I don't care if the Bible, my family, my friends, and even random strangers all agree that only an idiot would waste her time with this loser—I'm still not going to give him up." We've all seen it before. Some beautiful, seemingly intelligent young lady starts seeing a guy who treats her like dirt, and everyone sees it but her.

The worst case I have ever seen is a woman named Mary (not her real name). Mary has been in a relationship with a man for about fifteen years. In those fifteen years this man has never married her, cheated on her with several of her friends, made sexual advances toward her daughter, has never held down a steady job, and during one of his more hostile moments beat her within an inch of her life. And this is the abbreviated version! To top it all off, this man is not some charming, debonair, irresistible Don Juan. On the contrary, he is one of the most obnoxious people I have ever met. Yet Mary is drawn to him like a moth to a flame (more like a fly to one of those insect lights).

I am sure we all know our share of Marys. We all marvel as we watch them endure the abuse, each time wondering, *Will this be the last straw?* The question, however, is, why would any woman settle for this? If you ask Mary, she will probably quote the aforementioned axiom: "We don't choose who we fall in love with." Mary's decision to stay in this abusive, unsatisfying relationship has nothing to do with reason or common sense. It's all about that (allegedly) random force called love that brought her and her abuser together.

Myth #2: Love Is an Overwhelming Force

The handsome leading man takes his ravishing leading lady in his arms. He looks longingly into her eyes as though they hold the key to his very existence. Their chests heave as they try to catch their breath. She tries to resist (thinking of her husband who is blind to her true intentions), but he grabs her again and pulling her close says, "This thing is bigger than both of us." Sound familiar? I know I'm no romance novelist, but we've all seen and heard this so many times that it has become cliché. Love, according to the Greco-Roman myth, is an overwhelming force against which we mere mortals cannot hope to prevail. And even if we do, it will only lead to misery as we spend the balance of our days pining over the loss of our "one true love." Never mind the fact that we said "I do" to someone else.

It's one thing to see this myth played out on the silver screen, but seeing it in real life is quite another story. In the movies we are left with the impression that this overwhelming force only has a good side. All we see is the long-anticipated kiss as the credits roll. We never get to see the agony of the jilted lover or the dysfunction that haunts the children who wonder when Mom or Dad is going to fall out of love with them. Nor do we get to listen in a year later as the lovely couple, the adventure and mystique long over, has another fight because the means by which their relationship came about renders them unable to trust.

Myth #3: Love Is an Uncontrollable Force

"We just fell out of love." This was the answer I got when I asked a gentleman why his marriage ended after twenty years. I was expecting him to say something, anything, just not that. I was waiting for an excuse or an explanation. I thought he would say they hung in there until the kids were gone (although that would have been completely unacceptable). But he didn't say any of those things. He just shrugged his shoulders and blurted out, "We just fell out of love."

It was as though he was telling me something that was obvious. There was neither shame nor remorse in his countenance. He didn't avert his eyes or lower his head; he didn't follow up with an explanation or try to make it sound better. He just said it.

I wish I could say that this gentleman was unusual, but he is not. He is typical of many men and women who have resigned themselves to the idea that love is an uncontrollable force that sometimes goes away as quickly and mysteriously as it came. He is one of many casualties who drank deeply from the cistern of the Greco-Roman myth that never quenched his thirst.

Myth #4: Love Is a Sensual Force

From romance novels to feature films to sitcoms, love is equated with sex. Sex is the new marriage in modern media. Movies used to start with two strangers meeting and moving toward wedding bells and exchanging vows. Now the couple meets, has sex, and then after an acknowledgment that they have something "special" exchange phone numbers. The question most often asked of a film's female love interest is no longer, "Did he pop the question?" It's "Have you slept with him?"

This is merely the logical next step in the Greco-Roman love myth. Cupid's arrow has always led to sensual love; we just didn't get to see it portrayed so graphically. Nor has it ever been characterized by such nonchalance. What we are seeing is the Greco-Roman myth with the trappings removed. If sensual love is the ultimate end of romantic love, why bother with such formalities as courtship, propriety, and marriage?

In fact, who needs Cupid anymore? That's right, we have jettisoned the little cherub with the heart-shaped arrow in favor of a modernized, New Age concept. Now Cupid is the air we breathe. We don't need to wait for an arrow through the heart, just a willing partner with time to spare.

The End Result: Love Doesn't Translate

Perhaps the greatest problem with this kind of love is that it doesn't translate to other relationships. If love is a random, uncontrollable, overwhelming, sensual force, how do I love my kids? I have seen this problem in my own life with my daughter. Like most men, I went through a difficult season when my daughter began to walk into womanhood. How do I express love to this young woman if I believe that love is a sensual force? Is it best for me to stop hugging my daughter? Certainly she is going to have to stop sitting on my lap.

Unfortunately, my wrestling with these things created a sense of uncertainty and discomfort in my daughter. Sure, she was changing, but I was still Daddy, and in her mind she was still Daddy's little girl. She saw my caution as rejection. I had to learn how to be appropriate with my daughter without ceasing to be affectionate. The first step was to get over the Greco-Roman myth of romantic love. I had to view love biblically if I was going to be able to translate it from one relationship to another.

Another problem with this love myth is its tenuous nature. Can we blame children of divorce for wondering when Mom or Dad is going to stop loving them the same way they stopped loving each other? How do I love my job, my mother, my God? Better yet, how does my God love me? In fact, it is this Greco-Roman myth of romantic love that causes many to doubt God's love. What if God's love is as capricious as the love of Hollywood? Is God going to divorce me?

There must be a better way. Love must be more than the myth. The myth won't endure hardship, overcome adversity, or triumph over disaster. The myth brings no comfort to the woman whose beauty has faded, as she must live in constant fear that her husband will be zapped by this random, uncontrollable, overwhelming, sensual force as he looks upon the beauty of a younger woman. Nor can it assuage the fears of the man who loses his job, his confidence, and his wife's adoration. This love also offers nothing to the young couple trying to navigate the peaks and valleys of the early years of marriage.

Fortunately, there is a better way. God has given us a definition of love that transcends the myth. This love is transferable, in that it is the same whether it is directed toward a spouse, a child, a sibling, or God. It is also comforting, as it is not fickle or fragile like the myth. This love endures, overcomes, and triumphs. Better yet, this love satisfies completely.

Moses and the Biblical Portrait of Love

One of the best-known verses in the Bible is Deuteronomy 6:4. The *Shema* ("to hear") is a daily prayer uttered by devout Jews. The name

Shema is derived from the first Hebrew word in this passage: "Hear O Israel! The LORD is our God, the LORD is one!" However, the most popular part of the passage comes next: "You shall love the LORD your God with all your heart and with all your soul and with all your might" (v. 5). The three Hebrew words used here (translated *heart, soul,* and *might*) provide a clear biblical definition of love: *Love is an act of the will accompanied by emotion that leads to action on behalf of its object.*

Examining each of these words in the context of Moses' message in the book of Deuteronomy and in the witness of Scripture as a whole more than bears this definition out.

Love Is an Act of the Will

Love is a choice. Some people find this statement offensive because it just doesn't sound "romantic." That may be true, but our goal here is not romance—it's love. More specifically, our goal is God's idea of love, and that begins with the Bible. Moses says, "love the LORD your God with all your *heart*." This is one of those words we use without thinking. What does it mean to love someone with "all of your heart"? The heart is a muscle that pumps blood, and contrary to our terminology, the heart knows nothing, the heart feels nothing, and the heart sees nothing. Whenever we use phrases like "head knowledge vs. heart knowledge" or "I feel it in my heart," we are always using figurative language. We don't literally mean that the muscle in the middle of our chest has a mind of its own.

The Hebrew word for heart is *lebab*. While you may never use or hear that word again, I assure you it is very important. The word means "inner man, mind, or will." Remember, the heart is a muscle that pumps blood, so this has to be a figurative reference. Here we see that the word points to our will. Hence biblical love is *an act of the will*; it is a choice.

How many times have we watched an athlete dig deep within herself and do something extraordinary? When it happens, we say, "She has *heart*." On the other hand, when we see a team fall apart in the fourth quarter and blow a substantial lead, we may exclaim, "They just didn't have *heart*." This does not imply that the aforementioned woman had a blood-pumping muscle in the center of her chest that the losing team lacked. That would be ridiculous. What we mean is she showed incredible *will* and the team did not. In many ways we have the aforementioned Hebrew concept to thank for this figure of speech.

The problem is that over time we have forgotten that this is a figure of speech. Many of us have completely divorced the concept of love from the mind and will. We speak of the heart as though it were the opposite of the mind and the will when in fact the mind and will are precisely where true love resides. I can no more love without my mind than I could speak without my tongue.

Love Is Accompanied by Emotion

The fact that love is a choice does not negate its emotional aspects. Love is not void of emotion. In fact, show me a man or a woman who is unemotional about his or her prospective mate and I'll show you someone who has found the "wrong one!" If a man were to sit across from me for premarital counseling and tell me that he was committed to his fiancée but didn't necessarily feel anything emotionally, I'd tell him to keep looking.

This is not just true of prospective spouses and newlyweds. When my fifteenth anniversary arrived, I didn't stand at the door and grumpily hand my wife flowers and request her company as we "go and devour charred animal flesh in celebration of the covenantal bond that has united us these past 180 months." No! I looked her in the eyes and forgot everything I had planned to say! All I could do was shake my head and say, "Thank You, Jesus!"

My heart still races when I get close to my house after a ministry trip. I still have problems catching my breath at times when my wife touches me. I am still mesmerized when I watch her walk across a crowded room. In fact, I am having a difficult time fighting back tears as I write this paragraph. I am still extremely emotional about my wife.

While emotion is a large part of the love equation, it must not be the sum total. Although love is accompanied by emotion, *biblical love is not led by emotion*. Emotions change. There are days when my wife wants to wring my neck! There are other days when we just want to chuck it all. Newsflash: *Marriage is hard!* We are two unique individuals waging war against the flesh, the world, and the devil. And sometimes that leads to waging war against each other.

One of the sad by-products of the Greco-Roman myth of romantic love is the abundance of emotion-led marriages discarded on the trash heap of divorce. As a minister I have had several conversations with people who have chosen to walk away from marriages because their feelings have changed. Some people even blame it on God. How many times have we heard the now common excuse, "God wouldn't want me to stay in a marriage where I was miserable." The more honest version of that is, "When I said 'til death,' I meant the death of my personal satisfaction."

Love Leads to Action on Behalf of Its Object

In the words of that famous "theologian" Janet Jackson, "What have you done for me lately?" Of course, Janet was not singing about the biblical definition of love, but she was on to something. Moses says that we are to love the Lord our God with all of our heart (will), all of our soul (emotions), and all of our strength. This last term, *meod*, if translated literally, means *muchness or force*. The word implies effort or action.

Throughout Deuteronomy Moses connects loving God with keeping His commandments (6:5-6; 7:9; 10:12; 11:1, 13, 22; 13:3-4; 19:9; 30:6, 16, 20). The theme is, love and obey. This theme is repeated not only throughout the Old Testament but also in the New.

Jesus said, "If you love Me, you will keep My commandments" (John 14:15). In John 14:21 he said, "He who has My commandments and keeps them is the one who loves Me; and he who loves Me will be loved by My Father, and I will love him and will disclose Myself to him." Again, He said, "If you keep My commandments, you will abide in My love; just as I have kept My Father's commandments and abide in His love" (John 15:10). John, the author who recorded these statements, echoed them in his epistle (1 John 2:3-4; 3:22; 5:3). In fact, the theme of demonstrating love for the Lord by keeping His commandments permeates the epistle of 1 John.

In other words, if you want to know whether or not someone truly loves God, watch what he or she does. If a person does not do the things that God says are pleasing and acceptable, and in fact does the things that God abhors and forbids, and yet claims to love God, it will be tough to support that claim. In fact, John argues, "The one who says, 'I have come to know Him,' and does not keep His commandments, is a liar, and the truth is not in him; but whoever keeps His word, in him the love of God has truly been perfected" (1 John 2:4-5a).

Love is proved by our efforts. If I say I love God, there should be evidence in the things I do (or the way I expend my energy and effort). By the same token, if I say I love my wife, that should be evidenced by my actions. If my actions are self-centered, I am demonstrating love for me. However, if my actions are directed toward meeting her needs, then she truly is the object of my affections.

It took me a while to learn this, but once I did, it paid immediate dividends. I remember vividly the second time we built a house (that's right, we've been through it more than once). The builder couldn't believe that we were putting ourselves through the torture again. We told him that we were fine and that we looked forward to the experience. I vividly remember his response. He looked directly at me and said, "Yeah, you say that now, but wait until you have to go to *The Room*."

He was, of course, referring to the room where all the design options were chosen. This was the place where couples often came to tears or to blows as they tried to decide on paint, brick, trim, floor coverings, fixtures, and the dreaded upgrades. *The Room* is legendary. If you've ever been there, no explanation is required. If you haven't been there, no explanation is sufficient. You have to see it to believe it.

Nevertheless, I wasn't worried. I looked him in the eye and said, "We'll be fine." He looked back at me with a smile the size of Alaska, and with all the sarcasm he could muster he said, "I'll be here if you need me." Bridget and I went into *The Room*, and the game was on.

Thirty minutes later we emerged. The salesman, certain that we had reached an impasse and ready to lend a hand, asked, "How can I help?" You could have bought him for a nickel when I looked back at him and said, "No need; we're done." I tried not to gloat (being a Christian and all), but I must admit, I felt like "Neon" Deion Sanders after picking off a pass in the Super Bowl and returning it 99 yards *to the house*!

What was our secret? Why were we able to get in and out so quickly, and with selections that impressed even the most experienced sales staff and decorators? The answer is love. I took the time to find out exactly what Bridget was thinking. I asked questions, listened to the answers, watched her reactions when we were visiting model homes. I paid attention. By the time we got into the design room, I knew what she wanted. So all I had to do was gravitate toward the things I knew would catch her eye, match them up according to the skills I had acquired, and watch things come together.

I could have gone into *The Room* and said, "Baby, you pick out whatever you want." Had I done so, she would have been frustrated and angry. She would have been frustrated because the task would have been overwhelming. And she would have been angry because I had divorced myself from the process.

I could also have just taken over. I could have said, "Just relax and let me do this." Had I chosen that route, she would have been terrified. Her mind would have raced as she envisioned the masculine eyesore that she would have to call home.

I chose instead to discover what she wanted and help her find it. In doing so, I demonstrated my commitment to my wife, to our home, and to the building process. It was awesome! Now if only I could just string a few victories like that together . . . Unfortunately, there are still days when I blow it. I can vividly remember the year I bought Bridget a video camera for Christmas. That was not a banner year. I saw this thing and immediately thought, *Boy, we need one of those*. In an effort to kill two birds with one stone, I wrapped it up and put it under the tree. I wish I was a good enough writer to describe my wife's face when she opened that box. But enough about that. Let's get back to my victory in the war room.

What I was able to demonstrate that day was a love that *leads to action on behalf of its object*. I know my wife needs to hear me say, "I love you." However, I have begun to learn that it is equally important for her to see me doing things that demonstrate my love. The same can be said of my children. They, too, need to hear and see Daddy's love.

I learned the value of this principle in the summer of 2003. I was scheduled to preach at the Southern Baptist Convention Pastor's Conference. It was by far the most significant invitation I had ever received. I was going to be standing in front of the annual assembly of the world's largest Protestant denomination. Moreover, I would be sharing the platform with some of the biggest names in the evangelical world. It was an incredible honor. However, two months before the convention I learned that my children had aced the state theory exam and had earned the right to play in the State Piano Ensemble. I also learned that I couldn't attend the piano ensemble and preach at the SBC.

I knew what I had to do. I immediately picked up the telephone and called Dr. Mac Brunson, the president of that year's conference. I explained my situation and asked if he would be kind enough to remove me from the program. Mac graciously agreed. When I hung up the phone, my wife stared at me with a look that I am convinced every man should experience at least once in his lifetime. It was not a look of shock or surprise; it was a look of utter joy and appreciation. I had just said no to the biggest opportunity of my career, but that's not what she heard. She heard a resounding *YES* to the question, "Are the children and I really number one in your life?" She heard a hearty amen to the question, "Do you love us more than these?"

My wife later relayed the story to my children, and their response was perhaps more rewarding than hers. They simply looked at their mother as she fought back tears and said, "Cool." It was no big deal to them, partly because they had no idea what the SBC was and partly because they had no doubt that their dad would move heaven and earth for them and that they were second to nothing (except the Lord and their mom).

Advantages of the Biblical Model of Love

The Biblical Model of Love Is Volitional

What value is there in a love that is overwhelming and uncontrollable? What value is there in being told that someone is with you because they can't help it? I don't know about you, but it would bring me little comfort to know that the last fifteen years of my life were based on little more than chemical reactions. I find it far more comforting to know that my wife wakes up in the morning choosing to love me than I would to know that she woke up with a finger in the air trying to discern which way the romantic wind is blowing and wondering whether or not she had "fallen out of love" yet.

The Biblical Model of Love Is Transferable

One of the biggest problems with the Greco-Roman myth is that it does me absolutely no good in non-romantic relationships. The biblical model fits my relationship with my wife, my daughter, my son, my mother, my neighbor, and my God. In each of these situations I can love as *an act of the will accompanied by emotion that leads to action on behalf of its object.* Conversely, the overwhelming, uncontrollable, unpredictable, sensual nature of Greco-Roman romantic love is almost exclusively reserved for a lover or a spouse.

I must admit I didn't understand this when I became a father. I was excited about having a child, but I was scared to death that I wouldn't be able to love her. I loved my wife so much that I didn't think I had room to love another person. And what about other children? I wondered how I was going to spread my love around to everyone. Through discussions with other expectant couples, I have discovered that my dilemma was not unique.

However, the beauty of biblical love is that it is completely transferable. I love my wife as an act of the will, not as a response to a mystical force. If love were a force, I would have to spread it out. However, if love is a choice, I can choose to love my wife without compromising my ability to choose to love my son or my daughter. Moreover, since love is accompanied by emotion, my choice in each relationship brings its own emotional reward. Also, since love leads to action on behalf of its object, I can demonstrate my love to my wife in actions that in no way compromise my ability to act on behalf of my children.

The Biblical Model of Love Is Secure

What happens to a love that is based on sensuality when your spouse is disabled, or just unattractive? What happens when your spouse is on a business trip and Cupid strikes him with an errant arrow? What happens if your wife becomes "uncontrollably overwhelmed" in the presence of another man? The answer in the Greco-Roman myth is simple: "We don't choose who we fall in love with," so sometimes you have to just recognize that you have fallen out of love with one person and in love with another. After all, "Isn't that why they invented no-fault divorce?" It is the myth of romantic love that has given us such wonderful inventions as the prenuptial agreement.

Not so with biblical love. Biblical love says, "I choose to love you, and I'm not going anywhere." Biblical love knows nothing of backing out when things get tough. Biblical love gives without expecting, goes the extra mile, sacrifices for others, and views divorce as a tragic and unnecessary plague visited upon a culture that has settled for a lie. Biblical love is not constantly seeking the emotional high that often characterizes immature relationships but instead is content with the depth and breadth that only the love of a maturing, godly relationship can provide. Biblical love is not constantly looking for a *better* deal; it is too busy thanking God for the *real* deal.

I saw a tremendous example of this recently when I preached for a friend of mine, Dan Yeary, the pastor of North Phoenix Baptist Church. Dan and his wife have been married over thirty years. They are one of the godliest couples I have ever been around. Dan's bride has multiple sclerosis. For the last several years she has been confined to a wheelchair. She can no longer walk or care for herself. She is totally dependent on Dan.

I spent two days watching Dan Yeary, a man in his sixties, lift his wife in and out of her wheelchair and place her in her seat at church and at the restaurant where we ate. He has to lift her in and out of the car every time they go someplace. At dinner he had to help her eat her food, wipe her mouth, and adjust her in her chair more than once.

As I watched this couple, I was struck by how asinine it would be to blame some chemical reaction for the level of commitment this man displays on a daily basis. Three hundred and sixty-five days a year he has to care for his beloved, and he hasn't gone anywhere. You won't find that at the point of Cupid's arrow.

The Biblical Model of Love Satisfies

I would rather have a sandwich with Bridget than sex with another woman. I am completely satisfied with my wife. I am not looking for "that special feeling we used to have." I realize that what we share has grown and matured over the years. I don't expect that raw adrenaline rush of brand-new infatuation. Nor do I long for it. I have found something more substantive, more satisfying, and more rewarding. I have found something that doesn't ebb and flow like the tides. I have found real love.

I am not suggesting that I am immune to feminine wiles. To think that would be foolish. I constantly remind myself of the warning in 1 Corinthians 10:12: "Therefore let him who thinks he stands take heed that he does not fall." No, I am not a superman. I guard myself at every point. I am not alone with women if I can help it. I don't counsel women unless I am in a room with an open window through which someone on the outside can look in. I don't have intimate friendships with women outside of my family. I am very careful; some say I am too careful!

I don't take these precautions because I doubt my commitment to my wife. On the contrary, I take these precautions as a sign of that commitment. I want to avoid even the appearance of evil. I don't even want to leave room for accusations. Moreover, I don't want to give the enemy as much as an inch, let alone a foothold. Not to mention the fact that these safeguards stand as a constant reminder to my wife that I am committed to protecting the sanctity, purity, and exclusivity of our covenant. In other words, she understands that these safeguards are *an act of my will accompanied by emotion that has led to action on behalf of its object.*

People Are Watching

My wife and I were at dinner one night in a restaurant in Las Vegas. We were enjoying a two-day getaway filled with our two best pastimes (great food and incredible shows). We had just left a theater where we had seen an awe-inspiring performance by Cirque du Soleil. Afterward we had reservations at Emeril's; it was a dream date for both of us. We entered the restaurant laughing, talking, and holding hands. We were both all smiles. As we approached our table, I pulled Bridget's chair out (as I always do), helped her to her seat, then sat next to her as we continued to discuss our amazing day.

As we sat there, the woman at the next table asked my wife, "Are you two on your honeymoon?" Bridget and I looked at each other and smirked. "No, we've actually been married twelve years," Bridget responded. The woman nodded quizzically, then asked, "Anniversary?" Bridget shook her head no as she gave the woman a coy grin. The woman finally blurted out, "You must have won big at the tables." To which Bridget responded, "No, we don't gamble." Finally, ready to satisfy the woman's curiosity, Bridget smiled at her and said, "We just came out here to get away for a couple of days." "Must be nice!" the woman retorted as she gazed at her husband who had hardly heard a word.

What this woman thought she saw was the glow of full-blown Greco-Roman romantic love. She thought Cupid had just struck us with his arrow and we were in the throes of new passion. She just *knew* that we were newly married, or at least celebrating a landmark anniversary. She simply couldn't fathom why a couple married for twelve years (in a row) would behave the way we were behaving toward each other. She spent the rest of the evening looking at us in disbelief.

What she didn't realize is that opening my wife's door, pulling out her chair, looking attentively into her eyes when she speaks, and walking on the street-side of the sidewalk are all learned behaviors on my part. She was unaware that holding my hand, laughing at my jokes, laying her head on my shoulder, and dining at the restaurant of one of my favorite Food Network chefs were all efforts on Bridget's part to make the trip memorable for me. She was also oblivious to the fact that Bridget and I sit down and plan out a couple of these getaways each year, not because we are smitten, but because we are committed to doing the things that nurture our marriage, and we know that if we don't plan them, they won't happen.

She thought she was looking at a random, overwhelming, uncontrollable, sensual force when she was actually looking at *an act of the will accompanied by emotion leading to action on behalf of its object.* This woman was so used to the counterfeit that she didn't quite know what to make of the real thing when it was staring her in the face.

Unfortunately, this woman was not unusual. Even some Christians spend their days aimlessly wandering through life searching for the Greco-Roman myth. They bounce around from relationship to relationship hoping that "this will be *the one.*" Eventually, they "follow their heart" down the aisle, fully expecting happiness ever after. Then when the novelty has faded and their wedding vows are a distant memory, they take a deep breath, throw in the towel, and set off again, convinced that all they need to do is make a better choice next time. For others their commitment to marriage won't let them give up, so they trudge forward through years of agony occasionally interrupted by momentary glimpses of hope. In either case contentment never truly comes.

All the while, God has given us an answer. God has provided a love that will satisfy our deepest longings. We don't have to wait around for the violins and cellos. In fact, I can guarantee that those moments will be rare. All we have to do is embrace the biblical definition of love and begin to walk in it. First, we learn to love God. Next, we begin to express that same love toward others. Finally, that love begins to be reflected back to us. And the next thing you know, people start to ask, "Are you guys on your honeymoon?"

Take Action

1. Go back over the last few knock-down-drag-out arguments you and your spouse have had. Did you contemplate throwing in the towel? If you did, consider the truths discussed in this chapter, and ask yourself what it would cost for you to do that.

2. Consider your relationship from your children's perspective. Do they know that you and your spouse love each other? As they watch you and listen to you do they see a picture of biblical love, or do they see a picture of a fickle, unstable, insecure relationship that could fall apart at any time? If it is the latter, you may want to go

to your children and apologize for the picture you've painted and start to present another portrait.

3. If you are considering marriage, have you built your relationship upon the expectations of the Greco-Roman myth or the biblical mandate? What will you do to promote the latter and not the former in your marriage?

4

GIVE HIM YOUR HEART

"These words, which I am commanding you today, shall be on your heart."

DEUTERONOMY 6:6

A proper understanding of biblical love is the foundation upon which a child's spiritual life is built. However, that foundation is only the first step. If biblical love is the foundation, a biblical worldview is the frame. It is imperative that we prepare children to think biblically. A child without a biblical worldview is like a ballplayer without a playbook. He may have spectacular abilities that will allow him to make the occasional jaw-dropping play, but more often than not he will end up in the wrong place at the wrong time, and worse, not knowing how he got there or how to get back.

A Lesson from the Gridiron

I played football in college. My sophomore year I went through a coaching change. I spent one year under the leadership of head coach Jerry Burnt and his staff. Then out of the blue Coach Burnt was gone, and my teammates and I were introduced to the regime of Fred Goldsmith. Chances are you don't recognize either of these men by name. Needless to say, my university was far better known for its academics than for its football team, but to us it was a big deal.

From the outside coaching changes look simple enough. One man is on the sidelines yelling, "Come on, guys!" and it's just not working. Therefore you go get another man to stand on the sidelines and yell, "Let's go, guys!" and hope that he gets better results. Of course, anyone who has ever played football knows that's not the case. Changing coaches is a tremendous undertaking.

One of the most difficult components of a coaching change is adapting to philosophy and terminology. Football is a simple game, but there are several different ways to approach the art and science of getting that piece of pig across the chalk line (and stopping the other guy from doing the same). Some coaches emphasize speed; others prefer size. Some coaches want to throw the ball all over the place, while others want to grind it out on the ground with the running game. Moreover, some guys use words to describe plays, while others use numbers. In many ways learning a new coach's philosophy and terminology is like learning a new language (and some are more complicated than others). That's why some players can thrive under certain coaches but flounder with others.

In many ways salvation is like a coaching change. We go from one regime (the world, the flesh, and the devil) to another (Christ). Like a player faced with a new coach, we must learn our new playbook and our new coach's philosophy and terminology as quickly and as thoroughly as possible if we hope to succeed. Unfortunately, many Christians are either oblivious to the larger implications of these truths or never take the time to incorporate them into their everyday walk.

We must change not only our allegiance but also our language and thinking. I believe this is what Moses means when he says, "These words . . . shall be on your heart." This is not just a call to do what God says; this is a call to submit our very will to the will of God. As we saw in Chapter 3, the use of the Hebrew word for *heart* in this passage is used to indicate volition and will. This is a call to a complete worldview overhaul. Peter Craigie notes:

The Commandments, which provide the framework within which the Israelites could express their love of God, were to be *upon your heart*—that is, the people were to think on them and meditate about them, so that obedience would not be a matter of formal legalism, but a response based upon understanding.[1]

John Calvin, commenting on the same passage, puts an even finer point on the matter when he writes:

> He would have it implanted in their hearts, lest forgetfulness of it should ever steal over them; and by the word "heart" He designates the memory and other faculties of the mind; as though He had said that this was so great a treasure, that there was good cause why they should hide it in their hearts, or so fix this doctrine deeply in their minds that it should never escape.[2]

Hence, the goal of Moses' teaching was not to lead Israel toward rote memorization or wooden adherence to the Law. The goal was a change in the very way God's people thought.

When we come to God, everything changes. We begin to use words like *faith*, *salvation*, and *eternity*. More than that, our behaviors and attitudes begin to be transformed. In short, coming to faith means changing worldviews. I believe this truth has at least two very significant implications as it relates to raising godly children.

First, if following the Lord means changing our worldview, we must acquire a basic understanding of what a worldview entails. Second, if our worldview must change, the biblical worldview is not our default position. In other words, if biblical worldview thinking were normal for us, there would be no need to adapt our worldview when we come to faith. Thus it is essential that we learn what a worldview is in general and the biblical worldview in particular.

Researcher George Barna suggests that people do not get a biblical worldview simply by regularly attending church. He argues, "A biblical worldview must be both taught and caught—that is, it has to be explained and modeled. Clearly, there are huge segments of the Christian body that are missing the benefit of such a comprehensive and consistent expression of biblical truth."[3]

What Is a Worldview?

The term *worldview* has been tossed about in Christian circles with increasing frequency as of late. There have been numerous worldview books published in the last decade—*How Now Shall We Live?* by Charles Colson and Nancy Pearcey, *Total Truth* by Nancy Pearcey, *Think Like Jesus* by George Barna, *Worldviews in Conflict* by Ronald Nash, *Naming the Elephant* by James W. Sire, *Clash of Worlds* by David Burnett, and more. It's hard to walk through a Christian bookstore without bumping into a book with *worldview* in the title. Nevertheless, most Christians struggle to define the term. Perhaps the best way to work toward a definition of worldview is to look at what it does.

Our Glasses

A worldview, according to Francis Schaeffer, is the "grid through which [one] sees the world."[4] In other words, a worldview is like a pair of glasses. Think about the first time you put on a pair of colored shades or placed someone else's prescription lenses on your eyes. Immediately the world took on a new shade, or maybe even got bigger or smaller. That is exactly what a worldview does.

On September 11, 2001, people throughout the western world looked on in horror as news of the terrorist attacks spread. However, who can forget the pictures of Palestinian Muslims dancing in the streets and passing out sweets to the children as though it were a holiday? This is a prime example of the impact of worldview. My lens saw a tragedy while others saw a triumph.

I witnessed the same phenomenon as a young seminarian. I was a student at Southwestern Baptist Theological Seminary when the O.J. Simpson trial captured the attention of the entire nation. Not much was said in the halls, but when the verdict was read, people's actions spoke volumes. I specifically remember black students cheering while white students and faculty shook their heads in disgust and disbelief.

As I walked out of the lounge where many of us had gathered to hear the verdict, one of my friends, a white pastor in his mid-thirties, asked me, "What just happened in there?" He couldn't believe the stark contrast between the two groups of people in that room. They were all students at the same seminary, followers of the same Jesus, readers of the same Bible, but their worldviews were worlds apart. It was as though the two groups of people were looking at the same picture through entirely different lenses.

Our Assumptions

James Sire expands on this idea when he states, "Our ground-floor assumptions—ones that are so basic that none more basic can be conceived—compose our worldview."[5] Most people's worldview is not based on critical analysis but on assumption. We don't spend our formative years evaluating the merits of cultural assumptions. We simply see the way things are and fall in line.

I remember walking through the airport in London and watching a woman walking several feet behind her husband carrying bags like a pack mule. She was a very small woman covered from head to toe. She had two small children and several suitcases. I remember thinking, *What a jerk!* My western sense of chivalry was offended. I'm the guy who was taught to always walk on the outside of the woman when walking down the street, to always open doors, to wait for the lady to be seated before taking my seat, and a whole host of other things related to the proper treatment of women.

However, when that man looked at me through his cultural lens, he probably thought my wife (and the wives of the other westerners in the airport) was extremely disrespectful for walking with me as though she were my equal. He probably thought I was setting a bad example for my children and that my daughter would grow up to be a terrible wife to some man. We all have assumptions. There are things we take for granted that others would consider quite peculiar.

Our Big Picture

Chuck Colson and Nancy Pearcey put an even finer point on the matter in their book *How Now Shall We Live?* They define worldview as "the sum total of our beliefs about the world, the big picture that directs our daily decisions and actions."[6] The key to the Colson/

Pearcey definition is in the last line. Our worldview "directs our daily decisions and actions." You and I act upon what we believe.

Our children will ultimately act on what they believe too. If we do not give our children a biblical worldview, they will simply follow our rules while they are under our watchful eye, but as soon as they gain independence, they will begin to make decisions based upon their worldview. How many times have we seen this scenario played out? A young man or woman who was raised in a "good Christian home" goes off to college and loses his cotton-pickin' mind! What happened? It's actually quite simple; the restraints were removed, and his worldview took over.

Like most fathers, I have undertaken the arduous task of putting together a swing set for my children. I won't bore you with the details, but suffice it to say that I learned a valuable lesson about why they include instructions with such things.

Our worldview functions much like the set of instructions for a swing set. Each decision in our life is like a part of that swing set. By itself it may seem insignificant or even meaningless. However, when we look at the instructions (the big picture) we see where this seemingly insignificant piece fits. Your worldview is the set of instructions by which you determine the proper place for every thought, action, behavior, opinion, and decision in your life.

Why Our Kids Need a Biblical Worldview

In 2005 I started conducting conferences throughout the United States. The conferences were based on my first book, *The Ever-Loving Truth*. These weren't worldview conferences per se, but I did deal with the issue. After one of the conferences in Pensacola, Florida I received the following e-mail from a young lady I'll call Katy. She wrote:

> What made the situation so interesting to me was that not only was I trying to pay attention to what I was doing, I was actually reading *Ever-loving Truth* just before I slipped right back into "pluralistic, secular humanism," I believe it was called. We were discussing a book in my English class called "Of Mice and Men." (If you aren't familiar with the book, the general story line is about two men who travel together. One of them is mentally retarded and keeps getting into trouble and

doing very bad things without realizing it. When it becomes clear that the man is going to be caught, and killed, probably after being tormented and abused, his friend shoots him in the back of the head.) We had a discussion in class about whether this was right and if it could really be considered murder under the circumstances. So, immediately going on autopilot, I start to write down my usual answer—it wasn't really right but it was probably okay . . . and I realized. This is it! This is exactly what you were talking about. Through the entire discussion, not one person would admit that murder is murder is murder. Thou shall not kill. Period! But it was merciful, and it was for his own good and the circumstances. . . . I persisted throughout the conversation bringing up the undeniable—murder, but once I said the words "absolute truth," I was completely ignored. I was removed from intelligent conversation because I was being unreasonable. And I almost went along with it! Obviously, I'm still a long way from a true Christian worldview, but I'm trying, and I'm learning.

How would your child have fared in Katy's class? Better yet, how would you have done? Would you or your children be able to have an intelligent conversation with someone who wanted to know the biblical, theological, and philosophical foundation upon which you base your ethical decisions? Would you be able to "make a defense to everyone who asks you to give an account for the hope that is in you" (1 Peter 3:15)? I don't mean take time to sit down, gather your Bible study tools, do an Internet search, collect your thoughts, and present your argument. I mean, do you have the answers ready? Are they "on your heart"?

If your answer is no, you are not alone. Moreover, if your kids aren't quite there, they are not alone either. I teach a biblical worldview class at a local college, and I am continually amazed at how rare it is to find students who possess a biblical worldview. I am not talking about clueless eighteen-year-olds either. The college where I teach caters to older, nontraditional ministerial students. I regularly encounter pastors, Sunday school directors, youth ministers, and church leaders (most of whom are in their late thirties) who simply do not think biblically. What's worse, many of them are initially skeptical of and resistant to the biblical worldview.

In his research for the National Study of Youth and Religion,

Christian Smith found that "impressively articulate teens were few and far between." He continues, "The vast majority simply could not express themselves on matters of God, faith, religion, or spiritual life."[7] Anticipating questions about the general ability of these teens to articulate clearly on other issues, Smith writes:

> We do not believe that teenage inarticulacy about religious matters reflects any general teen incapacity to think and speak well. Many of the youth we interviewed were quite conversant when it came to many other views on salient issues in their lives about which they had been educated and practiced discussing, such as the dangers of drug abuse and STDs. Rather, our impression as interviewers was that many teen-agers could not articulate matters of faith because they have not been effectively educated in and provided opportunities to practice talking about their faith.[8]

Unfortunately, this should come as no surprise. Researcher George Barna found that less than 10 percent of self-proclaimed "born-again Christians" in America have a biblical worldview. What's worse, he found that only half (51 percent) of America's pastors have a biblical worldview. Lamenting his findings, Barna writes:

> The most important point is that you can't give people what you don't have. The low percentage of Christians who have a biblical world-view is a direct reflection of the fact that half of our primary religious teachers and leaders do not have one. In some denominations, the vast majority of clergy do not have a biblical worldview, and it shows up clearly in the data related to the theological views and moral choices of people who attend those churches.[9]

Unless these figures change, future generations are in trouble. A church filled with people who lack a biblical worldview is no church at all.

Basic Elements of a Worldview

Opinions vary as to what comprises a worldview. However, for our purposes we will limit the discussion to the five most basic elements: our view of God, man, truth, knowledge, and ethics. Teaching our children to think biblically in these five basic areas will go a long way toward establishing a foundation for biblical thinking in their lives.

In order to contextualize these ideas, we will examine them in light of the ongoing conflict in our culture between Secular Humanism and Christian Theism. Secular Humanism is the most popular worldview in our culture today (as you will recognize). In fact, many Christians in our society identify more readily with elements of Secular Humanism than they do with Christian Theism.

Another thing you will notice as we journey on is that the structural elements and core components of Secular Humanism explain a great deal of the current cultural conflict. Perhaps you have asked questions like, "Why is there such debate over teaching intelligent design alongside the theory of evolution?" or "How could anyone be opposed to a ban on partial birth abortion?" An even better question is, "In an election that saw Marriage Amendments (defining marriage as a relationship between a man and a woman, thus banning so-called gay marriage) pass overwhelmingly, why did the majority of eighteen- to twenty-four-year-olds vote against the measures?" All of these things come into clear focus when we understand the elements of the secular humanist worldview.

	SECULAR HUMANISM	CHRISTIAN THEISM
VIEW OF GOD	ATHEISM	THEISM
VIEW OF MAN	EVOLUTION	SPECIAL CREATION
VIEW OF TRUTH	RELATIVE	ABSOLUTE
VIEW OF KNOWLEDGE	SCIENTIFIC/ MATERIALISM/ NATURALISM	SCIENTIFIC/ GENERAL/NATURAL REVELATION
VIEW OF ETHICS	CULTURAL	ABSOLUTE

What Do You Believe About God?

The first question we must answer is, what is the nature of God? Secular Humanism takes an atheistic position on the question of God, while Christian Theism, as the name would imply, comes from a theistic or God-focused perspective. In other words, Secular Humanism (the dominant worldview in our culture) argues that there is no God, while Christian Theism believes in a personal God who created, rules, and interacts with the world.

It is often noted that the majority of Americans (some put the number as high as 90 percent) claim to believe in God. Thus it seems inconsistent to argue that Secular Humanism, with its inherent atheistic tendencies, is the dominant worldview in America. It is important to note that many secular humanists will claim to believe in God in some form, but their belief is usually a canard. Some argue that there must be some "higher power" or "guiding force" in the universe, but they fall short of declaring a belief in the God of the Bible. In his book *A New Christianity for a New World*, John Shelby Spong argues that our understanding of the modern scientific world makes it necessary for Christians to develop a new, "non-theistic" view of God. In other words, Spong, an admitted secular humanist, acknowledges the fact that the theistic view of God does not fit his worldview. But as an Episcopal priest he also acknowledges that blatant atheism doesn't quite fit his context. The problem, of course, is that this so-called "non-theistic" view of God bears no resemblance to the God of the Bible.

The God of the Bible is personal. The God of the Bible is not a force or an idea; He is a person. The God of the Bible is rational, relational, communicative, and emotional. The God of the Bible speaks to and through His prophets. He calls His people to Himself. He redeems lost sinners and judges the unrepentant.

The God of the Bible is sovereign. He knows every hair on your head, every blade of grass, every sparrow that flies, and every autumn leaf that falls. The God of the Bible never slumbers or sleeps. He is never caught off guard or surprised. The God of the Bible knows the end from the beginning. He knew all of our days before we were born.

The God of the Bible is holy. He cannot sin. He is the very source of truth and righteousness. There is no shadow in Him. God's very nature is good. God makes no mistakes and can do no wrong.

The God of the Bible is the Creator of the world. In the beginning God created the heavens and the earth. With these words the Bible announces one of its central themes in the first line of the first chapter of the first book. This may seem simple and insignificant, but in reality this is the core of the biblical worldview. If God created the world, Secular Humanism is not even a remote possibility. If God created the world, then God created man. If God created the world, then our view of truth, knowledge, and ethics must be shaped by this single fact. The biblical worldview rises and falls with this simple concept.

What Do You Believe About Man?

The second major question that a worldview must answer is, what is the nature of man? Secular Humanism views man as the end result of random evolutionary processes, while Christian Theism sees man as a special creation of God. This is seen clearly in the current evolution debate.

What is at stake here, however, is far more significant than whether we will teach intelligent design or not. This worldview element also cuts to the heart of the abortion debate. If man is merely a glorified single-celled organism run amok, he has no inherent worth, value, or dignity; ultimately man is then merely a cosmic accident, and the human community bestows any value he has upon him.

It is not difficult to see how this would lead to a radical view on abortion. Peter Singer, a renowned bioethicist at Princeton University, argues that abortion should be legal prior to "personhood." What makes this shocking is that Singer's definition of personhood would carry the abortion question not into the second or third trimester of a pregnancy but into the second year after birth. That's right, by Singer's definition my thirteen-month-old son (due to the fact that he cannot communicate or sustain his own life without help) has not yet reached personhood, and to take his life now would be no more problematic than a pre-birth abortion.

While this is shocking, I must ask a question: What is the difference between my thirteen-month-old son and a six-month-old fetus? The answer is, location. If it is acceptable to kill a child in the womb, it is also acceptable to do so outside the womb. Peter Singer is not being morbid; he is being consistent. The only difference between him and many Christians who take a pro-choice stance in the abortion debate is the coherence of his view of man. A quick look at the biblical picture of the nature of man makes this clear.

The Bible teaches that man is created in the image of God. In Genesis 1:26 the Bible records the words of the Triune God: "Let Us make man in Our image, according to Our likeness." He continues, "let them rule over the fish of the sea and over the birds of the sky and over the cattle and over all the earth, and over every creeping thing that creeps on the earth." Thus man was created as the crowning glory of the creation. This truth has several important implications, not the least of which is the dignity and value of every man.

As God's image-bearer man has inherent dignity and value. When you and I look into the eyes of another human being, we are looking at God's image-bearer. Regardless of race, color, creed, socioeconomic status, or even evil deeds, every man, woman, boy, and girl has inherent value due to his or her creation in the image of God. Secular Humanism cannot make this claim. If man is merely the result of a cosmic accident, there is no inherent dignity or value in human life. In fact, it was this type of evolutionary thinking that led to the atrocities of the Nazi regime in Hitler's Germany. If there are races of people who represent a higher level of evolution than others, then it is incumbent on the more evolved race to dominate and/or exterminate the less evolved. While most secular humanists would abhor such thinking, my question to them would be, on what grounds?

In Adam, man fell into sin. Some argue that man is basically good. I have always believed those people don't have kids of their own. If they did, they couldn't make such a statement with a straight face. Don't get me wrong—I love my children. However, I am also not naive. I know that my children (like all children) are sinners from the word go. The Bible leaves no room for debate on this issue.

Behold, I was brought forth in iniquity, and in sin my mother conceived me. (Psalm 51:5)

"There is none righteous, not even one; there is none who understands, there is none who seeks for God; all have turned aside, together they have become useless; there is none who does good, there is not even one." (Romans 3:10-12)

All have sinned and fall short of the glory of God. (Romans 3:23)

Apart from the redemptive work of Christ, man remains in his sin. Perhaps nothing sets the biblical worldview apart like this simple truth. Nowhere else do we find an answer to man's sin problem. Other religions and worldviews seem to suggest that all one must do to be righteous is have a religious experience, then try to do more good than bad and hope for the best in the end. Again the Bible offers a clear answer.

> *For the wages of sin is death, but the free gift of God is eternal life in Christ Jesus our Lord. (Romans 6:23)*

> *For Christ also died for sins once for all, the just for the unjust, so that He might bring us to God, having been put to death in the flesh, but made alive in the spirit. (1 Peter 3:18)*

> *For He rescued us from the domain of darkness, and transferred us to the kingdom of His beloved Son, in whom we have redemption, the forgiveness of sins. He is the image of the invisible God, the firstborn of all creation. (Colossians 1:13-15)*

> *For there is one God, and one mediator also between God and men, the man Christ Jesus, who gave Himself as a ransom for all, the testimony given at the proper time. (1 Timothy 2:5-6)*

What Do You Believe About Truth?

The third major question we must answer is, what is the nature of truth? Secular Humanism believes truth is relative. In other words, what's true for me is not necessarily true for you. Christian Theism sees truth as objective and absolute. My co-teacher, Paul Shockley, has one of the best definitions of truth I have ever encountered. He defines truth as:

> That which corresponds to reality, identifies things as they actually are, can never fail, diminish, change, or be extinguished, must be able to be expressed in propositional statements, and is sourced in the God of the Bible who is the Author of all truth.

Each element of this definition could be developed into an entire chapter. However, for our purposes it provides enough foundational information to see the difference between Secular Humanism's view of truth and that of Christian Theism.

Unfortunately, this is one area where we are clearly losing the battle. The Nehemiah Institute (like the Barna Group) has discovered that some 85 percent of Christian teens do not believe in the existence of absolute truth. These young people, who identify themselves as followers of Christ, believe that truth is situational and relative. This is precisely the reason worldview training is so crucial for our children. I have had numerous conversations with Christian high school and college students who struggle at this point. I don't think most parents have the slightest idea how difficult it is to grow up in today's philosophical climate and to hold on to any concept of absolute truth.

What Do You Believe About Knowledge?

The fourth major question our worldview must answer is, how do we know what we know? Secular Humanism (and its component, Naturalistic Materialism) is based on the assumption that nature is a closed system, and therefore all knowledge is derived from the study of this closed system through reason and the scientific method. Christian Theism, on the other hand, holds that God created the world and everything in it; therefore, our pursuit of knowledge must balance reason and revelation.

This is not to say that Christian Theism is anti-science. On the contrary, it was Christian Theism that gave rise to science. Scientists such as Galileo and Copernicus believed in an intelligent, orderly Creator whose creation could and must be studied in an orderly fashion. It is Naturalism (with its insistence on the world materializing out of nothing) that flies in the face of true science. If the world has no purpose or design, what good is science? If there are no absolutes, how can we rely on our scientific discoveries?

We come to know truth through God's revelation in creation. This is called general revelation. God has spoken to man through the created order. The Bible is filled with beautiful expressions of this truth.

The heavens are telling of the glory of God; and their expanse is declaring the work of His hands. (Psalm 19:1)

And the heavens declare His righteousness, for God Himself is judge. (Psalm 50:6)

For the wrath of God is revealed from heaven against all ungodliness and unrighteousness of men who suppress the truth in unrighteousness, because that which is known about God is evident within them; for God made it evident to them. For since the creation of the world His invisible attributes, His eternal power and divine nature, have been clearly seen, being understood through what has been made, so that they are without excuse. (Romans 1:18-20)

Christian Theism does not divorce knowledge from revelation. It is important that we realize that God has designed the world in such a way that we can understand something about Him through true scientific research.

One of the most tragic developments of our day is the abandonment of the hard sciences by the Christian community. Teaching our children what the Bible says about creation and giving them a biblical worldview should ignite a renewed interest in biology, geology, astronomy, chemistry, and physics. The secular humanists are at a distinct disadvantage due to the inconsistency of their worldview. Christian Theists must once again take their place at the forefront of scientific inquiry in pursuit of a better understanding of the world and the God who created it.

We come to know truth through God's revelation in His Word. This is special revelation. God has given us the universe and all of its glory, but that pales in comparison to His self-revelation in the Bible. God has communicated directly to man through His Word. "But know this first of all, that no prophecy of Scripture is a matter of one's own interpretation, for no prophecy was ever made by an act of human will, but men moved by the Holy Spirit spoke from God" (2 Peter 1:20-21).

What Do You Believe About Ethics?

The final question our worldview must answer is, how do we determine right and wrong? Secular Humanism views ethics as cultural and negotiable. In other words, what is ethical in America in the twenty-first century was not necessarily ethical in Germany in the twentieth century or in ancient Rome in the first century. Thus many history professors are unwilling to call what Hitler, Mussolini, Pol Pot, or Nero did unethical. Those rulers were merely acting in accordance with the ethics of their time and circumstances. Christian Theism, however, views ethics as timeless and absolute.

God determines what is right and what is wrong. Humanism begins with man as its starting point and works its way out from there. Thus the humanistic view of ethics begins with what works for me. This has led to Pragmatism (the view that results, rather than theories and principles, determine proper action) and Utilitarianism (the view that the greatest happiness of the greatest number should be the criterion of the virtue of action).[10] Sadly, these philosophies are as prevalent in much of the church growth movement as they are in modern politics, law, marketing, and education.

God's Word gives us clear instruction on ethics. "All Scripture is inspired by God and profitable for teaching, for reproof, for correction, for training in righteousness; so that the man of God may be adequate, equipped for every good work" (2 Timothy 3:16-17). God's Word is sufficient to equip us to do the good works (ethics) to which He calls us. Peter echoes and expands this thought when he writes:

> . . . *seeing that His divine power has granted to us everything pertaining to life and godliness, through the true knowledge of Him who called us by His own glory and excellence. For by these He has granted to us His precious and magnificent promises, so that by them you may become partakers of the divine nature, having escaped the corruption that is in the world by lust. (2 Peter 1:3-4)*

Note Peter's reference to "the true knowledge" and "His precious and magnificent promises." These are references to God's revelation. We know God through His Word. We have access to the promises of God through His Word. In other words, God has granted to us all of the information we need to live ethically, and it begins with true knowledge and the promises of God, both of which are found in His Word.

Ethics transcend time and culture. Truth knows no boundaries or borders. Biblical ethical principles can be applied universally. If it is wrong to commit adultery in Pakistan, it is also wrong to do it in Australia. If it was wrong to commit adultery in ancient Israel, it is also wrong in modern America. Local laws, customs, and penalties may be different, but the principle God outlined in the Seventh Commandment knows no boundaries.

A family cannot function properly unless all of its members are committed to the same game plan. The method of choice seems to be group negotiation with a view toward "what works best for us." This, however, is no substitute for prayerful submission to God's plan for the institution He created.

Watch Out for Legalism

Sometimes we fall into the trap of substituting legalism for a biblical worldview. For example, we set hard and fast rules for what our children wear, watch, see, and hear but never take the time to develop the kind of thinking that would guide them in such decisions. Don't get me wrong. I believe wholeheartedly that parents must diligently protect their children from ungodly influences. I also believe that limits must be set and rules must be established. I am simply suggesting that limits and rules are insufficient in and of themselves.

If all I give my children is limits and rules, they will do what I tell them as long as I am around. But once they leave my home, they will live in accordance with their worldview, not my rules. Thus I must spend as much time shaping and molding their thinking as I do making rules. Legalism simply sets up external, extra-biblical standards that take the place of biblical thinking.

When *The Passion of the Christ* was released, I made several phone calls encouraging friends and family to go see the movie. Bridget and I had seen it early on and were completely blown away. I also made what I must admit was a rather facetious phone call to a pastor friend of mine. He was on staff at a church where I had preached numerous times over the years. I called him at his office and inquired as to whether or not he had seen the film. He responded with a resounding yes!

After he and I shared a few comments about the movie, I posed the question I had really called to ask: "Is your pastor recommending that his members go see this *R-rated* movie?" He immediately broke into almost uncontrollable laughter as he remembered an incident that occurred after one of my sermons at the church. When he finally caught his breath, he said, "I had almost forgotten about that."

What was so funny? During one of my sermons I addressed the issue of legalism. At one point I raised the issue of R-rated movies as an example of modern-day legalism. I said, "Some people will watch *Titanic* seven times and never even blush at the sight of Kate Winslet's naked breasts but refuse to watch *Schindler's List* because it is rated R!"

I went on to argue that *Titanic* was inappropriate regardless of Hollywood's PG-13 rating, and *Schindler's List* deserved our attention even though it accurately depicted gruesome historical events. My point was that rating systems allow us to turn off our minds and cease to take responsibility for what we watch. I suggested that we examine the content of movies and make educated, responsible decisions about what we watch instead of falling into a legalistic trap that ends up excusing some godless viewings while sometimes preventing us from examining films that could enrich our lives in spite of the fact that they don't pull punches when it comes to historical facts.

This did not sit well with the pastor. He called me into his office a few days later and asked me to apologize. When I asked for an explanation as to what I had done that required an apology, he simply said that several members had written e-mails or made phone calls saying they were offended by what I said. I asked him if I had violated anything in the text from which I preached. He said no. In fact, he said he had listened to my message twice and found nothing unbiblical. Nevertheless he thought I should apologize for the sake of those who were offended. Of course, I refused.

Fast forward two years, and this same pastor who asked me to apologize for suggesting that an R-rating did not necessarily eliminate a movie for Christians was recommending an R-rated movie to his congregation! Of course, he would argue that this film is merely an accurate depiction of the violent death of Christ and has redemptive value because of its content. However, that does not change the fact that he violated his own R-rating rule. If he believed the rule, he should have condemned *The Passion of the Christ.*

This is a prime example of what is wrong with legalism. When we begin to make hard-and-fast rules based upon cultural norms rather than on the Bible, we will always end up in trouble. Have you ever been to a church that didn't allow women to wear pants? How about one that doesn't allow its members to go dancing? I have. And when I brought up the very passages they used to justify their positions and demonstrated that the passages actually contradicted their stance, all I got was, "Well, that's just the way we believe . . ." *Lord, help us!*

It is very important that we live by biblical standards. However, it is equally important that we continually examine those standards to ensure that we don't fall prey to legalism. And if we do have convictions that are not necessarily scriptural, we should admit it. We must be able to say, "This is a personal conviction to which I hold myself, not a standard to which God holds us all."

The next time you sit down for a family meal, open your book to this chapter (the page with the chart), pull out a piece of paper and a pen, and ask your children a few simple questions about their view of God, truth, knowledge, man, and ethics. Ask them where they get their answers. Push them on their source of authority. Ask for book, chapter, and verse.

If your children can answer these questions from a biblical perspective with any degree of confidence, then you (and they) are truly blessed. In fact, you need to be writing books on this subject rather than just reading them. On the other hand, if your family is anything like most American Christian families, this exercise will be an eye-opener. But do not be discouraged. You are merely becoming aware of the harsh reality that so many in the Christian community have ignored for far too long. Our children are not being equipped to resist the secular humanist onslaught of our post-Christian culture.

After you have assessed your children's worldview, you are well on your way to equipping them to think biblically. Just as when you are fixing your car, discovering the problem is half the battle. Once you know that your children struggle with their view of man, you can grab your Bible, look up key verses dealing with the subject, and teach the Word. If you feel like you need help, jump on the World Wide Web. Dozens of sites will help you address biblical worldview issues (here are a few sites to get you started: nehemiahinstitute.com, reformed. org, americanvision.org).

On a more holistic note, you may just want to get a handle on all five areas and make them the outline for your teaching over the next five weeks (or five months). Just make it a point to give your children a firm grasp on all of the worldview categories regardless of where they are right now. You will be amazed at how many areas of everyday life you will address along the way.

Take Action

1. Make a copy of the chart in this chapter, and add a blank column. Gather your children together, and ask them their views on the five key worldview categories. Fill in the empty column, and compare it to the other two columns.
2. Discuss the differences between Christian Theism and Secular Humanism and how your family's answers line up with each.
3. Discuss the logical conclusions of each worldview as it relates to contemporary issues.

5

TEACH THE WORD AT HOME

"You shall teach [God's Word] diligently to your sons."
DEUTERONOMY 6:7

Moses saw the home as the principal delivery system for the transmittal of God's truth from generation to generation. There is no hint here—or anywhere else in the Bible—of the multigenerational teaching of the truths of God being abdicated by parents in favor of "trained professionals." That is not to say that parents should reject any help. If I believed that, I wouldn't have written this book. However, we must be careful not to shift the responsibility for our children's biblical training onto anyone else.

The Way Things Are

As we have seen, Christian Smith's work on the National Study of Youth and Religion is both revealing and convicting. Unfortunately, as his research clearly shows, we are doing a poor job of raising our children in the "discipline and instruction of the Lord" (Ephesians 6:4). Part of the problem is the way we spend our time.

> Religious faith and practice in American teenagers' lives operate in a social and institutional environment that is highly competitive for time, attention and energy. Religious interests and values in teens' lives typically compete against those of school, homework, television, other media, sports, romantic relationships, paid work, and more.[1]

Far too many families have pushed the study of the Scriptures to the back burner. In fact, in many instances, there is no room for Bible study at all.

As Smith points out, "many religious teens in the United States appear to engage in few religious practices."[2] This is especially true when it comes to prayer and the study of the Word. His answer?

> [E]ven basic practices like regular Bible reading and personal prayer seem clearly associated with stronger and deeper faith commitment among youth. We suspect that youth educators and ministers will not get far with youth in other words, unless regular and intentional religious practices become an important part of their larger faith formation.[3]

Please don't miss Smith's last point. "Youth educators and ministers will not get far . . ." Smith is absolutely correct. We simply cannot fail to give our children the basic tools they need and expect the "professionals" to get the job done for us.

However, don't miss another important point. "[E]ven basic practices like Bible reading" have an impact on our children's faith commitment. That's right, it doesn't take much. You can impact your child's faith-life by reading and teaching the Bible at home. More importantly, God has entrusted and commissioned you (not the youth minister or the Sunday school teacher) with this awesome task.

I wish I could say my wife and I understood this from day one, but we did not. It was years before we understood the significance of daily time in the Word as a family. Oh, to have those days back. How I long for another opportunity to lay the foundation. However, I am so blessed to know that God can meet us right where we are and make up for lost time.

God Sent Them Home with You

I will never forget the day we brought my daughter Jasmine home. It was my junior year in college. I was struggling to balance marriage, college, and football when God dropped a baby into the mix. Bridget and I had only been married ten months when she was born. I was terrified!

I remember vividly the way I felt as I stood there wiping Bridget's brow and encouraging her as she battled through labor. We were so young then. I was just twenty-one. As the night went on, the moment of truth arrived. The doctor looked up and said, "I can see the head; give me one more good push." I immediately left Bridget's side and walked around to get a better view of this incredible moment. God was about to deliver another life into the world, and I was there to see it!

As Jasmine emerged, I remember two distinct thoughts that came to my mind. The first was, "Please wash her off." Then I remember thinking, "I can't believe I am this child's father." This was *my* daughter. Suddenly I became weak in the knees.

When the time came for us to take her home, I couldn't believe it. I just stood there looking at the nurse as she placed this beautiful, helpless creature in my arms. She pushed Bridget out of the hospital in the obligatory wheelchair, helped her into the car, and offered words of encouragement as I nervously locked my daughter into her safety seat. As I sat down behind the wheel of our brand-new 1989 Geo Metro, I remember thinking, "I can't believe they're leaving her with us!"

As I started the car, I nervously looked around waiting for someone to come running out of the hospital shouting, "Stop them! They're getting away with that baby!" But it didn't happen. I started the car, put it in gear, and drove off toward our apartment where the three of us would embark on a lifelong adventure together. I was somebody's father! The thought overwhelmed and excited me all at the same time. I remember thinking about all the things we had to do for this little girl. She had to be fed, changed, clothed, educated, and protected. She had to be brought up in the "nurture and admonition of the Lord" (Ephesians 6:4, KJV). And the only people on whom this obligation fell were my wife and me. This little girl was *our responsibility*.

That doesn't mean we would be the only ones who would teach, protect, and nurture her. On the contrary, we have had numerous partners in the process over the years. I am grateful for grandparents, aunts, uncles, and family friends who have walked with us through the ups and downs. However, when it is all said and done, my wife and I are ultimately responsible and accountable for this child with which the Lord has entrusted us.

Assuming Responsibility

Imagine your boss came into your office and said, "Congratulations, you have just been promoted." What if that promotion meant stepping into a job for which you felt inadequate and/or unprepared? How would you respond? Would you say, "Thank you, sir, but I am not up to the task"? Or would you say, "Thank you, sir, I'll do my best"? I think most of us would welcome the challenge and rise to the occasion.

As parents, that's exactly what God said to us when He gave us children. He said, "Congratulations, you've just been promoted to the position of parent." That means that everything God requires of parents is part of your new job description. At this point you have two choices. You can either say, "Thank You, God, but You must have taken momentary leave of Your senses. There's no way I can train my children in the Word." Or you can say, "Thank You, God. I know You don't make mistakes, and if You gave me this child, You will also give me everything I need to bring her up in the discipline and instruction of the Lord."

I wish I could say that my response was the latter. However, I must admit that I was terrified. I was a twenty-one-year-old college junior who had been married for ten months. I remember looking at one of my professors and asking, "What am I going to do?" He looked back at me and said, "You are going to do the same thing fathers have been doing for thousands of years." Suddenly it dawned on me—I wasn't the first man to become a father while he was in college. I could handle this. I wasn't sure how, but I knew that with God's help I could handle this.

My professor's words of encouragement have echoed in my mind for the past fifteen years. I am still trying to navigate my role as a husband and father, but I am sure that God has given me what I need to accomplish the task to which I have been called.

Teaching Is the Best Teacher

As homeschool parents, my wife and I are often asked how we homeschool two high-school-aged children. Many families believe they could never teach their children at home past the third grade! I cannot tell you how many times I have heard the standard line, "By the time they reach high school, they'll be past anything I could handle."

Whenever my wife and I encounter such comments we merely reply, "You only have to stay a week ahead." I love to see the look on people's faces when they realize the simple yet profound truth of this statement. All we really need to do to teach our children is stay a step ahead of them. Of course, this means that we must be in a constant state of learning, but it is doable. The same is true in teaching the Bible.

So many parents think they don't have enough Bible knowledge to teach their children. Nothing could be further from the truth. If you can read, you can teach your children God's Word. All you have to do is stay a step ahead of them. Don't be afraid. God has given you everything you need to do this. You don't have to be a seminary-trained theologian to read the Bible and talk about what it means. Besides, God would not have given you the responsibility unless He knew you could handle it. One of the oft-forgotten Reformation doctrines is the doctrine of the *perspicuity* (or understandability) of the Bible. God has given us the Bible in an understandable form. We do not have to break codes or unravel riddles in order to understand the basic teaching of God's Word.

The Role of the Home in Teaching the Bible

Contrary to popular belief, the home, not the church, has been entrusted with the primary responsibility of teaching children the Bible. In our age of professionalism we tend to hire out virtually every parental responsibility. We want Johnny to succeed at sports, so we hire a professional for private lessons. We want Susie to get into a good college, so we hire a special tutor to boost her SAT score. We want our children to be upstanding citizens and Christians, so we hire a children's pastor or youth minister.

There is nothing wrong with wanting our children to succeed (as long as we have a biblical view of success). Nor is there anything inherently wrong with seeking help when we need it. However, we have gone beyond seeking help to abdicating our responsibility. Unfortunately, this abdication has become so common in spiritual matters that words like these from John Bunyan sound foreign:

> [C]oncerning the spiritual state of his family; [the father] ought to be very diligent and cautious, doing his utmost both to increase faith where it is begun, and to begin it where it is not. Therefore, he must diligently and frequently bring before his family the things of God, from His Holy Word, in accordance with what is suitable for each person. And let no man question his authority from the Word of God for such a practice.[4]

Both of my older children play classical piano. They have a teacher who is very serious about her craft. She insists that her students practice daily, attend lessons weekly, be evaluated at a piano guild, participate in at least one concert and one contest annually, and pass the annual state theory exam.

While each of these requirements is challenging, the one that requires the greatest level of parental encouragement is the state theory exam. However, my oldest child recently had a breakthrough. She realized that her commitment to and subsequent grasp of music theory was the catalyst for her recent growth as a player. She realized that the notes on the page represented what she was to play but theory was the why. Now she is poised not only to play music but to compose it as well.

If giving our children a biblical worldview is the why of family driven faith, giving them biblical instruction is the what. Our worldview shapes the way we think, but learning and memorizing the Scriptures determine what we think. For example, a child with a biblical worldview may understand the inherent dignity of his parents as human beings created in the image of God, but a child with biblical instruction also knows that the God who created his parents says, "Honor your mother and father." It is not an either/or proposition but a both/and mandate. We must give our children a biblical worldview, *and* we must instruct them in the Word of God. In fact, without the Word of God there is no biblical worldview.

One could argue that Chapters 4 and 5 should be reversed. And if we were speaking strictly about the development of a child's understanding of spiritual things, I would agree. However, when we look at things from the perspective of the parent, it is a much different proposition. As a parent I must start with the big picture in mind before I can fill in the details. If we continue with the foundation and frame illustration in the previous chapter (biblical love is the foundation, and a biblical worldview is the frame), then biblical instruction would be the detail of the home.

Several years ago Hillary Clinton made headlines with her *It Takes a Village* campaign.[5] This, of course, was borrowed from the familiar African proverb, "It takes a village to raise a child." However, the Hillary Clinton version sounds more like, "It takes big, intrusive government programs and bureaucrats to raise a child." Recently another U.S. Senator, Rick Santorum, issued a shot across the bow when he wrote *It Takes a Family*. However, the Hillary Clinton model has taken root. We have come to believe that parenting is a task best left to professionals. Unfortunately, this mentality is not limited to the culture at large; the church has also been affected.

Just a few generations ago a man was considered spiritually responsible if he led his family before the throne of God in prayer, read and taught the Scriptures at home, and led family devotions (among other things). Today parents are considered responsible if they find the church with the best-staffed nursery and the most up-to-date youth ministry. In fact, there is a rule in church growth circles known as the 3 P's: If you want to grow your church, concentrate on parking, preaching, and preschool. I am not suggesting that previous generations accomplished their parenting tasks perfectly. On the contrary, had they done their job we wouldn't be in the mess we are in now. However, the paradigm seems to have shifted away from parental responsibility, and the standard has been lowered considerably.

Home Training

When I was a boy, my mother had a saying for kids (including me) who misbehaved in public. She would look at the child and say, "That child needs some home training." In fact, when we would visit other people, she would often remind me to be on my best behavior by looking at me with one of those mommy looks and saying, "Act like you've had some home training."

Mom never explained exactly what home training was, but I always had a good idea. I knew that home training had to do with the way I behaved. I later learned that home training was directly related to whether or not I internalized the values my mother tried to instill. In other words, my mother was attempting to shape me into a civilized, thoughtful, well-mannered human being. That is what home training is all about.

Home Training Basics

I have since discovered that there is a home training manual. It is called the Holy Bible. God has given us everything we need for life and godliness (2 Timothy 3:16-17; 2 Peter 1:3), and that includes training and teaching our children. Anyone who has read the book of Proverbs knows that the Bible is filled with valuable child-training information. God has not left us in the dark on this issue. He wants us to know how to raise our children. But how do we go about teaching our children this vast, often intimidating book that most of us have a difficult time understanding ourselves?

Read the Bible

I often meet people who complain about the Bible's complexity or lack of relevance (or both). However, when I ask them how much of the Bible they've actually read, they usually begin to backtrack. It is amazing to me that people read a few verses of the Bible (out of context) and simply write the whole thing off as complex and/or irrelevant. Imagine someone reading Shakespeare's line about "a rose by any other word" and deciding that *Romeo and Juliet* is a poor example of tragic drama and Shakespeare himself wasn't much of a writer. Listen to what the Bible has to say about its place in our lives.

The Bible is our source of wisdom: "The mouth of the righteous utters wisdom, and his tongue speaks justice. The law of his God is in his heart; his steps do not slip" (Psalm 37:30-31). *The Bible is our source of righteousness*: "Your word I have treasured in my heart, that I may not sin against You" (Psalm 119:11). *The Bible is our source of direction*: "Your word is a lamp to my feet and a light to my path" (Psalm 119:105). *The Bible is our source of hope*: "For whatever was written in earlier times was written for our instruction, so that through perseverance and the encouragement of the Scriptures we might have hope" (Romans 15:4).

Our ultimate prayer for our children should be for them to utter the words of Psalm 40:8: "I delight to do your will, O my God; Your Law is within my heart." However, this will not happen unless we read the Bible at home. We must get our kids into the Word of God if we intend to get the Word of God into our kids. It won't happen by osmosis.

In our home we read through the Bible night by night. In the morning we have our time of family worship and catechism, but the evenings are a lot simpler. We just get on a schedule and work our way from Genesis to the maps. There are plenty of tools to help along the way. In fact, there is a one-year Bible designed to give you the Bible in daily doses and keep you on track to finish in a year. There are also numerous web sites that will send you a daily reminder of what sections you should read. I don't care what methodology you use as long as you are reading. You don't even have to do it in a year. You could slow down and do a two-year pace if you want. What matters is that you *read the Bible*.

Why is reading the Bible so important? That is a legitimate question. Let me offer a few answers. First, *the Bible is the very Word of God*. In 2 Timothy 3:16 Paul writes: "All Scripture is inspired by God and profitable for teaching, for reproof, for correction, for training in righteousness." The Bible is not just a good book—it's God's Book. In fact, the Bible is the plumb line against which we measure all other books.

Second, *the Bible is God's primary tool in preparing us for a life of godliness and service*. Paul continues in 2 Timothy 3:17, ". . . so that the man of God may be adequate, equipped for every good work." Peter echoes this idea in 2 Peter. 1:3 when he writes, ". . . seeing that His divine power has granted to us everything pertaining to life and godliness, through the true knowledge of Him who called us by His own glory and excellence."

Third, *the Bible is an agent by which God conforms us to the very image of Christ*. Second Peter 1:4 tells us, "For by these He has granted to us His precious and magnificent promises, so that by them you may become partakers of the divine nature, having escaped the corruption that is in the world by lust." Peter makes reference to "true knowledge" (v. 3) and "precious and magnificent promises" (v. 4). There is no doubt that the revelation of which Peter speaks is accessed through the Bible. I don't know about you, but I want to be like Jesus. More importantly, I want to raise sons and daughters who are like Jesus. God will use the Bible to make that happen. Reading the Bible will lead us to the true knowledge of the Lord. Reading the Bible will expose us to the "precious and magnificent promises" of the Lord. God will use the Bible to transform our lives.

Fourth, *the Bible is a change agent*. Hebrews 4:12 reads, "For the word of God is living and active and sharper than any two-edged sword, and piercing as far as the division of soul and spirit, of both joints and marrow, and able to judge the thoughts and intentions of the heart." You may not be able to change your son's heart, but the Word of God can. Try all you want, but you can't reach that sullen teenage daughter of yours the way the Bible can.

> Reading and memorizing Scripture and the catechisms of the church results in incredible development of children, both spiritually and intellectually. What families regard as important is evidenced by the manner in which they spend their time. Therefore, regular family worship shows the children that their parents believe that Jesus Christ is central to all of life. This practice leaves a legacy that will benefit thousands in generations to come.[6]

The Word of God changes lives! Don't take my word for it. Start reading it as a family and see for yourself.

Q & A

My family and I recently worked through R. C. Sproul's book *Essential Truths of the Christian Faith* during our breakfast devotionals. The book is divided into 102 small chapters, each one dealing with a great doctrine of the faith. Reading the daily chapter took no more than five or ten minutes. However, we often spent half an hour or more discussing the truths we read.

I wouldn't trade those morning discussions for anything. I absolutely love sitting around the breakfast table with my family, discussing the great doctrines of the Christian faith and their implications for the way we live our lives. In fact, we discovered that the children enjoy it as much as my wife and I do. Now we are working through Starr Meade's book *Training Hearts and Teaching Minds*. It is a daily devotional based on the Westminster Shorter Catechism. The type and level of questions we have encountered recently has been amazing.

Some time ago Bridget raised an issue that we needed to discuss as a family. The children sat and listened; they even added their two cents. At the end of the discussion Bridget and I rose from the table (about to head for our room to get ready for the day) when our eleven-year-old son chimed in, "Aren't we going to do the book today?" "Yeah, we forgot our devotion," Jasmine added as Trey reached over and grabbed the familiar text from the bay window next to the table. Bridget looked at me with a smile and said, "Yeah, Daddy, I can't believe you were going to leave the table without our morning devotional."

The fact is, my children weren't hungry little theologians who couldn't wait to tackle another complicated theological truth. They were just a couple of kids who had questions. As their parents we found an avenue for providing answers. All kids wonder about theology. What child hasn't asked questions like "Who made God?" or "If Jesus is God, how can He be the *Son of God*?" These are theological questions, and one of the greatest things we can do as parents is provide opportunities for those questions to be asked and answered. But how do we create such a place?

First, give your children permission to ask biblical questions. Bridget and I have been blessed with very inquisitive children. I say blessed because their inquisitive nature makes them very teachable. However, I must admit that we haven't always seen it as a blessing. Let's be honest—one can only take so much, "Daddy, why is that?" Eventually we all learn how to say, "That's just the way it is."

However, if you want your children to learn biblical truths, you are going to have to give them permission to ask biblical questions. That means we can't say it's OK with our lips but tell them something different with our attitude. We must demonstrate a genuine willingness and desire to hear our children out. Parents who huff and puff when their children ask biblical questions are saying, "Don't bother me, kid, I'm busy."

Second, validate your child's honest biblical questions. One of the best things you can say to an inquisitive child who asks you a theological question is, "That's a great question." Or better yet, you might say, "I have often wondered that myself." This not only lets the child know that it's alright to ask legitimate questions but affirms the factual nature of the Christian faith. Think about it. What if you kept asking someone about his or her faith but he or she never acknowledged or tried to answer your questions? Eventually you would assume that the person either didn't know very much about his or her faith or that there wasn't much to be known. The same is true with our children.

In fact, you may be reading this book right now looking for answers because no one cared enough or knew enough about the Christian faith to validate the legitimate questions you asked along the way. Perhaps you grew up believing that one must accept Christianity on "blind faith" but later realized there had to be more to it than that. Or maybe you had well-meaning parents who taught you things that turned out to be false. Although this may be common, it is not biblical.

The Bible gives a beautiful example of the kind of attitude we should have toward those to whom we teach the faith in the prologue to Luke's Gospel:

> *Inasmuch as many have undertaken to compile an account of the things accomplished among us, just as they were handed down to us by those*

who from the beginning were eyewitnesses and servants of the word, it seemed fitting for me as well, having investigated everything carefully from the beginning, to write it out for you in consecutive order, most excellent Theophilus; so that you may know the exact truth about the things you have been taught. (Luke 1:1-4, emphasis added)

Note Luke's choice of words and phrases: *compile, eyewitnesses, investigated, carefully, consecutive order, exact truth.* This is not the stuff of fairy tale or legend. This is solid, verifiable, historically reliable truth! Let your children know that our faith can stand up to their questions.

Third, answer your child's biblical question. It's one thing to validate a question; it's quite another to answer it. A child who is encouraged to ask biblical questions and has those questions validated but unanswered may get the idea that the Bible has no answers or that his parents don't. In either case a very important authority in the child's life will be undermined.

I have told the story of my journey to faith so many times that those closest to me know it by rote. That story is important to me for many reasons—not least of which is the fact that I was lost, but now I'm found. However, one of the most important elements of my story is the fact that the young man who shared the message of Christ with me took the time to answer all of my questions (over a period of three weeks).

Sometimes those answers were on the tip of his tongue. However, I distinctly remember that on more than one occasion he had to admit that he didn't have an answer. But he didn't stop there. He always followed up with, "but I will find out." Eventually he would find the answer to my questions. This process taught me two things that have greatly impacted my Christian walk.

First, I learned that being a Christian doesn't mean you have all of the answers. In fact, the more I walk with Christ, the more I realize that I have more questions than I do answers, a lot more. Paul alludes to this reality when he writes, "For now we see in a mirror dimly, but then face to face; now I know in part, but then I will know fully just as I also have been fully known" (1 Corinthians 13:12).

Second, I learned that Christianity stands up to scrutiny. Steve didn't try to convince me to stop asking questions. Nor did he cop out by claiming that I had to close my mind in order to exercise my faith. He went and found answers. Granted, there are some questions that can't be answered (like, why did God do things the way He did?). However, those things are unanswerable because of the infinite nature of God and the finitude of man.

Fourth, teach your children to answer their own questions when they can. When my daughter was fourteen she began to work with a writing tutor. She has always been a very gifted writer, and she was finished with tenth and eleventh grade English by the time she was fourteen. Her tutor had developed a composition course that was part biblical worldview, part critical thinking, part creative writing, and part research methodology. It was a perfect fit. Jasmine met with the tutor once a week, and Bridget and I worked with her on the daily nuts and bolts.

One of the greatest blessings of this course was the day I realized my daughter and I had begun sharing a library. She walked into my office one day with a determined look on her face and said, "Daddy, I just *love* your office" as she diligently searched for a book on comparative religions. It was one of the greatest moments she and I had ever shared. My little girl had gone from "Daddy, what does this verse mean?" to "Daddy, where can I find information on Mormon theology?" She had begun to seek her own answers!

I have to admit my daughter's act of independence was a bittersweet moment. Part of me was excited about the achievement of one of many parental goals. However, another part of me was sad to see the little girl we brought home from the hospital getting smaller in the rearview mirror. But if my goal is to send my children forth as arrows (or nuclear missiles) bent on making a significant impact in the world for the cause of Christ, they are eventually going to have to know the Lord for themselves and think His thoughts after Him without me looking over their shoulders.

Books, Books, Books

Collect books that will help you teach the Bible. We all read to our children even before they can understand what we're reading. Many times we have sat down with a colorful cardboard book in front of a wide-eyed infant who can do little more than stare and coo at all the pretty colors. Eventually, though, that child learns to speak, and then to read, and he simply cannot wait for his favorite bedtime book. Why not make some of those early books tools for teaching biblical truth?

I love *Green Eggs and Ham* as much as the next guy (probably more), but there are many more things we have to communicate to the young, impressionable minds with which the Lord entrusts us. There are hundreds of books designed to help parents teach the Bible to their children.

Collect books that will help your children understand the Bible. If we commit ourselves to reading the Bible as a family, the questions will inevitably come. Be prepared by having books on hand that will help you answer them. For example, find a good Bible dictionary to look up key words in the Bible. You will also need a Bible encyclopedia. The encyclopedia will give you a broader understanding of key biblical terms, names, and concepts. It is also good to have a concordance on hand. A concordance is a handy tool to help you search for Bible verses by looking up key words. For instance, if you want to know where the Bible talks about holiness, just look up the word in a concordance, and it will show you every verse that contains that key word. A Bible atlas is another helpful tool. When you read about a specific place in the Bible, a Bible atlas will show you exactly where it is. Finally, you'll need a good commentary. There are many other books and tools out there, but these will get you started.

Collect books that help your children think biblically. When my oldest was small, my wife found a collection of books called Help Me Be Good. Each book was dedicated to a specific behavior such as telling the truth, sharing, or obeying parents. The books followed familiar characters through challenging episodes in which they learned lessons the hard way. By the end of the book the message was clear, and we would talk to our children about the benefit of exhibiting the behavior about which they had just read.

Books like this have become increasingly important as other influences continue to undermine biblical faith and morality. If we don't teach our children how to behave, Bart Simpson will. Turn off the TV, and hand your kids a book. This was a lesson we learned the hard way.

Our children used to watch more television than I care to admit. Then we moved to England. TV in England was so bad that we got cable so we didn't have to watch regular television at night. Eventually we just didn't watch. We occasionally rented videos, but for the most part we became a family of readers. I can't tell you what a difference that made in our children's lives. Now our children are limited to four hours per week—only on weekends—and to be honest, unless something special is on, they tend not to use all of that.

Collect books that will connect your children to the church and its history. One of the greatest gifts my wife gave each of our children is an introduction to and love for Christian biography. Our children love to read about *real* men and women who lived long ago and left their mark on the world as they faithfully followed Christ. Jasmine got her hands on *Foxe's Book of Martyrs* about a year ago, and she was hooked. She wouldn't stop talking about the men and women who laid down their lives for the cause of Christ and the incredible encouragement their stories were to her.

Find books about men of faith that will inspire your sons and women of faith with whom your daughters can identify. It is important for our sons and daughters to have targets to aim for. There is nothing as inspiring as people whose lives were very ordinary but who were used by God to do something extraordinary.

Home Training Takes Commitment, Time, and Effort

My good friends Matt and Lisa Bullen have five incredible kids. Their children are by no means perfect, but they are among the most respectful, thoughtful, resourceful, and well-behaved children I have ever met. In fact, the Bullens are legends of sorts around our church. New members are always commenting on the behavior and disposition of the Bullen kids.

The Bullens attended a Bible study Bridget and I hosted in our home. It was an eight-week study on marriage attended by eight families ranging from newlyweds to a couple who had been married more than thirty years. During one of our discussion times, the subject turned to training godly children. Matt Bullen leaned in and said, "You know what I'm tired of? I'm tired of people looking at our five children and saying, 'You guys are so lucky you got five good children.'" Matt's point was simple. Raising godly children is not a matter of luck; it is a matter of work.

All children are shaped in iniquity and conceived in sin (Psalm 51:5). Proverbs 22:15 says, "Foolishness is bound up in the heart of a child; the rod of discipline will remove it far from him." This is not true only of those children whose parents weren't "lucky" enough to get good ones. This is true of all children. Thus it is not lucky parents but the diligent ones who will end up with a child who brings them praise instead of shame.

But what is it about the Bullen family that separates them from others? The answer to this question is simple. They put in the time. The children were taught first-time obedience from the time they could crawl. They have been taught what the Bible says about wisdom versus foolishness since before they could fully understand it. They have had a family altar since before they were born, and they live under the constant watchful eye of two parents who are completely devoted to the idea of partnering with God to produce godliness in their children.

There is no magic bullet when it comes to raising godly children. There is, however, a detailed road map. The Bible gives us everything we need in order to get the job done right. Make a commitment right now to teach the Bible in your home. Pray that the Lord will give you the courage, conviction, and endurance to see it through. Start with one day a week if that is all you can carve out. If necessary, make it a point to read the Bible during your evening meal each day. You may also want to consider a time of Bible reading at bedtime as you put the kids down. Whatever you do, read the Bible in your home.

Take Action

1. Make a commitment to read through a book in the Bible with your family over the next week. Try to carve out a specific time each day to just read the text aloud.
2. Buy a Bible for every member of your family.
3. Once you have established a habit of reading the Bible, try to find a family devotional or a short family Bible study you can go through as a family.

6

LIVE THE WORD AT HOME

You shall . . . talk of them [God's words] when you sit in your house and when you walk by the way and when you lie down and when you rise up.

DEUTERONOMY 6:7

Moses makes it clear that multigenerational faithfulness is an all-day, everyday process. We must teach our children at all times. Moreover, we are always to teach according to the commandments of God. This may sound simple, but I assure you it is profound. If this is true, then the Bible must govern the method and manner I employ in training and discipling my children. I cannot simply use cultural, secular humanist methods and expect to reap biblical results.

When I raise this issue Christian parents will often ask, "Does the Bible really have specific instructions on raising children?" I have two responses to this question. First, the very nature of the Bible would suggest that this question must be answered in the affirmative. As we have seen earlier, the Bible makes it clear that "All Scripture is breathed out by God and profitable for teaching, for reproof, for correction, and for training in righteousness, that the man of God may be competent, equipped for every good work" (2 Timothy 3:16-17, ESV). The discipleship, discipline, and training of our children are definitely among the good works for which the Bible equips believers.

The second response to this question is based on the mountains of Bible passages dealing either directly or indirectly with raising children. The book of Proverbs, for example, is a treasure trove of information for parents wondering what to do. There are also numerous examples in the Bible of godly parents who got it right and others who blew it. Both cases give us insight into what it takes to parent effectively. Not to mention the foundation upon which this entire book rests, the book of Deuteronomy.

In Deuteronomy 6:7 Moses commands God's people to practice biblical instruction with their children "when you sit in your house and when you walk by the way and when you lie down and when you rise up." In other words, there is to be no sense of categorization in life that places biblical truth on one side and parenting on the other. We are called upon to employ biblical truth in every aspect of our lives, especially as it pertains to multigenerational faithfulness and the discipleship of our kids.

Paul: A New Take on an Old Truth

I have been amazed recently at the prominent role that the book of Deuteronomy plays in the New Testament. A quick look at the Scriptures quoted by Jesus and the apostles leads to the inevitable conclusion that Deuteronomy was and is a very important book. A case in point is Ephesians 6. Here Paul harkens back to Deuteronomy 5 as he instructs Christian parents on raising children. His teaching is a prime example of what I mean when I say that the Bible gives specific instructions to parents.

> *Children, obey your parents in the Lord, for this is right. Honor your father and mother (which is the first commandment with a promise), so that it may be well with you, and that you may live long on the earth. Fathers, do not provoke your children to anger, but bring them up in the discipline and instruction of the Lord. (vv. 1-4)*

From this passage of Scripture we can extrapolate at least three distinct phases of preparation for our children. Phase 1 is the discipline and training phase. Phase 2 is what I like to call the catechism phase. Finally, in phase 3, we begin discipleship.

Discipline and Training

Paul makes these comments in the middle of his discussion of authority and submission. He has just given three contrasts in 5:15-18, culminating in the contrast between being filled with wine and being filled with the Spirit. In verses 19-21 he gives three conditions that exemplify the Spirit-filled life. The third condition is that we "be subject to one another in the fear of Christ" (v. 21). After this he gives three contexts where this submission is lived out. First he addresses the submission of the wife to her husband (5:22-33). Next he turns to the obedience of children to parents (6:1-4). Finally he turns his attention to servants and masters (6:5-9).

What this means is that the degree to which children properly respond to the authority of their parents is indicative of the degree to which they are filled with the Spirit. In other words, obedience is a spiritual issue. Thus teaching my children to obey is not optional; it is a biblical mandate. This gives us a great deal of practical ammunition that can and must be employed in our effort to live by the Word on a daily basis. Practically it means we must devote ourselves to teaching and expecting our children to do what they are told, when they are told, with a respectful attitude.

Do What They Are Told

We've all been there. You tell your two-year-old to do something in front of the pastor's wife and she sticks out her tongue, yells "no," and takes off running in the other direction. Usually the person watching will try to alleviate our embarrassment by saying something like, "They sure are a handful at that age." Or maybe they will say, "Mine used to do the same thing." Everyone smiles, you run off after the child, and it's never brought up again. Eventually you learn that everyone is willing to accept this behavior, or at least to make comments that suggest their acceptance.

The only problem with this scenario is that it clearly violates the principles laid out in God's Word. It is not OK for our toddlers to be characterized by rank disobedience. Moreover, if we do not deal with this when they are toddlers, our children will grow up to be disobedient, disrespectful, obnoxious teens whom no one wants to be around. More importantly, they will have established a behavior pattern that mitigates against the Spirit-filled life. Remember, a young man or woman who is filled with the Spirit will be marked by obedience to his or her parents.

While it is beyond the scope of this book to give step-by-step instructions in biblical child training, I will say that we must learn to correct such behavior in our children whenever we see it. If we continue to let little Susie get away with open defiance, she will grow up to be openly defiant. Bridget and I learned this the hard way with our firstborn. We were inconsistent with her as a toddler, and we had a mess on our hands. By the time she was ten we had to go back and completely retrain her. We simply didn't know there was a better way. No one had ever taught us the importance of this biblical mandate.

Do It When They Are Told

An even tougher lesson to learn is the principle of first-time obedience. I can remember standing in a grocery store counting to three as I waited for one of my children to put down a box of cereal that he knew he wasn't supposed to pick up. After the child put the box back, a woman in the store who had been watching complimented me. She said, "I'm impressed. I didn't think you were going to win that one." I was one proud dad. That is, until I learned that what I was doing was settling for less than obedience.

A friend of ours asked me a very simple question one day. "When should your child do what he or she is told?" he asked after watching me go through my counting routine. "When I tell them," I replied. He looked down at the child who had just complied prior to the count of three and asked me a question that rocked my world. "Then why do you count?" That hit me like a ton of bricks. I was teaching my child *delayed* obedience. I may as well have said, "Sweetheart, you only have to obey Daddy when it's serious enough for him to count to three." That wasn't what I was after. More importantly, that isn't what God is after. Our Heavenly Father doesn't count to three when

He gives us a command. It is not a sin to disobey God when He counts to three; it is simply a sin not to obey God. And delayed obedience is disobedience.

This is a difficult principle to understand because we often overlook the punishment our sins deserve and ultimately received in the cross of Christ (or will receive during an eternity separated from God in hell). However, whether God smites us immediately as He did Ananias and Sapphira (Acts 5) or appears to let it slide, we can rest assured that every sin receives just recompense (Romans 3:21-26). Thus, in the economy of God every act of disobedience is ultimately punished whether we see it immediately or not. That is why it is important to teach our children that every instruction is to be obeyed right away. As they get older, they may be allowed to enter into discussion about our instructions, but that discussion should follow an act of obedience, not determine whether or not they are convinced of our position.

I also learned that my yelling was doing the same thing. When I would yell at my children, I was teaching them that they didn't have to do what I said whenever I said it, just when it was important enough (or I was mad enough) to raise my voice. What's worse, I was undermining my wife's authority in the home because she wasn't as big and scary and didn't have as deep a voice as me. Thus my word (thundered through the house) became the standard for eliciting obedience.

We do not want our children to do what we say with conditions attached. We want them to obey, period. Learning not to repeat ourselves, not to yell, not to call the offending child by all three of his or her names, but to speak in clear, level tones and follow through with consequences for every act of disobedience has completely transformed our home. No, our children are not perfect, but they understand what obedience is and fully expect a consequence if they fall short of doing what they are told when they are told to do it.

Do It with a Respectful Attitude

The last child-training principle Paul imparts in this passage comes in verse 2: "Honor your father and mother." Hence we see that children are to be trained to do what they are told, when they are told to do it, with a respectful attitude. This is huge. This means that if you tell your teenager to do something and she huffs, puffs, smacks her lips, and slams the door on her way to do it, she has still missed God's best and needs to be corrected.

When I first became a Christian, I thought all Christians were sold-out, fire-breathing, truth-telling, water-walking followers of the Lord Jesus Christ. I also believed that I should be able to trust anything that was written by a Christian author and published by a Christian publisher. I soon discovered that I was wrong.

Most Christians in our culture live like everyone else. There is little distinction between our lives and the lives of the pagans down the street. We wear the same clothes, watch the same movies, read the same books, send our children to the same schools, and sign the same divorce decrees as everyone else. Furthermore, there ought to be a sign posted in every Christian bookstore that reads, "The views expressed in these books do not necessarily express the views of our Lord and Savior Jesus Christ." I'm not saying, don't read Christian books. I'm just saying, read with discernment.

Let's face it—living in accordance with the Word of God is not the default position for most Christians. It is much easier to drift along in the milieu of mediocrity than it is to swim upstream. In fact, after a while the norm changes, and we become less passionate (some would say fanatical) again.

However, if we are to experience multigenerational faithfulness we must come to a place where we throw off the shackles of our culture and live in the fullness that is found only in Christ. We must be people who live the Word in our homes. Unfortunately, this is not as easy as it sounds. In fact, even leaders in this movement called Christianity often find it difficult to break the ties that bind.

As a result, the "Christian" marketplace is filled with perilous advice. One cannot be too careful when perusing the aisles for something to read (or to watch). Sometimes well-meaning professionals give advice that is less than biblical. Two examples immediately come to mind.

"Christian" Psychology and the Discipline Dilemma

One of the areas where Christians adopt a cultural rather than a biblical perspective is the area of discipline and child training. It seems that someone has successfully circumvented the part of many American Christians' brains when it comes to applying biblical principles to the subject of teaching our children to behave appropriately. Unfortunately, this flaw is not limited to the masses. Even well-educated, Bible-believing, Christian "experts" fall prey to this blind spot.

I recently heard Christian psychologist John Rosemond give a radio interview and was thoroughly impressed. So impressed that I immediately ordered the CD of the interview and a copy of his book. As I read the Introduction, I was hooked. The author writes:

> I am a heretic within my profession. My views on child rearing and family life are "psychologically incorrect." They rock the boat, upset the applecart, and provoke often vitriolic response. The simple explanation is that I have been willing to publicly state my disdain for the child-rearing ideology propounded since the 1950's by mainstream psychology.[1]

Rosemond went on to explain in his book, as well as in his radio interview, that he considers the Bible to be the best parenting book in the world. What refreshing words from a psychologist! He went on to lay the axe to the root of the problem by addressing everything from democratic parenting, no-fault divorce, feminism, and political correctness to "homosexual rights," sex ed curricula, and the mental health profession. And this was all in the Introduction! I could tell right off that this was my kind of guy.

Unfortunately, my euphoria didn't last. About halfway through the book I ran into a buzz saw. In Rosemond's chapter on "The Respectful Child" he transitions from a section titled "Give 'Em Reasons, but Don't Reason," in which he addresses the popular idea of reasoning with children, to a section titled "Give 'Em the Last Word." In this section Rosemond explains how he answers parents who frequently ask him what to do with children who always seem to want the last word:

> I say, "By all means, give them the last word," to which these parents, taken aback, usually respond, "You're kidding, right?" *Au contraire*. I am for a change being completely serious. You have a child who wants

the last word? So, what's new? All of God's children want the last word. You do, I do, our kids do. Such is the nature of being human.[2]

He then gives anecdotal support for his position in the form of a story about an encounter he had with his then sixteen-year-old daughter. Rosemond asked his daughter to clean the house for a dinner party; she refused. His response? "I vacuumed. I cleaned the bathroom. I didn't say a thing to Amy. For six days, that is."[3] Rosemond didn't address the issue until the following Friday when he "came home in the early evening to find Amy and her best friend, Angie, getting ready to go out."[4] It was then that he decided it was time to punish his daughter for her rebellion. He told her she couldn't go out. He went on to explain that his decision was based on her actions the previous week. Rosemond records Amy's reaction:

> She blew her stack. I can't print what she said, not because it isn't appropriate for a book on family values, but because it was gibberish. Very loud gibberish. In the midst of her tirade, I said, "Sorry," and started to leave the room. She called after me, "I'm going out anyway, and you can't stop me!"[5]

He continues:

> She stormed. She fumed. She went outside to the driveway to see if I'd follow. I didn't. She and Angie talked for a while, then Angie got in her car and drove off. Amy sat on the steps for a while, then came in, went to her room and stayed in there the rest of the night.[6]

As I read this passage, the only thing I could think of was the words of the apostle Paul in Ephesians 6, "Fathers, do not provoke your children to anger." Thus, in a book on what to do as a parent we find a prime example of what the Bible says we should not do. Again I cannot overemphasize the fact that this is one of the good guys. Rosemond actually does a great job of outlining a biblical approach to parenting. I just think he missed this point.

In another anecdotal story Rosemond records the experience of a single mother from Dayton, Ohio who had, in his words, "been touched by the god of common sense." She had learned to give her daughter the last word.

> Shelly would yell something disrespectful and, getting no response, something equally insolent. Then she'd pout. But, mom told me, if left to "stew in her own juices," Shelly would eventually do as she'd been told. Needless to say . . . Shelly still didn't like the fact that she wasn't free to do as she pleased, but we haven't had an argument since I began letting her have the last word, and that was three years ago![7]

So what's the big deal? Evidently this parenting philosophy works, right? Rosemond's daughter got the message, and this single mom hasn't had an argument with her daughter in three years. What seems to be the problem? I'll tell you the problem. Better yet; I'll let the Bible tell you:

> *Honor your father and your mother, as the* LORD *your God has commanded you, that your days may be prolonged and that it may go well with you on the land which the* LORD *your God gives you. (Deuteronomy 5:16)*

> *Children, obey your parents in the Lord, for this is right. Honor your father and mother (which is the first commandment with a promise), so that it may be well with you, and that you may live long on the earth. (Ephesians 6:1-3)*

> *Children, be obedient to your parents in all things, for this is well-pleasing to the Lord. (Colossians 3:20)*

The problem with this approach is that it seemingly ignores (and thus violates) the Fifth Commandment. It is not enough for our children to eventually do what we tell them; they *must* honor us. It is not all right for our sons and daughters to shout at us, stomp their feet, slam doors, or walk out of the house. God has spoken on this issue, and we must strive for full obedience.

By giving his daughter the silent treatment for several days before responding, Rosemond also ignores principles such as, "fathers, do not provoke your children to anger" (Ephesians 6:4; Colossians 3:21), and "Be angry, and yet do not sin; do not let the sun go down on your anger" (Ephesians 4:26). He has also taught his daughter to do the same, as evidenced by her silence toward him. This is simply not a biblical approach to discipline. We are not talking about peripheral issues here, but the core of the Bible's teaching concerning the role of children in the home.

Rosemond gives us insight into the philosophical underpinnings of his approach when he writes:

> Whenever I had foolishly engaged in the game of "Who Gets the Last Word?" I had lost control of myself, relinquished my authority, and accomplished nothing. You want your children's respect? Then retain your authority. It's that simple. Give them the last word and get more than you ever insisted upon in return.[8]

I agree that it is wrong for parents to lose control when disciplining their children. I also agree that doing so compromises our authority. However, I think Rosemond has addressed the wrong issue here, and the consequences are frightful. Instead of working on his temper and properly restoring his parental authority, he chose to allow his children to violate the Fifth Commandment and thus risked undermining God's authority in order to salvage his own.

Again, I liked Rosemond's book. In fact, before I got to the aforementioned section I recommended it to several of my closest friends. Subsequently I have continued to recommend it with a caveat, as I do not think this issue renders the rest of his work useless. This is not some left-wing, tree-hugging, pacifist parent. This is a respected spokesperson within the Christian community. This is a psychologist who puts his own profession in the crosshairs and shows no mercy. However, on this issue I couldn't disagree more. If we are going to live by the Word in our homes, we can't use the Bible as a jumping-off point; it must be our law, our guide, our model, and our source. We must submit ourselves to its teaching from pillar to post. And that includes the way we discipline our children.

The Fifth Commandment and Child Training

One of the keys to understanding Paul's teaching on the training and discipleship of children is to understand the commandment to which he refers in Ephesians 6.

The Position of the Fifth Commandment

The Ten Commandments are given in Deuteronomy 5. However, those commandments are divided into two sections. The first four commandments are what some theologians refer to as vertical commandments. "You shall have no other gods before Me." "You shall not make for yourself an idol." "You shall not take the name of the LORD your God in vain." "Observe the sabbath day to keep it holy." These four commandments deal with our relationship with God.

The next six commandments are concerned with our horizontal relationships. They deal with such issues as murder, committing adultery, stealing, bearing false witness, and coveting. However, the first of these horizontal commandments is the Fifth Commandment: "Honor your father and your mother." Before the prohibition against murder, against adultery, against stealing, God gives a word about proper respect for parents. The mere position of this commandment shows the importance that the Lord put on the family in the grand scheme of things.

The Promise of the Fifth Commandment

In addition to its position, the Fifth Commandment is significant in its promise. The first four commandments have no promises attached. However, when God wrote the Fifth Commandment, He added a step that had not yet accompanied any of the vertical commandments. For the first time God says do this so that "your days may be prolonged and that it may go well with you on the land which the LORD your God gives you."

Of course, there are promises inherent in all of the commandments. God certainly blesses us when we abstain from idolatry or adultery. Moreover, there is the inherent blessing that accompanies all godliness. However, when it comes to honoring one's parents, the promise is not assumed but is stated. Highlight this truth for your children. Marvel with them over the beauty of the promise that God has in store for those who show due respect to their parents. Chasten them when they are not respectful, and ask them whether or not their behavior is worthy of the promise.

The Purpose of the Fifth Commandment

Perhaps the most significant aspect of the Fifth Commandment is its purpose. I have often looked at Ephesians 6:2-3 and thought the promise was for my individual children. "Jasmine," I would say, "if you honor me, you will live a long and prosperous life." Or I would use it in the negative: "Trey, the Bible says that if you honor me, you will live long. That means if you don't do what I say, I'll take you out." How many times have we viewed these words from this perspective?

The key to understanding the role of the family in discipling children is understanding the purpose of the Fifth Commandment. This commandment was not given for the sake of the individual child as much as it was given for the sake of the community. The Fifth Commandment was the foundation upon which the concept of multigenerational faithfulness is built. God designed the family to disciple children and insure the faithfulness and perpetuation of the community of faith throughout the ages. In other words, God says to us (through the Fifth Commandment), "If you want to continue to exist as the people of God in the midst of the pagan land that I am about to give you, you will have to do so by training and discipling your children."

This is the linchpin in every argument I have made or will make in this book. God has designed your family—not the youth group, not the children's ministry, not the Christian school, but your family—as the principal discipling agent in your children's lives. The most important job you have as a parent is to train and disciple your children. This truth completely transformed the way Bridget and I viewed our role as parents. Suddenly we realized that if we raised our children to be great doctors, lawyers, athletes, or musicians but did not train them to honor us and obey God, we would have failed. Thus we had to rethink our schedule, our priorities, everything. In fact, this is one of the key truths that led us to home education. It was inconceivable to us that we could accomplish this monumental task without giving our children an education that completely embraced and undergirded this philosophy.

The Catechism Phase

In verse 4 of Ephesians 6 Paul puts the cookies on the bottom shelf. Here he states in no uncertain terms what the role and responsibility of the Christian parent is expected to be. After contextualizing his teaching on children in verse 1, he ties it to the commandments in verses 2 and 3. Then in verse 4 he gives us the bottom line. Parents, your job is to teach your children to behave like Christians and to believe like Christians.

Phase 1 in living by the Word in the rearing of children is training and discipline. Once we have that base covered, we can move on to phase 2—catechism. I hesitate to even use the word *catechism* since, frankly, so many Christians today either don't know what it means or think it has something to do with a particular branch of Christianity. In fact, until recently Bridget and I didn't really understand catechism ourselves. We are good Southern Baptists who had never heard of such a thing. But catechism is merely basic instruction in Christian doctrine using questions and answers.

The goal of catechism is to impart biblical theology. Through a series of questions and answers the child slowly learns what to believe and, more importantly, why. Catechism is not a magic bean or a silver bullet. We still have to work at teaching our children. However, the catechism is an invaluable tool that facilitates the process. More importantly, the catechism lays the foundation for the discipleship that is to follow. Without catechism our discipleship is reduced to a list of moralisms.

For instance, what if I tell my sons not to engage in premarital sex but do not give them the biblical and theological foundation upon which to build such a decision? Unfortunately, this is precisely the way I was taught. I was told that I should not have sex with girls because I was too young and I could get someone pregnant. Of course, what this also meant was that when I was older I could justify the practice if I took the proper precautions. Thus I was no longer too young, and no one was going to get pregnant.

Compare this to instruction based upon an understanding of the sanctity of marriage, the dignity of the opposite sex, my role as a protector of what Peter calls the "weaker" marriage partner (1 Peter 3:7), the biblical purposes for which sex was given, and a host of other theological principles, and the difference is astonishing. For instance, the Westminster Shorter Catechism addresses the issue of sexual purity from the perspective of the Seventh Commandment:

> Q: What is the Seventh Commandment?
> A: The Seventh Command is, "You shall not commit adultery."
> Q: What is required in the Seventh Commandment?
> A: The Seventh Commandment requires the preservation of our own and our neighbor's chastity in heart, speech and behavior.
> Q: What is forbidden in the Seventh Commandment?
> A: The Seventh Commandment forbids all unchaste thoughts, words, and actions.

This is a far cry from "Don't get anyone pregnant." That is not to say that children armed with this information will never violate the principles they have been taught, but it will require thought-out rebellion as opposed to the logical assumption that the activity is justifiable.

Catechism is merely a track to run on. So many of our children have little idea what they believe or why they believe it. Couple this with the fact that they are fallen human beings whose natural bent is to sin and they live in a culture that glorifies, justifies, and promotes such sin, and it is not difficult to see their dilemma. Failing to catechize our children is tantamount to surrendering to the culture. Walking in holiness is difficult enough when we know what is right; let's not make things tougher than they already are.

I had a conversation recently with a pastor who was at his wit's end with his oldest son. The young man was clean-cut, pleasant, and very well mannered. However, there was an obvious tension between the boy and his father. When I sat down with the two of them, I realized that this pastor had not discipled his son. The young man was well versed in church language, but he did not have a grasp on biblical Christianity.

Some Useful Tools

A number of wonderful catechisms are available—Westminster, Heidelberg, Spurgeon's, etc.—and a simple Web search will provide you with more information than you ever thought possible. One thing we have found very useful is the *Truth and Grace Memory Book* material from Founders Press (available at www.founders.org). This is not really the place for discussing the pros and cons of each catechism. I simply want to implore you to find a good tool for teaching your children biblical theology. I just happen to think catechism is about the best way to do it. However, even if you choose not to use a formal catechism, you must catechize your children. In other words, if you do not find something that fits your theology, make one of your own. Our children are developing a theology whether we are teaching them or not. As you saw in the worldview section, everyone has basic, underlying assumptions about the nature of God, man, truth, knowledge, and ethics. Failing to catechize our children only makes it that much easier for the Secular Humanism with which they are constantly bombarded in school, on television, and through friends, neighbors, and coaches to take root and become the guiding principle by which they live.

The Discipleship Phase

The third phase in living by the Word in raising our children is discipleship. We have asked for and received their heart in the discipline and training phase. We then captured their minds in the catechism phase. Now it is time to take their hand in the discipleship phase. In this phase we teach our children what to do with what they have learned.

The discipleship phase is dependent upon the other two phases. For instance, if you have not gotten a handle on discipline and training, you will be left with a young man or woman who is disrespectful and/or disobedient, and you cannot disciple someone in that condition. Discipleship is built on trust and respect. Moreover, if you have not taken care of the catechism phase, you do not have a track to run on. Discipleship is the application of what we believe. If our children do not know what we believe or why we believe it, they will have a difficult time understanding why one lifestyle choice is superior to another.

Imagine trying to teach someone how to cook chicken marsala (one of my favorite dishes) when they don't know the difference between a pot and a pan. Or how could you teach someone how to play Bach's *Cello Suite No. 3 in C Major* without first teaching them music theory? This is precisely the kind of leap we often take with our teenagers when we try to teach them how to behave like Christians before teaching them to believe like Christians. We try to walk them through the process of choosing a college before we have given them a basic understanding of what the Bible has to say about education and the pursuit of knowledge. We talk to them about the importance of sharing their faith with unbelievers without having given them a firm grasp on soteriology.

The Importance of Discipleship

One of the greatest blessings in my Christian life is the fact that I was actually discipled as a young believer. Two teammates of mine, Brent Knapton and Max Moss, took about a semester teaching me the basics of Christian life. Another friend and teammate, Otis Latin, loved me enough to allow me to share his parents with me while I was away at college. The first Christian family I ever heard talk about family devotions was the Latins. These early experiences laid a foundation in my Christian life that has borne much fruit. It has also given me an appreciation for the importance of biblical discipleship.

Unfortunately, this experience represents the exception to the rule. Most Christians have never been discipled. The ones who claim they have been often refer to a series of classes they took at their church in a room with twenty other people. Rarely do I meet the man or woman who has had mature Christians spend significant time with him or her with the express purpose of showing him or her how to live the Christian life. Hence many of us find it difficult to think in terms of discipling our own children.

Education: The Forgotten Key to Discipleship

In a seemingly obscure New Testament passage of Scripture, Jesus says some of the most profound words concerning education and discipleship in the entire Bible. Luke records His words in his Gospel: "A pupil is not above his teacher; but everyone, after he has been fully trained, will be like his teacher" (6:40). This is the New Testament version of Proverbs 22:6 ("Train up a child in the way he should go and when he is old he will not depart from it"). This raises one of the most important questions Christian parents will face concerning the discipleship of their children. Whom will your children resemble at the completion of their "formal" education?

Education and the Knowledge of God

Before you run off screaming, "Another homeschool dad trying to convince us all to do what he does," let me assure you of a couple of things. First, I would never suggest that everyone should educate his or her children the same way we educate ours. Second, I don't want to make it that easy. I want you to think about what the Bible has to say on the subject and wrestle with the decision you have to make. That being said, let's look at some key biblical passages and their implications.

Proverbs 1:7 is foundational to our discussion. Solomon tells us, "The fear of the LORD is the beginning of knowledge" (cf. Job 28:28; Psalm 111:10; Proverbs 9:10; 15:33; Ecclesiastes 12:13). In other words, our educational choice has to be based on the fact that God cannot and must not be ignored in the process. Any educational system that denies the existence, preeminence, and primacy of God is in violation of this biblical principle and is detracting from, rather than contributing to, the discipleship process.

Education and the Great Commission

Many object to homeschooling or private Christian schools based on the fact that God has called us to be "salt" and "light" and to evangelize the world. Ironically, this is precisely why we chose homeschooling. The Great Commission states: "Go therefore and make disciples of all the nations, baptizing them in the name of the Father and the Son and the Holy Spirit, *teaching them to obey all that I commanded you*" (Matthew 28:19-20, emphasis added). How is this likely apart from Christian education? How can I effectively "make disciples" of my children if I send them off to the government school forty-five to fifty hours per week? The Nehemiah Institute, The National Study of Youth and Religion, and the Barna Report have shown us clearly that our children do not even understand—let alone obey—all that the Lord has commanded.

Moreover, how can our children evangelize our government schools if they don't know what they believe and why they believe it? Not to mention that all of the evidence currently points to the fact that our children are the evangelized, not the evangelists, in our nation's schools. They are the ones being carried away by every wind of doctrine.

Education and Worldview Development

One of the clearest issues in the education debate is the question of worldview development. The Nehemiah Institute continues to demonstrate year after year that Christian children in government schools who actually retain anything close to a biblical worldview are the rare exception and not the rule.[9] This makes even more sense when measured against Scripture.

> *And do not be conformed to this world, but be transformed by the renewing of your mind, so that you may prove what the will of God is, that which is good and acceptable and perfect. (Romans 12:2)*

> *See to it that no one takes you captive through philosophy and empty deception, according to the tradition of men, according to the elementary principles of the world, rather than according to Christ. (Colossians 2:8)*

> *O Timothy, guard what has been entrusted to you, avoiding worldly and empty chatter and the opposing arguments of what is falsely called "knowledge"—which some have professed and thus gone astray from the faith. (1 Timothy 6:20-21)*

Clearly, believers are to avoid unnecessary exposure to worldview influences that would contradict and/or undermine biblical truth. Again, any educational choice we make must take this biblical principle into account.

Education and Morality

Contrary to popular opinion, there is no such thing as amoral education. All education teaches and shapes morality. It is impossible to separate one's view of God, man, truth, knowledge, and ethics from the educational process. Every day that our children sit behind a desk, they are either being taught to know, love, and obey God or they are being taught to love and obey someone or something that has usurped God's proper role.

If you think your child is above such influence, think again. The Bible clearly warns believers about the dangers of association with immoral/amoral influences.

> *Do not be deceived: "Bad company corrupts good morals." (1 Corinthians 15:33)*

> *Do not be bound together with unbelievers; for what partnership have righteousness and lawlessness, or what fellowship has light with darkness? Or what harmony has Christ with Belial, or what has a believer in common with an unbeliever? (2 Corinthians 6:14-15)*

> *How blessed is the man who does not walk in the counsel of the wicked,*
> *Nor stand in the path of sinners,*
> *Nor sit in the seat of scoffers!*
> *But his delight is in the law of the LORD,*
> *And in His law he meditates day and night.*
> *He will be like a tree firmly planted by streams of water,*
> *Which yields its fruit in its season*
> *And its leaf does not wither;*
> *And in whatever he does, he prospers. (Psalm 1:1-3)*

Psalm 1 has to be one of the most poignant passages in the entire Bible in terms of the evaluation of immoral educational influence. We must not allow our children to stand, sit, or walk with those who deny biblical truth and morality. Instead we must place them in situations that will aid them in meditating on the law of the Lord "day and night."

Education and Accountability

While I wish every believer could experience the rich reward of educating his or her children at home, I know that will not always be the case. However, I want to make one point clear. We can no longer coast along and ignore biblical truth when deciding where and how to educate our children. The Bible is not silent on this issue. Do everything in your power to place your child in an educational environment that supplements and facilitates their discipleship. Do everything in your power to avoid the influence of government schools that are incapable of bringing our children up in "the discipline and instruction of the Lord" (Ephesians 6:4).

Let me be clear—I applaud men and women whom God has called to teach in government schools. These people are front-line warriors, and they need to be right where they are. However, there is a big difference between sending fully trained disciples into enemy territory and sending recruits to our enemy's training camp. If we do the latter, we shouldn't be surprised when they come home wearing the enemy's uniform and charging the hill of our home while waving an enemy flag.

Recently one of America's most widely syndicated columnists, Cal Thomas, addressed the issue of sex and drug use in government schools. Thomas outlined a three-step strategy for rescuing our children:

> Step one is to *pull them from the government schools* that serve as hothouses for this kind of behavior and thinking. Step two is to reduce lavish lifestyles so that parents work less and invest more time in their children, with one parent actually staying home to make the home a safe haven. Step three is no television in the home. Television has become hostile to the things most parents want their children to believe and embrace. It is deadly to their moral development; it encourages disrespect for fathers and undermines those things that used to make families a strong, positive cultural force (emphasis mine).[10]

Thomas continues:

The government schools and the sex and entertainment industries aren't about to fix the problem. The responsibility to properly raise children belongs to parents. *The state and various interest groups have no right to develop the moral fiber of a child* and, in fact, they are speedily undermining that development (emphasis mine).[11]

If this is the first time you have heard someone speak so plainly about the issue, get used to it. The handwriting is on the wall, and silence is no longer an option. As Southern Baptist Theological Seminary president Al Mohler boldly proclaimed, "It is time for responsible [Baptists] to develop an exit strategy from public schools." Seminary presidents and syndicated columnists are making bold statements about the need for Christian parents (and essentially all responsible parents) to get their children out of government schools. Amazing!

To the single mother with four children and two jobs whose husband left without providing any means of long-term support, let me say two things. First, my heart breaks for you. I wish I could afford to stand in the gap for every one of you and protect your children, but I cannot. I must entrust that duty to a sovereign God who is not surprised by your circumstances.

Second, I apologize to you on behalf of many in the Christian community who have failed to grasp a vision for providing affordable educational alternatives for people in your situation. I wish I could change that overnight, but I cannot. I can, however, continue to blow the trumpet and call a sleeping giant to wake up and recognize what we are doing to our children and yours by allowing them to stay in secular humanist boot camps one day longer than they absolutely have to.

In fact, a dear friend of mine, Bruce Shortt, and I offered a resolution at a recent Southern Baptist Convention annual meeting calling for parents to investigate public schools and remove Christian students from schools that were found to be promoting a radical homosexual agenda. One of the things we called for in the resolution was the establishment of affordable educational alternatives for those trapped in failing schools. You would have thought we were calling for Baptists to eat their young!

The powers-that-be in the convention threw us under the proverbial bus! We were accused of lacking passion for evangelism, compassion for the poor, and appreciation for schoolteachers (despite the fact that our resolution addressed each one of these issues). I know that this is a hot-button issue that makes people's blood boil. However, I cannot ignore the data, and I will not ignore the Scriptures. My soul yearns for the day when Christians recognize the central role of education in the discipleship of our children and the incredible opportunity we have to truly evangelize people looking for something better than American schools that rank sixteenth out of seventeen industrialized nations in math and science and place our children at risk for school violence, drug abuse, student/teacher sex abuse (which is far worse than anything the Catholic Church has experienced),[12] homosexual propaganda, sexual promiscuity, teen pregnancy, and functional illiteracy. Oh, how I long to see the day when Christian schools are seen as cities on the hill that beckon to parents looking for something better, saying, "On Christ the solid rock we stand, all other ground is sinking sand."

Take Action

1. Read and reread the biblical texts concerning parenting quoted in this chapter. Look at their context, their background, etc. Then ask yourself if the parenting philosophy to which you adhere lines up with the biblical teaching. If not, how do you need to change?
2. Memorize the Ten Commandments with your children. Ask them how each commandment applies to their lives. Then go back to the Fifth Commandment and ask them how they can obey it each day.
3. Sit down with your spouse, and write down your expectations concerning the discipline and discipleship of your children. After each of you has written your list, compare, contrast, and synthesize the lists.
4. Compare the aforementioned list to the work you did in action step #1.

7

MARK THE HOME AS GOD'S TERRITORY

You shall write them on the doorposts of your house and on your gates.

DEUTERONOMY 6:9

I have often wondered why I remember my mother's Buddhism so vividly. I know I was around Christian people—or at least people who went to church and claimed to be Christians—but none of their practices had the long-term impact on me that my mother's did. I know this is due in part to the frequency and proximity of my mother's worship. However, I have also come to realize that there was something more. Something else embedded my mother's practices deep in the recesses of my mind.

Then I began to study Deuteronomy 6. I couldn't quite wrap my mind around the application of the principles in verse 9. This is a specific expression of the general principle of the whole passage. There should be tangible things in and about the homes of God's people that distinguish them from the homes of others.

Memories from My Mother

I don't remember when my mother became a Buddhist. We have often discussed the multilayered experiences that led her in that direction, but I do not have any personal recollection of a day when things suddenly changed. I do, however, remember the elements of her religion very vividly.

We had a very small apartment in Los Angeles. The two physical features that stand out in my mind are my mother's extensive collection of albums that seemed to cover a complete wall in our living room and the black lacquer box on the opposite side of the room near our dinette set.

Inside that box was a golden statue of Buddha and a scroll with strange Asian writing. There was also a place for incense, which my mother would burn whenever she chanted. There was a place for fruit (which I never understood), a string of pearl-like beads, and a small gong or bell. This was nearly thirty years ago, but I can see that box in my mind's eye as though it was yesterday.

I also remember seeing my mother open that box, kneel on the floor in front of it, and begin her daily ritual. She would bow, light the incense, ring the bell, and begin to chant her mantra. While she chanted, she would rub the beads together in her hands. I can almost hear the sound of the bell, the clicking of the beads, and my mother's monotone voice as she chanted the same mantra over and over for what seemed like hours at a time.

My mother became a Christian within six months of my conversion, but I still remember her previous religious expressions vividly. Why? *My mother's Buddhism engaged, stimulated, and made a lasting impression on every one of my five senses.* That black box, the golden Buddha, the scroll, and the sight of my mother kneeling and bowing engaged my sense of sight. The sound of the bell, the beads, and the mantra engaged my sense of hearing. The incense engaged my sense of smell, the beads engaged my sense of touch, and the fruit in the box next to Buddha engaged my sense of taste.

Imagine the impact that Moses' teaching had on the children of Israel in the Promised Land. Children moved into a strange land with strange sights, smells, tastes, textures, and sounds, and they had to somehow retain their distinction. How did they do that? Every time they walked up to their gates, they saw symbols of their faith. Their doorposts proclaimed their distinction. The annual feasts with bitter herbs, lamb, and unleavened bread continually hearkened back to their roots in the Exodus event. Moreover, the nations that surrounded them saw, heard, tasted, touched, and smelled the difference. That is what it means to mark our homes as God's territory.

The World Knows This Is True

Walk into a doctor's office and what do you see? Look on the walls and you see diplomas and awards. You also see posters representing the doctor's specialty. In a pediatrician's office you will see babies at different phases of life. In an obstetrician's office you will see the enigmatic picture of the baby leaving the birth canal. From the time you walk into the office, you will be bombarded with images designed to comfort and reassure. By the time you see the doctor, you know that he is trained and board-certified, what his specialty is, and how long he's been doing this. All of this from a well-marked office.

The same is true in virtually every industry. Walk into any business and you are bombarded with their latest awards, a poster naming the employee of the month, their company motto, music designed to put you in the proper mood, and employees trained to communicate the company philosophy in the way they dress, speak, and maintain their work space. There is even an Asian fad called Feng Shui sweeping the nation. As one web site puts it:

> Feng Shui is about understanding the secrets of how energy moves in our surroundings and how the style of our buildings and interiors affect us at a subtle level. It involves harnessing beneficial chi to enhance the success and good fortune of the individual.[1]

Even non-believing Eastern mystics understand the spiritual significance of one's surroundings (although they are completely at odds with the truth of God's Word). How much more should the children of God, armed with a biblical mandate, mark their homes as God's territory!

Engaging the Eyes

I have had the privilege of taking my family to many marvelous places. However, if I had to name the top ten I would have to include the

Louvre Museum in Paris. We were living in England at the time, and we hopped over to Paris to see the sights. While the whole trip was quite exciting, words can barely describe the moment we came face-to-face with the *Mona Lisa*. I couldn't believe we were standing there. Even my son Trey (then eight years old) thought that was cool. It was one of the most memorable days we've ever spent together as a family.

One of the things that struck me about that day was the inordinate number of religious paintings. I was suddenly reminded that there was a period in history when anyone who wanted to be considered a serious painter, a grand master, painted biblical themes. We saw the Bible displayed in vivid, artistic form like we had never seen before. Everywhere we looked we saw another painting of Mary, Jesus, the wedding feast, the crucifixion, angels, or the Last Supper. It was there that I felt the full weight of the potential of Christian art to lift and even captivate the human spirit. I was moved emotionally and spiritually by what I saw. To this day I still remember many of those images. I believe Christians should make an effort to fill their homes with such moving pieces.

I know we can't all afford the works of the grand masters, but we can all afford a decent painting, poster, or Christian symbol here and there. My mother and I were poor, but she somehow managed to buy a Buddha. Find a way to place beautiful pieces of art in your home that will engage your children's eyes in the worship of Almighty God and remind them of who, and whose, they are.

You can also accomplish this through picture frames with Christian symbols or messages or plaques with verses of Scripture. One friend of ours has Scripture verses written across the border of her kitchen as a constant reminder of God's presence in their home. Others have framed christening or baby dedication gowns on the wall as a constant reminder of their commitment to raise their children in the nurture and admonition of the Lord. The possibilities are endless. Use your imagination, and mark your home.

Engaging the Sense of Hearing

Not long ago we took a family road trip up to Dallas to visit Bridget's family. The kids were in the back talking, snacking, and doing what kids do on long road trips. Bridget and I were in the front enjoying the familiar scenery (what little there is between Houston and Dallas) and engaging in the kind of sporadic conversation typical of four-hour drives. Suddenly a familiar song came on the radio. It was one of those blasts from the past that you don't hear every day. I don't remember what song it was, but I know it was played on the radio incessantly during our early years together. Without a word the two of us grinned, grabbed one another's hand, and drifted back in time for a few moments.

Music is an incredible medium. With a few notes we can be transported to another time and place. There are songs that remind me of my boyhood, songs that remind me of my courtship, and songs that remind me of all-nighters preparing for midterm exams. There are also songs that remind me of spiritual landmarks in my life. The same will be true of our children.

Music is very important to our family. We frequently turn on the CD player while we eat our meals or play games. Sometimes we play music all day long as the children do their schoolwork and Bridget and I go about our work. We also play songs of the faith as we ride along in the car. It is as though we are creating a soundtrack for our lives. I want my sons and daughters to hear the songs of the faith twenty years from now and smile as they remember the home in which they grew up and the spiritual formation that took place there.

Engaging the Senses of Taste and Smell

There is no such thing as Christian food. I know my Southern Baptist friends beg to differ (we call chicken "the gospel bird"), but fried chicken is not a "Christian" dish. However, that does not mean that food is off-limits when it comes to engaging the senses in the worship of Almighty God in our homes.

Alistair Begg is one of my favorite preachers. I don't know if it is his rich Scottish accent or the fact that he handles the biblical text with a level of care, accuracy, passion, power, and attention to detail that few can match, but I love to hear him preach. I vividly remember one of his messages at a pastors' conference where he was illustrating the importance of a reverent attitude toward worship. He illustrated the point by telling the story of Saturday nights in his boyhood home. I could almost smell the Sunday dinner as he described in great detail his vivid memory of every aspect of the meal as at least part of it was prepared the night before in order to avoid any extra hindrance on the Lord's Day.

As a man in his fifties he is still reminded of the smells of Sunday when he was a child. What a blessed gift his parents gave him. Even something as small as preparing a special Sunday meal on a regular basis can impact your child's future recollection of their Godward journey in the days of their youth.

Engaging the Sense of Touch

Have you ever walked into a home with one of those enormous family Bibles? I mean the kind you have to open with both hands. Those things are amazing. Some people have had them in their family for generations. I love to leaf through the pages and see the records of births, weddings, baptisms, and deaths. What an incredible reminder of God's providence in the life of a family. Moreover, it is a tremendous way to engage the sense of touch. Nothing feels quite like the pages of an old Bible.

Many families require their children to play a musical instrument. Unfortunately, many of us see this requirement merely as a way to "broaden our children's horizons" or increase their scores in subjects like math. There is far more to it than that. What better way to engage God through the sense of touch than to learn songs of the faith on your instrument of choice? We can either view our children's music education as an edge we give them, as making them properly cultured, or as a tool to help them engage with God.

I must admit, I didn't understand this when we started. I just wanted our children to be able to play the piano. I wanted them to read music and understand music theory so they could choose later in life whether it was something they wanted to pursue. I had no concept of using the piano as a tool to bring my children closer to God. That is, until I began to learn myself.

If you are thinking about giving your child music lessons, I encourage you to do so. More importantly, I encourage you to find a teacher who knows and follows Christ and who is as committed to the music of Zion as he or she is to the technical aspects of the instrument itself. This can be an incredible experience for you and your child, and God can use it in tremendous ways to make Himself known as your sons and daughters place their hands on their instruments and "make a joyful noise to the LORD" (Psalm 95:1-2, ESV).

While art, music, and food engage the senses in magnificent and meaningful ways, there is one activity that far exceeds them all and engages several senses at once.

The Family Altar: A Multisensory Expression of Faith

A funny thing happened on the way out of my children's last piano recital. One of the parents looked at me and said, "I thought *all* of Mrs. Heidi's students had to play at the recital." Several other parents looked on, nodding their approval, as my kids' piano teacher walked up grinning like a Cheshire cat and took me by the arm. The next thing I knew, I was walking toward the piano with several couples following closely behind. I had been found out. Someone had spilled the beans. It was no longer a secret that I was learning to play the piano.

After I muddled through a few songs, everyone clapped and patted me on the back. They were very kind and supportive. One woman smiled and asked, "What made you start taking piano?" To which I responded, "I just wanted to lead my family in worship." Her smile got even bigger, and she almost burst into tears. My wife was way ahead of her as she was already on her way out of the sanctuary to get a tissue.

I knew Bridget was proud of me, but I had no idea how much it meant to her. She later told me that her tears were the closest she could come to describing the difference our daily time around the piano was making in our family. She was right. I don't think I am a skillful enough writer to put our experience into words. All I can say is our days have not been the same.

While we only recently added the piano to our family worship time, we have been gathering for Bible study, prayer, and songs for years. However, we didn't start out this way. I can remember a time when we did not worship together as a family. I thought my children would get all they needed from church. After all, that's why we hire children's workers, isn't it? Then I came to grips with the fact that family worship is an essential part of family life. Arthur Pink (1886–1952) put it better than I could when he wrote:

> It is not enough that we pray as private individuals in our closets; we are required to honor God in our families as well. At least twice each day, in the morning and in the evening the whole household should be gathered together to bow before the Lord parents and children, master and servant to confess their sins, to give thanks for God's mercies, to seek His help and blessing. Nothing must be allowed to interfere with this duty: all other domestic arrangements are to bend to it. The head of the house is the one to lead the devotions, but if he be absent, or seriously ill, or an unbeliever, then the wife would take his place. Under no circumstances should family worship be omitted. If we would enjoy the blessing of God upon our family, then let its members gather together daily for praise and prayer. "Them that honour Me I will honour" is His promise.[2]

At first blush, Pink's admonition seems a bit extreme. However, after a closer examination of passages such as Deuteronomy 6:7 we see that Pink is not off base at all. Moses commands God's people to teach His commandments to their children "when you sit in your house and when you walk by the way and when you lie down and when you rise up." In other words, family worship is ultimately an all-day, everyday affair.

Tara Lipinski is a Houston legend who won an Olympic Gold Medal in figure skating. Tara's commitment is legendary. Like many figure skaters, she woke up before dawn every morning to get to the ice rink before school. She would also practice for several hours in the evenings. Tara was fifteen when she won her medal.

Millions of young athletes' families cart them all over town to practice softball, baseball, football, soccer, Tai Kwon Do, and on and on. In fact, this level of commitment and activity is so common that we have a name for the women who run themselves ragged making sure their children make it to and from their practices, recitals, and games. We call them soccer moms.

Why is it that Christian families think nothing of a lifestyle that demands hours per week traipsing across town, blood, sweat, and tears from our children, and thousands of dollars each year from our bank accounts, but the idea of a twenty-minute daily commitment to family worship immediately strikes them as too much to ask? I fear that we have lost our way. Christianity has become so marginal in our culture that even those who claim allegiance to Christ have very little to show for it in terms of time and commitment.

I must admit that arriving at a consistent commitment to daily family worship was not easy for our family. We, like every other family, have so many things to do that the time often gets away from us. However, once we decided that our time in the Word was more important and would have a more lasting impact than anything else we could possibly do, we decided to make our family devotions the immovable object in our family life. If school or meals or free time or anything else has to move, it can. However, when we rise (or at least right after breakfast) and before we lie down in the evening, we will spend time together around the Word of God.

This is not to say that family worship twice a day is a definitive mandate. It is not. Some families may worship together three times a day, others three times a month. However, the crucial issue is that we make time to gather together before the throne of God. The benefits are myriad.

> Nothing will spur a father toward godly, spiritual discipline in his own walk with Christ more than leading his family in worship. In order to teach his wife and children, he will have to study the Scriptures on his own. A godly woman will be encouraged and inspired as she sees her husband take responsibility and lead in family worship. This practice sets a tone of harmony and love in the household and is a source of strength when they go through affliction together. As they pray for each other their mutual love is strengthened.[3]

It all comes down to a simple question: Why are we here? Does our family exist to prepare children for the Major Leagues? If so, then baseball will be the center of our family's universe, and everything will bow to the whims and wishes of the baseball god. Does our family exist to produce socialites? If so, then our family must revolve around the social calendars of our overloaded teenagers and their hectic schedules. However, if our family exists to glorify and honor God and to lay a biblical foundation in the lives of our children, then we must not allow anything to interfere with our commitment to family worship, prayer, and Bible study.

To quote Pink once more:

> An old writer well said, "A family without prayer is like a house without a roof, open and exposed to all the storms of Heaven." All our domestic comforts and temporal mercies issue from the loving-kindness of the Lord, and the best we can do in return is to gratefully acknowledge, together, His goodness to us as a family. Excuses against the discharge of this sacred duty are idle and worthless. Of what avail will it be when we render an account to God for the stewardship of our families to say that we had not time available, working hard from morn till eve? The more pressing be our temporal duties, the greater our need of seeking spiritual succor. Nor may any Christian plead that he is not qualified for such a work: gifts and talents are developed by use and not by neglect.

I must admit that these words cut me to the quick. Too many times I have allowed the cares of this world to crowd out the things of God in my family. Too many times I have allowed the business of the family schedule to dictate the amount of time we would devote to God. All I can do is fall on the mercy of God and be grateful for another day to seek His face.

I know these words sound foreign to most of us. At least they would have to me a few years ago. I was a seminary graduate, an ordained minister, on staff at a local church, preaching to thousands of people across the country, and I did not understand this principle! My family and I ran ourselves ragged trying to do all of the things that modern families think they must do in order to have healthy, happy, well-balanced (read: spoiled) children. We had more soccer practices, piano practices, play dates, church activities, birthday parties, cook-outs, and meetings than you could shake a stick at. We were fortunate to have family devotions once a month, let alone once a day.

The sad thing about our condition is that we were still among the top-tier Christian parents. At least we were homeschooling our children and had Bible in their curriculum. At least we were in church regularly. At least our daughter wasn't dressing like a streetwalker, and our son wasn't a thug or a partying drunkard. But the bottom line was that we were not building a lasting foundation in our children's lives. We weren't teaching them to live Christianity—we were just teaching them to play at it. We were teaching them that church was a good excursion, but nothing more. We were showing them that Jesus owned our Sundays and our Wednesdays, but not our home. It wasn't until we began to have regular family worship that things began to change.

I cannot tell you exactly when we began to worship on a daily basis, but I can tell you that it changed us forever. I distinctly remember watching my son run around gathering up Bibles one day as he anxiously anticipated our family worship, and I said to myself, *How could we have missed this?* Now we feel like something is missing (and it is) when we don't gather together to worship the Lord.

Where Do We Begin? (Seven Steps)

Family Worship Must Be Born of Conviction

You must be convinced that this is something you need, and you must be convicted that this is something required of you as a parent who is responsible for bringing your children up in "the discipline and instruction of the Lord" (Ephesians 6:4). If you are not convicted of this truth, you will not follow through. If you read the words of this chapter and dismiss them as overzealous or fanatical, you will not implement family worship. However, if the things you have read to this point ring true to you and line up with what you read in the Scriptures, then you are well on your way.

We tried to establish family devotions in the past, but it never lasted long. We would gather together for singing, prayer, Bible reading, etc., but it was never consistent. We would do fine for a few days and then miss a day, then another, and another. Eventually we would be right back where we started. It was not until we began to read about the importance of family worship and hang around families who were committed to regular devotions that we finally turned the corner.

Family Worship Begins with the Head of the Household

Mom, if your husband hasn't read this book, do not—I repeat, *do not*—hit him over the head with it. The last thing you want to do is rush in and demand that he start leading the family in worship on a daily basis. First of all, that would clearly violate the principles in 1 Peter 3:1-2:

> *In the same way, you wives, be submissive to your own husbands so that even if any of them are disobedient to the word, they may be won without a word by the behavior of their wives, as they observe your chaste and respectful behavior.*

If you want God's blessing, you must do things God's way. Moreover, forcing your husband to take the lead would contradict the first principle (it must be born of conviction, not coercion or guilt). Try to get your husband to read this chapter, and allow the Lord to use it in his life as you prayerfully and respectfully wait on the Lord. However, if you are a single mom, then you are the head of the household, so go for it!

This is not to say that Mom should never lead family worship. On the contrary, there are times when she must. In fact, during my eight to ten days a month when I'm traveling, my wife leads family worship. However, as the head of the household, family worship will usually rise and fall with me. And if I am committed to family worship, my wife and children will likely follow suit.

Family Worship Must Be Scheduled

If we do not plan family worship, we will skip it. In our home, family worship happens right after breakfast and right before bed each day. That way if we have to start the day earlier or later, family worship doesn't get scrapped because of time. This will also turn family worship into a habit. Of course, that doesn't mean you want it to be a rote exercise, but you do want it to be a regular practice.

This is especially important when you begin to implement family worship. It has been said that it takes thirty days to form a habit. Try getting on a rigid schedule for the next thirty days in order to form a habit of family worship. It is very important that you get started and see it through. Scheduling your time will go a long way toward establishing a pattern.

Family Worship Must Be Simple

Family worship does not have to be a big production. You do not have to produce PowerPoint slides or an order of service. All you need is a commitment to gather together and the Word of God. In the mornings we sing a few songs around the piano, and then we read through a devotional book (usually a catechism). In the evenings we read through the Bible. We simply start where we left off and read on a pace that will get us through the Bible in a year. Keep it simple. Don Whitney notes that "there are three elements to family worship: read the Bible, pray, and sing."[4]

One of the benefits of keeping things simple is that it doesn't take much to add a little zing from time to time to keep things interesting. Every once in a while I will add a new element in order to spice things up. And sometimes I will remove an element in order to simplify things even further. Don't outthink yourself on this.

Family Worship Must Be Natural

Family worship is not the time for you to do your best George Beverly Shea or Darlene Zschech impression. Just be you. Remember, God sent your children home with you, so He must want you to be the one to lead them. If God wanted George Beverly Shea to lead your children in family worship, they would have been born into the Shea family instead of yours. Choose songs that you and your family love to sing. Study materials that fit your situation in life.

This is also important because children can detect a lack of authenticity. They know when we're faking it. They live with us all day every day; so when we do something that is out of character, it sticks out like a sore thumb. Moreover, if we are not careful we will teach our children not to be themselves before God. Just be natural.

Family Worship Must Be Mandatory

No rogue members of the family get to skip out on family worship. If that sullen teenager thinks this is something that doesn't register on his cool meter, just inform him that it doesn't have to. I do recognize that this will be difficult for some families at first, but I assure you it will be to your benefit and to the benefit of your children if you make this mandatory for everyone in the house. If your teenager does not want to participate, then you have rebellion on your hands, and that must be handled separately, but family worship is not an option.

I do not mean to make light of this situation. I know that teenagers can be difficult. Nor am I suggesting that all you have to do is make a rule and the child's rebellion will melt away. You know better than that. The fact is that rebellion must be handled biblically and emphatically. My point here is that the rebellion is a separate issue. Take, for example, a child with a bad attitude about algebra. We wouldn't think for a moment that the answer was to simply avoid algebra. We would continue to teach the child algebra while we worked on the rebellion. The same must be true of family worship. Family worship is no less important than algebra; in fact it's more important. Make it mandatory, and stand your ground.

Family Worship Must Be Participatory

Make sure family worship is not a performance by one gifted member of the family that is merely observed by everyone else. Invite your children to join in singing, choosing songs, reading Scripture, discussing issues, and praying. You will be amazed at how willing your children are to participate in family worship and at how much (and how fast) they will grow in the process. Participatory family worship can even touch the heart of that resistant teen. Get them all involved and engaged in the process.

What Difference Will It Make? (Seven Blessings)

Family Worship Honors God

God is always honored when His people bless His name. Family worship gives us occasion to do that daily as opposed to weekly and with the members of our household as well as with our church family. It also gives us occasion to involve our whole household in the process. Bridget and I love it when we have overnight guests. There is something special about bringing friends and family along with us as we worship. I believe God is honored in the process.

Interestingly, our children seem to take family worship more seriously when we have guests. I think it reminds them of how special our daily time is, and unfortunately how rare it is as well. Suddenly they realize that we have an opportunity to share this special family activity with others. More importantly, it is an opportunity to give another family a vision for family worship and for honoring God in our homes.

Family Worship Will Draw Your Family Closer to God

This is crucial since God's promise of salvation has connotations for the entire household (John 4:53; Acts 11:14; 16:31). Of course, this does not guarantee the salvation of everyone in our household, but it certainly doesn't hurt. God ordains both the ends and the means of salvation, and we must do everything in our power to move our children toward faith in God. I believe wholeheartedly that salvation is a sovereign, monergistic work of God's grace from beginning to end. I also believe that I must do everything in my power to employ the biblical means through which salvation is brought about. Thus we must be committed to proclaiming the gospel to our children with a view toward their conversion.

It also goes without saying that a family that prays, reads the Bible, and sings praise to God together will be closer to God than a family that does none of these. To quote Pink once more:

> The advantages and blessings of family worship are incalculable. First, family worship will prevent much sin. It awes the soul, conveys a sense of God's majesty and authority, sets solemn truths before the mind, brings down benefits from God on the home.

God will honor the family that honors Him. And He will strengthen the bonds that tie their hearts to one another and to Him.

Family Worship Will Draw Your Family Closer to One Another

Nothing draws a family together like prayer. Prayer is one of the crucial elements of family worship, and it is amazing how something so simple can have such a profound effect on family dynamics. It is difficult to harbor ill will toward my wife when I am praying for her every day. It is difficult for the children to be at each other's throats when they are regularly called upon to voice prayers for one another.

What's more, singing together is a tremendous bonding agent. There is something powerful about the blending of our voices as we sing praises to God. My daughter and I found out that we sound pretty good when we harmonize together. In fact, we have been known to pull off the occasional duet for visitors. Sometimes when I'm just sitting at the piano practicing, she will come up behind me, lay her hands on my shoulders, and sing with me. I wouldn't trade those moments for anything.

Family Worship Will Lay a Foundation for Multigenerational Faithfulness

Family traditions are powerful. Many of us put up a flag on Memorial Day, barbecue on Labor Day, and cut down our own tree at Christmas simply because that's what our family did when we were growing up. Our family traditions do not guarantee that our children and grandchildren will follow in our footsteps, but they do lean in that direction. There are no guarantees that our children will conduct family worship in their homes with their families, but we do know this: Children who grow up in homes that had daily family worship will see it as the norm.

Many times we have met people from different parts of the country who have completely different views of family time. One family likes to fish together, another likes to hunt, still another likes to play golf. This is simply who they are. More often than not, these things were instilled in them through regular participation in their home. Their dad was a fisherman who regularly took them out. Or their dad was a hunter who couldn't wait for deer season. In any case all it took was a parent (or grandparent) with a sincere passion and regular commitment. You can accomplish the same thing in the area of family worship. Fishing, hunting, and golf are all great pastimes, but I would much rather instill the habit of family worship in my children and my children's children.

Family Worship Will Expose Spiritual Weaknesses in Your Home

I believe one of the greatest crutches in the church is the nursery. Parents who have neglected to train their children have very little encouragement to do so when there is a place to hide them. The father who should be up in arms by the time he gets home from church because of the embarrassment to which his child subjected him ends up going home with a clear conscience while the nursery worker takes a handful of aspirin.

Unlike the church, where unruly children can be pawned off on nursery workers, family worship offers no such reprieve. If you practice daily family worship, you will be forced to recognize such behavior and correct it. Moreover, the rebellious, disrespectful attitudes of older children will come to the surface. It may not be pretty, but it is necessary.

You may think this is a reason not to engage in family worship, but nothing could be further from the truth. If we do not address such attitudes and behaviors, they become ingrained in our children's character. It may be expedient to avoid such confrontations, but the price of looking the other way is far higher than the price of facing up to the problem now. John Bunyan offers stern and encouraging words for those who find themselves face-to-face with such an unruly child:

> [Y]ou must rule them, and not let them rule you! You are set over them by God, and you are to use the authority, which God has given you, both to rebuke their wickedness, and to show them the evil of their rebelling against the Lord. This is what Eli did, though not enough; and likewise did David [1 Samuel 2:24-25; 1 Chronicles 28:9]. Also, you must tell them how sad your state was when you were in their condition, and so labor to rescue them out of the snare of the devil [Mark 5:19].[5]

Family Worship Will Serve as a Training Ground for Smaller Children

Personally, family worship forces us to teach our toddler to sit quietly for extended periods of time and to receive correction in a worship setting. For us, it has also borne much fruit as we see even our smallest children participate in corporate worship at church since the practice is no longer foreign to them. I will never forget the first time our youngest son, Elijah, recognized a song in church that we had used several times at home. He was about thirteen months old at the time. The congregation began to sing, and he lit up like a Christmas tree! He began to flail his arms, and he smiled so big I thought he was going to pull a muscle in his face. It was an incredible moment.

Our little one is far from perfect. We still have to correct him in church, and he still gets distracted at times. However, he is able to make it through the service without major incident. In his world it's just a larger version of what he does at home every day. We have the privilege of being part of a family-integrated church,[6] and it is amazing how quickly children adapt to being in the service when worship becomes a part of their lives.

Recently, Bridget and the kids were able to join me when I preached at a church in the Houston area. I love to take the family along with me whenever I can, so this was a treat for all of us. I had to preach three services that morning, so I knew it would be a test for little Elijah. When Bridget arrived, I was already at the church and in my seat. As she approached the sanctuary a young lady spotted her carrying the baby and made a beeline for her. The woman was polite and courteous. She smiled at Bridget and the kids and then said, "We have a nursery for the little one." Bridget smiled back and said, "Thank you, but we'll be fine."

The woman became a bit more assertive and informed Bridget, "The nursery is staffed by child-care professionals, and they have age-specific activities for the baby. I'm sure he will be fine." Bridget became a bit agitated and told the woman that Elijah sat through church every week and would not be a problem. Doubtlessly feeling that she had failed at her assignment (which was obviously to see to it that no babies or toddlers made it into the sanctuary), the woman moved aside and with a parting gesture said, "The nursery is right down that hall should you change your mind."

As it turns out, I used a closing illustration that day in which I told the amazing story of Elijah's adoption. When I was done, I pointed to him as he sat there in his mother's lap completely unnoticed until that very moment. Elijah sat through all three services that day, and at the end of each one of them young mothers approached my wife to compliment him and ask her what in the world she had done to get him to remain so quiet. Each time Bridget smiled and said, "He sits through family worship every day." Of course, now that I've written this in a book he will probably throw a fit in the middle of my next family conference.

Family Worship Will Make Corporate Worship More Meaningful

Much modern worship has become passive and entertainment-driven. We sit in plush theater seats watching the show, hoping that this week's version will at least equal, if not exceed, the presentation we witnessed the week before. Musicians have their sets down to a T. The media crew has their lighting, sound, and set cues timed to the minute. The drama team knows which song they will follow, and the preacher— excuse me, the speaker—has his talk timed out perfectly so the video clip comes at precisely the right moment. All of this to ensure that the service will start at 11 o'clock sharp and end at 12 o'clock dull (as one of my seminary professors used to say).

If there was ever a time for families to engage in simple, heartfelt, participatory, community-based, New Testament worship, it is now. If you are in a church that has resisted the temptation to professionalize worship, you are blessed. If not, my heart goes out to you. In any event, family worship will deepen your appreciation for biblical worship and make the corporate experience that much richer. However, I must caution you—family worship also has a tendency to open your eyes to the shallow, mundane, worldly aspects of the modern "worship" scene.

Through intentionally marking our home with things that will engage the senses of our children and through engaging in regular family worship, we can turn our homes into sanctuaries for the worship of Almighty God. No longer will our lives be subdivided and compartmentalized with the sacred on Sunday mornings (and Wednesday nights) and the secular dominating every other moment. Our lives can be fully engulfed with the presence and priority of God. That will go a long way toward establishing family driven faith.

Take Action

1. Take inventory of the things marking your home. If there are things that need to go, take action. If there are things that need to be featured more prominently, do so. If you need to add some strategic pieces, do that as well.
2. Think about a weekly meal that will mark Sunday as the Lord's Day.
3. Fill your house with the songs of Zion. Try to play Christian music in your home at least one day this week.
4. Start having weekly family worship. Mark out one day a week to sing, pray, read Scripture, and encourage one another in the Lord. Let your family know this will be a regular occurrence.

8

ENJOY THE GIFTS WITHOUT FORGETTING THE GIVER

Many Christians live and work in this world, as if their Christianity was a low priority in life, and this world and its pleasures were all important; when indeed the things of this world are fleeting and Christianity is the one thing we need most.

JOHN BUNYAN

Then watch yourself, that you do not forget the LORD who brought you from the land of Egypt, out of the house of slavery" (Deuteronomy 6:12). I have always found it interesting that as Moses stood before the people, preparing them to go into the Promised Land, he not only warned them about the dangers of their pagan neighbors' beliefs, he also warned them about their attitude toward God's provision. He knew that the pull of prosperity would be as great as the pull of paganism.

This same concept prompted Jesus to issue one of His most famous warnings: "It is easier for a camel to go through the eye of a needle than for a rich man to enter the kingdom of God" (Matthew 19:24; Mark 10:25; Luke 18:25). The magnitude of Jesus' statement is even greater when viewed in context. The rich young ruler who wanted to know how to "obtain eternal life" had just confronted Jesus. The entire story is a case study in the power of prosperity. The young man missed heaven because "he was extremely rich" (Luke 18:23).

We hear this sentiment again in Jesus' admonition, "No one can serve two masters" (Matthew 6:24; Luke 16:13). The context is a discussion about serving both God and money. Jesus makes it clear that prosperity is often a hindrance to spiritual commitment.

Paul echoes this concept when he asserts, "The love of money is a root of all sorts of evil" (1 Timothy 6:10). Of course, it is important to note that he does not call *money* the root of all evil; it is the *love of money* that is the culprit. This is a key point. God is not against your having things. He is, however, against things having you. Moses was not calling Israel to forsake prosperity; he was merely warning them not to elevate the gift above the Giver.

This is a word that we Americans desperately need to hear. We are among the wealthiest people on the planet, and we have a tendency to equate financial prosperity with God's approval. We say of the wealthy among us, "God has really blessed his business" or "The Lord has really prospered her," not realizing that in some instances prosperity has become a curse that has driven a wedge between the person and God. In many ways we resemble the church at Laodicea in Revelation 3, about whom Jesus says:

> *I know your deeds, that you are neither cold nor hot; I wish that you were cold or hot. So because you are lukewarm, and neither hot nor cold, I will spit you out of My mouth. Because you say, "I am rich, and have become wealthy, and have need of nothing," and you do not know that you are wretched and miserable and poor and blind and naked . . . (Revelation 3:15-17)*

Wealth has an uncanny way of driving a wedge between a man and his God (or a man and his family). I know personally that it was much easier for me to pray when I was poor than it is now that my family and I are doing well. When we first got married, we would pray for our next day's meal. Now our refrigerator never gets that low. We used to pray for rent money; now we worry when there's not enough in savings to pay the mortgage in case of an emergency. We used to pray that none of us got sick because we didn't have insurance; now we just fuss about how high our premiums have risen.

If we aren't careful, we begin to trust in our own resources rather than trusting in God. Isaiah offers a stern warning to those who fall prey to this kind of false trust:

> *Woe to those who go down to Egypt for help*
> *and rely on horses,*
> *and trust in chariots because they are many*
> *and in horsemen because they are very strong,*
> *but they do not look to the Holy One of Israel,*
> *nor seek the LORD! (Isaiah 31:1)*

That is a poignant picture of the American church. We live in the wealthiest, most powerful nation in the history of the world, and we have forgotten what it means to trust in God. We have church buildings that rival professional sports arenas (some of them actually were sports arenas), church budgets that rival the gross domestic product of some small countries, church staffs that rival those of Fortune 500 companies, church stage productions that resemble Hollywood sets, and church programs that we rely on more than on God. We have "gone down to Egypt for help" and have come to a place where we "rely on horses and trust in chariots because they are many and in horsemen because they are very strong." We have adopted a "more must be better" mentality.

Consequently, many Christians believe the best thing they can do for their family is provide them with more stuff. So we continue to accumulate as though accumulation is the answer. All the while our children are screaming at us from beneath the piles of untouched toys and unworn clothes begging for a few minutes of our time. Time we simply don't have because we are too busy trying to find that one thing we can add to the pile that will make the screaming stop.

Families on the Altar of Prosperity

I used to be an ESPN fanatic. In fact, I am of the opinion that ESPN stands for Every Saved Person Needs it! I love to watch the big game, the latest news, and the greatest highlights. I also like to hear the story behind the story. I love the personal interviews with players, coaches, and owners. Recently I watched one such interview with John Fox (head coach of the Carolina Panthers), Dennis Green (then head coach of the Arizona Cardinals), Steve Mariucci (then head coach of the Detroit Lions), and Brian Billick (head coach of the Baltimore Ravens). The coaches were seated together around a table discussing the ins and outs, ups and downs of coaching in the NFL. The conversations aired over a course of several days, and they were all very insightful. However, one episode in particular caught my attention. The coaches discussed the difficulty of balancing their responsibility as coaches with the demands of family life.

Stuart Scott introduced the segment by recounting the story of an NFL coach who once asked an assistant to stop the film and run back a play during a film session. After pausing the tape, the coach exclaimed, "I didn't know John had gotten so big." Scott went on to note, "John was the coach's son." The moral of the story was that the coach, like many in his profession, had missed seeing his son grow up. Unfortunately, this is not unusual. A couple of years ago Joe Gibbs returned to Washington, D.C. to coach the Redskins. However, many forget that the reason he left earlier was because, as he put it, he walked into his son's room one night to tuck him in and the boy was grown! He, too, had in many ways missed out on his kids' lives.

Several of the coaches in the aforementioned segment effectively tap-danced around the harm their absence has caused and is causing their families, particularly their children. I want to address these issues. However, I must say at the outset that I am not picking on coaches. As you will see, I am merely using this example because it provides ample opportunity to address several of the issues surrounding our choices when it comes to work and family.

This phenomenon is not limited to the coaching profession. Businessmen, lawyers, doctors, ministers—it is not unusual for men in our society to sacrifice their families on the altar of success. Even the great Billy Graham admitted in his autobiography that his success as an evangelist was often purchased with his failure as a father. In fact, I went through my own personal battle in this area. I had to struggle with the idea of balancing my time on the road doing "the

Lord's work" and my time at home being God's man. These coaches will merely serve as practical examples of where, when, and why we often make and then justify poor choices in this area.

Four specific issues were raised in the discussion that I think capture the essence of what is wrong with the way we ineffectively juxtapose family and career. First, one coach referred to other professions (specifically the military) where transfers are a way of life. Second, one of the coaches said his son is about to go off to college and wants to be a coach. Third, another coach referred to the "trade-off" from which his children benefit. Finally, when asked, "How do you balance family life with the heavy demands of the coaching profession?" the coaches passed the buck to their wives. In fact, Brian Billick stated, "We don't; our wives do."

These statements struck me because they sound eerily familiar. In fact, I have heard these exact statements from ministers. I have heard ministers justify their absence by pointing to their son's decision to join the ministry or the trade-off from which their children benefit or the fact that their wives make up for their absence. In all cases, the excuses ring hollow.

Other Families Suffer Worse Than Ours

First, let's address the coach's assertion that there are other professions where families have to move frequently. This is true. However, it is also a very poor excuse. How many times have we told our children, "You can't justify your bad behavior by pointing to someone else's worse behavior"? That would be like saying, "Sure, I robbed the bank, but there are a lot of guys out there who steal." The issue is not whether there are many careers that cost families as much or even more than ours. The issue is whether we have made an unreasonable compromise. Moving around is not a sin. However, running around from town to town, chasing the almighty dollar regardless of the price your family pays, is inexcusable.

I had a rough childhood. I grew up in the projects of south-central Los Angeles without a father. My mother was only a teenager when I was born, and we were seldom able to rely on anyone for help. However, as rough as my childhood was, it pales in comparison to my wife's. When we married, I learned that she had endured unspeakable abuse as a child. Things went on in her home that I wouldn't dare write in this book. Needless to say, the emotional scars she and her sisters carried into adulthood were significant.

When I learned what had happened to my wife, I began to view my childhood from an entirely different perspective. I realized that as bad as things were, they could have been worse. But that didn't change the fact that my father abandoned my mother and me. Nor did it change the number of times I walked around with patches covering holes in the knees of my pants because my mother couldn't afford to replace them. The fact that there is someone out there who endured more than I did does not eliminate my father's culpability. Furthermore, it does not change the fact that I have had to overcome significant obstacles in my journey to maturity. The scars in my life are as real as they were before I learned that "other families suffer worse than ours."

My Kids Want to Be Like Me

The second issue is similar in that the coach asserts that our children's eventual decision to pursue our career justifies the price they paid for our choices. Think of the logic when applied to another career: "My kid wants to be a mobster like me, so it must not be that bad." Our children love and admire us even when we neglect and mistreat them. My father's absence didn't change the fact that I wanted to be a football player *just like my dad*. Nonetheless, my desire to follow in his footsteps did not counteract his neglect.

There is a deeper problem here. This statement expresses an "end justifies the means" mentality about family life. Sometimes we act as if the only thing that matters is that our children end up being productive members of society. While this is important, it is shortsighted. I don't just want my children to be productive—I want them to be godly. I want my son to have a clear picture of what it means for a man to love his wife "as Christ loved the church and gave Himself up for her" (Ephesians 5:25). I want my daughter to know what a husband and father looks like. Moreover, I want to share something with my wife that transcends a mortgage and some offspring.

The Benefits Outweigh the Costs

Third, the coaches, like many of us, pointed to the trade-off factor. As one coach put it, "They may not have dad at home to tuck them in or read them stories . . . [but] there are other benefits like being on the sidelines and in the locker room." Great! "I wasn't there for you, but you got to meet some big stars along the way." I call this the "good outweighs the bad" excuse. Again, I believe these men, like all of us who at one time or another made such excuses, mean well. They did not enter their profession to spite their families. They are just hard-working guys who have gone further in their careers than most and have been rewarded with big contracts, fame, notoriety, and a schedule that would kill a mule.

There is no difference between this response from the coach and that of a busy business executive who says, "Yes, I am gone a lot, but how many other kids get to fly in private jets and vacation in Maui?" The problem, of course, is that God designed the family to operate with the input of a father, and no amount of money, toys, or fringe benefits can replace a godly father.

Momma Will Fix It

Finally, one coach argued that the key to balancing family and careers was his wife. In other words, we take care of business and leave our wives to take care of our kids. This is perhaps the most common excuse of them all. I can't tell you how many times I have talked to dads and husbands who excuse their absence by pointing to their wife's superhuman ability to function as mom and dad in the home while he chases the American Dream.

This is also one of the most common excuses I hear from ministers. As an itinerant preacher, I travel a great deal. At one time I traveled too much. It was not uncommon for me to be gone fifteen to twenty days a month on top of my responsibilities at church or school. In fact, during my last semester at seminary I took twenty-one hours of classes (remember, this was graduate school and nine hours was full-time), worked full-time as the Minister of Missions at a 5,000-member church, and traveled the country preaching in revivals and Bible conferences, all while we built our first home. I was an idiot! However, if anyone asked about my family, I would simply laud the herculean effort my wife was making on the home front.

Eventually things came to a head, and something had to be done. I had to find a better way. And that is precisely what I did. My wife and I sat down with a calendar and a calculator and made some tough decisions that changed our marriage and our family's future. Eventually we came up with a set of criteria that cut my travel down to ten to twelve days per month (now down to eight to ten), and my full-time church position became part-time. Eventually I found another position in a different church that fit even better. Additionally, I established an office at home in order to make up for my time away. Eventually we found a schedule that allowed me to pay the bills, participate in our family life, and take full advantage of my gifts and calling from God.

A Better Way

The first step toward finding a better way is deciding what is important from a biblical perspective. We could have sat down and written out what each of us wanted from the other and tried to negotiate. However, we decided a long time ago that as fallen human beings, what we want is usually selfish and falls far short of God's best for our lives. Therefore we dug into the Scriptures and came up with some guidelines.

God Is Not Opposed to Prosperity

There are many truths to be discovered in Deuteronomy 6. However, the idea that God is opposed to prosperity is not one of them. In fact, based on verses 10-11, one could argue to the contrary:

> *Then it shall come about when the LORD your God brings you into the land which He swore to your fathers, Abraham, Isaac and Jacob, to give you, great and splendid cities which you did not build, and houses full of all good things which you did not fill, and hewn cisterns which you did not dig, vineyards and olive trees which you did not plant, and you eat and are satisfied.*

Here we see God's intent to fulfill His promise to the patriarchs by ushering the children of Israel into the *prosperous* land of Canaan. He uses phrases like "great and splendid." He makes reference to "vineyards," "olive trees," "houses," and "land." It is obvious that God was inviting Israel to live in prosperity, not poverty.

As a father, it is not a sin to provide nice things for my family. Nor is it a sin for me to work hard toward that end. In fact, not to do so would make a man "worse than an infidel" (1 Timothy 5:8, KJV). The issue here is balance.

Prosperity vs. Idolatry

The warning about prosperity in verses 12-15 is as frightening as the previous verses are encouraging. Moses states:

> [T]hen watch yourself, that you do not forget the LORD who brought you from the land of Egypt, out of the house of slavery. You shall fear only the LORD your God; and you shall worship Him and swear by His name. You shall not follow other gods, any of the gods of the peoples who surround you, for the LORD your God in the midst of you is a jealous God; otherwise the anger of the LORD your God will be kindled against you, and He will wipe you off the face of the earth.

Our pursuit of prosperity can turn into idolatry if we are not careful. It is easy to keep our eyes a little too focused on the prize.

This principle brought our family to a crossroads. We had to decide what was essential and what was enough. Had we not come to this point, we would have ended up right back where we started. If we pursued prosperity without the fear of idolatry, we would end up making a mockery of the God who gives us the ability to create wealth (Deuteronomy 8:18; Proverbs 10:22). On the other hand, if we shunned prosperity for fear of idolatry, we would run the risk of being ungrateful. Israel would have been just as wrong to reject God's gift of the Promised Land as they would if they were to worship the gift above the Giver. How, then, do we overcome the tension between prosperity and idolatry?

Be a Good Steward of Your Gifts

God has gifted every believer. Moreover, each person has unique skills, abilities, and aptitudes. Each of us must discover and utilize these gifts for the glory of God, the benefit of mankind, and the support of our families. Imagine a world where Albert Einstein chose to be a cobbler, the Wright brothers practiced law, George Washington forsook politics for farming, Booker T. Washington became a banker, and Michael Jordan, Tiger Woods, and Hank Aaron were fishermen. What a tragedy! It is just as tragic when any one of us fails to discover our God-given gifts, talents, abilities, and aptitudes.

This may seem simple, but there is a deeper truth here. If I do what I do because it fits what God gave me, I am being a steward. If I do it because there's money in it, I am on my way to idolatry. There is a difference between the man who goes into medicine because science, service, and humanity course through his veins and the man who sees it as a lucrative career. One man is pursuing the best the world has to offer; the other is pursuing the best he has to offer the world.

Prosper as God Allows

There are two sides to prospering as God allows. The first is affirmative, and the second is negative. In the affirmative, God intends for us to prosper. We are to do the best we can with what we have. If you are a doctor, be the best doctor you can be. If you are a plumber, be the best plumber you can be. Don't be lazy; don't cheat your boss, yourself, or your Lord. The negative aspect of this admonition is more complicated. Just as there is godly prosperity, there is ungodly prosperity. Our prosperity must be in accordance with the will, nature, and authority of God.

During my sophomore year of college I saw the hand of God sweep across the campus of the small liberal arts university I attended. The school had no religious affiliation; in fact, there was an antagonistic atmosphere toward Christianity. Nevertheless, scores of young men and women were coming to faith in Christ. I saw numerous lives radically changed, including my own. One of my most profound memories is of a conversation I had with a teammate on the football team named Paul (not his real name).

Paul was a fifth-year senior. He was a good football player, but he didn't have the tools to play at the next level. He was, however, an incredible student at a top-tier university. He was about to graduate with a degree in business management and finance. He was intelligent, articulate, and handsome; he had it all. He also had several job offers. The reason I remember Paul in the context of the revival we experienced on our campus is because his newfound faith in Christ had a profound impact on his career decision. You see, the best offer Paul had, financially, was from a beer distributor. The compensation package was head and shoulders above any other offer he was considering. This was a great job for a young man right out of college. This was the fast track to the big time.

There was, however, a more pertinent question for Paul. Would taking this job honor God? In other words, would taking this job constitute prospering as God allows? It would have been easy for Paul to justify taking the job. He could have fallen back on the standard, "Well, I prayed for God to open a door, and this is an open door." But he didn't. He took a job that paid less money and had fewer benefits but allowed him to sleep better at night.

Not all prosperity is godly prosperity. We must constantly ask ourselves tough questions. We must seek wise, godly counsel. In short, we must do everything within our power to see to it that we prosper as God allows.

Prioritize Your Family

My family and I had just flown home from a family trip. We were sitting on the airport shuttle heading back to our car for the much-anticipated ride home. As we sat there soaking in the Houston humidity as it welcomed us back, I couldn't help but overhear the conversation going on just behind us. Now, I'm not usually one to eavesdrop, but this time I couldn't resist. The conversation involved two businessmen who had just returned from their respective business trips.

One man was traveling with his wife who had come along with him since his schedule had required him to be away so much lately. The two men exchanged pleasantries and then began to discuss their respective schedules. The gentleman traveling alone said he traveled about 180 days a year. The gentleman traveling with his wife looked at her, then turned back to the other gentleman, and commented, "That's about where I am." The two men shook their heads. Then the gentleman traveling with his wife said, "That's why she came with me this time; we just haven't seen much of each other lately." The other gentleman responded, "I know what you mean." The wife chimed in, "Do you have any children?" The other man nodded in affirmation. "So do we," the woman replied. Then they all exchanged glances and nods without words. The silence was deafening.

I wasn't sure if my wife was listening until our eyes met. She looked at me, smiled, squeezed my hand, and laid her head on my shoulder. It was one of the most meaningful things she had ever said to me, and she hadn't said a word. With that glance she said, "Remember when you were on the road that much?" With that squeeze of my hand she said, "Remember how you changed your schedule because you refused to sacrifice your family on the altar of your ministry?" And with her head on my shoulder she said, "No amount of money, success, notoriety, or fame would be worth what we have now."

As an itinerant preacher I make my living on the road. Hence traveling is not optional for me. There are, however, things I can do to balance out my life. Over the past five years I have traveled about ten to twelve days per month. I have an office at home. I participate fully in my children's lives. I make a lot less money than I could. And I wouldn't trade any of it. I have served on several church staffs throughout my years in ministry. However, in recent years I have only taken positions that would allow me to keep my family life in balance. Most recently I served as a teaching pastor at a church in the Houston area. I was able to bring my gifts and abilities to bear in the life of the church, but my office was still at my house. In a few years my children will be gone, and I will be free to travel as much as I want. For now I have to realize that plenty of people can preach at events across the country that I choose not to add to my schedule, but no one can replace me as Bridget's husband and Elijah and Trey and Jasmine's dad. How dare I pour my life into equipping other families at the expense of my own!

I can't tell you what to do with your schedule. That is between you and God. I can, however, say that anything that causes you to sacrifice your family on the altar of prosperity is not of God. Ask the tough questions; give honest answers; make hard choices. That's the only way to walk in obedience in this area.

This brings me to what has perhaps become the most controversial issue facing the prosperous American Christian family: should Mom work outside of the home? I want to answer that question in two ways. First, we must seek to understand what the Bible teaches on the matter. Next, we must discover the motives behind our current practices. Only then can we arrive at an appropriate answer to this pressing question.

Being a Wife and Mother Is an Honorable Calling

My wife, Bridget, taught school for six years. She loved the children she taught and thought of teaching as much more than a job. However, over time she was convinced that she needed to be home with our kids full-time. Eventually she quit and became a full-time mom without a second job.

During the transition the hardest thing for her to get used to was answering the question, "What do you do?" At first she gave the standard, "I don't work" response. She then graduated to the "I don't work *outside the home*" response. Eventually, though, as she began to understand the impact her presence was having on our children, her attitude changed. She no longer viewed herself as a schoolteacher who had given up her career. She now saw herself as a mother who had embraced a higher calling. Ask my wife what she does today, and you are likely to see her eyes light up as she proudly asserts, "I am raising and teaching my three children."

Being a wife and mother is nothing to be ashamed of. I find it difficult to make that statement—not because I don't believe it, but because I can't imagine how motherhood has fallen so far out of favor in our culture. I don't understand why such a statement is necessary. Why would a woman be ashamed of the fact that she is investing her life in shaping the future? Why should a woman be ashamed of her role as COO of the home? When did we begin to tell women they lacked value if they refused to leave the lion's share of their children's daily lives to the "professionals" down at the day care?

You Only Get One Shot at Parenting

Over the past few years I have become more aware of the deficiencies in my life brought on by my father's absence. There are several lessons I have had to learn on my own. I had no idea how to treat my wife, and later my children. I had no idea what a family was supposed to look like. I had to learn on my own. I could not be re-parented. My parents couldn't regroup and try again. Once I was grown it was a done deal.

Parenting is a tough job, and we have a limited amount of time to accomplish a lifetime of work. As I write this chapter, my daughter is finishing her last year of high school, and my oldest son has about three years left (the babies haven't started yet). When that time comes, it will be nearly impossible to undo things that were done badly or redo things that were missed. Sure, I will still have a relationship with my children, but for the most part the die will have been cast. I don't know about you, but that thought drives me to my knees! I want to take advantage of every opportunity, every teachable moment. Bridget and I want to have the greatest possible impact while we can. Again, this doesn't mean that Bridget can't go to work outside the home. It does, however, mean that the choices we make must take our awesome responsibility into consideration.

You Can't Have It All . . . and You Don't Need It All

The movie *Mona Lisa Smile* ought to have a subtitle: *A Feminist Manifesto*. The theme of the movie was, "You can have it all!" You can be a lawyer in the courtroom, a queen in the bedroom, a gourmet in the kitchen, and a first-rate mother all in one. This is simply untrue. Being a wife and mother is a full-time job, and a full-time job + a full-time job = something gets neglected, and that something is almost always the family.

I know this is not PC. In fact, you don't even have to be a flaming liberal feminist to find what I am suggesting offensive. For decades we have been told that women *can* have it all. Moreover, we have been told that they *should* have it all. What we haven't been told is the high price that they and their children have paid for "it all." On Mother's Day 2004 the following story ran on our local nightly news:

> On Mother's Day, working moms spoke out about the pressures they face.
>
> A survey by online recruiting firm CareerBuilder.com found that one-third of working mothers interviewed are dissatisfied with the balance between work and family life. Fifty-three percent say they missed at least one major event in their child's life because of work in the past year.
>
> Nearly half said they're preoccupied with work while at home, while many say they often work weekends. Mary Delaney, chief sales officer at Career Builder and a mother of three, said one way to balance time is to set boundaries and priorities *at both home and at work*. She said some companies are helping, by allowing flexible schedules, telecommuting and more generous personal time policies [emphasis mine].[1]

Ironically, one of the most poignant statements I've ever heard on this issue came from Oprah Winfrey. I have always thought of Oprah as a typical feminist. What's more, her New Age spirituality gives me the creeps. Nevertheless, I must give credit where credit is due. In a May 4, 2004 show on parents who push their children toward stage and screen, Oprah confessed that she chose not to have children because she knew that she could not possibly balance parenting and a high-demand career. While something tells me she will end up regretting her choice, I still applaud her candid evaluation. Oprah Winfrey understood something that I wish many women would admit: *You can't have it all!* And that's okay because you don't need it all.

Again, I am not saying that any mother who works outside the home is sinning. That is for each family to decide as they wrestle with the Scriptures and their circumstances. I know there are many mothers who have to work. My mother, like far too many women, was left to raise a child alone. She did not have the luxury of being a stay-at-home mom. My mother had to put food on the table.

Other women's husbands have died or are disabled. Some women have chosen career paths that allow them to work when their children are at school, and others work part-time or as volunteers. All of this is in keeping with the Proverbs 31 woman:

> *She is like merchant ships;*
> *She brings her food from afar.*
> *She rises also while it is still night*
> *and gives food to her household*
> *and portions to her maidens.*
> *She considers a field and buys it;*
> *from her earnings she plants a vineyard.*
> *She girds herself with strength*
> *and makes her arms strong.*
> *She senses that her gain is good;*
> *her lamp does not go out at night. (vv. 14-18)*

The ultimate question, however, is, "Are we both working because we have to or because we don't think our house is big enough or our car new enough or our bank accounts fat enough?" If it is the latter, we have crossed the line. That is when our children have been sacrificed on the altar of prosperity. That is when Moses' warning echoes through the halls of history: "Then watch yourself, that you do not forget the LORD who brought you from the land of Egypt, out of the house of slavery."

A Life Invested Is Never Wasted

My mother graduated from college at age forty-nine. She graduated so late in life because she became a mother at age eighteen and later found herself raising a son alone. As I watched her walk across the stage, I could not hold back the tears. For the first time in my life I understood her sacrifice. My mother had put her life on hold in order to invest in me. She did whatever she had to in order to see to it that I became a responsible, productive man. At one point, realizing that life in the projects of south-central Los Angeles was not the best environment for me, she packed up everything we owned, and we moved across the country to Buford, South Carolina to live with her oldest brother, a retired Marine Corps drill instructor.

My mother was still a very young woman in her late twenties. As I look back on it, small-town South Carolina couldn't have been a place she wanted to be. But it was the place her son needed to be, and that was all that mattered.

My mother could have been anything she wanted to be. And she was. She was my mother. When she saw to it that I became a man, she went on with her life. She didn't just finish college, she excelled, graduating with honors! After the graduation ceremony, students, professors, and administrators all came by to congratulate my mom. Most of them had tears in their eyes. People I had never met came up to me to tell me how much of an inspiration she had been to them. She is a brilliant, courageous woman, and I am proud to call her my mother.

Mothers, don't let the world rob you of the incredible joy of a life invested in your children. They are your mark on the world. They are your legacy, your testimony, and your contribution to mankind. Don't let some other woman steal your influence. Remember, "The hand that rocks the cradle is the hand that rules the world." That saying didn't just show up one day. That proverb is the result of centuries of observation. A mother's influence is unmatched. I pray that every mother reading these words has the privilege of someday looking into the eyes of a man who has the level of admiration and gratitude for her that I hold in my soul for Frances Baucham. If so, motherhood will never again be forsaken to the degree that it has been in our time.

A Lesson from an Old Coach

I recently made a phone call to one of my old coaches from high school. Coach was one of the most influential men in my life. He was one of those men who took the coaching profession seriously. He was always at school before sunup and was one of the last to leave. He traveled an hour each way to get to work every day. He was one of those coaches who led by example and made his players want to win for him.

Over the years Coach and I have kept in contact. Every once in a while I'd pick up the phone and catch up with Coach. Recently I discovered that he had fallen on hard times. He had finally retired and didn't know what to do with himself. What's worse, his marriage of over twenty-five years had recently ended. At first I wondered what could possibly have gone wrong. Then it dawned on me. We saw a committed coach who arrived early every morning; his wife saw a man who was never home when she got up in the morning. We saw him as committed; she saw him as overextended. We saw him as a confidant who was always there for us; his children saw a man who was more of a father to strangers than he was to them.

Now he spends his nights alone missing the woman who spent a quarter of a century missing him. He sits at home reminiscing about the house he was so committed to that he drove an hour to work every day rather than moving. He yearns for time with his kids, but that time is scarce because they are busy doing what he didn't—spending time with their families. His days are spent with his elderly father, and occasionally he has a chance to watch his grandkids play ballgames, something I'm sure he wishes he had done more with his children.

Every once in a while someone from the past calls and asks, "How's it going, Coach?" A few minutes later the reminiscing is over, the voice from the past is gone, and Coach is alone with his memories. And all he has to show for it are a few trophies, a couple of pictures, and some patches on an old, faded jacket.

I cried when I got off the phone that night. I felt like I had just watched the climax of an M. Night Shyamalan movie. All of the pictures came together, and I finally saw the truth that had been there all along. This man who had meant the world to me had sacrificed his family on the altar of his career, and I was oblivious to it. I considered it normal, even admirable. Suddenly, all these years later, I went from admiring Coach to feeling sorry for him. I saw the trade-off, and it wasn't worth it. The occasional thanks of strangers will never dull the pain of years missed with your family. Needless to say, when I got off the phone with Coach, I spent some time with my kids. It turns out Coach still had lessons to teach.

Take Action

1. Sit down with your children, and ask them if they think you spend enough time with them. If they say no, ask yourself why not.
2. Take a look at your calendar. Do you have time written down for your family? Do they appear as much as they should?

3. Make a commitment to plan at least one family vacation and one getaway with your spouse each year. It doesn't have to be fancy or expensive. You can take a trip in the car or go to a family camp in the summer. Just get it on the calendar, and don't let anything interfere.
4. Make a commitment to sitting down for at least one meal a day as a family. It sounds simple, but making time to share a meal together each day is a great way to establish family cohesion.

9

THE COMING REVIVAL: IS THE CHURCH READY FOR FAMILY DRIVEN FAITH?

Family driven faith is about more than just being a better parent. This is a complete lifestyle and worldview overhaul. If we believe that God calls us to worship Him without rivals, build our homes on a foundation of biblical love, adopt a biblical worldview, teach the Word in our homes, mark our homes as God's territory, and keep our prosperity in check, then we must also believe that God intends for the church to aid and not hinder families in this process. Unfortunately there are times when this is not the case. I say unfortunately because we may be missing out on a tremendous revival.

My favorite definition of revival came from the pen of Alvin L. Reid and Malcolm McDow (professors of evangelism at Southwestern and Southeastern Seminaries respectively) in their book, *Firefall*. According to Reid and McDow, "Revival is God's invasion into the lives of one or more of His people in order to awaken them spiritually for kingdom ministry."[1] It is on the basis of this definition that I believe that the recent rise in parental awareness, desperation over the future of our families, churches, and communities, the homeschool movement, and the family-integrated church movement constitutes a modern revival on the American landscape. All across this country men and women have been "awaken[ed] spiritually" to the "kingdom ministry" of total commitment to the education and discipleship of their children and their children's children.

Speaking as someone who has experienced this revival firsthand, I can say without reservation that our decision to homeschool our children was a spiritual awakening in our family. We opened our eyes one day, and our daughter was no longer a baby. She was a ten-year-old fourth grader at a private Christian school who was beginning to develop some attitudes and ideas that displeased her mother and me. And as we anticipated the day when she would reach youth group age, we were mortified as we thought about our little girl walking into that segment of congregational life. Immediately we got on our faces and sought God's wisdom on how to be good stewards of the time we had left with all of our children. The status quo simply would not do.

We were well aware of the academic advantages to home education, but it was the spiritual, emotional, and interpersonal aspects that pushed us over the edge. Hence we opted out of the school culture and eventually the typical church youth culture. In other words, this revival in our family led us to a crisis of faith as our newfound commitment caused a clash of cultures between our family and our church. Unfortunately we were not alone in our experience.

Sometimes families who adopt the philosophies outlined in this book (which I believe are those outlined in Deuteronomy 6) are made to feel like outsiders. Women who break the unwritten two child per family rule are often greeted with questions like, "Haven't you guys figured out what causes that?" Fathers who choose to emphasize their sons' spiritual growth at the expense of their participation in the all-consuming pursuit of sports sometimes find themselves being alienated by other dads. Children who don't attend the local public high school are often looked down upon because they don't know the latest catch phrases or wear the latest designs. The pursuit of family driven faith can be costly.

One family that reminded me of the high cost of such pursuit attended a conference I recently conducted. The first member of the family I met was Jean, a homeschooling mother. She and her husband were very active in their local church and worked tirelessly in their community. Their children were astonishing. They were all extremely well mannered, highly intelligent, personable, and to top it off all accomplished musicians. They were a modern-day von Trapp family. More importantly, there were six of them! One could not help but be impressed.

I met Jean and her husband while conducting a conference at their church. She and several of her children were volunteer workers. When I spotted the older children (three teenagers) working at the product table, I knew right away they were different. I walked up and asked them, "Are you guys homeschoolers?" They smiled, and the oldest daughter spoke up and asked, "How could you tell?" "I'm a home-school dad, and I've gotten to a place where I can spot homeschool kids a mile away," I replied. I am not saying that homeschool kids are better or worse than other children. They are just different. Especially those whose families have made their educational decision based upon lifestyle and worldview choices as opposed to just academics.

As the conference went on, I shared much of the same information I share at all of my conferences. I talked about biblical worldview, the validity of the Bible, the historicity of the resurrection, etc. And as usual I shared several personal stories about our family. Over the course of the two-day conference I bragged on my wife and my kids and mentioned the fact that we are committed to home education as a component of discipleship and multigenerational faithfulness. I didn't make a special push or give an altar call for those who wanted to bring their kids home for the rest of their education. I just talked about my life, which happened to include things like family worship, family discipleship, and family-based missions and evangelism. I just shared my story. However, to Jean I had done much more than that.

She came up to me at the end of the conference with tears streaming down her face. There was a crowd of people around, but she didn't seem to care. "Can I hug you?" she asked with her arms spread out like she was going through pre-game warm-ups. "Sure," I said, wondering what was waiting for me on the other side of the hug. After she hugged me, she wiped her face and said, "We have been in this church for years, and this is the first time that our lifestyle has been validated from that pulpit." By now her children had joined her and were shaking their heads in agreement as they too began to fight back tears. "We don't think we're better than anybody else at this church. We just love children and believe they are a blessing from God. We just believe that we are accountable to God for their physical, spiritual, emotional, and intellectual well-being." By now the kids could no longer hold back the tears. She took a deep breath and said, "It means the world to me that my children got to hear you articulate the truths that we live by."

I knew exactly what Jean was talking about. I had been on the other side of the snide remarks. I had sat down at dinner with church staff members who talked about families like hers (and mine for that matter) with utter disdain. I have heard women say (with a straight face), "I could never do that with my kids; we just don't get along well enough." Or "I just don't think I have the right temperament to spend that much time with my children." Again, this is not a question of homeschool versus non-homeschool. The question is whether or not we are willing to adjust our entire lifestyle around the incredible responsibility God has given us to prepare our children to be launched from our homes as arrows (or ballistic missiles) aimed at the kingdom of darkness. And if we do so, will there be a church there to wrap its arms around us, encourage us, equip us, and cheer us on?

In case you think this discussion is just a homeschool issue, read what a gentleman wrote to me in an e-mail after I visited his church in the Midwest.

> I'll start with the basics: I am in the Air Force (meaning, I am not a wealthy man), have been for 19 years as an aerospace engineer. I'm a Lt. Col. now and make a decent living, but when we started having children I was a Captain, making [a] whole lot less. We made the decision very early (before children) that mom (Master's degree in elementary education) would stop teaching and stay home to raise the children—as an educator, she saw first-hand the impact day care had on kids—not good. We didn't know we were going to have 7 at the start, but we knew we were going to let God be the guide in that area and whatever he sent our way, we'd gladly take!
>
> So how do we make it? [It's] easier now than [it was] in the beginning when I made less money, but still we must do without some things. No elaborate vacations, no brand-new [cars], little new furniture, no Disney cruises, no plasma TV, no cable TV, no high speed

Internet, no X-Box, no home theater system, no time-share in Vail. My middle-aged TV (with rabbit ear antenna) broke last week—it may be months before we find a way to replace it—but most of what comes over the airwaves I'd just as soon miss anyway. Do I feel deprived? Not at all. We live in a very nice home in a very safe neighborhood, have access to a great Christian school, strong church involvement, and a wonderful network of friends—so, we have it pretty good I think.

I have to admit I was initially taken aback by this e-mail. In a time when families are getting smaller, houses are getting bigger, lives are getting busier, and children are taking a backseat to the pursuit of "more important" things, this military man and his wife have completely bucked the trend. I am humbled by their commitment.

God is truly turning the hearts of fathers toward their children. Anyone who has been around the Christian church in America knows that these people are way outside the mainstream. The lifestyle choices they have made are not the kind we typically hear about in Sunday school. Something has happened to these folks. Something that God ordained.

Looking for a Church

I didn't know it at the time, but in 2003 my family and I embarked on one of the most difficult spiritual journeys of our lives. We set out to find a church! I had been on staff at numerous churches, but we hadn't had to find a church to attend as members since our first year of marriage. We had always joined the church where I worked. This time, however, we had to find a church to plant our lives and serve in apart from any official commitment. This time we had to ask much tougher questions. It took us more than a year of praying, searching, questioning, and struggling. At times we were discouraged, frustrated, and even disillusioned. We went through peaks and valleys (mostly valleys) as we searched the fourth-largest city in America for a church. And not just any church—we were looking for a Southern Baptist, elder-led, family-integrated church that practiced church discipline and verse-by-verse, systematic exposition (expository preaching through books or large sections of the Bible) and believed in church planting. Did I mention that it took a while?

Everywhere we went people bombarded us with pamphlets outlining the incredible benefits their church had to offer. And since we had our teenage daughter in tow, the pitch always included, "And we have a great youth group." Of course, we knew exactly what that meant. We were about to be freaks again. You see, once we adopted a multigenerational family philosophy, that completely changed the way we looked at the church. If the Bible clearly gives parents the responsibility of discipling their children, what role does the church play in the process? And if the church is not playing that role, what options do those of us pursuing family driven faith have?

The journey that followed led us down a long, winding, and lonely road filled with self-examination, theological reflection, isolation, and eventually vindication. What follows is an attempt to explain that journey, to warn those who dare to travel this road, and perhaps to awaken a sleeping giant. I am not out to change the church overnight, but I do believe the church must change. I just pray that the Lord will allow me to live long enough to see it.

Flaws in the Contemporary Model

The church in America is in trouble. Teens are abandoning the faith in astounding numbers. Birth rates are plummeting as our attitude toward children continues to sour. The overwhelming majority of those who call themselves Christians do not think biblically, and the answer given most often is better youth ministry. In case you don't think this is a major issue, consider the following statistics. With a birth rate hovering around two children per family, a biblical worldview rate below 10 percent, and about 75 percent of our teens leaving the church by the end of their freshman year in college (using the more optimistic estimates from Chapter 1), it currently takes two Christian families in one generation to get a single Christian into the next generation. "Houston, we have a problem."

	Generation 1	Generation 2	Generation 3	Generation 4
2 children/family @75% departure	4,000,000	1,000,000	250,000	62,500

At this rate our current evangelistic strategies amount to little more than pouring water into a bucket with a giant hole in the bottom. The only way for the church to remain even is to reach three lost people for every one Christian. There is just one problem—the best we can muster right now is reaching one lost person for every forty or more Christians.[2] In short, if things do not change, the church in America will continue to decline precipitously over the next few generations.

Researcher Roger Dudley has studied church attendance and patterns of church affiliation among youth. His work is both poignant and alarming. Dudley captures the magnitude of the contemporary problem:

> According to Wieting (1975), "A recurrent focus of social philosophy since Plato's *Republic* has been the threat posed by the possibility that the young might not adopt the essential wisdom and values of that society. . . . If a society is to continue its existence beyond one generation, the members must transmit what they consider to be necessary knowledge and values. The continuity of a social system by definition requires transmission between generations." Applying this to institutional religion, churches and other religious communities must be vitally concerned with retaining the children from member families— in other words, preventing youth dropout is a major consideration for any religious group that desires a future.[3]

At times it seems our only answer has been more and bigger evangelistic events and improved church structures to manage the flow of our children from the front door to the back. By the way, the news is even worse than it sounds. Rainer and his team discovered that "If our research approximates eternal realities, nearly one-half of all church members may not be Christians."[4] As one who has been in pastoral ministry for over fifteen years, I'd say the truth is probably much worse than Rainer's numbers indicate.

So what's the problem? Where and how did we drop the ball? Talk to a college pastor about the freshman fallout rates, and he will tell you, "We do the best we can, but by the time we get them from the youth ministry, it's too late." Talk to a high school pastor and he'll tell you, "We have to do a better job in our junior high ministry." Of course, the junior high pastor is going to blame the children's minister, who will in turn pass the buck to the preschool minister. I believe there is a more fundamental question that we must ask. Could it be that the paradigm itself is broken? Could it be that we have established systems designed to meet the wrong needs and attack the wrong problems?

In order to answer these questions, let's examine a typical youth ministry mission statement:

- Our Purpose: To see unbelieving students become committed followers of Jesus Christ.
- Our Plan: We desire to achieve our purpose through Evangelizing, Equipping, and Engaging the students of [this] Church and of the surrounding community.
- Evangelize: We are committed to exposing the middle school and high school students to the message of Jesus Christ. It is also the role of every committed follower to reach out to those God has placed around them. We challenge the students to take the gospel with them everywhere they go (Colossians 4:2-6).
- Equip: We want to teach, mature, and train those who are seeking to become committed followers. Equipping them to reach out to their peers (Ephesians 4:11-13).
- Engage: We want to provide opportunities for our committed students to be actively involved in ministering to one another. Our goal is to bring glory to God and to multiply committed followers (Ephesians 2:10).
- Our Vision: To evangelize, equip, and engage as many middle school and high school students for Jesus Christ as possible.

This mission statement is typical of those found in youth ministry. I took it directly from the web site of a leading evangelical church whose youth ministry serves as a model for churches throughout the country. In fact, this statement is repeated on numerous youth ministry sites (sometimes word for word).

At first glance this mission statement looks incredible. This ministry appears to have covered all of the bases. They have a plan, a purpose, and a vision. They move from evangelizing to equipping, then engaging. They use Scripture to back up their approach. They have a clear, concise vision and have obviously thought things through. This is a ministry headed by trained, dedicated professionals who love teenagers and are passionate about seeing young people grow in their walk with Christ. I know because I have met them. I've been to this church, and I have talked with the men who implement this strategy.

There's just one problem with the aforementioned mission statement. It makes absolutely no mention of parents! This ministry sets out to do for teens what God commands parents to do. Think about it. It is *not* the job of the youth pastor to evangelize my child—that's my job. It is *not* the youth pastor's job to equip (disciple) my child—it's mine. And it is *not* the youth pastor's job to send my child out to engage the world; you guessed it—that's my job too. Ironically, the guys running this ministry completely agree! I sat down to lunch with one of them, and he told me very plainly that he saw the evangelism, discipleship, and mobilization of teenagers as a parental responsibility.

I'm not saying that I wouldn't welcome help, advice, mentoring, and/or support from someone who has raised teenagers, has proven himself as a parent, and is well trained and competent in handling the Scriptures. I am more than happy to rely on such help to assist and undergird me in my task. I am also pleased to have other significant adults in my teenagers' lives. However, I am not about to turn my children over to a youth pastor for their discipleship. Again, that is my job (Ephesians 6:1-4).

I simply cannot ignore the biblical mandate in favor of the cultural norm. This is especially the case when our attitudes reflect those described by youth ministry guru Mike Yaconelli:

> Every week local churches looking for someone—anyone—to work with their youth place ads like this one at nearby seminaries. Never mind that most seminary students do not belong to local churches, are overwhelmed with school work and are sorting out their own faith; these churches are desperate to find someone who will "do something" with their kids. Punch on to the job listings on the Youth Specialties Web site and you find the same phenomenon: hundreds of churches are eager to find someone who will form their children in the Christian faith. What's happened? Why are we so eager to hand the spiritual

development of our young people to the first person we find who can locate the New Testament and needs a little part-time work?[5]

Unfortunately, many parents fuel this attitude. It seems many parents yearn for someone to give their children what they, for some reason, are unable, unequipped, or unwilling to provide. This is also fueled by the growing consensus that views teen rebellion and the generation gap as the norm. Youth ministers feel pressured by the expectations placed on them by parents and pastors alike. They know the drill.

One day you visit a church, your teen goes off to the youth service, your little one goes off to children's church, the baby goes to the nursery, and you and your spouse get a great seat in a plush auditorium with first-class music, professional drama, a relevant, encouraging, application-oriented, non-threatening talk, and you get it all in just under an hour. Moreover, you look at the brochures, and it's right there in black and white: "Our youth ministry exists to do the job that you've neglected all these years." What a deal! We don't have to keep the little one quiet, we get our needs met, and to top it off, the youth guy is going to disciple my teenager (whom I don't even like right now). Who cares if the youth guy has only been married a few months and has never even attempted to disciple a child of his own. "Count me in!"

I realize that this is an exaggeration, but the fact is, it wouldn't matter if the youth pastor were a forty-year-old Ph.D. with five children of his own whom he had raised successfully. That still would not justify the abdication of parental responsibility. Let me set the record straight. While I believe the vast majority of those who shepherd segregated portions of congregations are well meaning and would never presume to replace parents in their biblical role, I believe the modern American practice of systematic age segregation goes beyond the biblical mandate. I believe it is a product of the American educational system, and in some instances it actually works against families as opposed to helping them pursue multigenerational faithfulness. I believe the church's emphasis ought to be on equipping parents to disciple their children instead of doing it on their behalf. I see at least three significant problems with the current approach.

First, *there is no clear biblical mandate for the current approach*. I have to choose my words carefully here, since I do not wish to intimate that churches with youth ministries are heretical or unbiblical. I fully recognize that many of the things we do in church today are not found in the Bible. We would be hard pressed to find a church building (as we know it), a pulpit, or a microphone in the book of Acts. So I am not arguing that the fact that something is not specifically mentioned in Scripture means it is absolutely forbidden in today's church.

What's more, some of my best friends throughout the years have been youth pastors. Most of these men did the best they could to line up everything they did with the Scriptures. And I only knew these guys by virtue of my participation in many of their events. So I am not saying they are denying the Bible. In fact, pick up a youth ministry book in your local bookstore and you will find dozens of biblical references. However, you will also discover that a number of those references are taken out of context.

Take, for example, Doug Fields's popular book, *Purpose-Driven Youth Ministry*. Fields uses biblical principles to teach youth ministers how to be successful in their field, but he does so by taking general principles (in this case the five purposes of Rick Warren's *Purpose-Driven Church*) and applying them to the youth ministry model. Fields states:

> Any youth ministry is capable of growth when it is built on *God's purposes for the church*. The material in this chapter will help you discover *God's five purposes of a healthy ministry*. These purposes are the vital component—the cornerstone—for constructing a youth ministry that enjoys long-term health and growth [emphasis added].[6]

Note how Fields begins with a general principle (God's five purposes for the church) and simply applies it to youth ministry. This is a common practice. It has to be. To do anything different would require specific biblical teaching on the subject, and it simply does not exist. That is not to say that Doug Fields (or any other youth ministry proponent) is a bad person or a heretic. He is simply operating on the basis of a cultural assumption that is readily accepted by everyone—well, almost everyone—and thus he sees no problem with this form of application.

Second, *the current approach may actually work against the biblical model*. Even the most avid supporters of the segregated model admit that it has often had damaging effects on family dynamics. Even Mike Yaconelli, who was an avid supporter and exponent of the segregated model, lamented:

> [T]he curtain must be pulled back. If we are to keep young people involved in the church and if we are to renew our congregations, we first must acknowledge that many of our current forms of youth ministry are *destructive* [emphasis added].[7]

That's right, he said "destructive." Yaconelli's criticism was sweeping in that he condemned all three of what he considers to be the main youth ministry models (the entertainment model, the charismatic youth leader model, and what he called the information-based model). While his critique is surprising in general, his critique of the charismatic youth leader model was particularly poignant:

> The youth-leader-as-savior approach, extrapolated from parachurch ministries like Young Life and Youth for Christ, has *generally been destructive for all concerned*. Alone and segregated from the church community, youth ministers are soon exhausted. Expected to be walking icons of the risen Christ, they are not allowed to be fallible, and their own need for Christian nurture goes unmet. Left as the *sole mediator between the adult and youth congregations*, youth ministers quickly become isolated, lonely and spiritually alienated. And even with the most well-intentioned ministers, the bait-and-switch strategy rarely works—teenagers often accept the youth minister as their personal savior but are rarely able to transfer their devotion to Jesus Christ [emphasis added].[8]

While I do not agree with Yaconelli's ultimate solution, his critique is important nonetheless. How can this extra-biblical isolationism produce biblical fruit? For example, it is common in both high school and college ministries to have a Titus 2 approach. In other words, these groups encourage older teens (or college students) to mentor younger teens. This sounds great on the surface, but listen to what Paul says about the Titus 2 woman in light of the contemporary segregated model:

Older women likewise are to be reverent in their behavior, not malicious gossips nor enslaved to much wine, teaching what is good, so that they may encourage the young women to love their husbands, to love their children, to be sensible, pure, workers at home, kind, being subject to their own husbands, so that the word of God will not be dishonored. (vv. 3-5)

How can the older women instruct the younger women if everyone is in a Sunday school class with people within nine months of their own age? Better yet, how can this type of mentoring ever happen if most of the younger women are across the parking lot in the youth building? An even better question is, how much of our time do we spend in our youth and/or college ministries teaching young women about motherhood, homemaking, child-rearing, and biblical submission? There was no mention of this type of ministry in the aforementioned mission statement.

Regardless of your position on Titus 2, don't miss the point. It is difficult to establish a biblical format for a ministry that is not outlined in the Bible. Thus youth ministers are some of the most frustrated people in church work. I am constantly bombarded with e-mails and phone calls from young men who have thrown up their hands as they realize the magnitude of their dilemma. As one youth minister from North Carolina put it, "If I become too pastoral, the kids won't be entertained, and they will go down the street to the guy with all the bells and whistles. If I become too evangelistic, I get complaints about the shallowness of the group and the post-youth ministry dropout rate. I can't win."

This explains why parents who take their disciple-making mandate seriously are beginning to be skeptical about turning their children over to the youth ministry. How does a mother build biblical truth into her daughter's life, nurture her, guard her, and encourage her toward the application of that truth, then send her into an environment that will oftentimes by its very nature be hostile or at least ambivalent toward that truth? How does a father raise his son to respect young women and protect their purity only to send him off to the youth building with exposed midriffs, low-cut tops, and skin-tight jeans? Again, this is not universal. However, it is prevalent. And before you blame the youth pastor, know that there are young men out there who have lost their jobs for drawing the line on issues such as immodest dress.

If you are a parent, I feel your pain! I understand the desire to raise kids who fit in and how difficult that is to balance with the desire to foster a sense of purity and holiness. If you are a minister in one of these contexts, I know your story. I've been present during some parent meetings where the youth guy was told, "We just pay you to entertain them, not to be the fashion police." Unfortunately, there appear to be very few winners in the current scenario.

Third, *the current approach isn't working*. Remember, we have already established that in our current condition we are losing the overwhelming majority of our youth by the end of their freshman year in college (see Chapter 1), less than 10 percent of churched teens have a biblical worldview (see Chapter 6), and nearly half of all church members are probably not born again (more than that if worldview is any indicator). The retention rate is not highest among those in youth groups; it is highest among those whose parents (particularly fathers) actually disciple them. Ask any youth pastor and he'll tell you. The kids who stay are the ones whose parents are investing in them, the ones who aren't counting on two hours a week in the youth building to offset forty-five to fifty hours a week in the classroom and on the sports field.

Of course, there are anecdotal stories of young people whose lives were changed in the segregated community. We will always have those stories. The fact of the matter is that God can hit a straight lick with a crooked stick. He can use our feeble efforts and still get His job done. However, the end does not justify the means. A youth pastor who heard about my philosophy called me on the telephone several months ago to share one of these anecdotal stories. He told me about a young girl who came from a terrible background. Her story sounded like something from a Lifetime original series. There was sex, drugs, abuse, abandonment—you name it, this girl had been through it. But God used this youth pastor to touch her life. She was now in college walking with God and standing up to philosophy professors in defense of her faith. What could I say to that?

I asked him what kind of church he was a part of. He told me it was a conservative evangelical congregation. I asked about their music. He said it was traditional. I asked about the preaching at his church. He said their pastor was an old-fashioned, no-nonsense Bible preacher. I asked him what he thought about the modern seeker-driven Church Growth movement. He gave me a litany of reasons why he disagreed with what he called the "manipulative, market-driven, man-centered practices" and explained that he was not a fan. I asked him why. He said that the methodologies were not biblical. I said, "But they are reaching a lot of people."

At this point the lights went on. He realized exactly what I was doing. It was like an intellectual checkmate. He either had to admit that he was guilty of the same thing he was accusing the seeker-driven movement of or demonstrate that his ministry was based on clear biblical teaching and not market-driven, man-centered methodologies. He was also forced to admit that anecdotal stories about people whose lives were changed, while compelling, do not justify one's methodology.

Objections to This Stance

I probably don't have to tell you that most people disagree with me on this issue. As I have made my feelings about youth ministry (and systematic segregation in general) known, I have been challenged and criticized throughout the country. I have also had some very interesting discussions as I have been invited to lecture in youth ministry classes in colleges and seminaries over the past several years. However, what I have never had is a conversation with a person presenting the argument for segregated youth/children's ministry from an open Bible. I have never had a professor, a student, a youth pastor, or anyone else show me book, chapter, and verse in defense of the contemporary model. I have, however, heard numerous objections. Allow me to share a few.

We need youth ministry for parents who don't disciple their children. This is the most common objection offered against my position. As I have argued throughout this book, the data clearly points to the fact that Christian parents are not discipling their children. This is a fact that cannot be denied. Mike Yaconelli has bemoaned this point:

> Youth leader and writer Mike Yaconelli explains that he is reluctant to adopt the family-based approach because there aren't enough parents available who place their faith high as a top priority for their children. They are in favor of Christianity, he says, as long as they think it is going to make their kid into a nice person. But as soon as it becomes genuine Christian faith, they start to worry. This generation of parents is ambitious for its children, and can't let anything get in the way of their future "success."[9]

However, to argue that parents' failure to do the job that God called them to do gives us the right and/or responsibility to do it for them is a *non sequitur*. This type of reasoning would have the church establish ministries in charge of picking baby names on behalf of parents who weren't good at it. How about this radical idea: Teach families to do what the Bible tells them to do and then hold them accountable for it.

Paul makes the role of church leaders clear when he writes, "And He gave some as apostles, and some as prophets, and some as evangelists, and some as pastors and teachers, *for the equipping of the saints for the work of service*, to the building up of the body of Christ" (Ephesians 4:11-12, emphasis mine). The job of the church is to equip the saints to do their jobs, not to do it for them. (More in the next chapter about how churches can structure family ministries to address the needs of these children.)

We need youth ministry for kids who don't have Christian parents. I find this to be the most compelling argument. Millions of teens are being raised in non-Christian homes, and they desperately need to hear the gospel. More importantly, they need to be discipled and educated biblically. They need to be brought up in "the discipline and instruction of the Lord" (Ephesians 6:4).

Having said that, I do not believe that our current structure is the most efficient or effective way to accomplish this task. Kids who don't have Christian parents would be much better off participating in church services with intact Christian families (perhaps families with children their age) who can model worship and family for them than they would be in a pack of teens, 90 percent of whom, according to studies cited earlier, do not possess a biblical worldview. I would much rather have little Johnny sitting with me, my wife, and my children than have him over in the youth building or in the youth section of the sanctuary.

Why not let your children be leaders in the youth group and disciple other kids? Here they point back to Titus 2. However, it is not my child's job to disciple other people's children, any more than it is the youth pastor's job to disciple mine. My children are the "young women" and "young men" of the Titus 2 equation. What they need right now is mentoring and discipleship. Sure, they have relationships with other children at church, and they do exert influence.

Again, I'm amazed at how the current model has become so adept at taking Scripture out of context. I visited one church that had a Titus 2 program in their youth ministry. They had juniors and seniors assigned to younger kids (junior high) as Titus 2 mentors. When I asked the youth pastor whether or not they were teaching the principles lined out in Titus 2, he looked at me like I was from the moon. When I read the passage and refreshed his memory, he laughed. He thought it was ridiculous for me to expect these high school juniors and seniors to mentor their younger peers on subjects like housekeeping, submission, and child-rearing. I agreed with him wholeheartedly. Tragically, he did not quite understand why I thought he was misapplying the Scripture in this particular instance.

What about youth evangelism? Surprisingly, this is the weakest objection to the anti-youth ministry argument. Alvin Reid, chair of the Evangelism Department at Southeastern Baptist Theological Seminary (and my doctoral thesis supervisor), addressed this issue in his book, *Raising the Bar*. Reid, who is a proponent of youth ministry, notes, "The largest rise of full-time youth ministers in history has been accompanied by the biggest decline in youth evangelism effectiveness."[10]

Reid's argument goes beyond the lack of conversions or baptisms to the more significant issue of disciple-making. He notes:

> For the past three decades, then, youth ministry has exploded across America, accompanied by a rise in the number of degrees in youth ministry granted by colleges and seminaries, an abundance of books and other resources, and a network of cottage industries devoted solely to youth ministry. Yet those same three decades have failed to produce a generation of young people who graduate from high school or leave youth groups ready to change the world for Christ.[11]

Thus it is hard to argue that being against youth ministry constitutes being against youth evangelism. In fact, one could argue the opposite. It is the youth ministry movement that has dropped the ball in evangelism. Evangelism is not about getting young people to walk an aisle and sign a card, only to apostatize once they get to college. Evangelism is about making disciples (Matthew 28:19-20). The most effective way to make disciples of teens is to make disciples of their parents and teach them to do what God commands, which includes evangelizing and discipling their children.

Of course, this model flies in the face of what most churches believe youth ministry is all about. Mark DeVries, author of *Family-Based Youth Ministry*, offers a candid assessment of the desired outcomes of youth ministry:

> Most youth ministries that I've seen are vastly undercapitalized financially and in terms of staff and volunteers. Plus, most youth pastors work with unclear job expectations—other than that their parking lot evaluation has to be positive. We feel guilty as mainliners talking about numbers, but people are always out in the parking lot of the church evaluating youth pastors based on how many kids are showing up. A senior pastor once said to me. "I don't care about numbers, just give me a quality program." He was lying. If I had two kids show up, and I was making a full-time salary, he would care about numbers. Eventually I learned that I needed to have 100 kids there for him to feel like I was doing my job.[12]

We can deny it all we want, but the bottom line is still the bottom line in youth ministry. The overwhelming majority of the people who make professions of faith and are baptized do so before age eighteen. Thus youth ministry is the force that fills the pool. Never mind the fact that the overwhelming majority of those we have baptized know neither the gospel nor the Christ of the Scriptures and have a world-view that is more closely aligned with Marxist Socialism than it is with Christian Theism. Our numbers look good on the annual report, and apparently that's what matters most.

A New Approach

A number of churches and Christian organizations are waking up to the need for family-based ministry. Pamela Smith McCall has out-lined a number of these family-based approaches in a 2001 article in *Christian Century*. She highlighted the ministry of Tim Tahtinen, a youth pastor from Wisconsin who says, "Churches should focus their energies on putting parents and youth together in family-based youth ministry." Or that of the Youth and Family Institute at Augsburg College in Minneapolis, which "has endorsed the notion that families, particularly parents, are the primary source of faith development."[13]

Tahtinen is part of a growing number of youth pastors who have seen the handwriting on the wall. They recognize the failure of the segregated youth ministry model and the importance of parents in faith formation. Hence they are moving toward a modified, family-centered approach. And these are not isolated occurrences. These ministries represent the contemporary attempt to address the harsh realities with which all of us who love and want the best for the next generation must wrestle. All of the data point to the same conclusion. If you truly want children to grow up to walk with God, you simply cannot ignore the importance of their parents. Failure to do so has resulted in an unreached generation, as is evidenced by the existence of such movements as the Emerging/Emergent Church.

The Emerging/Emergent Church and a Lost Generation

Unless you've been hiding under a rock, you have probably heard about the Emerging (or Emergent) Church movement. However, if you are like most people, you have very little idea what the movement is about. Sure, you have seen the Gen-X services popping up all over the place. You have probably noticed the resurgence in the more mystical approach to worship in an effort to capture the postmodern culture. However, you may not be aware of the philosophical and theological basis underlying this effort to recapture a generation.

D. A. Carson wrote a very insightful and helpful book on the topic. In *Becoming Conversant with the Emerging Church*, Carson explains that this is primarily a protest movement. This protest, he explains, takes place on three fronts:

> The emerging church movement is characterized by a fair bit of protest against traditional evangelicalism and, more broadly, against all that it understands by modernism. But some of its proponents add another front of protest—namely, the seeker-sensitive church, the megachurch.[14]

Carson's critique of the movement is developed along four lines: "the emerging church's tendency toward reductionism, its condemnation of confessional Christianity, some theological shallowness and intellectual incoherence, and particularization of those three issues."[15]

A glance behind the polite, academic language reveals what is at times a scathing rebuke. Carson paints a picture of a movement that is far from harmless. While there are elements of the Emerging Church movement that are refreshing and even encouraging, this is often overshadowed by the "reductionism" and especially the "condemnation of confessional Christianity." When one protests orthodoxy, the end result can be antinomianism and/or heresy.

I'm sure that by now you are asking, what does the Emerging Church movement have to do with family driven faith? Everything! Especially when we understand that the Emerging Church movement is by and large a movement geared toward twenty-somethings. This movement was birthed out of the need created by the church's failure to retain what those in it consider the "emergent" (read: young adult) generation. Dan Kimball's experience is typical in this regard. He moved toward the Emergent movement when he discovered that

"Many of our graduating seniors were also having a hard time connecting with the church's existing college ministry and integrating with the main adult services of the church."[16]

In other words, Kimball's reforms were birthed out of the aforementioned failures of the contemporary church. In fact, he makes it clear that the children who experienced the type of discipleship outlined in this book were not his targets, nor did they need to be. "The churched teenagers who were raised in Christian homes that taught them Judeo-Christian values and had a history with contemporary Christian culture, values and language seemed more likely to make the transition."[17] Amazing! When kids are discipled and integrated into the Christian community, they tend to remain in the fold.

Thus the Emerging Church movement is an attempt to address the same issues raised in this book. However, their attempts are different in at least one very important way. The Emerging Church movement is one of immediacy, whereas family driven faith is a long-term process. Imagine a dying man lying on an emergency room table. The man is bleeding internally and is in danger of bleeding to death. However, the man also has a prominent growth on the side of his head. While the growth needs attention, it will be useless to fix it if you don't stop the bleeding.

I believe the absence of twenty-somethings in the church is a visible, very disturbing growth. Is it a problem? Absolutely. Does it need to be addressed? Certainly. However, if we fill our churches with young adults but ignore the more crucial issue of children continuing to abandon the faith due to our failure to adequately disciple them, we will merely have cleaned up our image while ignoring an acute, life-threatening tragedy. We must go beyond quick fixes to a complete paradigm overhaul.

In other words, this is not a problem that will be fixed by fads, programs, or personalities. This is a problem that must be addressed one home at a time. The answer to our current crisis is a renewed commitment to biblical evangelism and discipleship in and through our homes. You and I as individual parents must begin to take responsibility for the spiritual well-being and development of our children. We must commit ourselves to family driven faith. More importantly, our churches must facilitate this commitment. In the next chapter I will introduce a ministry model that is doing precisely that.

Take Action

1. Have you turned over the discipleship of your child to someone else? If so, work toward partnering with others who will equip and encourage you rather than do the work for you.
2. Are you fully aware of the theology, philosophy, and ecclesiology of the other spiritual influences in your child's life? If not, get up to speed immediately.
3. Write a family mission statement concerning the spiritual development of your children.

A RADICAL DEPARTURE FROM THE NORM

The family-based youth ministry approach is a promising sign. The Christian community appears to be coming to grips with the harsh realities concerning the failure of the current system. More importantly, there appears to be a consensus about the centrality of the parental relationship in the discipleship process. However, there is another movement lurking beneath the radar of which those interested in family driven faith need to be aware.

The purpose of this chapter is to give you hope. There is something on the horizon that will revolutionize the way we think of the church and the family. I have the privilege of serving as an elder in a church that is unlike any other I have ever known. In fact, it is unlike anything most people in our culture have ever known. Our church has no youth ministers, children's ministers, or nursery. We do not divide families into component parts. We do not separate the mature women from the young teenage girls who need their guidance. We do not separate the toddler from his parents during worship. In fact, we don't even do it in Bible study. We see the church as a family of families.

The Family-Integrated Church

During my last year at Southeastern Seminary, my thesis supervisor, Alvin Reid, and I began to discuss and debate the state of youth ministry. Reid wrote his dissertation on the Jesus Movement of the late 1960s and early 1970s. This movement was a demographic revival that touched the lives of scores of young men and women. This was also, as Reid noted in *Raising the Bar*, the greatest period of growth in the number of youth ministers, youth ministry degrees, and para-church organizations devoted to the evangelization and discipleship of teens.[1]

It was these conversations—and the research that followed—that led me to question the status quo. Initially all I could do was theorize about what the church would look like without systematic segrega-tion. That is, until I met David Allen Black. Dr. Reid suggested that I read Black's book, *The Myth of Adolescence*. When I read it, I knew I had found an ally and mentor in the struggle. Dr. Black taught in the New Testament Department at Southeastern, and the two of us became close friends.

It was Dr. Black who first introduced me to the term *family-inte-grated church*. He also sent me to the web site of Hope Chapel in Sacramento, California. At the time Hope Chapel was a twenty-year-old family-integrated church. Their web site was a storehouse of infor-mation. It was obvious from the articles on their site that they, unlike many reactionary family-integration movements, had examined their theology, ecclesiology, and methodology thoroughly.[2] Much of what we have included on our church web site (gracefamilybaptist.net) was inspired by the work of Hope Chapel.

For the first time in my quest, the family-integrated church was more than theory. I had finally found a living, breathing example of a church operating by this paradigm. Eventually I found Vision Forum Ministries and the National Center for Family-Integrated Churches. As it turns out, there are hundreds of family-integrated churches throughout the country. They come in all shapes and sizes (although the overwhelming majority are white, suburban congregations). They also come in a variety of theological and denominational forms. However, all of these churches share cer-tain basic distinctives.

Distinctives of the Family-Integrated Church

Families Worship Together

Walk into a family-integrated church, and the first thing you will notice is the presence of babies. We don't realize it, but we have been desensitized to the absence of babies. We're used to corporate worship being a largely adult affair. In fact, I preached in a church not long ago that had a sign up that read, "Please silence all cell phones, pagers, and children under four." In other words, "No babies, please!"

Once you get over the inordinate number of babies, your attention will probably be drawn to the absence of a teen section in the sanctuary. What's more, you will notice that the teenagers are actually sitting with their families, and rather large families at that. It won't take long to realize that you're not in Kansas anymore. This is not your normal church gathering.

No Systematic Segregation

Another distinctive of the family-integrated church is its insistence on the integration of all ages in virtually all of its activities. This stands in stark contrast to other "family-based" ministries. For example, Mark DeVries, the champion of family-based youth ministry, admits that his approach is not one of integration but occasional participation of parents into his ministry to their children. On the Family Based Youth Ministry (FBYM) web site he explains:

> Most people confuse the starting of a family based youth ministry with a *radical change in programming*. But the truth is that those who implement these principals [sic] without radically changing their program find that they meet much less resistance. It is therefore recommended that churches seeking to begin a family based youth ministry simply begin experimenting with one family based program at a time, until something clicks. For example, you might try a parent/youth Sunday school class for a few weeks, or you could sponsor a parent training event [emphasis added].[3]

Note DeVries's emphasis on implementing family-based principles without any change in programming. In other words, his is a systematically segregated youth ministry that merely acknowledges the importance of parents.

Elsewhere DeVries clarifies this issue when he admits that his ministry looks like any other youth ministry:

> Now, if you look at our regular programming, you'd probably come away saying, "Hey, that looks like an average, ordinary, garden variety youth ministry. What's so 'family based' about that?" The truth is that FBYM is not about what the programming looks like. It's about what you use the programming for. And we try to point as much of our programming as possible in the direction of giving kids and adults excuses to interact together.[4]

Thus there is a world of difference between the family-based youth ministry movement and the family-integrated church. I applaud DeVries for his efforts. He is absolutely correct in his assessment of the contemporary mode, and I wish him well as he works toward a more family-based approach. We need more ministries to work toward the integration of youth and their parents. However, this does not constitute family integration.

I make this observation not to discredit DeVries but to point out a common misconception. I have had numerous conversations with people who have heard about the family-integrated movement but have no idea what it is. Unfortunately, the idea of segregation is so ingrained in the minds of Christians in our culture that they cannot conceive of a church without age-graded Sunday school classes, children's church, and youth service on Wednesday night (and now on Sunday mornings in some places). Thus they hear about the family-based movement and its emphasis on including parents and think that must be what the family-integrated model is all about.

The family-integrated church movement is easily distinguishable in its insistence on integration as an ecclesiological principle. I recently had to clarify this point with the pastor of a megachurch in the South. He had discussed the issue of family-integrated churches with a prospective member. When the man with whom he was speaking used the term family-integrated church, the pastor had no reference point from which to evaluate the man's comments. The pastor, whose church is what I would call very family-friendly or family-based, told the man that they were a family-integrated church. He didn't understand why the man disagreed.

Later, when I came to preach at his church, the pastor noticed that I used the term *family-integrated* to describe our church. "Explain that term for me, please," he asked with a rather perplexed look on his face. I explained the distinctives of a family-integrated church, and he immediately understood the conversation gap in the previous interaction between him and the prospective member. This church had a children's worship service, a junior high ministry, a high school ministry, a weekly youth service, segregated Sunday school classes, segregated mission trips, youth camps, and dozens of other segregated ministries. However, because of their emphasis on increasing the involvement of parents, his church had taken a monumental step beyond that of every other megachurch of which he was aware. Thus he figured they were as family-integrated as they come.

Again, this is not a knock against that pastor. This merely illustrates the need to delineate the difference between the movement toward family-based or family-friendly approaches to the contemporary model and the family-integrated paradigm. This is a reformation, a paradigm shift. This is a complete departure from current norms in the way we do church. There is no systematic age segregation in the family-integrated church!

Evangelism and Discipleship in and Through Homes

The family is the evangelism and discipleship arm of the family-integrated church. This is the aspect of the family-integrated paradigm that critics find most disturbing. As I talk to pastors, professors, youth ministers, and parents around the country, this is the point at which they look at me with incredulity. "You actually trust parents to evangelize and disciple their kids?" one youth minister asked me. "Yes," I responded confidently. "Why shouldn't I expect it when the Bible clearly does?" At this point he shook his head and admitted, "I know that's what the Bible teaches, but I also know parents, and I haven't met a handful that were capable of doing what you propose."

The only thing sadder than these comments is the fact that I have heard them no less than a dozen times, a dozen different ways, from a dozen different men in the academic, pastoral, and parachurch worlds. There seems to be a general consensus that it is unreasonable to expect families to function the way the Bible clearly says they should. Perhaps it is because we have spent the last thirty years telling parents, "We're trained professionals. Please don't try this at home." Now three decades later we are amazed by the fact that families (many of whom were raised in the segregated church environment and were discipled apart from their homes) are inept when it comes to evangelizing and discipling their own children. I love to tell these skeptics about what we've seen in the lives of our men.

Everywhere I go churches are trying to crack the code in men's ministry. Some churches try big events where they bring in top-flight speakers and musicians. Others opt for weekly Bible studies geared toward practical, real-life issues. Some churches host hunting and wild game dinners. Still others opt for the weekly accountability meeting/small group approach. All of these emphases are designed to answer one question: How do we get our men to engage? Ironically, these approaches all leave out the preeminent biblical mandate that God has given to men—the mandate to love their wives as Christ loved the church and to bring their children up in the nurture and admonition of the Lord (see Ephesians 5:25–6:4). We fail to hold men's feet to the fire and to equip, expect, and encourage them to stand at the helm of their families and plot the course. No wonder men today feel they have less status and challenge in life!

Dave Black sheds light on the irony of this situation in his book *The Myth of Adolescence*. He notes: "No wonder [men] pour themselves into their work, looking for something to challenge their male longing for importance and purpose!"[5] As Nancy Pearcey notes, the passivity and absence of men (in a religious sense) is unique to Western Christianity: "In Eastern Orthodoxy, the membership is roughly balanced, and in Judaism and Islam men are actually predominate. So the pattern cannot be explained by saying that men are just naturally less religious than women."[6]

I am convinced that holding men accountable for the evangelism and discipleship of their families does more to motivate and engage them than any weekly Bible study ever could. Telling a man to show up to a weekly meeting is not a challenge worth attaining. Asking him to cook some eggs for the monthly men's breakfast will not provide him with that sense of accomplishment he seeks. But unleash him to evangelize and disciple his family, and he will have his mountain to climb. Tom Eldredge put it well: "The church can best minister to children by equipping the father, and assisting his helper, his wife. An overflow of love in the home will reach out to the community."[7] This is true. In fact, I have seen it firsthand.

Tim was new to our church. He had just been with us a few months when he came to his first Father's Council meeting. The men meet once a month for fellowship, prayer, vision casting, church business, etc. Sometimes we have times of testimony. This particular Wednesday night, Tim couldn't hold it in. He simply had to share what was on his heart. He took a deep breath, raised his hand, and with a deep sigh began to speak.

"I'm not much for speaking in public, but if I don't get this out, I'm afraid I might burst," he said as he nervously wiped his hands on the sides of his jeans. He went on to tell us how he had been the superintendent of the Sunday school at his previous church (a prominent megachurch in the Houston area) and was considered one of the leaders in that body. However, upon coming to Grace, he began to realize that the standard by which he was being measured was not very high. His eyes welled up with tears as he began to confess that he had never led his family in worship, Bible study, catechism, or anything else before joining Grace.

In fact, it never dawned on him that he should be doing those things. He had done them in church every week (Sunday school, Sunday morning worship, Sunday evening, Wednesday night); they even educated their daughters at home. However, no one had ever told him it was his job to disciple his family. One day, after being at Grace for a few weeks, his daughters approached him and asked, "Daddy, why are we the only family in our church that doesn't have family worship or do catechism?" He admitted that his knee-jerk reaction was to protest, "I'm sure we're not the 'only' ones." However, he thought better of it. He simply said, "I don't know girls, but that's going to change."

The next week he sought out one of the elders during the fellowship meal and asked, "How do I start family worship and catechism?" Since this is a question that is regularly asked around our church, the answer came quickly. Armed with a renewed determination and thorough instruction, Tim began to lead his family in worship and catechism the very next day. As he recounted the story to the men, he could no longer hold back the tears. "Men, I have a successful business, a great marriage, and four beautiful daughters. I have also been at what most laymen would consider the pinnacle of Christian service. However, I wouldn't trade anything for the way my wife and children look at me now." He went on to say that for the first time in his life he felt like a hero at home.

The rest of the men looked around at each other with huge smiles on their faces. Then one of our deacons broke the silence. "Brother, there aren't but a handful of men in this room who weren't exactly where you are when we started out here," he said as he recounted his own story. We have heard that testimony dozens of times at Men's Meeting, and it never gets old. Something amazing happens when you watch a family transform before your eyes because Dad was challenged to do what God called, created, and equipped him to do. These blessings have also borne fruit through men evangelizing their wives and children and even their neighbors. We constantly hear stories of friends, relatives, and neighbors who gladly hear the gospel from these men whose lives and families have obviously been transformed. Nothing forced, nothing coerced—just men who have a renewed passion and can't wait to tell about it.

Emphasis on Education as a Key Component of Discipleship

Perhaps the most prominent aspect of the family-integrated church movement is the disproportionate number of homeschool families it attracts. In fact, when I run into people who have heard about the family-integrated model, one of the first questions they ask is, "Are most of your folks homeschoolers?" This is due to the fact that the family-integrated church paradigm is based upon many of the same principles that drive the home education movement. Families who have decided to shoulder the responsibility for their children's education find it refreshing that a church would expect them to do the same in the area of discipleship.

More than 85 percent of Christians in America send their children to government schools.[8] That number is staggering. However, it has been the norm for so long that we fail to see its significance. Imagine if 85 percent of Christians voted. Better yet, imagine if 85 percent of Christians witnessed or tithed or showed up regularly at the churches where their names are on the rolls. I guarantee you there would be headline stories in every Christian publication if any one of those things happened anytime soon. It is almost impossible to get 85 percent of Christians to participate in any single activity. However, a whopping 85 percent make the same educational choice.

Thus, a movement that attracts primarily homeschool families is truly an anomaly.[9] One would think that family-integrated churches put signs outside that read, "Only homeschoolers need apply for membership." But that is not the case. The model is simply built on some of the same assumptions and principles that form the foundation upon which the Christian home education (and classical worldview school) movement is built.

Because these movements are based on education as a component of discipleship, they look beyond merely academic pursuits toward theological training and preparation. Unfortunately, many forms of Christian education have forgotten or abandoned this principle, thus finding themselves on the horns of a dilemma. David Baker and Cornelius Riordan face this harsh reality in their research on the impact of declining theological content and goals in Catholic education:

> Catholic schools are on the verge of becoming a system of proprietary schools that educate growing numbers of non-Catholics, children from the wealthiest strata of the society, and increasing numbers of children who do not consider themselves religious at all. In short, the old common Catholic school is fast becoming an elite private school in which *indoctrination into the faith* seems to be taking a back seat to academic preparation (emphasis added).[10]

Baker and Riordan have seen where this all leads. If we stop teaching our children in the faith, we will cease to exist as a community of faith. It's that simple. We cannot continue to send our children to Caesar for their education and be surprised when they come home as Romans. More importantly, we cannot continue to use Caesar's methods in our Christian schools and expect a different outcome. Education is inseparable from discipleship (Luke 6:40).

At our church we are unapologetic about the fact that we teach families the consequences of their educational choices. The Nehemiah Institute has demonstrated since 1988 that education is the greatest shaper of worldview. Thus their findings consistently show wide gaps between the worldviews of Christian children educated by the government and those educated by their parents and/or truly Christian schools. How can we know this information and remain silent? Especially when Jesus said, "Whoever causes one of these little ones who believe to stumble, it would be better for him if, with a heavy millstone hung around his neck, he had been cast into the sea" (Mark 9:42).

Many in the Jewish community are beginning to face the music when it comes to the catastrophic losses in the younger generations. Antony Gordon and Richard Horowitz offer a sobering assessment of the future of the Jewish community if things do not change:

> Based upon the data and the various population studies that are now available, it appears that an extraordinary disintegration of the American Jewish community is in process. There was a time when every Jew could take it for granted that he or she would have Jewish grandchildren with whom to share Seders, Sabbath and other Jewish moments. However, the clear data indicates that this expectation is no longer well founded. Indeed, our studies show that within a short period of time the entire complexion of the American Jewish community will be altered inexorably.[11]

Gordon and Horowitz have seen the future, and if things remain as they are, it is a future where the Jewish community will have carved out a spot on the Endangered Species List. With staggering graphics, charts, and statistics, they paint a bleak picture that cannot be ignored:

Sample Population Count

	Average Children Per Family	Intermarriage Rate	First Generation	Second Generation	Third Generation	Fourth Generation
Orthodox	6.4	3%	100	295	874	2588
Modern Orthodox	3.23	3%	100	151	228	346
Conservative	1.82	37%	100	62	38	24
Reform	1.72	53%	100	51	26	13
Unaffiliated	1.62	72%	100	36	13	5

The research targeted three key quantifiable elements of Jewish survival: *intermarriage rates, birth rates*, and levels of *Jewish education*. When all of these factors are tabulated and correlated, a troubling picture emerges of the future of American Jewry. Skyrocketing intermarriage rates, declining birth rates, and inadequate Jewish education continue to decimate the American Jewish people [emphasis added].[12]

Admittedly, these are not terms in which we are accustomed to thinking. When was the last time you heard a sermon on birth rates? Most Christians do not think about the community of Christ-followers as a heritage to be preserved. We don't even think in terms of intermarriage rates as a component of continuity. However, the work of these two Jewish researchers is not only insightful—it is prophetic.

No less than *The Wall Street Journal* ran a front-page story about the issue of birth rates, intermarriage, and the survival of faith in an article entitled "Zoroastrians Turn to Internet Dating to Rescue Religion: Declining Numbers Threaten the Future of Ancient Faith."[13] This issue is front-and-center in the culture war. It is also in line with the guiding principles of the family-integrated church movement. This movement seeks to address issues of intermarriage, birth rates, and religious education by promoting a biblical view of marriage and family, evangelism, discipleship, Christian education, and biblically qualified leadership.

Guiding Principles of the Family-Integrated Church

I am not naive. I do not expect mainstream churches to jump ship and turn into family-integrated churches. In fact, when I talk to people who are interested in doing so, I tell them it is one of the easiest ways

I know for a guy to get fired. When I have the opportunity to share this paradigm with classrooms full of youth ministers in our nation's colleges and seminaries, there are always a few guys who ask, "What can I do to get our church to move in this direction?" At that point I look at them with my best Dirty Harry stare and say, "If you go back and try to move your church in this direction, the parents will kill you, and the pastor will fire your dead body!"

I have met men who lost their jobs because they tried to move their youth ministry toward family integration. I have also met pastors who lost their jobs trying to end age segregation in their churches. Let me say it again, this is a paradigm shift. We are not talking about a new program; we are talking about a complete overhaul of the philosophy that is accepted in our churches, colleges, seminaries, and homes as the only way to do it. This is not a church growth scheme that pastors will pick up at a megachurch conference and come home with ideas about adding a new pastoral staff member. In fact, the family-integrated model requires less staff, not more.

There are, however, several principles that transcend methodology. I believe any church can become more family-integrated if the leaders are willing to get behind a few simple, biblical concepts. If you are a church leader, I offer these as suggestions that can be implemented immediately to change the culture of your church. If you are not in church leadership, I offer these things to you as a prayer list. Begin to cry out to God for these truths to come to the fore in your church. Talk about these things with your friends. Start to implement them in your home. Perhaps God will use you as a catalyst to wake the sleeping giant and move your church toward family integration.

Promote a Biblical View of Marriage and Family

As any mother who walks into the average American church with six or seven children will tell you, the pagan, secular humanist culture at large is not alone in its negative attitude toward children. Moreover, look at the divorce rates among Christians compared to those of non-Christians, and you will see that our attitudes about and commitment to marriage is anything but exemplary. To say that we need to promote a biblical view of marriage and family is almost an understatement. We must stem the tide.

> In a culture that seems to be going in the opposite direction, we must affirm in word and practice the gift of children as a "heritage from the Lord" (Psalm 127:3). Godly parents will be disciple-makers beginning in the home. They will understand that no greater investment can be made than that they would raise a brood of godly children who will live for Jesus just like they saw in Mom, and especially Dad. Our churches must train parents to evangelize and disciple their children.[14]

If we are to change the world, we must first change the church. Currently there is no distinguishable difference between the way our culture views marriage and family and the way we do in the church. We do not have to change every congregation into a family-integrated church, but we do have to promote a biblical view of marriage and family. We must do this by holding marriage in high esteem, welcoming and celebrating children, and placing a premium on family.

Our churches must hold marriage in high esteem. When Bridget and I got married, many of our Christian friends mourned. To them we had broken an unwritten rule by getting married before graduating from college. Ironically, our non-Christian friends—while they did not necessarily agree with our decision—respected the fact that we were doing something that was to them distinctly Christian. Many of them were encouraged to see Christian people doing something outside the mainstream.

I do not have a problem with young people being told to wait until the proper time for marriage. The problem is that college graduation is a completely arbitrary, secular, unbiblical standard. Our message must be biblical. When you are biblically qualified and ready for marriage and God sends you a mate who meets the same standard, get married. We must not mourn when young people get married young. "He who finds a wife finds a good thing and obtains favor from the LORD" (Proverbs 18:22). If he finds her before the arbitrary cultural marker of college graduation, so be it. Marriage is not an albatross around the neck of a young person; it is a crowning jewel. Let's celebrate it as such.

Our churches must welcome and celebrate children. Oh, that our churches would celebrate children as the psalmist did:

> *Behold, children are a gift of the* LORD,
> *The fruit of the womb is a reward.*
> *Like arrows in the hand of a warrior,*
> *So are the children of one's youth.*
> *How blessed is the man whose quiver is full of them;*
> *They will not be ashamed*
> *When they speak with their enemies in the gate. (Psalm 127:3-5)*

Perhaps if we believed this we would celebrate children as the blessings they are. I recently addressed this issue in a sermon I delivered to over a thousand pastors. At the end of my message a young woman in her twenties stopped me in the hall. Her eyes were filled with tears, and she could barely speak. She simply mouthed the words "Thank you" as she tried to gather her composure. She took a deep breath and said, "My husband is a young pastor in a rural church. We recently found out we were pregnant, and when we told the church, many members of the congregation said, 'But you guys are so young.'"

This young woman's experience is repeated all over our land. Somehow we have come to believe that children are a burden instead of a blessing. If our churches are going to stem the tide of cultural and moral decay, we must change our disposition toward children. We decry the work of abortionists but seldom say a word to the intentionally childless couples who slay even the possibility of life in the womb. Not to mention those who, like Bridget and me, bought the materialistic lie and cut off the possibility of future offspring due to "the rising cost of a college education" and the prospect of actually needing all those seats in our massive SUVs or all of the bedrooms in our giant homes. *Lord, make us a people who eagerly accept your mandate to "be fruitful and multiply" (Genesis 1:28).*

Our churches must place a premium on family. I had lunch several months ago with a college minister who was in the midst of a family crisis. It turns out his daughter had been skipping church for over a month. "How?" I asked in disbelief. "It really wasn't hard," he replied. I do not remember the conversation word for word, but I will never forget the general content:

> "She went to Sunday school at 9:15 while we were in worship, then she attended the 10:50 (contemporary) service. Her mother and I went to the 9:15 (traditional) worship service, then went to Sunday school at 10:50. Once she turned sixteen, we started going to church in separate cars since she would sometimes stay behind to hang out with her friends or pick them up on the way. On Wednesday nights she went to youth service, then eventually to the college service. Her mom was in the choir, and I worked in AWANA, so we would also drive separate cars on Wednesdays. It wasn't until her Sunday school teacher asked if there was anything wrong with her that we realized she wasn't going to church."

This church believed it was placing a premium on families because it had activities for people of all ages. However, what was happening was having the opposite effect. Individual members of families were being kept so busy in their age/season of life group activities that they were members of completely different congregations. This man was so disconnected from his daughter that he did not know she was skipping church until her Sunday school teacher said something. And this wasn't some detached, uninvolved dad. This was an active member of the church! In fact, it was his activity (and that of each of his family members) that kept him in the dark about his daughter's circumstances.

Again I know that it is impossible for every church to move toward complete family integration, but it is my prayer that we can at least foster an environment where families can still come to church in the same car. I invite you to join me in praying to that end. If you are a church leader, I invite you to put feet to those prayers.

Promote Family Worship/Discipleship

As a member of the Southern Baptist Convention, I am ashamed to admit that there is research suggesting that 9 percent of Southern Baptists do not devote one hour a year to family worship. I am even more embarrassed to admit that until a few years ago my family and I were part of that statistic. We had the occasional Sunday when we were not able to get to church and instead held worship at home. However, it was not a part of our lifestyle. We were not a worshiping family.

Moreover, both Christian Smith and George Barna have confirmed the fact that Christian families are not engaging in any type of meaningful discipleship. According to Barna:

> Parents are not so much unwilling to provide more substantive training to their children as they are ill equipped to do such work. According to the research, parents typically have no plan for the spiritual development of their children, do not consider it a priority, have little or no training in how to nurture a child's faith, have no related standards or goals that they are seeking to satisfy, and experience no accountability for their efforts.[15]

Again, in some ways this was me a few years ago. While I was well equipped for the job, I had no plan, no standards, no goals, and no accountability when it came to the discipleship of my children. What's worse, I wasn't expected to. Thus I was silent on the issue.

People get tired of hearing me talk about family worship and discipleship. Sometimes I don't even realize I am doing it. It is just such a normal, natural part of my everyday life that I talk about it without thinking. More importantly, I have seen the transformation in my own home and in the lives of my wife and children. I have also seen the incredible impact it has had on families at our church who for the first time in their lives are part of a community of believers where family worship and discipleship is the norm.

Join the reformation! Begin to worship regularly with your family. Once you do, and you have seen the benefits in both you and your family, begin to export it. Tell others about the tremendous impact that family worship has had on you and show them the way. Put a plug in whenever you can. If you are in a position of leadership in your church, model this biblical practice for others to see, and encourage them along the way.

Promote Christian Education

Christian education is a critical tool in the culture war. More importantly, it is a critical tool in the evangelism and discipleship of the next generation. This is evidenced by Jesus' words in Luke 6:40, "A pupil is not above his teacher; but everyone, after he has been fully trained, will be like his teacher." Even Muslims understand the power of Christian education. Sheikh Ahmad Al Katani, in an interview on the infamous Al Jazeera television network, responded to the fact that six million African Muslims a year are converting to Christianity. According to Katani, the culprit is not large evangelistic crusades but Christian education. After making a statement concerning the success of educational evangelism in Africa, Katani noted:

> My honored sir, you have to build the worshipper before you build the mosque. What should happen is that schools should be built first, which are the primary source of spreading Islam and to protect the Muslim using education not a mosque building. The mosque will come as a secondary stage. This is one of the mistakes that we commit; we are proud of building a mosque for example in Dar Al Salam, but believe me my dear sir, had we used that money to build a school it would have been a lot more beneficial. Build the worshipper before you build the mosque and the prophet—Allah's prayers and peace be upon him—spent ten years of his ministry without building a mosque, but instead he was preparing men. After the prophet entered the second stage of his ministry he built a mosque. . . . I say this and I take full responsibility for it; building a school comes before building a mosque. Build the worshipper before you build the mosque. Take for example yourself; you go to the mosque five times a day and if you added all that time it would equal an hour or maybe two hours if you include the Friday prayer. However, if I ask you how long you stayed at school, you will reply that you spent years in middle school and years in high school. Likewise the African goes to the mosque, *but if we built him a school where he could spend most of his time, and provided specialized educators we could at least stop this dangerous Christian missionary octopus*[16] [emphasis added].

The Sheikh is acknowledging what many American Christians choose to ignore. The greatest impact we can have on a life is through education. For too long we have been committed to forms of evangelism that ignore the crucial discipleship element explicit in the Great Commission. We have been called to make disciples, not converts. And the most effective means of discipling the next generation is education.

How could it be anything but beneficial for Christian children to be taught in an environment that acknowledges Almighty God and views every subject from the perspective of Christian Theism? Richard Baxter said it well: "This is the sanctification of your studies, when they are devoted to God, and when He is the end, the object, and the life of them all."[17] We can promote Christian education in our churches through carefully studying the issue, discovering the impact education is having on the children in our congregation, providing affordable educational alternatives, and reaching out to the home-school community.

First, make an honest effort to study what the Bible says about education. The Bible is not silent on the issue of education. Therefore, I disagree with those who say that we should just remain on the sidelines while Christian families make the educational choice (public school, private school, or home school) that best suits them. If the Bible addresses the issue, I cannot remain silent. I implore you to sit down with your Bible and allow the text to speak on the issue (see Chapter 6). There will never be consensus on this issue, but there should be a discussion based on a clear examination of the relevant texts.

Second, test the worldview of the children in your church. What if you discovered (like every church that has used the PEERS test to evaluate the worldview of their teens) that less than 10 percent of the students in your church have a biblical worldview? What if you also discovered that the number one cause was where and how those teens were educated? Many churches don't even want to know the answers to these questions because the education issue is such a political hot potato in the church. However, we cannot continue to hide our heads in the sand. If the kids in your church are being dragged down into Secular Humanism and Marxist Socialism, I would hope that you would want to know. Moreover, I would hope that you would take action.

Third, find and support affordable educational alternatives. From homeschool co-ops to the one-room schoolhouse, there are a number of affordable alternatives out there waiting to be discovered. Children wasting away in failing schools in our urban centers are waiting for someone to show them a better way. Perhaps your church can open that door. Admittedly this is not an easy task. However, I am sure that a community of believers that routinely raises millions of dollars to build sanctuaries for one-day-a-week use can find a few coins to help parents give their children a Christian education.

Finally, we must reach out to and embrace the homeschool community. According to the Home School Legal Defense Association, more than half of the parents who homeschool their children in this country are not Christians. Only 15 percent are evangelicals. The homeschool community is a tremendous mission field. Perhaps your church can start a homeschool support group or a Sunday school class for homeschoolers. Or you could do something as simple as recognizing home-educated children at special school-oriented events. As I have said, many homeschool families feel isolated and abandoned by their local church. It would not take much to remedy that problem.

Promote Biblically Qualified Leadership

As Tom Eldredge notes, "The commitments church leaders make in the areas of family and the education of their children are some of the first fruits the world examines when it seeks to verify the sincerity of the spoken Christian testimony."[18] However, the same cannot be said of the average Pastoral Search Committee. The search for a pastor has begun to resemble the search for a corporate CEO more closely than it does the New Testament model.

I am embarrassed to tell you how many times people have asked me to explain what I mean when I talk about "biblically qualified" leaders. Perhaps the worst case was a young woman who was serving on a Pastoral Search Committee. She and eleven other members of her church had been charged with the responsibility of recommending a replacement for their recently retired pastor. I say this was the worst case because this woman was in a position to influence her church's future by recommending its next pastor, but she didn't know where to go to find the qualifications for which she and her colleagues should be looking! And no, she was not the only one on the committee in that predicament.

In fact, I am convinced that most search committees are either ignorant of or ambivalent toward the biblical qualifications for pastors/elders. This is evidenced by the glut of unqualified ministers and the enigmatic euphemism *PK*, or preacher's kid. Pastors are so notoriously inept at raising children that we have a name for their wayward offspring. This is particularly problematic in light of the fact that while there are many character qualities the Bible calls us to look for, there are only two *skills* required of a pastor: He must be able to teach, and he must manage his household well.[19] God is definitely not silent on the issue of pastoral qualifications:

> *It is a trustworthy statement: if any man aspires to the office of overseer, it is a fine work he desires to do. An overseer, then, must be above reproach, the husband of one wife, temperate, prudent, respectable, hospitable, able to teach, not addicted to wine or pugnacious, but gentle, peaceable, free from the love of money. He must be one who manages his own household well, keeping his children under control with all dignity (but if a man does not know how to manage his own household, how will he take care of the church of God?), and not a new convert, so that he will not become conceited and fall into the condemnation incurred by the devil. And he must have a good reputation with those outside the church, so that he will not fall into reproach and the snare of the devil. (1 Timothy 3:1-7, emphasis mine)*

Paul's letter to Titus puts an even finer point on the matter. Concerning the ability to teach, he encourages Titus to find men who are "holding fast the faithful word which is in accordance with the teaching, so that he will be able both to exhort in sound doctrine and to refute those who contradict" (1:9). Thus those who would serve in the office of pastor/elder must have sound doctrine and theology, the ability to communicate truth effectively, and enough of a grasp on apologetics to refute those who would contradict the basic truths of the faith.

This is a far cry from the requirements I recently read from a church seeking a pastor on churchstaffing.com. According to this "contemporary" church, the ideal candidate "must be willing to incorporate creative elements like drama, testimony and video into topically relevant messages." This has absolutely nothing to do with the biblical requirements for pastors/elders. What's worse, it does nothing to ensure the doctrinal and theological integrity of the preaching and teaching ministry of the church.

As far as we have fallen on the issue of being "able to teach," we have fared much worse on the clear mandate to choose men who manage their households well. In fact, the current practice of choosing a pastor completely circumvents this requirement. The scenario goes something like this: We put a committee together, and they begin to take resumés. They evaluate the resumés for their cosmetic and corporate appeal (size of previous church, reputation of seminary degree, etc.) and then narrow the list. Once the list has been narrowed down, the committee will listen to sermons on CD and/or travel to hear the candidates in person.

If they are sufficiently impressed, they will call the candidate in for an interview. This interview will usually consist of a few perfunctory questions about the candidate's theology (usually no more than necessary to find out if they are of the same denominational affiliation and general theological ilk), but the bulk of the time in the interview is geared toward discovering the candidate's strategy for growing churches and satisfying the worship, programming, and building needs of the majority of the people in the congregation.

If the candidate performs well, the committee will make a recommendation to the leadership team, then to the rest of the church. After this, the candidate will be brought there "in view of a call." This means he will put on his best suit, bring his best sermon, preach it, and the church will vote on whether or not to call him as their pastor.

The problems with this process are myriad. However, one problem stands out above the rest. This process completely ignores the second requirement of a pastor/elder. As John MacArthur astutely observes, "to find out if a man is qualified for leadership in the church, look first at his influence on his own children."[20] When do we examine the man's family? When does the committee enter his home and observe him as he conducts family worship? When does the committee spend time with his wife and children to ascertain the level of impact he has had on their spiritual development through intentional and consistent discipleship and mentoring? When do we find out whether or not this man "manages his own household" well or whether "his children are believers and not open to the charge of debauchery or insubordination" (Titus 1:6, ESV)?

If these questions seem foreign to you, you are not alone. There is very little interest in the biblical qualifications of pastors these days. Just peruse the Internet job sites, and you will quickly discover that most churches are looking for the same thing Enron was looking for when they hired the team that brought about their downfall.

The problem with the current approach is twofold. First, it ignores or contradicts the biblical mandate. Second, hiring pastors who do not meet the biblical requirements will lead to decay in the body as a whole. Richard Baxter put it best:

> If you are ungodly and teach not your families the fear of God, nor contradict the sins of the company you are in, nor turn the stream of their vain talking, nor deal with them plainly about their salvation, they will take it as if you preached to them that such things are needless, and that they may boldly do so as well as you.[21]

"A mist in the pulpit becomes a fog in the pew," as the old saying goes. If we ever expect our churches to lead the way in family restoration, we must begin by holding those who lead to a higher standard. Not an impossible, unreasonable, or legalistic standard, but a biblical one. Is it too much to ask a man to demonstrate his evangelistic commitment by leading his children to faith? Is it too much to ask a man to demonstrate his commitment to and penchant for discipleship by raising children who are obedient and respectful and know what they believe and why? Is it too much to ask a man to demonstrate enough influence on his family to guide his children into adulthood as faithful followers of Christ?[22] In other words, is it too much to ask a man who will lead God's people to model the kind of parenting to which every believer should aspire? Or to put it another way, do we really believe that elders must be "examples to the flock" (1 Peter 5:3)?

The Long Road Home

Again, we probably can't all go out and transform our congregations into family-integrated churches. Nor do I think we need to. At Grace we have found a paradigm that answers most of the questions and concerns about multigenerational faithfulness and, more importantly, is closely aligned with the biblical model. However, our church is not perfect. We discover new weaknesses each day. And I am sure we will discover still more tomorrow.

Thus I did not write this chapter as a blueprint to be followed to the letter. I simply wanted to raise the relevant issues and offer some solutions that have proven effective. I also wanted to offer some answers to the questions I have received over the past few years as I have preached and lectured on the topic. Therefore, while most people will not share the distinctives of a family-integrated church, we can agree on the guiding principles. We can and we must promote a biblical view of marriage and family, family worship and discipleship, Christian education, and biblically qualified leadership.

The harsh reality is that unless we radically change the way we view the church and the family, we will not see an end to the decimation of both institutions in our culture. However, I believe that the tide is turning. I have shared this message all across our land, and the response has been overwhelming. Pastors have stopped me in the halls at conferences to ask me what to do to move their churches toward family integration. Moms and dads have brought pictures of children who have gone astray. Grandparents have looked me in the eye and said, "I wish someone had told me this thirty years ago." The recurring theme is, "Why has no one taught us these things?"

Ironically, nothing I've shared in this book is new. Richard Baxter was singing the same tune in the 1600s. He noted:

> You are not likely to see any general reformation, till you procure family reformation. Some little religion there may be here and there; but while it is confined to single persons, and is not promoted in families, it will not prosper, nor promise future increase.[23]

I have simply tried to remind God's people of what He has said on the subject of multigenerational faithfulness. The exciting thing is that God's people appear to be in the perfect position to hear His truth and act on it. The evidence is sobering. The answer is simple. The time is now. We will either win the culture one family at a time or will continue to lose the culture one family at a time. Either way the family is the key.

Take Action

1. Take inventory of the way you and your family worship. Are you and your children truly worshiping together? Are you members of different congregations in the same building? Are you operating under the same doctrine and theology?
2. Talk about the differences between your worship experience and that of your children (if they attend a different service).
3. If your children do not worship with you, ask them to start.
4. Think about starting a small group for families.

Church Leaders

1. Look at the overall structure of your church, and honestly evaluate the amount of time you are asking families to spend apart.
2. Take advantage of every opportunity you get to celebrate the gift of children.
3. Consider starting a family-integrated cell group or Sunday school class.
4. Reevaluate your hiring practices in light of the biblical mandate.

NOTES

Chapter 1: The Lay of the Land

1. T. C. Pinkney, *Report to the Southern Baptist Convention Executive Committee,* Nashville, Tennessee, September 18, 2001. Pinkney reported that 70 percent of teenagers involved in church youth groups stop attending church within two years of their high school graduation. See also the 2002 *Report of the Southern Baptist Council on Family Life,* which reported that 88 percent of the children in evangelical homes leave church at the age of eighteen.

2. George Barna, *A Biblical Worldview Has a Radical Effect on a Person's Life* (The Barna Group, 2003), accessed March 29 2005); available from http://www.barna.org/FlexPage.aspx?Page=BarnaUpdate&BarnaUpdateID=154.

3. Ibid.

4. Christian Smith and Melinda Lundquist Denton, *Soul Searching* (New York: Oxford University Press, 2005), 270.

5. Ibid., 115.

6. Thom Rainer, "A Resurgence Not Yet Realized: Evangelistic Effectiveness in the Southern Baptist Convention Since 1979," *The Southern Baptist Journal of Theology*, Vol. 9, No. 1, Spring 2005, 63. Rainer's research revealed that 31 percent of those who responded to diagnostic questions gave answers indicating that they definitely were not Christians, while another 14 percent were too ambiguous to classify.

7. Smith, *Soul Searching*, 131.

8. Ibid., 130.

9. Ibid.

10. George Barna, *Parents Describe How They Raise Their Children* (The Barna Group, 2005, accessed March 1, 2005); available from http://www.barna.org/FlexPage.aspx?Page=BarnaUpdate&BarnaUpdateID=183.

11. Ibid.

12. R. Albert Mohler, quoted in Baptist Press Online, http://www.bpnews.net/bpnews.asp?ID=18611. Accessed August 15, 2005. Mohler's comments were made on the June 22 broadcast of the *FamilyLife Today* radio program.

13. Al Mohler, "First Person: Deliberate Childlessness & Moral Rebellion." Baptist

Press Online, http://www.bpnews.net/bpnews.asp?ID=21298. Accessed August 15, 2005.

Chapter 2: A God with No Rivals

1. What follows is actually the combination of three very similar stories with a few names changed to protect the identities of the people involved, and with a random sport chosen for the same purpose. However, the encounter is real and has actually taken place numerous times with many different families.

Chapter 4: Give Him Your Heart

1. Peter C. Craigie, "The Book of Deuteronomy," *The New International Commentary on the Old Testament*, R. K. Harrison and Robert L. Hubbard, Jr., eds. (Grand Rapids, MI: Wm. B. Eerdmans, 1976), 170.

2. John Calvin, *Harmony of the Law*, Vol. I; http://www.ccel.org/c/calvin/comment3/comm_vol03/htm/v.xv.htm. Accessed August 30, 2005.

3. The Barna Group; http://www.barna.org/FlexPage.aspx?Page=BarnaUpdate&BarnaUpdateID=156.

4. Francis Schaeffer, *How Should We Then Live?* (Old Tappan, NJ: Revell, 1976; Wheaton, IL: Crossway Books, 1983).

5. James Sire, *Naming the Elephant* (Downers Grove, IL: InterVarsity, 2004).

6. Charles Colson and Nancy Pearcey, *How Now Shall We Live?* (Wheaton, IL: Tyndale, 2004).

7. Christian Smith and Melinda Lundquist Denton, *Soul Searching* (New York: Oxford University Press, 2005), 133.

8. Ibid.

9. Adapted from the Barna Group; http://www.barna.org/FlexPage.aspx?Page=BarnaUpdate&BarnaUpdateID=156. Accessed October 7, 2004.

10. Encarta® World English Dictionary, Microsoft Corporation, 1999.

Chapter 5: Teach the Word at Home

1. Christian Smith and Melinda Lundquist Denton, *Soul Searching* (New York: Oxford University Press, 2005), 28.

2. Ibid., 269.

3. Ibid., 269-270.

4. John Bunyan, "Christian Family"; http://www.biblebb.com/files/JB-001.htm.

5. Hillary Rodham Clinton, *It Takes A Village and Other Lessons Children Teach Us* (New York: Touchstone Books, 1996).

6. David Wegener, "A Father's Role in Family Worship," *Journal of Biblical Manhood and Womanhood*, Vol. 3, Issue 4, 1998.

Chapter 6: Live the Word at Home

1. John Rosemond, *A Family of Value* (Kansas City: Andrew & McMeel, 1995), 2.

2. Ibid., 144.

3. Ibid., 148.

4. Ibid.

5. Ibid.

6. Ibid., 149.

7. Ibid., 150.

8. Ibid., 149.

9. The Nehemiah Institute has been conducting worldview tests since 1988. The PEERS Test places respondents into one of four categories (Christian Worldview, Moderately Christian, Secular Humanism, Socialism). According to their results Christian students who attend public schools consistently score between Secular Humanism and Socialism. View a PowerPoint presentation of their results at www.nehemiahinstitute.com.

10. Cal Thomas, "Steamy Teen Love in Tampa," *Jewish World Review*, December 15, 2005; www.jewishworldreview.com/cols/thomas121505.asp. Accessed December 19, 2005.

11. Ibid.

12. Bruce Shortt, *The Harsh Truth About Public Schools* (Vallecito, CA: Chalcedon, 2004), 192-194.

Chapter 7: Mark the Home as God's Territory

1. See http://www.naturallyconnected.com.au/fengshui.htm. Related to this is the belief about chi, which according to eastern mystical belief is the energy or force that surrounds the earth and connects people to one another and their surroundings. This is closely tied to the concepts of Monism (all is one) and Pantheism (all is god).

2. A. W. Pink, *Family Worship* (accessed April 9, 2005); available from http://www.mountzion.org/fgb/Fall99/FgbF1-99.html.

3. David Wegener, "The Father's Role in Family Worship," *Journal of Biblical Manhood and Womanhood*, Vol. 3, Issue 4, 1998.

4. Donald S. Whitney, *Family Worship: In the Bible, in History, and in Your Home* (Shepherdsville, KY: Center for Biblical Spirituality, 2006), 37.

5. John Bunyan, "Christian Family"; http://www.biblebb.com/files/JB-001.htm.

6. This term is used to describe churches that do not segregate their members by age. There are no classes just for young married couples or teens or senior adults. There are no youth groups or KidZones. We view the church as a family of families and expect families to worship together and teach the Scriptures in their homes (hence no Sunday school). The children to whom I refer often

come from families who have never had their kids in worship with them until they came to our church. For more information on the family-integrated church movement, see www.visionforumministries.com or visit our church web site at www.gracecommunityinfo.org.

Chapter 8: Enjoy the Gifts Without Forgetting the Giver

1. The story aired May 9, 2004 in Houston on KPRC, channel 2 and was later transcribed at http://www.click2houston.com/family/3287972/detail.html. Accessed May 10, 2004. Associated Press, copyright © 2004.

Chapter 9: The Coming Revival: Is the Church Ready for Family Driven Faith?

1. Malcolm McDow and Alvin L. Reid, *Firefall: How God Has Shaped History Through Revivals* (Nashville: Broadman & Holman, 1997).

2. Tom Rainer, "A Resurgence Not Yet Realized: Evangelistic Effectiveness in the Southern Baptist Convention Since 1979," *The Southern Baptist Journal of Theology*, 9, No. 1, 2005.

3. Roger L. Dudley, "Indicators of Commitment to the Church: A Longitudinal Study of Church-Affiliated Youth," *Adolescence*, 28, No. 109, 1993; http://www.questia.com/PM.qst?a=o&d=5000179401. Accessed December 20, 2005.

4. Rainer, "A Resurgence Not Yet Realized," 63. Again, Rainer is working with Southern Baptists, but the numbers can be presumed to be at least as bad for other denominations.

5. Mike Yaconelli, "Youth Ministry: A Contemplative Approach," *The Christian Century*, April 21, 1999, 450; http://www.questia.com/PM.qst?a=o&d=5001255487. Yaconelli was co-founder of Youth Specialties, Inc. and an avid exponent of youth ministry. Although toward the end of his life he saw and admitted the failures of the model, he sought reforms through mysticism and the "new spirituality." He became a key voice in what has become the Emerging Church movement.

6. Doug Fields, *Purpose-Driven Youth Ministry* (Grand Rapids, MI: Zondervan, 1998).

7. Mike Yaconelli, "Youth Ministry: A Contemplative Approach," 450.

8. Ibid.

9. Pamela Smith McCall, "All in the Family," *The Christian Century*, April 18, 2001, 22; http://www.questia.com/PM.qst?a=o&d=5000988811. Accessed February 4, 2006.

10. Alvin Reid, *Raising the Bar: Ministry to Youth in the New Millennium* (Grand Rapids, MI: Kregel, 2004).

11. Ibid.

12. Mark DeVries, quoted in, "Passing It On: Reflections on Youth Ministry,"

The Christian Century, October 4, 2003; http://www.questia.com/PM.qst?a=o&d=5002019458. Accessed February 3, 2006.

13. Pamela Smith McCall, "All in the Family," *The Christian Century*, April 18, 2001, 22; http://www.questia.com/PM.qst?a=o&d=5000988811. Accessed February 4, 2006.

14. D. A. Carson, *Becoming Conversant with the Emerging Church* (Grand Rapids, MI: Zondervan, 2005).

15. Ibid.

16. Dan Kimball, *The Emerging Church: Vintage Christianity for New Generations* (Grand Rapids, MI: Zondervan, 2003).

17. Ibid.

Chapter 10: A Radical Departure from the Norm

1. Alvin Reid, *Raising the Bar: Ministry to Youth in the New Millennium* (Grand Rapids, MI: Kregel, 2004).

2. Many so-called family-integrated churches are merely cloisters of homeschool families that have grown weary of the segregated methodologies of most churches. Many of these groups classify themselves as house churches, although they lack many of the fundamental elements of the house church movement. These cloisters are often introverted and have little interest in missions and/or evangelism. This is not what I am referring to here.

3. See http://www.familybasedym.com/about_faq.php.

4. Ibid.

5. David Allen Black, *The Myth of Adolescence: Raising Responsible Children in an Irresponsible Society* (Yorba Linda, CA: Davidson Press, 1999).

6. Nancy Pearcey, *Total Truth: Liberating Christianity from Its Cultural Captivity* (Wheaton, IL: Crossway Books, 2004).

7. Tom Eldredge, *Safely Home* (San Antonio, TX: The Vision Forum, Inc., 2003).

8. Bruce Shortt, *The Harsh Truth About Public Schools* (Vallecito, CA: Chalcedon, 2004).

9. Approximately 90 percent of the families at Grace Community Church in Magnolia, Texas (the church I serve) educate their children at home.

10. David P. Baker and Cornelius Riordan, "The 'Eliting' of the Common American Catholic School and the National Education Crisis," *Phi Delta Kappan*, 80, No. 1; http://www.questia.com/PM.qst?a=o&d=5001373454. Accessed December 20, 2005.

11. Antony Gordon and Richard Horowitz, *Will Your Grandchildren Be Jewish? Intermarriage Rates & Statistics for Orthodox, Modern Orthodox, Conservative, Reform & Unaffiliated Jews*; http://www.simpletoremember.com/vitals/Will YourGrandchildrenBeJews.htm. Accessed November 23, 2005.

12. Ibid.

13. Peter Wonacott, "Zoroastrians Turn to Internet Dating to Rescue Religion: Declining Numbers Threaten the Future of Ancient Faith," *The Wall Street Journal*, February 6, 2006.

14. Daniel Akin, "The Future of Southern Baptists: Mandates for What We Should Be in the Twenty-First Century," *The Southern Baptist Journal of Theology*, 9, No. 1 (2005).

15. George Barna, *Parents Accept Responsibility for Their Child's Spiritual Development but Struggle with Effectiveness* (The Barna Group, 2003; http://www.barna.org/FlexPage.aspx?Page=BarnaUpdate&BarnaUpdateID=138). Accessed December 10, 2004.

16. The English translation of the interview is available at http://www.former muslims.com/forum/viewtopic.php?t=972.

17. Richard Baxter, *The Reformed Pastor* (Edinburgh, Scotland: Banner of Truth, 1979).

18. Eldredge, *Safely Home*.

19. See Titus 1:5-9; 1 Timothy 3:1-7; 1 Peter 5:1-4. There are numerous character qualities required of those who would serve as pastor/elder but only two skills.

20. John MacArthur, *Titus*, The MacArthur New Testament Commentary (Chicago: Moody Press, 1996).

21. Baxter, *The Reformed Pastor*.

22. MacArthur, *Titus*.

23. Baxter, *The Reformed Pastor*.

RECOMMENDED READING

Akin, Daniel. "The Future of Southern Baptists: Mandates for What We Should Be in the Twenty-First Century." *The Southern Baptist Journal of Theology* 9, No. 1 (2005): 70-85.

Barna, George. *A Biblical Worldview Has a Radical Effect on a Person's Life*. Ventura, CA: The Barna Group, 2003; accessed March 29, 2005; available from http://www.barna.org/FlexPage.aspx?Page=BarnaUpdate&BarnaUpdateID=154.

_____. *Parents Accept Responsibility for Their Child's Spiritual Development but Struggle with Effectiveness*. Ventura, CA: The Barna Group, 2003; accessed December 10, 2004; available from http://www.barna.org/FlexPage.aspx?Page=BarnaUpdate&BarnaUpdateID=138.

_____. *Parents Describe How They Raise Their Children*. Ventura, CA: The Barna Group, 2005; accessed March 1, 2005; available from http://www.barna.org/FlexPage.aspx?Page=BarnaUpdate&BarnaUpdateID=183.

Baxter, Richard. *The Reformed Pastor*. Edinburgh, Scotland: Banner of Truth, 1979.

Black, David Allen. *The Myth of Adolescence: Raising Responsible Children in an Irresponsible Society*. Yorba Linda, CA: Davidson Press, 1999.

Carson, D. A. *Becoming Conversant with the Emerging Church*. Grand Rapids, MI: Zondervan, 2005.

Eldredge, Tom. *Safely Home*. San Antonio, TX: The Vision Forum, Inc., 2003.

Fields, Doug. *Purpose-Driven Youth Ministry*. Grand Rapids, MI: Zondervan, 1998.

Gordon, Antony, and Richard Horowitz. *Will Your Grandchildren Be Jewish? Intermarriage Rates & Statistics for Orthodox, Modern Orthodox, Conservative, Reform & Unaffiliated Jews 2005*; accessed November 23, 2005; available from http://www.simpletoremember.com/vitals/WillYourGrandchildrenBeJews.htm.

Kimball, Dan. *The Emerging Church: Vintage Christianity for New Generations.* Grand Rapids, MI: Zondervan, 2003.

MacArthur, John. *Titus*, The MacArthur New Testament Commentary. Chicago: Moody Press, 1996.

McDow, Malcolm, and Alvin Reid. *Firefall: How God Has Shaped History Through Revivals.* Nashville: Broadman & Holman, 1997.

Pearcey, Nancy. *Total Truth: Liberating Christianity from Its Cultural Captivity.* Wheaton, IL: Crossway Books, 2004.

Pink, A. W. *Family Worship*; accessed April 9, 2005; available from http://www. mountzion.org/fgb/Fall99/FgbF1-99.html.

Rainer, Tom. "A Resurgence Not Yet Realized: Evangelistic Effectiveness in the Southern Baptist Convention Since 1979." *The Southern Baptist Journal of Theology* 9, No. 1 (2005): 54-69.

Reid, Alvin. *Raising the Bar: Ministry to Youth in the New Millennium.* Grand Rapids, MI: Kregel, 2004.

Shortt, Bruce. *The Harsh Truth About Public Schools.* Vallecito, CA: Chalcedon, 2004.

Whitney, Donald S. *Family Worship: In the Bible, in History, and in Your Home.* Shepherdsville, KY: Center for Biblical Spirituality, 2006.

Wonacott, Peter. "Zoroastrians Turn to Internet Dating to Rescue Religion: Declining Numbers Threaten the Future of Ancient Faith; Fertility Drugs in Mumbai." *The Wall Street Journal*, February 6, 2006.

INTRODUCTION TO
OPERATIONS MANAGEMENT

THE IRWIN SERIES IN
OPERATIONS MANAGEMENT

EDITOR
HOWARD L. TIMMS
Indiana University

INTRODUCTION TO OPERATIONS MANAGEMENT

Howard L. Timms, P.E., D.B.A.

Professor of Management
Graduate School of Business
Indiana University

1967
RICHARD D. IRWIN, INC.
Homewood, Illinois

PREFACE

ABOUT THE SERIES

THE "OPERATIONS FUNCTION" is defined as the "production function" in all types of organized activity, not just business firms. The following term equivalencies between business and nonbusiness organizations are employed in the Series: production function—operations function; marketing —distribution; firm—organization; profit—benefit/cost or cost/effectiveness; customer—user. As in the case of business firms, the word "product" equates with "output," and both mean goods and/or services. All these terms are used in appropriate context throughout the Series.

The plan for this series of short paperbacks in Operations Management was conceived in the fall of 1964. It called for dividing the subject of operations management, broadly defined, into logical divisions and engaging a recognized specialist in each division to write a small (150 to 160 pages) book about his subject.

The general specifications for each book called for de-emphasis of overlapping materials, with the bulk of the book confined to a rigorous treatment of the material unique to the subject. Thus each book treats its specialty in reasonable depth—much more so than could be done in a chapter or two of a full-length general text on operations or production management.

In addition, the subject matter of the books was to be integrated so that a combination of them suitable to the instructor could be used in his basic or general course in operations management in lieu of a single full-length general book. On the other hand, each book was to be self-contained enough to be highly useful in a specialized course in the subject, perhaps along with a full-length book, or along with supplementary readings from the journal literature which are cited heavily throughout the Series.

To accomplish all this, it was agreed that a "decision systems" (integrated decision processes) approach would be followed throughout the series. The first book in the series, *Introduction to Operations Management*, would cover background materials appropriate for the series and develop the concept of "decision systems." In this Introduction book would appear much of the general materials not covered in the other books.

Finally, to integrate specific parts of all the books so that any combination would "hang together" as a unit, the coordinating editor would write the Introduction book, provide his draft to the other authors, who would then write their drafts. These drafts would then be reviewed twice by the coordinating editor, who would provide substantive suggestions to the authors, together with cross-referencing materials and footnotes, and finally revise his Introduction book.

Those who are familiar with the busy schedule of a modern professor can appreciate why this process required almost two years. However, we believe this lengthy process has produced a unique series—not a set of handbooks, but a set of condensed textbooks, all of which are explicitly integrated with each other.

Various combinations of the books in the series are appropriate for use in a first course in operations management, production management, or industrial management at both the undergraduate and masters level in schools of business, industrial engineering, and industrial management. And, as mentioned above, each of the books on a specialized subject is appropriate for a follow-on course in that specialty. In the preface to each book, the author suggests how his text may be used in particular courses.

A single instructor's manual contains the solutions for all the problems in all the books employing problems or exercises. A number of the other books contain annotated case references.

ABOUT THE INTRODUCTION BOOK

The purpose of this book is to provide background knowledge to help the reader understand the development of appropriate decision systems for the major managerial problems facing the professional manager. These decision systems are developed fully in books 2 through 9 of this series. Throughout this Introduction book, appropriate cross-references to various parts of the other books are made. This serves to show how the subjects of all the books are interrelated.

A brief preview of each of the five chapters of this book may serve the reader in following the development of the subject. Chapter 1 deals with the main term in the title of this book and the series: "Operations." Chapter 2 deals with the next substantive term: "Management." The heart of the professional manager's work is *making decisions* in the many perplexing problem situations facing him. Accordingly, Chapter 3 deals with "Decision Theory." Because an appropriate managerial decision is one that is made as an integral part of a system of decisions, the "Systems Theory" of Chapter 4 offers an appropriate background. Finally, Chapter 5 brings together and synthesizes the subjects of Chapters 1 through 4 under the heading, "Decision Systems for Operations Management." This Chapter features the development of a general decision system that provides a framework for the specific decision systems developed in the other books in the Series.

USE OF THE INTRODUCTION BOOK

This text may be put to a number of uses. It may, for instance, serve as the central text in a general (first) course in management, with other materials of the instructor's choice accompanying it. These may be case materials, parts of full-length general management texts, or selected articles from the literature. The copious footnote references and annotated supplementary readings at the end of each chapter serve to provide choices for this purpose.

The book, while written to serve as an introduction for books in operations management, is useful for a general course in management for at least two reasons. First, three of the five chapters are on subjects directly relevant, and indeed central, to management in general, namely: "Management Theory," "Decision Theory," and "Systems Theory." Second, the final chapter—"Decision Systems for Operations Management"—builds a decision framework that serves to show how major managerial decisions in all the major functions—marketing, finance, personnel, purchasing, and others—are integrated in a systems approach. This puts the student in an appropriate posture, at the end of a general management course, for embarking upon functional courses such as marketing, finance, etc. He has command of a framework that enables him to better integrate the materials of these basic functional courses.

Finally, the Introduction book might well be used along with each of the other books in this series in follow-on specialty courses, such as the ones on quality control, purchasing, etc. This is appropriate for the same reasons given above. The last chapter especially would provide a framework into which the specialty materials may be integrated.

ACKNOWLEDGMENTS

Without the guidance and encouragement of Professor John F. Mee, this series would have collapsed at one of many critical junctures during the lengthy production process. Without the persistent help of William D. Crawford, the publisher's Vice President and Executive Editor, the critical problems could not have been overcome. My full gratitude must go to the series authors for their patience and cooperation. When my suggestions irked their professional sensibilities, their replies were gentlemanly and constructive.

To W. George Pinnell, Dean of the Graduate School of Business, Indiana University, and R. Stansbury Stockton, Chairman of the school's Department of Production Management and Industrial Engineering, go special thanks for encouragement through relief from minor chores of professorship. Finally, to my friend and colleague, Arthur M. Weimer, Vice Chairman of ARAC, must go many thanks for his understanding and help during the period of coordinating this series.

Bloomington, Indiana   HOWARD L. TIMMS
March, 1967

TABLE OF CONTENTS

Chapter 1

THE OPERATIONS FUNCTION

OPERATIONS DEFINED

THE TITLE "Vice President for Operations" is sometimes used in business, often in manufacturing firms. In many of these cases "operations" is the equivalent of "production" in the manufacturing firm. In other cases "operations" includes production and marketing, with the finance and personnel functions organized separately along with other organization units that serve the entire company.

At least one variation of the latter case known to the writer is one in which "operations" includes production and *physical* distribution of the product through field warehouses and dealers to the ultimate customer, but not the other functions conducted by the field warehouses and dealers.

In other cases the term "operations" refers to the nonmanagerial, sometimes called "operative," work of the business. This definition would imply that a book on operations *management* would treat the subject of "foremanship" or "supervision"—the first, or last (depending upon how you interpret organization structure) level of management. This is not the approach taken in this text or others in this series.

The term "operations" is often used in railroads, airlines, and other service-producing (as opposed to goods-producing) industries to identify the work associated with creating or producing the firm's output. This is equivalent to the economist's term "production function" as applied to business firms.[1]

The term "operations" is also frequently applied to the work of producing the output of a nonbusiness organization such as a government

---

[1] For a fuller explanation see Howard L. Timms, *The Production Function in Business* (rev. ed.; Homewood, Ill.: Richard D. Irwin, Inc., 1966), pp. 8–10.

1

agency, and in other nonprofit institutions. In these nonbusiness institutions, the benefit/cost measure associated with producing and distributing the organization's output takes the place of the revenue/cost, or profit, measure used by business organizations. In this and other texts in the series *the term "operations" is used to identify the "production function" in any organization*, business or nonbusiness. It identifies the work of creating or producing the output of the organization. Accordingly the terms "operations" and "production function" are often used interchangeably in this text and others in the series.

The term "management" refers to all levels in the management structure of the organization from top management (sometimes referred to as administration) through middle management and including "operative management." The term "management" is also defined broadly to include the various specialized activities often organized as staff units within the total management structure, such as industrial engineering. These staff groups play a prominent role in the decision-making processes for which line management is ultimately responsible. Accordingly, a decision-making approach to the subject of production in all types of organizations appropriately includes a treatment of the decision systems employed by specialists such as industrial engineers, cost accountants, and others. The design of this Series in Operations Management reflects this approach.

SYSTEMS VIEW OF OPERATIONS

So-called management scientists,[2] particularly those with a background in the physical sciences and engineering, find a useful analogy for the organization (any kind) in the so-called servosystem. The organization is regarded as a communication system closed on the users' (of the organization's output) needs and desires, as shown in Figure 1–1.

In this concept of the organization, users' needs and desires are assessed by the organization. Then products, processes, and distribution methods are planned so as to meet these needs and desires effectively and efficiently. The planning information flows to operations, where the plans are carried out and the product (goods or service) is produced. The product is then promoted so that users are aware of its existence and how it will serve their needs and desires. Finally, the product is distributed to them; at this time the needs and desires of users are filled.

This closed-loop communication system should operate continuously if the organization is to be most effective and efficient. As users' needs and desires change, the changes should be discerned as quickly as possible by management, plans revised, operations changed accordingly, and promoting and distributing techniques altered to serve best the revised

---

[2] Management science, along with operations research, is explained more fully in Chapter 3.

FIGURE 1–1
The Organization as a Servosystem

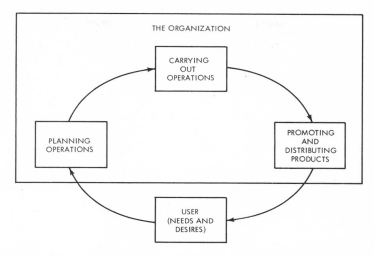

needs and desires. This concept of the organization as a dynamic feed-back system that is constantly "tuned in" to the users' needs, and that reacts immediately and correctly to changes, is extremely useful for solving problems in the operation of the organization, for organizing its work, and particularly for designing effective communication procedures.

Figure 1–1 introduces the concept of a servosystem that is basic to our treatment of the subject of managerial decision making in operations. First, note that *the concept clearly implies that the organization is, or should be, "market" oriented.* The organization stays in existence by filling needs and desires of users, not by producing products that few people want.

All successful organizations promote and distribute their output. The term "distribution" is the equivalent of "marketing" in a business firm. Many nonbusiness organizations, particularly governmental bodies, do not market their output in the sense of selling it to users. In fact, services that cannot readily be sold to the public, such as fire protection, are most likely to be provided by the government. However, even the government agency must promote its output if distribution is to be successful. The United States Departments of Commerce and Agriculture regularly mail out pamphlets explaining their new and revised services. Television is often resorted to, particularly in the case of entirely new services, thus emulating the promotional techniques of the business firm. An example is the case of Medicare, in which the prospective users (public over 65 years old) were not being reached in a mail campaign. Promotional techniques straight out of "Madison Avenue" were finally required to get eligible people to register for the service. Thus every organization must promote, in one form or another, its output if its distribution is to be accomplished effectively.

A second and very important aspect of the concept of the organization as a servosystem is the element of feedback in a dynamic user situation. Needs and desires of users change frequently and sometimes for fickle reasons in a complex society. If the organization is to provide successfully products that users want in the face of their dynamically changing needs and desires, management must be in constant communication with the users. The nature of the changes in needs and desires must be fed back into the planning process wherein the nature of the product and its production and distribution are determined for a period ahead. This feedback process obviously is crucial to the continued success of the organization.

The requirement of feedback from the organization's environment pervades all aspects of its operation. Already the perceptive reader will have decided that Figure 1–1 is quite "simpleminded." Not only must there be feedback from users; but also from other sectors comprising the organization's environment: suppliers, labor markets, capital markets, government, competitive firms, etc. Moreover, there must be *feedback between functions within the organization:* from the distribution people to the production people, and vice versa; from both of these groups to the finance people and vice versa, and from all of these to the personnel management people and vice versa, and so on.

Thus, from the standpoint of managerial decision making, *the going concern is a network of feedback systems,* sort of "wheels within wheels" of communications procedures. These wheels must be well designed, must mesh properly, must turn smoothly, must tend not to break down, or when they do, must let responsible managers know when and where the breakdown has occurred and hopefully what sort of "fix" is required. This latter aspect of *self-correction* is the reason for the prefix *servo* in servosystem.

Rather than going further into the subject of servosystems now, let us get back on the track of the operations function, reserving for Chapter 4 a comprehensive treatment of the servosystem or, more simply, the systems concept with its ubiquitous "feedback."

SUBFUNCTIONS OF THE OPERATIONS FUNCTION

Our purpose in this section is to abstract from the work of various types of institutions *the unique subfunctions of operations.* In so doing we shall arrange a very large amount of descriptive information about production in such a manner as to make it useful in the analysis of *operations* problems in all kinds of institutions. Figure 1–2 shows the basic subfunctions of production. The production function is indicated by solid lines; the distribution function is indicated in part by dashed lines.

Product Planning—Goods and Services

It is clear that every organization must plan its product to meet user's needs and desires, as shown earlier in Figure 1–1. Product specifications must be determined *before* detailed methods of producing these specifications can be determined. Rational product planning calls for research to determine the needs and desires of users, and then to translate this information into product specifications. *The specifications that express users' needs and desires may be called general specifications to distinguish them from the technical specifications usually needed for production purposes.* This distinction is shown in Figure 1–2.

FIGURE 1–2
Subfunctions of Operations

For instance, surveys may indicate that next year housewives will desire pastel colored refrigerators in sizes from 7 cubic feet to 12 cubic feet, including a freezing compartment. These are a few of the many general, as opposed to technical, specifications that describe customer needs and desires in refrigerators. Inasmuch as distribution is directly concerned with the demand side of the organization, and since *the general specifications of the product define what is demanded by users,* the activity of deciding the product general specifications is a distribution function as shown in Figure 1–2.

In order to produce the product in accordance with the general specifications that define users' needs and desires, technical specifications are often required, if only to express the general specifications in production language. In the case of a highly technical product ʻsuch as an aircraft, these technical specifications are quite extensive and complex. Decision making in this area is highly technological and is related primarily to the production processes, that is, to the acquisition of inputs and the conversion of these inputs into a product that will meet the general specifications set up by the distribution function. Since *deciding technical specifications is directly concerned with producing the product, this activity is considered a production or operations subfunction* as indicated in Figure 1–2.

Technical specifications apply to service-type products as well as to goods. For instance, the terms of an insurance policy describe the form of protection from risk that the buyer receives. Planning this kind of a product requires, in addition to determining the general specifications describing customer needs and desires, a highly technical type of decision making involving actuarial science.

Another service-type organization that is becoming increasingly well known is the government agency. In a sense it provides a kind of professional service to the public as prescribed by law. The law that brings the agency into existence spells out the public's needs and desires—the general specifications of the agency's product. Presumably the legislators have surveyed their constituents sufficiently well to stipulate in the law appropriate general specifications. The agency then goes on to develop detailed technical specifications for the services it produces.

Often users' conflicting interests bring about lawsuits in respect to the agency's right to specify as it does in certain situations. The details of the technical specifications are challenged by the plaintiff. This often happens in a "friendly suit" brought to clarify the nature (specifications) of the agency's service. The courts have generally been quite loathe to interfere with the agency's "product planning" function. This accounts in great part for the strength of our "fourth branch of government," the various executive agencies.

It is clear from this explanation of Figure 1–2 that the product planning function lies precisely at the interface of the operations (production) function and the distribution function of the organization. Since the distribution function is concerned primarily with the demand (users' needs and desires) side of the institution, the general specifications for the product are the responsibility of the distribution function. This distinction is made in Figure 1–2 by indicating the demand side in dashed lines. This explains why most books on marketing or distribution contain one or more chapters on product planning. On the other hand, general specifications for the product usually are not detailed and specific enough for production purposes, especially in the case of complex products. Accordingly, technical specifications are required for this purpose, and these are the responsibility of the production or operations function. Thus production books (and this series) also contain one or more chapters (or a book) on product planning.[3]

In order to develop further the thinking behind the model of Figure 1–2, let us break down all kinds of organizations into a relatively few classifications. There are many ways of doing this. For our purpose the following classification is useful: (1) by types of product (goods or service) and (2) by major function, for example, manufacturing, marketing, finance, transportation, professional service, and so on. Let us now proceed to examine each of these classifications for the purpose of identifying the remaining subfunctions of the operations (production) function.

Acquisition and Conversion of Inputs—Goods

Most of us, when we think of products, think of the various tangible goods produced by manufacturing firms—fabricated wood or metal goods, processed metals, chemicals, foods, and fabrics. In these organizations, raw materials are sent through a series of operations, collectively called a process, that convert the materials through successively different forms to the final form in which it is sold to the immediate customer, say the wholesaler.

Goods are sometimes classified as *consumer goods* and *producer goods*. The former ultimately are used or consumed by individuals or households. The latter, producer goods such as machine tools, are used by producers to make other goods. In a very real sense, producer goods are actually consumed by the user firm. Their consumption is relatively slow, however. A machine tool may operate for 20 years before its usefulness is exhausted.

Chain of Producer-Distributors. Goods are often produced through a long chain of organizations. The chain begins with the extractor (including the farmer) of basic raw materials from the earth, its waters, and its atmosphere. The chain includes a series of organizations that successively convert the product into the form, and at the time and place, desired by the *next immediate user* until finally the last organization in the chain converts the product into the final form desired by the *ultimate user* where and when he wants it. This is shown diagrammatically in Figure 1–3.

The chain shown in Figure 1–3 is sometimes more usefully conceived as a chain of functions rather than of organizations. From the standpoint of *functional analysis* and decision making, as opposed to institutional analysis, the concept of a chain of functions is quite useful. Also, a chain of functions implies time and place characteristics in their outputs, thus

[3] The subject of product planning is treated fully in L. N. Goslin, *The Product Planning System* (Irwin Series in Operations Management [Homewood, Ill.: Richard D. Irwin, Inc., 1967]).

FIGURE 1–3
Chain of Producer-Distributors of Goods

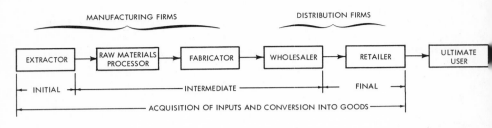

enabling us to employ meaningfully the economist's concept of "utilities" inherent in an output. That is, every product may be characterized as providing form, time, and place utilities to the user. This concept is employed in subsequent explanations of operations in various types of organizations. *Our interest in this text is in the functional aspects of operations conducted throughout the chain, not the institutional aspects.* Some goods, such as producer goods, do not move through so long a chain of organizations as that shown in Figure 1–3. They are sold by the fabricator directly to the ultimate user. Nevertheless, all the functions required to provide the product in the final form, and at the time and place desired by the ultimate user, are performed, *regardless of the number of organizations in the chain.*

Operations in Manufacturing Firms. In this class of organization, which includes the extractors, processors, and fabricators illustrated in Figure 1–3, various *inputs are acquired,* such as raw materials, physical facilities, and human skills. These inputs are then organized and operated as sets of conversion operations, called processes, that *convert* the inputs into a finished good or several goods simultaneously (joint products). The operations comprising the conversion process usually are called "stages" by the economist.[4]

In manufacturing, the spatial and time aspects of the conversion process can be extremely complex. Various raw materials may be sent through a number of processing work stations performing at varying rates in rather widely separated places. The outputs of these conversion processes are in semifinished form, for example outputs of work stations[5]

---

[4] Professor Nadler calls these conversion processes "work systems." See G. Nadler, *Work Systems Design: The IDEALS Concept* (Irwin Series in Operations Management [Homewood, Ill.: Richard D. Irwin, Inc., 1967]). His concept of work systems also applies to the production of services as explained in his text.

[5] An unfortunate conflict in terminology has arisen because the term "operations" has in recent years become identified with production in any organization (as explained earlier). For many years the term "operation" was used in manufacturing to identify the activity done at a "work station." A combination of work stations constitutes a "process." Thus a manufacturing process is a set of work stations at each of which

2A, 2B, and 2C in Figure 1–4. These semifinished goods are then converted in various combinations at various rates to a higher stage of semifinished condition (output of work station 3 in Figure 1–4.) The converting continues until the product is in the final state in which it is sold by the manufacturer to his immediate customer, perhaps a wholesaler. This final state need not be, and often is not, the form in which the ultimate consumer purchases the good; nor does this final manufactured state exist at the appropriate time and place for the ultimate customer. This, of course, is the reason for the existence of other organizations in the chain of producer-distributors, for instance the wholesaler and the retailer shown earlier in Figure 1–3.

FIGURE 1–4

Conversion Processes in a Manufacturing Firm

LEGEND: ◯ = A CONVERSION WORK STATION ⇨ = FLOW OF MATERIALS

Each of the numbered work stations shown in Figure 1–4 has unique inputs and often a unique rate of conversion into outputs that are of a form, and at the place and time, appropriate for the next conversion work station. For instance, *the outputs of work stations 2A, 2B, and 2C become inputs to work station 3.* Hence, the provision of form, time, and place utilities in the product takes place in increments throughout the total conversion process *within* the manufacturing firm, as well as *between* firms in the chain of producer-distributors.

Planning and organizing these incremental steps or stages can be extremely complex. In other cases it can be relatively simple. It can range in complexity from the simple single-work station (single-stage) process of pressing finished metal ashtrays in a punch press to the complex operations required to refine crude oil into the joint products of gasoline, kerosene, and asphalt.

From this brief description of production in the manufacturing firm, we may abstract the basic subfunctions of (1) *acquiring inputs* and (2)

---

an operation is performed. While unfortunate, the conflict cannot be resolved by "turning back the clock." In any case, the conflict is not so great as to cause much difficulty.

converting them into an output in a form, and at a time and place, appropriate to the needs of the next work station (or organization) and finally of the ultimate user.

Perhaps this is the appropriate place to mention that one or more inputs to a work station may be acquired by purchase as well as by production. For instance, one of the inputs to work station 4 in Figure 1–4 is a purchased item. It is used as an input in work station 4 in the form in which it is acquired from the supplier.[6]

Operations in Marketing Firms. In the wholesaling and retailing types of firms, the same two basic functions take place as in manufacturing firms. That is, the firm produces an output and distributes this output. The production function is concerned with the supply side. The distribution function is concerned with the demand side. In the marketing type of business, the distribution (marketing) function predominates, hence the name "marketing firm." The conduct of the marketing function absorbs the bulk of the resources used by the marketing firm and thus demands the major attention of management. Nevertheless, *the production function is performed in the marketing firm.*

The product in its finished state at the manufacturing plant often is not in the final form nor at the appropriate place and time desired by the ultimate user. The wholesaling and retailing firms must complete the basic function of *converting* goods acquired from the manufacturer into the form and at the time and place desired by their immediate customers. In order to do this, the various needed *inputs must be acquired* at the appropriate time and place and in appropriate quantities. Furthermore, a conversion process takes place within the wholesaling or retailing firm similar to that in the manufacturing firm.

The retailer acquires his major input, goods, from the wholesaler in relatively small quantities, usually in advance of receiving customer's orders. These goods ordinarily are in bulk form, for example, cartons of canned peaches. Or the goods may be in semiassembled form, such as baby carriages with the handles, wheels, and tops unassembled for more economical packing and shipping by the wholesaler or the fabricator. The retailer then converts the goods from the form in which he acquired them into the form in which he sells them, for example, a single can of peaches or a completely assembled baby carriage.

Associated closely with the process of converting the form of the goods from their acquired state to the state in which they are sold to the im-

---

[6] The acquisition of physical and service inputs by purchase from suppliers is explained fully in Wilbur B. England, *The Purchasing System* (Irwin Series in Operations Management [Homewood, Ill.: Richard D. Irwin, Inc., 1967]). The acquisition of human skills (other than through purchased services)—the manning or personnel function—is not covered in this series. This function serves the entire firm: production, finance, distribution, etc., and in any case would require a full-length text in personnel management for proper treatment.

mediate customer is *the task of providing time and place utility in the goods.* A can of peaches in a carton misplaced in the storeroom of the retailer, or worse, on order with the wholesaler, is not in the most salable state. To set the stage most effectively for selling, the can of peaches should be placed where the customers can see it and rapidly gain possession of it. Potatoes in the farmer's storage bin in Idaho or Maine provide little time or place utility to a customer in Chicago.

Providing goods at the right time and place calls for scheduling receipt of the inputs at the proper time and scheduling internal processes such as receiving, counting, inspecting, storing, and transporting the goods to the point of sale, for example, the soft goods counter. The retailer will acquire the goods from the wholesaler by purchase if they are separate companies, by requisition if the wholesaler and the retailer are under common ownership. *All of the processes involved in acquiring and converting inputs can be considered production subfunctions* except for the decisions on final arrangement of the goods to catch the customer's eye at the point of sale. These latter decisions fall in the category of sales promotion.

A similar analysis can be made of the functions of the wholesaler in the chain of business institutions. The wholesaler acquires his major input, goods, along with other necessary inputs, in bulk form in advance of customers' orders and in relatively large quantities. He schedules the receipt of these inputs, receives them, inspects, stores, and finally transports the goods to the selling site. These internal processes provide form, time, and place utilities in the goods. They are the equivalent of the conversion processes of the manufacturer. The wholesaler's conversion process can range from what amounts to zero conversion to a rather complex series of processes, just as in manufacturing. Zero conversion applies to the case where the product is sold in exactly the same form as it is acquired. This is the case, also, for goods in retailing.

On the other hand, form conversion can be a rather complex set of processes in the wholesaling firm. For instance, the farm equipment wholesaler usually acquires farm implements in a disassembled condition called a "bundle." The implements are shipped in this form for economy in transportation and to minimize damage. The wholesaler receives and stores the implements in bundle form, displaying one completely assembled implement of each type for sales purposes. Upon receipt of a customer's order, he draws a bundle from stock and assembles it to fill the order. This conversion process can be simple or relatively complex, just as in the case of the manufacturer. On simple implements, it consists of one or two simple work systems. On others, it may consist of a number of somewhat complex work systems requiring relatively highly skilled operators and somewhat complex physical facilities as inputs. Finally, the implement may not be completely assembled. Certain components such as headlights may be shipped in a knockdown state for safety in transport

ailer (farm equipment dealer). Here the retailer and/or the
istomer must complete the conversion function.

ine range of form conversion in wholesaling and retailing firms
can vary from zero on up to a rather complex set of processes. *Actually,
the case of zero conversion is rare. Even where the good appears to be
sold in exactly the same form as it is acquired, inspection often takes
place to cull out the damaged and inferior items.* This inspection may be
a simple process of visually checking for obvious faults in the product as
it is received from the supplier, or it can be a more formal inspection as
in the case of the druggist spot-testing a newly opened container of a
chemical before he produces a prescription. In any case, conversion of
inputs resulting in relatively little change in the form of the product is
not the total conversion function of production. *Total conversion includes
changes in time and place characteristics of the goods.* This is done by
all wholesalers and retailers, as well as manufacturers.

Acquisition and Conversion of Inputs—Services

One can quickly think of businesses, and especially nonbusinesses
such as government agencies, whose products are not tangible goods,
but *intangibles that can be called services.* Examples are the financial
institutions that convert savings (money or near-moneys such as checks)
into various services such as savings, deposit, insurance or loan services.
Also, there are businesses producing various types of transportation
services such as railroad, trucking, and airline services. This section of
the chapter is devoted to an analysis of the functions of service organizations for the purpose of abstracting the unique activities constituting the
production or operations function.

Operations in Financial Institutions. The investment firm, such as
Diversified Investors, Inc., produces for its customer the service of
converting his savings into earning assets. These are the product of the
firm. The investment firm may have a "product line," just as the manufacturing firm does. For instance the output of the investment firm may
be AAA industrial bonds, municipal bonds, and blue chip stocks. The
investment firm may convert the input of customers' savings into products
in advance of receiving the individual customer's order. In other words,
the firm may carry an inventory of products for ready sale to individual
customers. Or it may convert the individual customer's savings into a
particular product only after receiving his order, thus not carrying an
inventory of that product. Or it may do both.

The commercial bank *acquires the input of savings* and, along with
other inputs such as physical facilities and human skills, *converts them
into various products,* such as time deposits, demand deposits, personal
loans, and business loans. Hence, the bank has its "product line." The
production function in commercial banks, as in other financial institu-

tions, is not easily identified in all its detail. Internal operation of financial institutions is heavily compromised by external factors such as governmental monetary policy and banking regulations.[7] Therefore, internal operations are heavily technological in nature.[8]

The financial firm gets its name because it deals in financial media. It produces time, form, and place characteristics in its product. The concept of form utility need not be confined to real goods; it can be applied usefully to an intangible output. The major input to a financial institution is savings, usually in the form of money or near-moneys such as checks. Its output is in other *forms* of money or near-moneys. The products also have time and place characteristics desired by customers. For instance, the demand deposit permits the user to cash a check at almost any place where he is known and at almost any time. These characteristics, together with the fact that checks are a safe and easy form in which to carry and send a medium of exchange through the mails, constitute the utilities of this product to the user.

As in the manufacturing firm and the marketing firm, the financial firm must *acquire inputs and convert them* into one or more products that are services in various forms and with peculiar time and place characteristics. Acquisition and conversion are major functions of producing the product. The inputs must be scheduled, received, inspected, recorded, stored, and transferred (physically and on the books of account) until the process of conversion into various outputs is completed. These functions include many of the internal operations of a bank and are subfunctions of the basic production functions of acquiring inputs and converting them into products with characteristics customers desire.

Operations in Transportation Firms. The railroad firm uses inputs of various kinds, for example the railbed, rolling stock, and human skills, to produce a product called transportation service. This product can take several forms which are the equivalent of a product line in goods. The forms may be passenger service of various types, such as commuter service and express service. Other forms may be freight service such as LCL service, "piggyback" service, and "fishyback" service.

In producing these various service products, the rail transportation firm *acquires various inputs* in the proper quantities and at the appropriate times and places for *conversion into a service* of the form and at the time and place desired by certain customers.

A similar analysis of other transportation firms such as motor transport

---

[7] For an analysis of bank operation in which, "By appropriate translation and adaptation of the concepts of the economic theory of the firm to banking, we have tried to come up with an operational model," see David A. Alhadeff and Charlotte P. Alhadeff, "An Integrated Model for Commercial Banks," *The Journal of Finance*, Vol. XII, No. 1 (March, 1957), pp. 24–43.

[8] In this text we use the term "technology" in its broadest sense; that is, it covers applied science of all types: engineering, medicine, law, accounting, and so forth.

and airline service can be made. In all of them, various inputs are acquired and converted into various forms of transportation service with various time and place characteristics. These acquisition and conversion functions are basic activities in producing the service output.

Operations in Professional Service Firms. Certain firms produce a class of service in which the unique input is specialized human skill of a professional nature. Examples are legal firms, certified public accounting firms, engineering consulting firms, and government agencies.

The legal firm provides the service of representing clients in legal matters. One major service, that of defending a client in court, requires that evidence be acquired and, through the specialized professional skill of the lawyer, converted into the form of an appropriate defense or complaint. The unique input is the skill of the lawyer. A necessary input that must be acquired is the information that constitutes evidence. The lawyer converts the raw evidence into a defense of the appropriate form and at the proper time and place, all as governed by legal codes and court procedure. Here we have an example of a chain involving two organizations: a legal firm dealing with a governmental body—the court.

The public accounting firm likewise acquires the input of information and, through the unique professional input of the accountant, converts this information into a form and at a time and place desired by the customer. For instance, a set of financial statements conforming to legal and professional specifications is placed in the hands of the customer's chief financial officer soon after the close of the accounting period.

In all of these professional service firms, *information of particular kinds, much of which comes voluntarily from the customer* or the user, must be acquired and, along with other inputs, converted into the final form desired by customers. And there is usually a time and location constraint involved in rendering the service. It would seem that the unique input in such firms is the professional skill involved in the conversion process. Although the informational input is necessary, the particular *kind* of information needed is usually determined by the professional himself. In all of these professional service firms, physical facilities are secondary inputs. Desks, books, typewriters, chairs, telephones, and other physical facilities are necessary to produce the service effectively and efficiently.

Operations in Miscellaneous Service Firms. There are a number of firms which are often called service firms, but which in fact may be considered producers of goods. For instance, there are firms calling themselves typing services, repair services, and laundry services.

The firm specializing in typing service acquires the input of information to be typed and, along with other inputs, converts this information into typed form. The conversion process calls for application of the specialized input, typing skill, to produce the product. Physical facilities such as desks, chairs, typewriters, and paper are necessary inputs.

Probably the unique input is the typewriter-typist combination. As opposed to professional service firms, the typing firm is a vocational service firm. Nevertheless, the *various inputs are acquired and converted into a product*—a typed manuscript of the form and at the time and place desired by the customer. Actually, a tangible good in the form of a typed manuscript is produced by this "service."

In a repair service business, goods needing repair are the unique input. The vocational skill of the repairman is brought to bear on this input, together with inputs of physical facilities such as tools, to provide a goods in the form (repaired) at the time and place desired by the customer.

In a laundry service business, the soiled clothes are the unique input. Together with the vocational skill of the laundryman and the inputs of various physical facilities such as laundering equipment, the soiled goods are converted through a series of operations into the form of clean goods.

TYPES OF PRODUCTION

In this section of the chapter our purpose is to classify the various types of production and analyze the unique characteristics of each type. This is no mere exercise in classification for its own sake. We do this because production, when observed across the board in all types of institutions, appears so utterly complex a subject as to be unmanageable. By observing the unique characteristics of various types of production, we can understand more fully the situations giving rise to the various problems associated with each type. Thus prepared, we can recognize the applicability of decision processes developed for any one type of production in all types of organizations.

Manufacturing Business—Model for Study of Production

Most texts on the subject of production have been concerned almost exclusively with the manufacturing type of business. In fact, the greater number have been concerned mostly with metalworking manufacture. The reason generally given for this preoccupation with metalworking is that production of complex metal goods, usually containing many components which are made into subassemblies and thence into the final product, poses the most complex set of problems of any type of production.[9] This is undoubtedly true.

A second reason is that fabrication of metal goods constitutes a significantly large segment of our gross national product (aggregate production of goods and services). This should be obvious, without citing figures, by merely looking about and observing all the metal goods

---

[9] See Franklin G. Moore, *Production Control* (2d ed.; New York: McGraw-Hill Book Co., Inc., 1959), p. 2.

in daily use in our society. The prevalence of metalworking production and the complexity deriving from its multistage nature serve to make the metalworking model a highly useful one. Perhaps the best testimony to this fact is the rapidly increasing use of trained industrial engineers in all types of organizations ranging as far afield from metalworking as banking, hospitals, and department stores.[10]

There is another reason for using metalworking as a model for studying production, one that is more germane to our purpose. The *economic* aspects of the production function in the multistage operations of metalworking are highly complex. It is assumed that the reader is familiar with simple, single-stage production functions as explained in principles of economics. In a text such as this, it is appropriate that we study the more complex production function. Therefore, we shall take many but not all of our problem situations from metalworking production. However, we will then go on to show, particularly in other books in this series, the applicability of these analytical processes to production in other types of organizations.

There is a final compelling reason for using metalworking as the model for a study of the production function. In many other types of firms the technological aspects (rather than the economic aspects) of problems are paramount in production. In extreme cases, there is no choice between alternative sets of inputs to achieve a desired output. Hence, there is no economic aspect involved. For instance, if there is only one technologically feasible way of producing penicillin, the economic aspects of this production function are severely circumscribed if not completely eliminated.

Since we are concerned in this text principally with the economic aspects of production[11] rather than the technological aspects, it is appropriate that we choose as our model that type of production in which the economic aspects usually govern the final choice of inputs. We are not concerned directly with selection and use of inputs where there is no choice except that which is strictly technological. If we were, we would be forced to get into the technological details of accounting, law, banking, engineering, and so on, for which there is insufficient space in one text.

Frequently in firms where the choice of inputs is largely constrained by technological considerations, managers lack an awareness of those internal situations where an economic choice of inputs does exist. In such cases they are relatively poor managers of the internal use of physical

---

[10] For a comprehensive description of the work of industrial engineers in all types of organizations see the entire issue of the *Journal of Industrial Engineering*, Vol. XV, No. 5 (September–October, 1964). See also, *ibid.*, Vol. XVI, No. 1 (January–February, 1964), p. 19, p. 30, and p. 65; also Vol. XVI, No. 2 (March–April, 1965), p. 65, p. 109, p. 119.

[11] Other texts in this series treat "behavioral" as well as economic considerations in operations.

facilities, human skills, and materials. Almost everyone has heard it said of a failure in a service business, for example a law firm, "He was a good lawyer but a poor manager." Only in relatively recent years have such firms been forced, under the pressure of competition, to learn the analytical methods of the economist and the industrial engineer. All indications are that this trend will continue and intensify—which it should for the benefit of society.

In analyzing the various types of production, we find that two broad classifications are useful: (1) production to order and (2) production for stock replenishment. Further, we find that three classifications *within* each of these two are useful: (1) jobbing or "slow-moving" production, (2) continuous production, and (3) intermittent production.[12]

Production to Order and for Stock

The first classification of production is related directly to the product planning function of production examined earlier in this chapter. If, in product planning, the product specifications cannot be determined in advance of dealing with the individual customer, production is to customer's order, not for stock in advance of the receipt of customers' orders. On the other hand, *if product specifications can be established with reasonable certainty that they will meet customer needs and desires without dealing directly with individual customers, production may be undertaken for stock in advance of the receipt of customers' orders.* For instance, the production of homes may be to order or for stock. When the builder puts up single homes to individual customers' specifications, he is producing "to order." When a builder puts up homes in advance of customers' orders (the so-called speculation builder), he is producing for stock. He owns a stock of homes.

The product specifications in production to order may be known in advance only in a very general way, if at all. Details may be almost completely unknown. For instance, a subcontracting machine shop may know only that its products will be metal goods requiring general machining processes. The sizes and shapes of the products and the types and unit amounts of the unique input, raw metals, are unknown. Product specifications, although generalized as machined metal goods, are particularized only when the individual customer comes to the producer with a request to produce a certain item. Therefore, this type of manufacturer cannot produce for stock in advance of dealing with particular customers.

---

[12] Many writers on the subject of production in the manufacturing firm, particularly the metalworking or fabricating type of firm, prefer the classification (1) intermittent production and (2) continuous production. Even with the restriction to metalworking firms, this classification is lacking in usefulness. It frequently forces the analyst into creating a large catchall type of production as a third classification.

At this point, a cautionary digression is appropriate. The reader who is acquainted with various types of manufacturing institutions may find it somewhat difficult at first to discern the unique types of production from a *functional* viewpoint. We are interested in the functional aspects of production, not the institutional aspects, as indicated earlier in the chapter. The reader is cautioned to keep this in mind, and the following example may help.

When an automobile manufacturer produces a special limousine for the President, some of the components are drawn from standard (specifications) stock, part of which was produced intermittently and part continuously. The special attachments that make the limousine "special," such as a rear-compartment writing desk and a refreshment cabinet, are produced and assembled to the customer's order, not for stock in advance of the customer's order.

Many goods-producing firms simultaneously carry on various types of production such as jobbing to order, continuous to order, intermittent for stock, or other combinations. Rarely if ever will a firm be found in which only one type of production exists for very long. The mix of production types varies through time in the typical firm. Because of the inherent flexibility of many of his inputs, the producer may change economically the types of production he undertakes from time to time as market conditions, particularly sales volume, change.

Hereafter we shall cite various institutions from whose mix of production we discern a certain type. When we do so, there is no implication that this is the only type of production performed by the firm. Furthermore, no attempt is made to classify institutions in terms of the type of production that predominates in them. This apparently can be done, although rarely very clearly. For instance, some people classify automobile manufacturers as continuous producers, presumably because the assembly line runs continuously. However, many components of the automobile are produced intermittently for stock, from which they are drawn to feed the assembly line. Just what criterion is used to indicate the predominance of continuous production over intermittent production in automobile manufacturing firms is not made clear.

In production to order, *the unique characteristic is the uncertainty of product specifications.* As a result, details of conversion operations, including types and unit amounts of input, are for the most part unknown. The builder of bridges may know that he will use steel in most of the orders he receives, but the particular types, for example I beams of certain metallurgical characteristics and sizes, he does not know until he initiates production—that is, until he performs the product planning function for a particular bridge.

Production to order is what is often called custom building. The implication is production to the individual customer's unique specifications, which typically are expected to be considerably different from those of other customers, at least from a production viewpoint. Additional examples of production of goods to order are the manufacture of observatory domes, Indianapolis Speedway racing cars, and electric turbine generator units for the power plants of large dams. *It will be noted that the above examples are all of the low-volume type. This is not the reason for their being classified as production to order, however. The reason is solely the uncertainty of product specifications.* Production to order may be undertaken when expected sales volume is high, as subsequent examples will indicate.

Production for stock, on the other hand, may be undertaken when the details of product specifications can be decided in advance of receiving customers' orders. Through market research the firm will decide the nature (general specifications) of the product, for example, cigarettes, that will satisfy most customers' needs and desires for some time to come. Then the general specifications will be refined and detailed for production purposes (technical specifications). Thus, the product planning function is essentially complete before individual customers' orders are received by the producer. The firm may then produce the product to replenish finished goods stock as it is depleted through sales to customers.

The unique aspect of production for stock is the certainty of product specifications. As a result, the conversion operations, including the types and amount of the various inputs per unit of product, can be determined in advance of the receipt of customers' orders. Furthermore, the acquisition of inputs can proceed without direct reference to individual orders for the product. Acquisition can be for stock because of the certainty of the details of input specifications.

It should be noted that *this two-way classification of production to order and for stock is a discrete classification. All production falls into one class or the other.* The two classes are not points on a continuum.

Influence of Sales Volume on Production

The second method of classifying production is related to *the expected sales volume or quantity of the product demanded by customers per period of time*, say one year or one selling season. If the demand for a product of particular specifications is expected to be very low, production will be done most economically on a so-called jobbing or slow-moving basis. If the demand is expected to be very large, as in the case of goods which are "mass marketed," production will be most economical when done on a continuous basis. If the expected demand is not of such volume as to warrant economically either continuous production or jobbing production, but something in between the two extremes, intermittent production of lots or batches is the economically appropriate type. *Thus we can have the three types of production: jobbing, continuous, and intermittent, taking place within the two broader types: production to order and production for stock.*

The expected sales volume heavily influences managerial decision making in all the subfunctions of production (and all other major functions of the firm). Expected volume of sales to particular specifications dictates the product specifications and the nature of the inputs used in the production process. This is a question of economics rather than one of technology. Obviously, it would be uneconomical to use a high-priced machine tool to perform a production operation on only a few goods a year, with the machine tool standing idle much of the time unless, of course, its use in this manner permits an offsetting cost reduction elsewhere in operations.

Furthermore, the extent or volume of the market dictates the degree to which specialized inputs can be used in conversion operations.[13] In extreme cases of low expected volume, machines, which are really only a highly specialized form of labor of a roundabout variety, cannot be used economically at all. Hand labor is the appropriate form to use. This is evident in various aspects of building construction work.

The influence of sales volume on the nature of the physical facilities used in production extends to the use of human skills and even to raw materials in goods production. In designing production processes, the technologically feasible *combinations* of inputs are the ones that are candidates for economical selection. Therefore, *the influence of the extent of the market extends to the choice of all inputs and their use.* Finally, since the product should be designed to facilitate low-cost production, given the product general specifications, the expected volume of sales plays a large role in product technical design.

Continuous and Discontinuous Production

Unlike the classification of production by certainty of product specifications into two discrete categories, namely to order and for stock, classification by volume actually does not lend itself to discrete categories as we have implied by identifying three types, namely jobbing, intermittent, and continuous. While there is a certain usefulness in three such classifications, as explained in other texts in this series, a strictly accurate designation would be "continuous and discontinuous." Actually, production can hardly be "classified" by volume, as in fact the volume of production can be anywhere along a continuum. *The point (or probability distribution) at which the expected sales volume lies on the continuum determines the degree of specialization and standardization*

---

[13] See George Stigler, "The Division of Labor Is Limited by the Extent of the Market," *Journal of Political Economy*, Vol. LIX, No. 3 (June, 1951), pp. 185–93.

that may be employed economically in designing the product and conversion processes, including the inputs.[14]

In specific cases of product and process design, the expected sales volume will enter into appropriately designed decision processes for product and process design as explained more fully in other texts in this series. These decision processes are designed to *yield unique quantitative answers to problems relating to the appropriate degree of specialization to employ* in product and conversion process design, including inputs.

REVIEW QUESTIONS

1. Explain the important aspects of the concept of the organization as a servo-system. How do these aspects help management?
2. Explain how production differs from distribution in respect to the provision of utilities to users.
3. Why can't product planning be considered solely a function of production?
4. What is the purpose of general specifications in product planning?
5. What is the purpose of technical specifications in product planning?
6. Should an organization that offers a service be concerned with technical specifications of its output? Explain.
7. What is the difference between a consumer good and a producer good?
8. Why is it useful to conceive of a chain of producer-distributors as a chain of functions rather than of institutions?
9. Briefly explain the conversion process in manufacturing firms.
10. What are the basic subfunctions of production in the manufacturing firm?
11. What distinguishes a marketing firm from a manufacturing firm?
12. Does the marketing firm perform a production function? Explain.
13. Explain the conversion process in a typical wholesaling firm.
14. What unique activities constitute the production function in financial institutions?
15. Do transportation firms perform any activities that might be considered a production function? Explain.
16. What is by far the most important input in professional service firms? In general, how is this input converted into a service that people want?
17. Why is it advantageous to classify the various types of production?
18. Why do most texts on the subject of production often concentrate on metalworking manufacturing?
19. What is the relationship between certainty of product specifications and production for stock?
20. What is the unique characteristic of production to order?
21. Which of the following products do you think are normally produced well

---

[14] This is the point of Stigler's article referred to in footnote reference 13.

in advance of customers' orders? Only for order? Think of situations where exceptions from the "normal" are possible.

a) Slide rules	*i*) Steel ingots
b) Men's suits	*j*) Dies
c) Hand-painted pictures	*k*) Sugar
d) Industrial boilers	*l*) Television sets
e) Engine-block milling machine	*m*) Kitchen cabinets
f) Textbooks	*n*) Legal cases
g) Insurance policies	*o*) Profit and loss statements
h) Ice cream sundaes	*p*) Service by the NLR Board

22. What is the relationship between sales volume and the type of production?

SUGGESTIONS FOR FURTHER STUDY

BOWMAN, EDWARD H., AND FETTER, ROBERT B. *Analysis for Production Management*, chap. i. Rev. ed. Homewood, Ill.: Richard D. Irwin, Inc., 1961.
    Chapter 1 contains a brief discussion of the functions of production and the major economic problems of production management.

BUFFA, ELWOOD S. *Modern Production Management*, chap. iii. New York: John Wiley & Sons, Inc., 1961.
    Chapter 3 presents a discussion of the production function in business as well as a generalized descriptive model of production.

DAVIS, RALPH CURRIER. *Industrial Organization and Management*, chap. xv. 3d ed. New York: Harper & Brothers, 1956.
    Chapter 15 is concerned primarily with production control but includes a good discussion of types of industry and types of production.

MEE, JOHN, F. "Marketing-Dominated Economy," *Business Horizons*, Vol. 7, No. 3 (Fall, 1964), pp. 63–64.
    Author briefly discusses the evolution of our "market-dominated" economy and what this means to the organization and operation of the business firm.

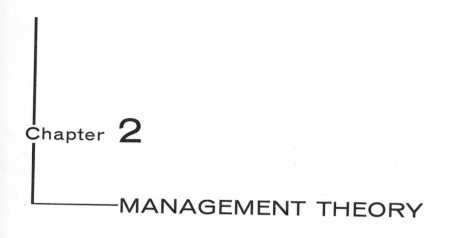

Chapter 2

MANAGEMENT THEORY

INTRODUCTION

CHAPTER 1 dealt with the nature of the operations function.

This chapter deals with the nature of managing, or management theory. This seems appropriate, as the text is concerned with the analysis of major problems arising in operations *management*.

In a very real sense, a logical system of thought about management is an abstraction from the actual complex practice of managing. If the abstraction is not too drastic, it ought to *provide a useful framework for discerning the major problems of operations management and for developing analytical processes for their solution.* In addition, a logical system of thought about management *provides a general model within which more particularized models for solving specific problems in operations can be built.* Finally, a logical system of thought about managing *facilitates effective communications.*

NATURE OF MANAGING

Thoughtful people have inquired into the nature of management, or managing, for many years. The history of this inquiry goes back to at least the turn of this century. Even earlier roots may be identified, such as Adam Smith's explanation of the effect of division of labor, or specialization, on productivity in his book, *The Wealth of Nations*, published in 1776. However, most students of management identify the beginning of the development of a theory or philosophy of management in the United States with Frederick W. Taylor, who in 1911 published *The Principles of Scientific Management.* At about the same time, Europeans were writing on the *process* of management. One of the earliest of these books was Henri Fayol's *Organization*, published in 1916.[1]

---

[1] For a comprehensive treatment of the development of management thought, see Harold F. Smiddy and Lionel Naum, "Evolution of a Science of Managing in America,"

Science versus Art in Managing

The practice of management is generally considered to fall within the social sciences, as opposed to the natural sciences, such as physics and chemistry. To the extent that managing is a science rather than an art, this is undoubtedly an appropriate way to view management. There are many, however, particularly those who view managing as essentially providing leadership, who consider management an art. On the other hand, there are those who firmly believe that management is a science, and make a strong case for it.[2]

Actually, modern management can usefully be characterized as a mixture of art and science. In this sense it is very much like the practice of engineering, or medicine, in which the basic sciences such as physics, chemistry, biology, physiology, etc., are applied to the solution of practical problems. A knowledge of underlying basic science is required, and in this sense at least, the practice of management, or engineering, or medicine, is scientific. However, the creativity, imagination, and intuition required to successfully *apply* the underlying sciences are undoubtedly art of some sort.

The question of theory arises as part of the question of whether management is a science or an art. Scientists in general would assert that if the practice of management is based upon theory, then it is a so-called *applied science*. Dutton and Starbuck state, ". . . in the general sense of the term, theory is necessary for reaching a decision on any cognitive problem. Both art and science require theory, the dividing line between them being largely a matter of communication." They go on to say, "The dividing line between science and art is not sharp. There is art in all science and science in all art. Some sciences contain a large element of artistry, psychoanalysis or the development of the hybrid corn plant being examples. On the other hand, most experienced painters know a good deal about the chemistry of pigments and many sculptors know a good bit about mechanics, metallurgy and geology."[3]

Perhaps the important point to make is that the *practice* of manage-

Management Science, Vol. I (October, 1954), pp. 1–31. See also Alan J. Levy, "New Developments in Management," *The Journal of Industrial Engineering*, Vol. XVI, No. 3 (May–June, 1965), pp. 171–77. For a comprehensive treatment of the interrelationships between the development of management thought and major social developments, see John F. Mee, *Management Thought in a Dynamic Economy* (New York: New York University Press, 1963).

2 See Luther Gulick, "Management Is a Science," *Academy of Management Journal*, Vol. 8, No. 1 (March, 1965), pp. 7–13.

3 John M. Dutton and William H. Starbuck, "On Managers and Theories," Purdue University, Herman C. Krannert Graduate School of Industrial Administration, Reprint Series No. 86, p. 4 (reprinted from *Management International* [Germany: Betriebswirtschaftlicher Verlag], 1963, No. 6, p. 27).

ment involves problem solving, devising
courses of action in many perplexing sit
finding the best combinations of scarce
objectives. Successful managers draw on ev
arrive at appropriate solutions to the many
economics, mathematics, psychology, socic
sciences. They often cannot, or at least do n
the ways in which they draw on the various
normally employ the method of the scienti
facts rather than conjecture. Their reasonin
based upon observation, their collective o
perience."[4]

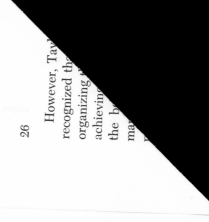

Definition of Management

There are on record many definitions of management offered by
qualified practitioners and observers. Dr. John F. Mee lists four such
definitions by recognized authorities.[5] These definitions are very much
alike, and all cite a similar *process* involved in managing. This process
includes *functions* such as *planning, organizing, integrating, coordinating,
measuring, and controlling.*

An early definition offered by Frederick W. Taylor, considered by
many to be the founder of modern scientific management, was as follows:
"[Management is] knowing exactly what you want men to do, and then
seeing that they do it in the best and cheapest way."[6] This definition,
emphasizing as it does "the best and cheapest way," reflects Taylor's
interest in efficiency. Input-output relationships occupied an important
part of Taylor's framework of managing. Therefore, his system is useful
in analyzing the economic aspects of the problems of production
management.[7] Perhaps Taylor's major contribution to management
thought was his *stress on the application of the scientific method* to the
solution of problems of management—particularly in production, where
a great deal of his business experience was gained.

---

[4] For other articles on the nature of the manager, see Laurence A. Appley, "The
Professional Manager," *Mechanical Engineering,* Vol. 86, No. 3 (March, 1965), pp.
38–39; Herbert Southoff, "What Is the Manager," *Harvard Business Review,* Vol. 42,
No. 6 (November–December, 1964), p. 24; S. Benjamin Prasad, "The Profile of the
Managerial Mind," *Academy of Management Journal,* Vol. 8, No. 1 (March, 1965),
pp. 44–47.

[5] Mee, *op. cit.,* pp. 9–10.

[6] Frederick W. Taylor, *Shop Management* (New York: Harper & Brothers, 1919),
p. 21.

[7] Some writers trace the origin of modern scientific management to the writings of
Charles Babbage in 1832. It is interesting to note that the title of his work, *On the
Economy of Machinery and Manufactures,* implied that economics, as well as human
relations, is a proper interest of managers.

lor's definition also stressed "seeing that they do it." He
t management is concerned with more than planning and
he use of resources for efficiency reasons. It is concerned with
performance on the part of the managed. Taylor recognized
havioral or motivational aspect of the problems of production
nagement. "No concise definition can fully describe an art [of
management], but the relations between employers and workers form
without question the most important part of this art."[8] However, the
public and many writers tended to focus on his treatment of efficiency,
his stress on the planning and organizing functions of management,
forgetting that he clearly saw management as being concerned with
people and their motivations.[9]

Since World War II, writers on the subject of management have
tended to swing over to the lightly stressed aspect of Taylor's definition.
They now stress relations between people as the central aspect of
managing. A number of writers define management as "the function of
getting things done through people." This would imply that management is not so much concerned with what people *should* do as with
ensuring that the job gets done. The emphasis here is on achieving
performance on the part of the managed. The swing away from the
economic aspects of the problems of the manager to the behavioral
aspects is probably a natural reaction to the earlier emphasis on efficiency
in the use of resources. It is certainly a healthy reaction which has led to
a fuller understanding and appreciation of what management is all about.
However, as often happens in human affairs, the pendulum has probably
swung too far. More will be said about this in the next section of this
chapter. For now, let us complete our treatment of the definition of
management.

A definition of management which indicates that the manager is
interested in choice in the use of *all* resources to achieve objectives is
quite realistic and useful. It permits a better integration of the disciplines
of economics and the behavioral sciences for the betterment of management practice. Accordingly, perhaps a return to a Taylor-type definition
of management, with its stress on both the economic choice of resources
and the behavioral aspects of management, is desirable. The definition
used in this text is: *Management is the practice of deciding for others
(the managed) the use of all resources, and getting others to implement
these decisions.* This definition also stresses the decision-making role of

---

[8] Taylor, *op cit.*, p. 21.

[9] Taylor did not stress what today is called the "behavioral" aspect of managing if
for no other reason than the behavioral sciences were undeveloped in his day. In fact,
even today many members of the so-called hard sciences (physics, chemistry, etc.)
question whether or not the so-called soft social or behavioral sciences ought to be
labeled "sciences." This is undoubtedly an extreme view of the matter.

management, and is therefore appropriate for the purposes of this text as stated in the preface.

EMERGING MANAGEMENT THEORY

Unfortunately, there is no single system of thought or theory of managing that is universally accepted as being definitive in all its details. Each writer believes his system is the most useful, and undoubtedly it is to him. At first impression, the student of management may be somewhat disconcerted with the apparent welter of opinion on the details of a suitable framework for thinking about management practice. Often the student's reaction is, "If the experts can't agree, how can I read their writings with confidence?" Implicit in this attitude is the student's desire to know the truth, an appropriate attitude. However, the student should recognize that the search for truth never ends. Just when it is believed that all that is worthwhile about a subject has been put in print, someone comes along with a breakthrough that clearly calls for a revision or reordering of past ideas. Paradoxically, a welter of differing opinion is a healthy condition for the growth of a sturdy body of knowledge on any subject.

Management Theory Jungle

During recent years the controversy over management theory has become so bitter as to cause one well-known representative of the so-called traditionalist school to characterize the situation as a jungle.[10] The traditionalist school of thought generally accepts and builds upon the system of thought developed largely by successful *practitioners* of management: Fayol, Mooney, Alvin Brown, Sheldon, and Urwick,[11] among others. These writers distilled from many years of observation of both successful and unsuccessful management practice what they believed to be rational concepts and principles that explain and permit prediction of management *practice* and enterprise *results.*

The opposing and newer "behavioral school," comprising for the most part academicians in the behavioral sciences (sociology, social psychology, cultural anthropology, and various branches of these "new" sciences) assert that the traditionalist body of thought and particularly the "principles" set forth are "armchair" and a priori, and thus not worthy of being called "theory." For the most part these academicians have had

[10] Harold Koontz, "The Management Theory Jungle," *Academy of Management Journal,* Vol. 4, No. 3 (December, 1961), pp. 174–88.

[11] On the other hand, Chester Barnard, a successful practitioner of management, provided many of the antecedents for the current behavioral school of thought. See his *The Functions of the Executive* (Cambridge, Mass.: Harvard University Press, 1938).

little experience in the practice of management and therefore appear not to appreciate the results of intelligent observation by management practitioners. They would prefer to see the theory develop through controlled experimentation and thus be more scientific.[12] This begs the question of whether or not it is possible to develop a *theory of applying underlying theory*. To date the physicists have not pressed engineers to develop a *theory of engineering* nor have the physiologists pressed the medical doctors to develop a *theory of medicine*. Nor have either tried to do it for them!

In their zeal to advance their thesis the behavioralists have, according to the traditionalists, spent more time tearing down the traditional body of thought than in advancing it through experimentation and testing. And thus, in spite of sober appeals to transcend the debate,[13] the controversy still rages.[14] In the writer's view, all the newer developments since the writings of the original traditionalists, such as operations research, management science, decision theory, behavioral theory of the firm, and so on, are *logical extensions* of the traditional management process. They complement and supplement the thought of the traditional school, rather than conflict with it. Until a given theory of management is universally recognized as definitive, the student should familiarize himself with existing thought. Before the advent of Einstein's theory of relativity, discerning physicists undoubtedly recognized that Newtonian physics was not the complete and last word, if only because there were gaps in his system of thought as evidenced by its failure to explain many natural phenomena. Nevertheless, they used the Newtonian system to the very great advantage of mankind until Einstein's theory proved more generally useful.

Because of the many differing versions of a useful framework for thinking about management, *it is necessary that one particular framework be selected at the start of this text*. Otherwise, author, instructors, and readers cannot hope to communicate effectively. Since the purpose of this presentation is *not* primarily to develop and defend a complete body

---

[12] Industrial engineers for many years have been conducting quite rigorous experiments in the physiological and anthropometric aspects of work, the findings from which form a generally accepted body of thought and principles useful for designing work systems. This is explained fully in Gerald Nadler, *Work Systems Design: The IDEALS Concept* (Irwin Series in Operations Management [Homewood, Ill.: Richard D. Irwin, Inc., 1967]).

[13] Paul J. Gordon, "Transcend the Current Debate on Administrative Theory," *Academy of Management Journal*, Vol. 6, No. 4 (December, 1963), pp. 290–302.

[14] Lyndall F. Urwick, "The Jungle of Management Theory," *Personnel*, Vol. 42, No. 3 (May–June, 1965), pp. 8–18. The student interested in reading further in this controversy will find copious references in this article. The various contributions to management thought by representatives of the various "schools," as presented at a symposium, are given in Harold Koontz (ed.), *Toward a Unified Theory of Management* (New York: McGraw-Hill Book Co., Inc., 1964).

of thought or theory of managing, but rather merely to get tuned in on the same wavelength, an abridged framework is presented here.

THE MANAGEMENT PROCESS

One widely accepted version of the nature of managing is called "the management process" and conceives of *three main steps or functions: planning, organizing, and controlling.*[15] This is a drastic abstraction from actual management work. Nevertheless, it is a useful one. It lies at the heart of the traditionalist school of thought. It is stressed in this text not because the ideas of the behavioral school are considered unworthy of inclusion here, or are somehow wrong, but because it is useful in a decision-making approach to the study of operations management. Various tenets of the behavioral school are also useful in a decision-making approach to any subject, and these are introduced in Chapter 3 where the subject of decision making is treated more fully. The behavioral aspects of management are also included at appropriate points in the other books in this series.

In the version of the management process stated above, the task of *establishing objectives* is taken for granted. The manager can hardly plan meaningfully if he has no idea of what he wants in the end. Omission of the obvious first step in a logical framework of the process of managing, that is, establishing objectives, would render the framework less useful from a decision-making viewpoint. The establishment of an appropriate objective is a necessary first step in problem solving. Analysis using the scientific method calls for the establishment of an objective in the first step of the method. Accordingly, on the grounds of usefulness, the framework of managing used in this text will define the first step in the management process as that of *establishing objectives.*

In the management process broken down into planning, organizing, and controlling, no unique step by management is considered necessary to *ensure performance* of planned work as organized. Most managers with line as opposed to specialized staff experience, probably would not consider this a very useful framework. They are well aware that overt and unique action on the part of the manager is necessary to get planned work underway and to sustain it. Giving the employee a wage often is not enough to accomplish this.[16] Somehow or other the employee must be

---

[15] See R. C. Davis, *Industrial Organization and Management* (New York: Harper & Brothers, 1957), p. 54. Compare the description of "at least six fundamental concepts and steps in the process of administration," George Albert Smith, Jr., and C. Roland Christensen, *Policy Formulation and Administration* (4th ed.; Homewood, Ill.: Richard D. Irwin, Inc., 1962), p. xviii.

[16] This is one of the important findings of the pioneering Hawthorne experiments as reported in F. J. Roethlisberger and William J. Dickson, *Management and the Worker* (Cambridge, Mass.: Harvard University Press, 1950).

motivated to act according to plan, and in this motivating process arise most of the human or behavioral aspects of management. Behavioral scientists probably would not find a framework of managing which assumes away the human aspects—or does not make them explicit—a very useful one.

Those who find it useful to conceive of a unique step in the management process to get performance underway characterize this function in various ways. Those with an authoritarian bent, such as exists to a significant degree in the military, would call this function *direction*. Others less inclined to authoritarianism might call it *supervision*. The behaviorist might call it *motivating*. If it is argued that the functions of planning, organizing, and controlling largely involve economic decision making in that they are concerned principally with choice in the use of scarce resources to achieve desired objectives,[17] then we must include *a unique function for achieving performance*—getting action on the part of the managed. This can be called direction, supervision, or motivating. In our framework it is called *motivating*.

While this text is devoted primarily to a study of the economic aspects of operations management problems, nevertheless the process used here as a model of managing includes the overt function *motivating*. The reason for this is, first, to stress the fact that the economic aspects of business problems are really only abstractions from larger problems that include behavioral or motivational aspects. There is more to managing than planning, organizing, and controlling the use of resources. Second, a framework of managing that includes the function of motivating is useful in building a model organization structure for the production function, as explained in the next section of this chapter.

The arguments presented above may now be summarized by stating that a useful description of the major functions involved in managing are: (1) establishing objectives, (2) planning the work of others (the managed) to achieve the objectives, (3) organizing the planned work so as to have it carried out most effectively and efficiently, (4) motivating (the managed) to carry out the planned work as organized, and (5) controlling the performance of work. This process *takes place at all levels in the hierarchy of management* and *within all departments of an enterprise*. Top management performs the process for the enterprise as a whole; lower level managers perform the process for their departments. The functions comprising the process are not mutually exclusive. On the contrary, they are highly interrelated as, for instance, when a manager plans the control function, or organizes for effective planning. Being

---

[17] See the section "Planning Is Economic" in Harold Koontz and Cyril O'Donnell, *Principles of Management* (2nd ed.; New York: McGraw-Hill Book Co., Inc., 1959), p. 465, and p. 472, "It is in connection with the managerial function of planning that economic theory has much to offer."

interrelated, the functions of management form a "system," a concept that is explained more fully in Chapter 4.

The remainder of this chapter concentrates on the organizing function in the management process. The other functions: establishing objectives, planning and controlling in operations management, are treated in depth in the other books in this series. Further, this text assumes as given "the skill and will to work" on the part of employees, as well as the availability of the needed skills.[18]

Nevertheless, in the following treatment of the organizing function, concepts from the behavioral school of thought are introduced, thus off-setting in part what might be considered a serious omission in not treating at all the very important management function of motivating employees. A full treatment of all the functions of management is best acquired in a *general* management course, which ideally should precede the study of operations management.

ORGANIZING FOR PRODUCTION

The purpose of this section of the chapter is to develop a model organization structure for *production managerial work*. There are several reasons for doing this. First, organizing has its economic aspects. A manager organizes to accomplish planned work efficiently as well as effectively. Second, many of the economic problems of production involve cost elements which are directly the result of the conduct of the production subfunctions. In turn, the conduct of the production functions depends upon their organization. We can generalize this by saying that managerial costs, particularly in a large firm, are significant elements of total cost; and managerial costs depend in great part upon the management organization structure. These points are developed fully in the last book in this series.[19]

Purposes of Organizing

Organization of activity is undertaken for the purpose of carrying out planned activities most effectively and efficiently. *When business activities require the attention of more than one man, the activities, or various aspects of each activity, must be divided between these men.* In fact, one can hardly say that a one-man business is a business *organization*, even though it is a business firm. *As soon as the firm has more than one member, it has an organization structure. The activities of the*

---

[18] This is consistent with the reservation concerning the acquisition of human skills expressed in footnote reference 6 in Chapter 1.

[19] Robert N. Anthony and James S. Hekimian, *Operations Cost Control* (Irwin Series in Operations Management [Homewood, Ill.: Richard D. Irwin, Inc., 1967]).

firm are divided in some fashion between the members. The division of activities may change from time to time as conditions dictate. This does not mean that there is no organization. It merely means that organization of work is changing. In fact, a desirable attribute of organization structure is flexibility.

If the president of a 50-man business were to plan the operation of the business but not organize his 49 men to carry out these plans, it goes without saying that the plans would not be carried out as effectively or as efficiently as they might be. To assume that the 49 men would somehow, on their own, find and maintain (with changing external conditions) an appropriate division of labor is unrealistic. To achieve effectiveness and efficiency, the president will divide the planned activities among the 49 men and himself. *Hence, dividing planned work is the primary aspect of organizing.*

The division of planned work is rarely if ever crisp and clear-cut, however. The professional manager will strive to divide work clearly, but he never can do this perfectly. The reason for this is simple. He wants the men to work together as one. This will also make for effectiveness and efficiency. However, working together as one is the antithesis of separate or divided duties. As soon as the president says, "Joe will do such-and-such work and Bill will do this work," he has brought on problems in communication and coordination because *all of the work of the firm is interrelated.* Actually, what the president does when he organizes is to abstract from the total work of the firm blocs of work which are somehow related and thus are more easily coordinated than other alternative combinations of blocs would be. However, the dividing line between one bloc and another is never absolutely clear. Where one type of work ends and another starts is never as clear as an organization chart implies.

Another purpose of organizing follows from the primary aspect of dividing work. It is the *assigning of responsibility and authority together with accountability to members of the firm for the various blocs of work.* Finally, descriptions of the detailed work involved in each bloc, which is commonly called an *organization unit,* serve as the basis for job evaluations, which in turn serve as the basis for wage structure. Our interest here is principally in the division of the firm's work to form the organization structure, and in the nature of the authority delegated in the production function.

Definition of Organizing

It follows from our examination of the purposes of organizing that this function of management is concerned with dividing planned work so that it may be performed in the most effective and efficient manner. We learned in Chapter 1 that conversion process inputs are used in combinations which are technologically appropriate. We are concerned with combinations of *all* inputs in the production function, not just human skill. Therefore, *organizing the production function must be concerned with all types of inputs.*[20] We may generalize this by saying that *organizing is the process of developing the most effective and efficient relationships between work, workplace, and people.* This is our working definition of organizing. The word "relationships" is a generalization which includes division of work, structure and systems of divided work, procedures that coordinate divided work, authority and responsibility for work.

At the top management level, organizing is concerned principally with structure, and especially with systems of large blocs of work. At the operative management level, organizing is concerned principally with procedures for blocs of *operative* (nonmanagerial) work. This chapter is concerned principally with structure of work and its economic implications. Later chapters are concerned first with organization *systems* and with analysis of the economic problems which arise in work systems and procedures.

Division of Business Work

Work normally is divided quite simply in small firms. The organization structure will be comprised of few blocs or organization units. In the very large firm, the total work of the company may be divided in many ways and combinations of ways, resulting in an organization structure having thousands of organization units. Division of work is directly related to the volume of the various types of work to be done. This in turn is directly related to the extent of the market served, as we learned in Chapter 1.

The work of the firm may be divided into organization units on the basis of (1) geographical location and (2) similarity of work. Further, there are many bases for establishing geographical location and many bases for establishing work similarity. Before getting into them we should understand the role of *grouping work* in organizing.

Grouping Related Work. Sometimes the distinction between *dividing* work and *grouping* work is a fine one. Nevertheless, there is a useful difference in the concepts. From a purely functional point of view the total work of the firm may be divided *ad infinitum*, for example on down to human micromotions and thoughts. *The really significant aspect of organizing is how the divided work is grouped to form organization units.*

Where a portion (division) of total work is very highly related to another portion, they are often but not always grouped to form an organization unit. Whether or not they should be grouped is essentially

---

[20] See Davis, *op. cit.*, p. 83. "We have noted that organizing involves things and physical conditions, as well as people." For another version of organizing see Koontz and O'Donnell, *op. cit.*, p. 36.

an economic question. *They will not be grouped if the volume of work for each of them makes it economically appropriate for each of them to specialize, that is, not merge.*

If the portions of work are divided from dissimilar basic business functions such as marketing and production, as in the case of product planning, the question arises as to which of the two—marketing or production—the grouped unit belongs. We may *generalize and say that product planning would be organized as a production subfunction in firms where product specifications are uniquely related to the conversion function.* This would be true generally in many types of manufacturing and professional service businesses. For instance, planning of the output in a public accounting firm is very closely related to the unique processes of accounting. On the other hand, where the conversion function is not so uniquely related to product specifications, as in warehousing goods, product planning often will be organized as a marketing function. This is true most frequently in marketing type firms.

Geographical Division of Work. The total activity of the business firm may be divided into geographical regions. For instance, the firm may have a domestic division and a foreign division. Within the domestic division, there may be a headquarters division, a West Coast division, a southern division, and others. Geographical division of work may be undertaken because of the regional location of particular inputs such as a supply of skilled labor or of raw materials that are uneconomically moved to another region.

Geographical organization of the total production function, for all of these reasons together, was illustrated earlier in the chain of producer-distributors of goods, Figure 1–3. In the long chain of firms, the extractor of materials is located at the source of the materials in nature, that is, at the oil field, on the farm, at the mine, on the ocean, in the forest. The processor is usually located where a strategic input exists and cannot be moved economically. For instance, processing aluminum ore into ingots requires a large source of water and power. The strategic input in many cases may be efficient transportation of bulk materials. Thus processors frequently are located near railroad intersections or water ports. Fabricators will locate near a unique labor supply, although with our rapidly increasing supply of all skills countrywide in America, this becomes less and less an economic consideration.

Wholesalers are located in a geographical position to serve economically a chosen market of retailers. Retailers in turn are located in a geographical position to serve economically a chosen consumer market. The problem of business location is an important economic problem and therefore is treated in greater detail in another text in this series.[21] In

---

[21] R. Reed, Jr., *Plant Location, Layout, and Maintenance* (Irwin Series in Operations Management [Homewood, Ill.: Richard D. Irwin, Inc., 1967]).

its broadest sense, it is a problem in organizing.

Division on the Basis of Work Similarity. There are many ways in which the total work of the firm may be divided and grouped into units of similar work. *Division of work may be on the basis of product similarity, process similarity, similarity of authority, and others.*

An example of work divided on the basis of similar product groups is General Dynamics Corporation which has its Electric Boat division making submarines, Consolidated Vultee Aircraft Division making airplanes, and other product group divisions. General Motors Corporation has its passenger automobile group, truck group, locomotive group, refrigeration group, and others. Division of work may be *by product* within a product group. For instance, in General Motors Corporation there is the Chevrolet division, Buick division and others within the automotive group.

Production work may be performed more economically when volume is very high by grouping operations *by product* in a continuous production line, for example a cement processing line. Production *work may be performed most economically when volume is low by grouping similar processes.* For instance, in jobbing and in intermittent production all welding work may be grouped, all typewriters may be grouped, and so forth. The optimal grouping of work is generally called "plant layout" in industry. This subject is explained in detail in a later book in the series.[22]

Sometimes a product group may require unique processing, as in making gears. Then grouping of all gear work may be considered either organizing by similar product or organizing by similar process. Actually it is both. In addition to organizing the production function on the basis of similar processes, the whole firm may be organized in this way. For instance, in the textile industry there are so-called commission mills, companies organized to do one process only, say weaving, or dyeing, or spinning yarn.

Division by Technological Function. The work of the firm may be organized on the basis of technologically similar work. That is, technologically similar work may be grouped together to form departments. In such cases the basic business functions: production, marketing, finance, and personnel are distributed throughout these departments, with no single basic business function performed completely in a single technological department. This is the case in many professional service firms and to a great extent in banking. *It is difficult to clearly discern just where, and thus how, the basic business functions are performed in a technologically organized business.* Researchers in bank organization and the organization structure of other types of service firms generally will sadly attest to this fact.

---

[22] *Ibid.*

Aside from the extreme case of complete organization by technological functions, as in a law firm, partial organization in this fashion can exist. For instance, the legal department of a large manufacturing firm is a technological staff unit reporting to the president because it serves the entire firm. It cannot be considered part of the marketing, or production, or finance, or personnel functions.

Division by Authority.   An obvious division of the work of the firm is *by managerial and nonmanagerial work.* Managerial work is differentiated by the fact that managers have authority to make decisions for others to follow. Nonmanagerial people have no such authority. They can make decisions for themselves only, not for others. This conforms to the definition of management given earlier in this chapter.

The *work of the firm is divided in such a way as to have a management group and a nonmanagerial, or operative, group.* In a tiny firm, the management "group" may be one man, that is, the owner-manager. This is the case in many service firms such as laundries, repair shops, legal firms, and in many retailers of goods such as men's clothing stores and gift shops.

In large firms the management group may consist of many organization units. In other words, the management group is itself divided. *Usually this division of managerial work is on the basis of authority such as line authority and staff authority.*[23] Line authority is that authority which should accompany *primary responsibility* for the conduct of a specific division of work, say marketing, production, finance, or personnel. Staff authority is that authority which should accompany *secondary responsibility* for the conduct of work. For instance, the top-line manager in production is primarily responsible for producing the output. The supervisor of production control, a staff group, is only secondarily responsible for the same thing. His group aids the line manager in discharging his responsibility.

Staff Organization Units.   There are many types of staff units which are needed to aid line management. In the very small firm, the top manager may regularly employ only a line organization. Occasionally, however, he may set up one man as a staff assistant to investigate a problem and report his findings. The line manager will make the decision from the findings, and then send the man back to his regular work. This is a temporary, or *ad hoc*, staff unit. Further, the staff unit is given only that authority (right to make decisions) necessary to gather the required information. This may be called *informational authority.*

---

[23] The subject of *dividing or "factoring" managerial work,* such as Prof. Herbert A. Simon calls it, on the basis of *authority* (the right to make decisions) is one aspect of the traditional theory with which the Simon school of behaviorists tends to agree. That is, they base their theory of management organization structure on decision making. See Herbert A. Simon, *Administrative Behavior* (rev. ed.; New York: The Macmillan Co., 1957).

The line manager may give the temporary staff unit or committee *advisory authority*. In such a case the unit is required to analyze the problem situation and advise the line manager on appropriate alternative solutions. The line manager will make the final decision.

Finally, the line manager may give the temporary staff unit or committee *functional authority*. That is, he will require the unit to make the final functional decision. In such a case the line manager has transferred his authority to make this particular decision to the staff or committee unit.

Where a class of problems recurs frequently, as in the large firm, the line manager will set up the staff unit or the committee on a permanent basis. Permanent specialization of labor becomes economically appropriate because of the large volume of this class of problem (remember Stigler's injunction). An example is the quality control staff in production, whose problems are examined in detail in a later book in this series.[24]

The permanent, or standing, committee differs from the permanent staff unit in that its members do other work in the firm on a permanent basis. The standing committee does not *operate* continuously as a committee, although it *exists* continuously. On the other hand, the permanent staff confines its activities to its staff work and operates continuously.

Work may bunch up on occasion for the permanent staff unit, and there is an economically optimum size of the unit. The problem of how large a permanent staff unit should be is solvable by application of waiting line theory, which is examined in detail in a later text in this series.[25]

Division by Managerial Function. It was established earlier in this chapter that the management process is comprised of the following functions: (1) establishing objectives, (2) planning, (3) organizing, (4) motivating, and (5) controlling. *Managerial work may be divided on the basis of these management functions.* For instance, a staff unit may be set up to specialize in managerial planning, or organizing, or both, or for control as in the case of the quality control department. The function of motivating *operative* production people normally will stay in the line organization unit, however.

There is more to the subject of organizing than we have reviewed here.[26] Nevertheless, this brief presentation of the rationale of organizing

---

[24] R. B. Fetter, *The Quality Control System* (Irwin Series in Operations Management [Homewood, Ill.: Richard D. Irwin, Inc., 1967]).

[25] R. Reed, Jr., *op. cit.*

[26] For those who wish to pursue this subject further, some of the latest articles by both "schools," behaviorists and traditionalists, are listed below. Be careful however; the semantics problem in the management theory jungle is a formidable one! Behaviorists seem to shy away from the use of the word "organizing," perhaps because of its authoritarian implications. More frequently they will discuss organizing within the context of the word "organization," which is often so broad as to include partial treatment of planning, motivating, and controlling. William Millman, "Some Unsettled

practice puts us in a position to develop models of organization structure for various types of production.

PRODUCTION MANAGEMENT ORGANIZATION

Highly developed organization structure for managing production is found, for the most part, in manufacturing firms of large size. Even in relatively small manufacturing firms, however, one may sometimes find in production a complex division of managerial labor into many staff organization units. For instance, a small producer of automated special-purpose heat-processing equipment had at one time more staff people than line people in the production management group. The reason for this lay in the very great amount of specialized technological decision making required in this type of business. Designing and building highly technical special-purpose production equipment required specialized organization units for product research, design, and field service. The amount of labor employed in just building each special-purpose machine in the shop was relatively small.

This example notwithstanding, small manufacturing firms may be characterized as having relatively few staff organization units in the production managerial group. The reason, of course, is found ultimately in the extent of the market. Volume of relatively few kinds of managerial work is sufficient for economical specialization in staff organization units.

In the large manufacturing firm, the total production function may first be divided geographically. This would occur in very large firms serving a very broadly distributed market. The production function may, in addition, be divided on a product basis, particularly if the entire firm is so divided. For instance in General Motors Corporation the Chevrolet division has its own production organization unit. The production function may, in addition, be divided on a process basis. For instance, most of Ford Motor Company's forging work was at one time done in a separate plant at Canton, Ohio, which did no other kind of production.

Finally, the production function may, in addition, be divided by types of production. For instance, products produced continuously may be in one plant, or one department of a plant; products produced on a jobbing basis in another. Products produced intermittently may be organized as a separate division or department of the company, particularly if it is the "similar process" type. Thus the large manufacturing firm uses *combinations* of the various bases for dividing and grouping the work of the firm into organization units.

Within each of these types of organization the subfunctions of production and the functions of management are performed. Products must be planned, conversion operations performed, and inputs acquired. Pro-

---

Questions in Organization Theory," *Academy of Management Journal*, Vol. 7, No. 3 (September, 1964), pp. 189–95; Otis Lipstreau and Kenneth A. Reed, "A New Look at the Organizational Implications of Automation," *ibid.*, pp. 24–31.

duction work must be managed, that is, objectives set, operative work planned and organized, people motivated, and their performance controlled. Rarely will one find the structure of *managerial* work for production based on the basic production subfunctions. That is, we rarely see division of labor as: product planning management, conversion management, and acquisition management, even though these are the subfunctions performed in production. Where division of *managerial* labor occurs, it is usually into line and staff units. *The staff units are set up to aid the line in carrying out the functions of management as opposed to the functions of production.*

Line Management Structure

In extremely small manufacturing firms with low volume of production managerial work, the organization structure for production management is mostly of the line type. Few staff organization units can be employed economically. Since production in the manufacturing type firm is concerned with goods—physical outputs—technological decision making of the type called engineering exists to a greater degree than in other types of firms, especially service firms.

In most small retailing and wholesaling businesses, while their unique input is goods, the amount of engineering decision making is not so large, nor is it so complex as to warrant specialized engineering units in the organization. In larger retailing firms and some large service firms such as banks, however, there apparently is enough of such work to employ economically at least one industrial engineer and his clerical group.

In the very small manufacturing firm involving relatively little and not very complex engineering analysis, this analysis is done by the line organization. Organization structure is frequently as shown at the left side of Figure 2–1, with the corresponding managerial process and types of decision making shown to the right.

The management functions are performed completely in the line organization. All planning, organizing, and so on, is performed by the production manager and managers under him. This work is *shared vertically.* Portions of the total planning function, portions of the organizing function, and so on, are assigned to each manager in the vertical line. Each of them establishes objectives, plans to achieve them, organizes the planned work, motivates the men under him, and controls their performance. All the functions of management are performed in some degree at each level of management.

From this it is obvious that a lower level manager cannot be concerned very much with *managerial organization structure* below him. There is less and less management structure to be concerned with at each progressively lower level of management. The organizing function of management at lower levels is more concerned with work procedures. These are relationships between work, workplace, and people. Thus

FIGURE 2–1

Line Organization for Production—Small Manufacturer

organizing at low management levels conforms to the definition given earlier in the chapter.

At each vertical level of management, decisions are made in respect to the aspects of the problems which come up in the performance of the management functions. For instance, when planning conversion operations, deciding which of various machines to use will have technological, economic, and human aspects. Economic choice must be made among alternatives which are technologically feasible and which humans can effectively (and willingly) operate. Figure 2–1 summarizes and integrates the foregoing concepts.

The supervisory level of management, often designated foremen in manufacturing, is frequently divided horizontally *on the basis of the division of operative work.* For instance, departmentalization of operative work will determine the number of foremen to employ. While this is horizontal division of work, it is still line management work, not staff.

As the number of operative departments increases, the span of effective management of the production manager may be violated. With more foremen to coordinate, he has little time left for his other management work. Coordinating the foremen is done principally through the establishment of formal and informal procedural and information systems. The design of these systems is *both* planning *and* organizing work combined at this level of management. With many foremen reporting to him, the production manager may have little time left for detailed control of production operations. Hence, he may divide his work vertically with an assistant manager, who is often called production superintendent or general foreman, to whom all foremen report.

Staff Management Structure

As the volume of business increases, the effective and efficient performance of the *management* functions may call for staff specialization rather than further lengthening the line organization. Lengthening of the line organization brings on problems in communication and in vertical coordination of management functions. These problems apparently grow as a multiple of, rather than directly with, each increase in the vertical organization. Accordingly by the time a production policy filters down through a long vertical chain it may be unrecognizable.

Also, managerial efficiency tends to diminish with lengthening line organization because of the failure to take advantage of specialization of managerial work in the form of staff units. When staff organization is warranted, it often takes place in the production organization *on the basis of the functions of management combined with technological considerations.*

FIGURE 2–2
**Line and Partial Staff Organization for Production—
Large Manufacturer**

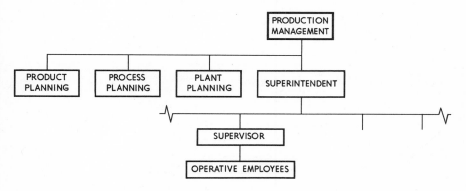

Planning and Organizing Production. Staff organization units may develop for *planning and organizing the operative work of production.* For instance, organization may be as shown in Figure 2–2. In an organization structure such as this the production manager has established three staff units to aid him in his work. One is for planning the product, that is, establishing product technical specifications. One is for planning conversion operations, that is, process planning. The third is for planning the plant, that is, all physical facilities other than process equipment.

In such an organization the production manager normally would give *functional* authority to the staff units. In other words, the staff units would be given authority to make the decisions necessary to effectively and efficiently carry out their planning responsibilities. The production manager will not give up all his planning authority, however. If he did, he would not be a manager, by definition. Usually he will always retain the authority to make policy decisions (standing plans).

The production manager in an organization such as that shown in Figure 2–2 has retained the function of *controlling* operative production work completely in the line units. Of course the head of each planning staff unit *must be the manager of his own department.* Accordingly, he will perform all the functions of management for his own department, unless division of his work is economically appropriate. If it is, he may employ only vertical division, that is, have an assistant. If warranted, he will employ staff units within his staff department. These are sometimes called "secondary staff units."

When the production manager employs staff units for planning, as shown in Figure 2–2, he usually gives up a portion of his organizing authority. This is particularly true in the case of establishing procedures. While the production manager usually will retain authority over the *structure* of the production *management* group, he usually will give up

FIGURE 2–3
Staff Engineering Departments in Manufacturing

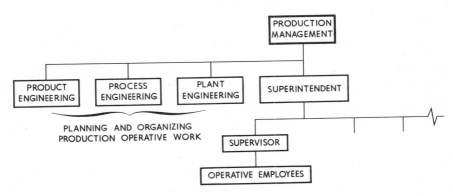

authority to the planning units to establish procedures for the *operative* work of production. The reason for this lies in the fact that planning and organizing for operative work tend to merge at this level. For instance, a process instruction is both a plan and an organization instruction. It establishes relationships between types of work, workplace, and people, for example a turning operation to be done on a lathe in a given department by a Class 1 machinist.

The production manager normally will hold on to some overall procedural authority by establishing coordination policies. For instance, he may require that all process instructions be cleared for ideas with the superintendent and bear his initials before they are issued. When the production manager has a satisfactory set of coordinating policies established, he will not require product and process instructions to come to him for review and release over his signature. He has delegated authority to do this to the appropriate staff unit and has advised lower line managers to this effect. This is the essence of functional staff authority.

Much of the work of planning and organizing production *operative* work in the manufacturing firm is technological. It is concerned in great part with physical matters. Therefore, it is engineering work. It involves deciding feasible designs of product, process, and plant. Accordingly, the planning and organizing staff units are frequently given the name "engineering," as shown in Figure 2–3.

Technological decision making is not the only aspect of planning and organizing, however. Throughout the planning and organizing work is the aspect of choosing among technologically feasible alternatives. This is the *economic* aspect of planning and organizing. When the engineer is given authority and responsibility to make these decisions, as well as the technological decisions, he is being asked to act like an economist. This accounts in part for the existence of well-known texts in "engineering economy."[27] Furthermore, the production manager should know how to make these economic decisions so that he may effectively guide and review the work of his staff groups.

Frequently the production manager will not delegate complete authority for making economic decisions to staff units, even though he may delegate full technological authority. In such cases the production manager will reserve to himself the authority to make the larger economic decisions. For instance, he may establish the policy that physical facilities costing more than $1,000 will be decided by him from technologically feasible alternatives developed by the engineering people.

The same division of decision making authority is frequently encountered in the motivational aspects of problems arising in planning and organizing production operative work. The production manager frequently will establish the policy that any problem which has significant motivational aspects will be decided finally by him. For instance, in the choice of foundry molding equipment, he may decide that a sand slinger will be used rather than a jolt-squeeze-rollover machine, if both will do the work with near equal effectiveness (a technological question). He may decide the problem this way because the slinger is far less noisy, even though it may be somewhat more costly to acquire and operate than the alternative machine.

Motivating Production Workers. Obviously, the production manager is fully responsible for effectively motivating all production operative employees. Normally he will not delegate any of this authority to staff units within his organization unless he sets up his own personnel department. However, he may not be allowed to do this. A high-level manager, perhaps the president, may consider it more appropriate to set up a centralized personnel department to serve all basic functions of the business. Such a structure will make for more uniformity in personnel policies and their implementation. Further, it very probably would be

---

[27] For an example, see Eugene L. Grant, *Principles of Engineering Economy* (3rd ed.; New York: The Ronald Press Company, 1950).

uneconomical to establish smaller separate personnel departments within each basic function of the business except in a very large firm. Even then they would normally take technical direction from a top management personnel unit which would establish personnel policies and general procedures for carrying them out.

In any case, each manager of an organization unit will be required to motivate the people in his unit to perform effectively and efficiently. For instance, the chief product engineer will be expected to perform this function for his department, as well as plan, organize, and control the internal work of his department.

Controlling Production. Finally, as volume of managerial work continues to grow, the production manager may establish staff units for control of operative production work. There is no reason to believe that the emergence of staff units for planning and organizing would precede units for controlling as shown back in Figure 2–3. The need may dictate control staff units prior to planning and organizing units.

Three types of control units may finally evolve: volume control, quality control and cost control. There are only four aspects of any kind of work, its quantity, its quality, its cost, and the time used. The time aspect is directly relevant to the quantity aspect, only indirectly relevant to the aspects of quality and cost. Hence, we normally think of the quantity of work per unit of time, or volume of work. *Therefore, we speak of volume control, quality control, and cost control.*

The term "volume control" is rarely if ever used in industry. In its place managers use the term "production control." This is actually a misnomer as there is more about production work to control than its quantity per unit of time, or volume. However, *to conform to industrial usage, we shall speak of production control when we are considering the quantity-time aspects of production.*

Integrating all that has been developed in the forgoing paragraphs on staff organization for production, we have the model organization structure for the fully developed production managerial group as shown in Figure 2–4. Here the division of the functions of management among staff units is highly developed. However, it was indicated earlier that not all planning, organizing, and controlling is delegated to the staff units. Some of each of these functions remain in the line organization, as dictated by the production manager. Remember, *he* decides organization structure to help him do *his* job well.

ORGANIZATION VARIANTS IN MANUFACTURING

The organization structure of Figure 2–4 is a *model* structure useful for analyzing the problems of production management. One could study the structure of many production organizations in various institutions and not find many exactly like Figure 2–4. This does not lessen its usefulness.

In fact, this model structure is useful as a *base* from which the practicing manager may *start* his thinking about organization structure for *his* particular production conditions, rather than a generalized set of conditions as posited above.

Organization structure should be flexible. It should change as conditions change within the organization, in the organization's environment, and in its production function. A structure that does not change over many years is probably a poor one. On the other hand, one that changes through the piling on of various units to meet transitory changes in conditions without ever eliminating some organization units has "grown like Topsy." It is probably overorganized, a condition that is relatively

FIGURE 2–4
Highly Developed Line and Staff Organization for Production

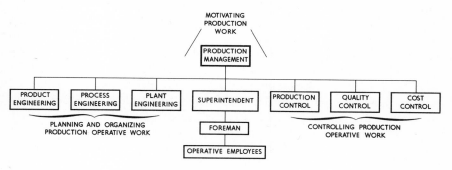

easy to slip into. Periodically, the production manager should reanalyze his organization structure—sort of clean house and start over again. The structure shown in Figure 2–4 is a useful *base* to which he may return in his thinking each time he reanalyzes structure.

It is difficult to generalize about the conditions which will cause actual organization structures to differ from the one shown in Figure 2–4. There are, however, some generalizations which are useful, even though one may find exceptions to them. Let us now examine some of these generalizations.

Industrial Engineering

Industrial engineering has been defined as "the engineering approach applied to all factors, including the human factor, involved in the production or distribution of products or services.[28] The range of activities for which the industrial engineering department is responsible varies

---

[28] H. B. Maynard, "Industrial Engineering," *Encyclopedia Americana*, Americana Corp., Vol. XV (1953), reported in H. B. Maynard (ed.), *Industrial Engineering Handbook* (New York: McGraw-Hill Book Co., Inc., 1963), p. 1–3. The American Institute

so widely in practice that we cannot generalize, or develop a model
of the function, on an *empirical* basis.[29] However, we can develop a model
which has some deductive, if not inductive, logic behind it. Such a model
will be useful for our purpose of understanding the problems of production management. We shall now proceed to develop this model.

An organization structure such as that shown in Figure 2–4, with seven
functions—one line and six staff—reporting to the production manager,
could be difficult to handle. Particularly if the volume of business
increases greatly, the production manager will find himself in conference
with top managers, for example the vice presidents and the president,
several hours each day. In fact, the production manager may wear two
hats. He may also be a vice president of the company. Together with
other vice presidents he will spend a great deal of time on top management problems, particularly those directly involving the production
function.

In such a case the production manager may have as little as four hours
a day to devote to the seven men under him, plus handling that portion
of the total managerial function which he retains for himself, that is, the
responsibility and authority that he does not delegate to his staff units or
share with his superintendent. This may result in less than 15 minutes a
day available to each of the seven men reporting to him. In other words,
the production manager's *span of effective management* may be violated.
One way of overcoming this condition is to have fewer men reporting to
him. This may be accomplished by *grouping* several of the staff functions
into one department headed by a supervisor who may be a trained
industrial engineer. This department may be named the "industrial
engineering department."

The functions combined to form this department will vary from firm
to firm depending upon conditions. The individual production manager
will decide this to suit his own peculiar situation. This accounts in great
part for the wide variety of work content in industrial engineering departments as reported in the references cited in footnote 10, Chapter 1. The
successful production manager will be guided by sound organizing
principles in grouping work to form the industrial engineering department. He will seek to group staff functions which are more closely related
than others until he has reduced the number of people reporting to him

of Industrial Engineers defines industrial engineering as follows: "Industrial Engineering is concerned with the design, improvement, and installation of integrated systems
of men, materials, and equipment; drawing upon specialized knowledge and skill in
the mathematical, physical, and social sciences, together with the principles and methods of engineering analysis and design, to specify, predict, and evaluate the results to
be obtained from such systems."

[29] For a series of articles in the *Journal of Industrial Engineering* describing the
wide range of responsibility of industrial engineering departments in various institutions, see footnote reference 10, Chapter 1.

to a manageable number. Two functions which are more closely related than others shown in Figure 2–4 are *process engineering* and *cost control.* Combining these will reduce the number reporting to the production manager to six.

If he desires a further reduction, production (volume) control may be included in the industrial engineering department. While one can find a degree of relatedness between *all* staff functions, as there necessarily must be between all the organization units of the firm, production control, process engineering, and cost control are more closely related than are

FIGURE 2–5

Production Organization Including Industrial Engineering

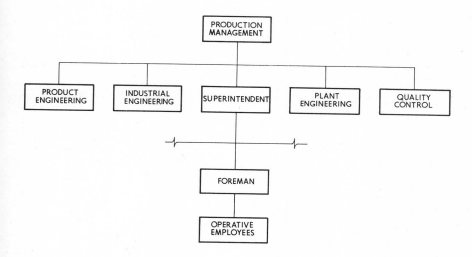

other combinations of the staff functions shown in Figure 2–4. Particular conditions in a given firm may violate this generality, however, resulting in variations in the work of the industrial engineering department from firm to firm.

The model of production management structure for use in this book, and others in this series may now be changed from that shown in Figure 2–4 to that shown in Figure 2–5. However, the texts in this series generally follow the breakdown of work indicated in Figure 2–4. For instance, process engineering is covered by Nadler's *Work Systems Design: The IDEALS Concept;* plant engineering is covered by Reed's *Plant Location, Layout, and Maintenance;* production control is covered by Greene's *Operations Planning and Control.* These authors are all professors and consultants in industrial engineering.

Project Organization

Large-scale production projects such as the development and production of the Polaris missile are normally executed by a project manager via a form of organization called *project organization*. In such an arrangement a unit, often called the project office, headed by a project manager, is given responsibility and authority to make key decisions in managing the project. This authority and responsibility is *ad hoc*, that is, it lasts only until the project is completed.

The project manager's responsibility and authority cuts across the traditional functional organization units such as production control, quality control, cost control, and so forth. Whereas in traditional functional organization authority-responsibility relationships are delegated downward through the vertical organization structure, in project organization these relationships are arranged laterally, cutting across the vertical functional organization lines. Thus the functional line manager may have to deal with several project managers whose projects are currently in process in the line manager's department. This he does in addition to dealing with his superior in the regular line organization performing the regular nonproject work.

The project manager exercises his authority principally by virtue of his professional expertise and his status in the overall organization. He normally cannot "command" the regular functional line managers in regard to specific aspects of the project. However, line managers recognize the importance of the project (hence project organization) and collaborate closely with the project manager. The latter relies heavily on the motivating function in the management process to achieve project objectives. The project manager participates heavily in the planning, organizing, and control functions of management *in respect to his project*. In particular, he normally exercises budgetary control over all aspects of the project. And, of course, the "power of the purse" is always significant.

Project organization is resorted to when the project, which is a task that is clearly differentiated from all other work of the firm, is a major one of significant importance. Significant importance can be caused by any one or more of several characteristics such *as size of the project, cost, technical complexity, and particularly complexity of coordinated effort*. In large production projects such as weapon systems, dams, or a highway network, a number of companies will participate in the project. In such cases coordinated effort is of crucial importance to the success of the project. The project manager will spend a great deal of time in coordinating the functional line departments of many companies in managing the project.

Project organization is not new, although one hears more about it today because of the increasing number of large-scale production projects, particularly those in our military and space efforts. One of the best known of these was the Manhattan Project (development of the atom bomb) during World War II.

Predecessors of the project manager were the project expediter and later the project coordinator. And of course companies have always used this organization arrangement under the heading of "special projects" for the same reasons given above. For instance, when a major addition to production capacity is undertaken, top management will often relieve a key man of his regular duties and give him authority to design the new plant and coordinate all the activities in acquiring and installing the physical facilities. In carrying out the project he normally will have authority to call on regular functional people for specific tasks. For instance he may delegate the design of the quality control system for the new plant to the quality control manager, or obtain a specialist from that department to carry out this task, after which the specialist goes back to his regular duties.[30]

Matrix Organization

A firm may employ more or less continuously several of the various bases for organizing work described earlier in the chapter. If, for instance, a company regularly produces large project contracts simultaneously along with its regular work, it may maintain project organization units on a continuous basis. Thus it will maintain a two-dimensional matrix organization, one dimension being the project organization and the other the regular functional line and staff organization. In companies, or divisions of companies, whose regular work is composed almost solely of large projects, the dominant organizational dimension will often be the project type, with the functional organization relegated almost completely to a support role.[31]

The concept of the matrix organization is not new, although again we hear more about it today because of the increasing use of project management together with, or superimposed upon, the regular functional organization. Wherever management finds it appropriate to *utilize simultaneously more than one of the bases for division of labor described earlier in the chapter*, a matrix organization is created. The matrix will have as many dimensions as there are bases of division of labor employed. Thus simultaneous organization by product, by similar process, and by

---

[30] For a full discussion of project management see David I. Cleland, "Why Project Management," *Business Horizons*, Vol. 7, No. 4 (Winter, 1964), pp. 81–87.

[31] For a description of such a situation in an aerospace company, see John F. Mee, "Matrix Organization," *Business Horizons*, Vol. 7, No. 2 (Summer, 1964), pp. 70–72. See also an example of matrix organization in an information center in Arthur M. Weimer and Howard L. Timms, "The Aerospace Research Applications Center," *ibid.*, pp. 93–100.

management function will be a three-dimensional matrix organization. Most large companies have always employed a multidimensional matrix organization.

REVIEW QUESTIONS

1. Why should the student spend his time studying management thought when the so-called experts cannot agree on an appropriate content?
2. What are five major functions involved in managing?
3. Define organizing. Why should organizing be concerned with more than just human skill?
4. Does the size of the firm significantly affect the manner in which its work is divided?
5. What criteria determine whether related work will be grouped to form an organization unit?
6. For what reasons might geographical division of work be undertaken?
7. In what ways can the total work of a firm be divided and grouped into units of similar work?
8. Define the types of authority a staff unit might have.
9. Discuss the various bases for organizing the work of production in a manufacturing firm.
10. When is a staff organization unit warranted in manufacturing production?
11. What staff organization units usually develop for planning and organizing the operative work of production? What type of authority do they typically have?
12. What is the distinction between product, process, and plant planning and product, process, and plant engineering?
13. Do staff organization units normally perform the management function of motivating operative workers? Why? Under what conditions?
14. What types of control units generally evolve for controlling production?
15. What production activities might be the responsibility of the industrial engineering department?
16. When might management resort to a project organization structure?
17. What is the basis of the project manager's authority? Why is this the case?
18. Under what conditions would a firm employ a matrix organization?

SUGGESTIONS FOR FURTHER STUDY

AYERS, E. D., AND RHODES, A. W. "The Role of the Plant Industrial Engineer," *Journal of Industrial Engineering*, Vol. XIV, No. 5 (September–October, 1963), pp. 268–73.

   Discusses how the industrial engineer serves management by providing the information and analysis of alternatives for decisions by management.

BEER, MICHAEL. "Organizational Size and Job Satisfaction," *Academy of Management Journal*, Vol. 7, No. 1 (March, 1964), pp. 34–44.

Author tests the hypothesis that job satisfaction is inversely related to organizational size.

ETZIONI, AMITAI. *Modern Organizations.* Englewood Cliffs, N.J.: Prentice-Hall, Inc., 1964.

Author presents the structuralist approach—a synthesis of the scientific management and the human relations school of organization theory—in discussing organizational goals, organizational structure, and organizations and their social environment.

FILLEY, ALAN C. "Common Misconceptions in Management," *Business Horizons*, Vol. 7, No. 3 (Fall, 1964), pp. 87–96.

Author discusses several common misconceptions in business management that, if corrected, might help the academician present a workable theory to managers.

FREDERICK, WILLIAM C. "The Next Development in Management Science: A General Theory," *Academy of Management Journal*, Vol. 6, No. 3 (September, 1963), pp. 212–19.

Author explains his belief that within 10 years an acceptable theory of management will evolve.

HAIRE, MASON (ed.). *Modern Organization Theory.* New York: John Wiley & Sons, Inc., 1959.

Distinguished authors such as Argyris, Likert, Cyert, Haire, March and others present their ideas on the latest and most significant factors in research and theory that are related to organizations.

MARCH, JAMES G., AND SIMON, HERBERT A. *Organizations.* New York: John Wiley & Sons, Inc., 1958.

Volume brings together into a single framework the diverse approaches of sociologists, scientific management adherents, administration theorists, social psychologists, and economists.

MEE, JOHN F. "Project Management," *Business Horizons*, Vol. 6, No. 3 (Fall, 1963), pp. 53–54.

Brief article discusses the history, necessity, and advantages of project management.

STIEGLITZ, HAROLD, AND JANGER, ALLEN R. *Top Management Organization in Divisionalized Companies.* Personnel Study No. 195. New York: National Industrial Conference Board, Inc., 1965.

A four-part report discussing the work reserved to top management in divisionalized and decentralized companies. Part 1 sets the perspective by analyzing the nature of the decentralized division. Part 2 discusses the functions of the chief executive and his office. Part 3 discusses work of the heads of the operating divisions. Part 4 discusses the nature of the corporate staff.

URWICK, LYNDALL F. "Management in Perspective: The Tactics of Jungle Warfare," *Academy of Management Journal*, Vol. 6, No. 4 (December, 1963), pp. 316–29.

Article discusses the history and aspects of the different definitions and approaches to the study of management theory.

YODER, DALE; MILES, RAYMOND E.; MCKIBBEN, LAWRENCE; BOYNTON, ROBERT

E.; AND ENGLAND, GEORGE W. "Managers' Theories of Management," *Academy of Management Journal*, Vol. 6, No. 3 (September, 1963), pp. 204–11.

Discusses the *What's Your Theory?* game; a game designed to help managers identify and establish their attitudes toward management theory.

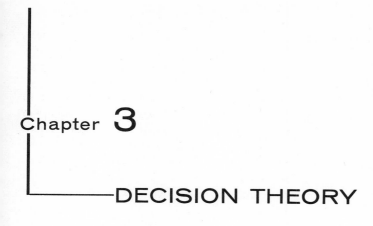

Chapter **3**

DECISION THEORY

INTRODUCTION

IN CHAPTER 2 the subject of managing was examined particularly as applied to production. There we referred to managerial decision making but deferred its fuller examination to this chapter. Here we shall examine the subject of *decision theory*, principally as it relates to production, working up to the concept of *systems*, which we go on to examine more fully in Chapter 4.

MANAGERIAL DECISION MAKING

Decision making is at the heart of the functions comprising the management process.[1] This was made clear in the definition of management given in Chapter 2. It is an easy step to recognize that *the manager makes decisions in establishing objectives;* he makes planning decisions, organizing decisions, motivating decisions, and control decisions. This was indicated back in Figure 2–1. In this sense modern decision theory is a logical extension of the traditionalist's "management process."

Analysis and Decision Making

Simon defines decision making as not merely the final act of choice among alternatives but rather a whole *process* leading up to and including choice. He conceives decision making as a process that includes three

---

[1] One prominent researcher and writer in the field of decision making takes "mild liberties with the use of the English language" by using "decision making" as though it were "synonymous with managing"—Herbert A. Simon, *The New Science of Management Decision* (New York: Harper & Bros., 1960), p. 1. One might define decision making broadly enough to warrant this synonym, but it is doubtful that there is much to be gained thereby.

principal phases: "finding occasions for making a decision; finding possible courses of action; and choosing among courses of action."[2] Thus "decision process" and "decision making" would be synonymous. Most practicing managers would question Simon's first phase, "finding occasions for making a decision." There is no lack of such occasions in successful management practice. Decision situations,[3] or problems, seem to engulf most managers even in the best-managed organizations; and there is little necessity for "finding occasions" for making decisions.[4]

Concerning the second phase of Simon's "decision process," the task of finding possible courses of action may be included as part of the task of *analyzing* the problem situation, that is, dissection and disclosing the elements of the situation, in the process of which alternative courses of action are revealed. Thus, one might rephrase Simon's definition and say that decision theory has two aspects: analysis and decision making. We shall employ this definition hereafter. However, for the sake of brevity we will usually identify the entire process by the name of its last stage, "decision making."

Objectives and Decision Making

The famous educational philosopher, John Dewey, is reported to have stated in his book *How We Think* three stages of problem solving: (1) What is the problem? (2) What are the alternatives? (3) Which alternative is best?[5] This process presumes the existence of a problem. As indicated in Chapter 2, however, we prefer to think that there can be no problem unless there is first an objective. Problems are obstacles standing in the way of achieving objectives. *The choice of objectives sets the stage for the kinds of problems that will arise and have to be decided.* Accordingly, it seems appropriate that we begin the subject of decision making with a study of objectives in management.

Hierarchy of Objectives. In the first step of the total decision process, establishment of an *immediate objective or criterion for decision making* is of primary importance. In order to appreciate this concept, we should

---

[2] *Ibid.*, p. 1. Simon labels these phases respectively: intelligence, design, and choice, *ibid.*, p. 2.

[3] A number of writers in the field of decision theory use the phrase "decision problems." This phrase is not used in this text as it seems somewhat redundant. A problem calls for a decision sooner or later. If a situation is such that a decision is not required, no problem exists.

[4] Simon states that this first phase, which he calls "intelligence," occupies a large part of executives' time, that is, they "spend a large fraction of their time surveying the economic, technical, political, and social environment to identify new conditions that call for new actions." *Ibid.*, p. 2. This is certainly true of top managers, but not true of lower level managers whose attention is expected to center on internal matters. In any case, this activity could be termed "analyzing the situation," and thus fits the definition used in this text.

[5] *Ibid.*, p. 3.

turn our attention to the concept of a hierarchy of objectives and its significance in decision making.

The existence of an objective at one management level in the organization poses problems for the next lower level. This level, in turn, must establish immediate objectives to solve these problems. The objectives so established pose problems for the next lower level of management, on down to the nonmanagerial employee.[6]

An example that is examined in detail in another book in this series[7] is the case of planning the production (volume) of goods. With the highest level economic objective in a business firm taken as a planned (maximum)

FIGURE 3–1
Hierarchy of Objectives in the Organization

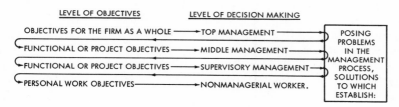

rate of return (profit) on investment (capital employed in the firm), this poses the problem of an optimum production schedule of finished goods. The quantities and due dates for each finished good in the product line, as established in this schedule,[8] are objectives that pose problems of scheduling the receipt of materials and their conversion into components. These schedules are in turn objectives that pose problems in placing orders (on suppliers for materials, on the shop departments for components) in sufficient time to hold stockouts at a tolerable level without carrying excessive inventory. Obviously this is a hierarchal problem. That is, the higher level subproblem must be solved before the lower level subproblems can be solved. Thus the hierarchy of objectives is essentially a "means-ends" chain, with "ends" equivalent to objectives and "means" equivalent to alternatives available to achieve the ends.[9]

This concept of a hierarchy of objectives in which prior-level objec-

---

[6] For a different treatment of the task of deciding objectives, see C. West Churchman, Russell L. Ackoff, and E. Leonard Arnoff, *Introduction to Operations Research* (New York: John Wiley & Sons, Inc., 1957), chap. vi, "Weighting Objectives."

[7] James H. Greene, *Operations Planning and Control* (Irwin Series in Operations Management [Homewood, Ill.: Richard D. Irwin, Inc., 1967]).

[8] This schedule for many years was called "the Master Schedule," and still is by many managers and writers, e.g., *ibid.*, although in recent years the term, "Production Plan" has been substituted by some writers for "Master Schedule."

[9] This terminology (means-ends) is employed by Gerald Nadler in his *Work Systems Design: The Ideals Concept* (Irwin Series in Operations Management [Homewood, Ill.: Richard D. Irwin, Inc., 1967]).

tives pose a set of problems for the next lower management level, the solutions for which pose objectives for the next lower level, may be shown schematically as in Figure 3–1. Note that the process ends when it reaches the nonmanagerial employee. Higher level objectives do not pose for him problems calling for solutions that establish objectives *for others.* In accordance with the definition of management given in Chapter 2, the nonmanagerial worker does not make decisions for others to carry out.

It is not always easy to determine an appropriate immediate objective for solving a problem, even though the higher level objective that posed the problem is clear. *An appropriate objective is one consistent with the objectives of the next higher organization unit.* If, then, the objectives of this organization unit are consistent with the objectives of even higher organization units, and so on up the hierarchy to the overall organization objective, a solution to the problem based on the objective so chosen will further the overall objective of the organization. Obviously the choice of the immediate objective is important. However difficult it may be to identify an appropriate immediate objective in a lower level problem, an objective *must* be settled upon in order to solve the problem.[10]

An objective that is not clearly and explicitly related to a higher level objective is sometimes called a "proximate objective." Such objectives are often arrived at intuitively. In fact their selection frequently requires a certain amount of so-called creative thinking. Granger states, "Establishing even a subobjective [lower level objective] within the framework of a broader objective is a creative act. It involves the conceptual creation of a number of possible subobjectives, testing them against the realities of (1) consistency with internal resources, (2) consistency with environmental conditions, and (3) effectiveness/cost relationships in accomplishing the broader objective."[11]

Sequential Decision Making

The hierarchy of objectives is *not* a consequence of a hierarchy of management with its various levels as shown in Figure 3–1. *The single manager of a very small organization would face the same set of hierarchal problems in solving the more complex problems of his organization.* For instance, the problem of planning aggregate production and the production of components cited in the previous section must also be faced by the single manager of the small firm. The hierarchal nature of the problem is not brought about by the existence of a management group with various levels.

---

[10] For a careful analysis of the hierarchy of objectives, see Charles H. Granger, "The Hierarchy of Objectives," *Harvard Business Review*, Vol. 42, No. 3 (May–June, 1964), pp. 63–74. This article establishes that, "There are objectives within objectives, within objectives. They all require painstaking definition and close analysis if they are to be useful separately and profitable as a whole."

[11] *Ibid.*, p. 69.

The hierarchal nature of many problems is caused *solely by their extreme complexity;* and in part because of this, organizations resort to specialization of managerial labor, not the other way around.[12] The planning of production volume in the aggregate and by items (end items, components, raw materials) has so many complex interrelated aspects that so-called management scientists and operations researchers have not yet been able to develop, except in very special cases, an operational model (set of simultaneous equations expressing the problem) that can be manipulated on the most powerful computer yet developed. Therefore, since a decision must be made, managers break such complex problems down into a *set of related subproblems.* They then solve each subproblem in its turn, knowing full well that the subproblem solutions are not strictly correct. This is true because only a *simultaneous solution* of all the subproblems would be correct.

The process of *successively solving interrelated subproblems comprising a large complex problem may be called sequential decision making.* This is the only method by which many of the complex problems can be solved with the present state of the art of decision making. Solutions to each subproblem in the set may be improved by iterating (repeating) the entire decision process for the whole set of problems. By this method the analyst achieves a series of successive approximations. *The more iterations, the closer the analyst approaches truly optimal solutions* to the subproblems comprising the set. This subject is treated more fully in Chapter 5 where we examine management decision systems that are designed to ensure that the interrelatedness of production subproblems is appropriately taken into account. Other books in this series examine the decision processes for many types of subproblems, explicitly taking into account their interrelated nature by treating them as decision subsystems.

Multiple Objectives

In many if not most managerial problem situations the task of decision making is compounded by the existence of multiple objectives. This is true throughout the hierarchy. For instance, in business organizations the primary top-level objective is usually profit maximization, or maximum rate of return (profit) on invested capital over the long term. On the other hand, some managements recognize other objectives at specific times. For instance, the owner-manager of a small manufacturing firm

---

[12] The reasoning of many writers in the behavioral school tends to be oriented to group activity, particularly in large organizations. This orientation sometimes causes them to explain certain decision processes as though they are brought about by division of labor or specialization. This is not always true by any means. The single-manager organization has hierarchal problems, and they are no less complex than the same problems in a large organization. What is yet to be done in decision theory is the development of a theory that applies to *all* sizes of management groups, including the single manager.

known to the writer insisted on trading monetary profit for psychic profit by operating his business in such a manner as to ensure long-term employment for his inept sons. Keeping them employed was a major objective of the father in the process of managing the business. Also, some writers and businessmen recognize a social objective as well as a profit objective in managing the firm.[13]

In the case of nonbusiness organizations, such as government agencies, multiple objectives are quite frequently involved. For instance, the U.S. Army Corps of Engineers in studying the feasibility of building a new dam and reservoir will try to achieve an optimal mix of the following objectives: flood control, recreation, conservation, and downstream flow control. All these objectives enter into the benefit part of the benefit/cost ratio by which a proposed reservoir is evaluated and, if approved, designed.

In various lower level operations problems multiple objectives frequently arise. This is especially true in designing optimal conversion processes. For instance, in addition to cost minimization, other objectives such as safety, capability of controlling quality, psychological receptivity, adaptability to change, and others are involved.[14] Often in process design the profit measure is not directly applicable, because there is no way of knowing what portion of the organization's total revenue is applicable to the process. For instance, how can one know how much revenue is earned by the drill press that drills two holes in a component of the product? To say that its revenue is proportional to its cost is to dodge the question completely. Actually, the task of establishing and ranking these objectives is much like that in public works projects in which the "benefit" measure is equivalent to "revenue."

The task of weighting multiple objectives so that they may serve collectively as a single objective is not an easy one that lends itself to rigorous formal analysis.[15] A number of the objectives in a multiple objective problem situation may be difficult to characterize numerically as one may do with profit, or revenue, or cost. In such cases index numbers or letters may be employed. But these usually reflect the subjective values of the decision maker rather than objective values. We shall return to this subject later in the chapter in the section on "Evaluating Courses of Action."

---

13 David Rockefeller, eminent banker, said in an address before the American Philosophical Society, Philadelphia, November 8, 1962, "In *social* terms the old concept that the owner of a business firm had a right to use his property as he pleased to maximize profits has evolved into the belief that ownership carries certain binding social obligations." Quoted in Charles F. Phillips, Jr., "What Is Wrong with Profit Maximization?" *Business Horizons*, Vol. 6, No. 4 (Winter, 1963), pp. 73–80.

14 Objectives such as these are sometimes termed "scales of value"—measures by which alternative courses of action are valued. Gerald Nadler employs this approach and terminology in his *Work Systems Design: The Ideals Concept, op. cit.*

15 For an explanation of the complexities involved and an approach to handling them, see Churchman, Ackoff, and Arnoff, *op. cit.*, chap. vi.

Another method of dealing with multiple objectives is to choose one that is considered paramount, such as cost minimization in process design, or flood control in dam design, then treat the other objectives as constraints in the problem.[16] For instance, maximum measures may be established for some of the other objectives beyond which the decision maker cannot go, and minimum measures set for the other objectives below which the decision maker may not go. Examples of this approach are given in the linear programming techniques applied by other authors in this series.

Planning Periods and Decision Making

Decision making at the various levels of management is concerned in varying degrees with the future. Top management should look forward furthest, that is, as far forward as it believes it can meaningfully interpret and predict the organization's environment. The length of the planning period will be influenced by the degree of uncertainty prevailing in the environmental situation ahead. The imminence of global war, for instance, would severely limit the length of the planning period. This time period is often called "the planning horizon."

Top management decisions should always be for longer periods ahead than should lower level decisions. In fact, the period ahead for which decisions are made will diminish through the various levels of management as shown in Figure 3–2. The length of the planning period, or time span, varies for different kinds of problems. For instance, decisions concerning additions to plant or installing a new plant normally require a longer planning and forecast period than do decisions on adding to capacity by merely purchasing another machine tool.[17]

The obvious corollary of Figure 3–2 is that higher level managers cannot reasonably expect lower level managers to make decisions for a period further ahead than the period for which the higher level makes decisions. The concept of the decreasing planning horizon down through the hierarchy of management is also valid for the hierarchal problem solved sequentially. *The subproblems should be arranged in sequence in*

---

16 Herbert A. Simon concludes in his paper "On the Concept of Organizational Goal," ". . . it is doubtful whether decisions are generally directed toward achieving *a* goal. It is easier, and clearer, to view decisions as being concerned with discovering courses of action that satisfy a whole set of constraints. It is this set, and not any one of its members, that is most accurately viewed as the goal of the action." *Administrative Science*, Vol. 9, No. 1 (June, 1964), p. 20. Professor Simon developed this conclusion in part by using a linear programing approach in his argument. Examples in later books in this series show how this can be done for lower level managerial problems that lend themselves to quantification, but not those in which social objectives are a constraint on profit maximization. In such a problem, quantification is generally impossible to achieve.

17 For examples of the length of planning period required for various types of problems, see John F. Magee, *Production Planning and Inventory Control* (New York: McGraw-Hill Book Co., Inc., 1958), pp. 109 and 119.

FIGURE 3–2

Planning Periods for Decision Making

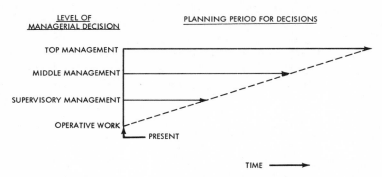

the order of their appropriate planning horizons, with the first subproblem in the sequence having the longest planning horizon.

Continuous Cycles in Decision Making

It must not be presumed that top management problems can be solved without reference to prior lower level solutions for the related subproblems. In other words top management does not start with a clean slate, say once a year, and solve its planning problems for the year ahead without reference to what has happened in lower level operations in the past year. On the contrary, top management will be guided by past performance in solving today's problems for tomorrow's performance of operations. Past performance is the result of past decisions at all levels

FIGURE 3–3

Continuous Cycles in Decision Making

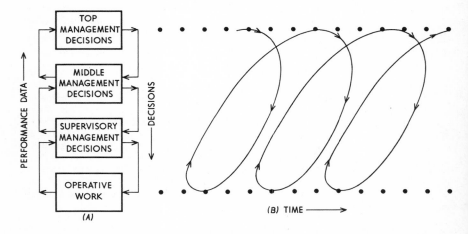

of management. Hence, *decision making in the going concern proceeds dynamically through time in an iterative fashion, as shown in Figure 3–3.*[18] There is nothing static about the operation of successful organizations, and thus appropriate decision processes must be the dynamic variety.

In Figure 3–3 (A), which is a condensation of Figure 3–1, decisions are shown as being made sequentially down through the various levels of management to operative work. Operative performance is primarily the result of these managerial decisions. Data on actual performance flows back up through the various levels of management and becomes input to the decisions at each management level for the next cycle of operations.

Cost of Decision Making

Managerial decision making costs money, of course. If the manager is willing to operate on the basis of snap judgments, he can get along with a much smaller management staff and thereby shift his managerial cost downward. To the extent that he can do this without raising costs elsewhere in operations, and/or lowering revenues, resulting in less profit or lower benefit/cost ratio, he should do so.

Sequential decision making in a series of subproblems, as described earlier, will yield solutions that are closer and closer to the optimal set of solutions for the series, as more iterations of the sequential decision process are performed. But *the greater the number of iterations, the more costly the decision.* Accordingly, there is a point of diminishing returns to analysis, beyond which the improvement in the solution is not worth the cost of achieving it.[19]

The same is true for the frequency of decision making. For instance, management could theoretically make a set of operating decisions once for a five-year planning period ahead, then sit back and take the consequences. Since the set of decisions is made only once, the cost of managerial decision making would be lower than, say, if the same set of decisions were made for each of the five years. On the other hand, the shorter (closer) the planning horizon, the lower the uncertainty, and the more likely the decisions will be good ones. Accordingly, management is willing to incur the higher cost of more frequent decision making (shorter planning horizons) for the lower cost associated with less uncertainty.

Much of the data entering into decisions, either directly as in a formal decision process, or indirectly as in the case of judgment, derive from past operations, as indicated in Figure 3–3 (A). The longer the planning period (horizon), the less likely that past operating data are valid or,

---

[18] See Exhibit II, Granger, *op. cit.*, p. 69 for a multicolored isometric figure that graphically depicts this concept of dynamism.

[19] Some iterative decision processes end in an optimal solution when a specific "test" indicates this solution has been attained. This is true in the case of linear programming, a decision process employed in a number of books in this series.

conversely, the greater the adjustment required in past data to make it valid for a future period. The shorter the planning horizon, the more valid are past operating data for making good planning decisions. For instance, if the organization's operations could be planned daily for the next day, the likelihood is good that yesterday's operating data would be valid for planning tomorrow's operations.

Daily planning would be more costly than, say, annual planning; but the costs associated with uncertainty and inappropriate data would be low. The manager tries to trade off all these costs and choose a planning horizon, and thus a frequency of planning decisions, that minimizes the total cost involved. As of today, decision theory tells us little about how to do this. The manager simply uses judgment.

Probability in Decision Making

Uncertainty was mentioned in earlier paragraphs in connection with the length of planning period for which decisions are made: the longer the planning period, the greater the uncertainty, and so forth. Probability theory is especially helpful when properly applied to problem situations involving uncertainty and the attendant risk. Certainty of an event occurring in the future implies no risk associated with this event. To the degree that there is uncertainty associated with the occurrence of the event there is risk involved.

Probability theory and associated mathematical statistical techniques may be employed to deal formally with uncertainty. These techniques enable the decision maker to employ past data generated by the organization's information system in a formal explicit manner, and thereby draw logical inferences about future events. Such techniques are employed in quality control and in production control, where the control system is designed to record, marshal, and retrieve data from past operations for statistical inferences about future operations.[20] The probability distributions developed from past data are tested to determine their relevance to future conditions, after which inferences may be made by appropriate mathematical manipulation involving the mean and variance of the distribution. Such probabilities derived from past data are termed "objective."

In problem situations where past data are not available to aid in establishing the probability distribution associated with a future event, the best the decision maker can do is draw on the judgment of people knowledgable in such events, principally from past experience with similar events. Their judgments ("highly likely, moderately likely, unlikely," etc.) are called "subjective" probabilities. They may be quantified and the techniques of mathematical statistics employed as in the case of

---

[20] Greene, *op. cit.*, Nadler, *op. cit.*, and Robert B. Fetter, *The Quality Control System* (Irwin Series in Operations Management [Homewood, Ill.: Richard D. Irwin, Inc., 1967]) employ these statistical techniques in their texts in this series.

objective probabilities. Subjective probabilities are often employed in higher level problems such as those associated with strategic questions in long-range planning. In particular, they may be used in the analysis of equipment investment problems—that is, adding and/or replacing production equipment.[21] Subjective probabilities are also employed usefully in new process design in which meaningful past data often is not available.[22]

Finally, it should be mentioned that in a hierarchal problem having a number of subproblems, some of which should be solved with the use of subjective probability measures or values arrived at by a number of different decision makers, considerable difficulty may occur. The difficulty results from the different "value structures" of individuals resulting from their differing backgrounds. To overcome or minimize this difficulty, group discussions by the decision makers involved are often mandatory. These discussions tend to develop consistency in value judgments. If reasonable consistency is not attained, an optimal solution to the hierarchal problem is unlikely.

ANALYTICAL METHODS

In spite of the fact that mankind has made billions of decisions, there is today no definitive, comprehensive theory of decision making that explains logically all aspects of the total decision process in all kinds of problem situations. Researches normally formulate hypotheses and conduct experiments in decision situations with which they are reasonably familiar. When they publish their findings and offer tentative conclusions, readers who are familiar with other decision situations that are quite different from the ones chosen by the researcher will challenge his conclusions, often with great conviction, and properly so. And to date the amount of research completed is far from sufficient to resolve all the challenges.

Like the field of management theory examined briefly in the previous chapter, the field of decision theory has a long way to go before it reaches the state of perfection of theory found in the "hard" sciences. This is true if only because in the hard sciences the problem of communications has largely been overcome. In the field of decision theory, as in management theory, there is still a tremendous problem in semantics to overcome.

Accordingly, no attempt is made in this chapter to examine all of the various methods by which man reaches a decision in any and every type of problem situation. Like the researcher mentioned above, this author will treat in a general way those analytical methods that have proved to be, or give considerable promise of being, effective in production problem situations, particularly the economic type. In subsequent

---

[21] Decision systems of this kind are explained in William T. Morris, *The Capacity Decision System* (Irwin Series in Operations Management [Homewood, Ill.: Richard D. Irwin, Inc., 1967]).

[22] Decision systems of this kind are explained in Nadler, *op. cit.*

texts in this series, these analytical methods are applied to specific problems that typically arise in the management of the production function.

Judgment and Intuition

We regularly hear, particularly from practicing managers, that judgment and intuition are the really important ingredients in effective decision making. There is a great mass of experience and evidence supporting this conclusion, all of which is summed up in the phrase, "You don't send a boy to do a man's job!" Even the most objective, skeptical researcher in the hard sciences normally acts on this principle in his own sphere.

Just what a person does when he exercises judgment or intuition is not clear. Apparently experience plays a large role in judgment. Just what else is involved and how experience is mixed with it to form a process leading to a decision is not fully understood. Since judgment is not understood, it can hardly be taught. About all that can be done to improve judgment is to practice it. Like a muscle, it seems to improve with use. This would seem logical since each use of judgment is an experience (mental), and experience apparently is an ingredient of judgment.

There are many who deprecate the role of judgment in effective decision making. They cite an increasing number of tests revealing different solutions, arrived at by judgment alone, to the same problem in the same situation by two equally educated and experienced practitioners in the same field. These test results presumably show that judgment or intuition is a poor basis for making decisions. Aside from the fact that "same" and "equally" are test conditions that are difficult to achieve, particularly in matters of education and experience (quality, as opposed to span of years, is of critical importance), the conclusion does not logically follow from such tests. A better test would be one in which the conditions were essentially the same except that one subject had no experience in the field and the other a great deal. Few such tests have been reported. Until a long series of such tests proves otherwise, it would seem that the better part of judgment would be to place a good deal of weight on the judgment factor in effective decision making.

Creative Thinking

This subject and its role in decision making has captured the interest of many researchers in recent years.[23] As expected, there are difficulties

---

[23] See the writings of eight distinguished behavioral scientists in Howard E. Gruber, Glen Terrel, and M. Wertheimer (eds.), *Contemporary Approaches to Creative Thinking* (New York: Atherton Press, 1962).

with semantics and the variety of frameworks implicit in the thinking of various writers in this field. Allen Newell, J. C. Shaw, and Herbert A. Simon state, "Interest has focused particularly on the more dramatic and mysterious aspects of creativity—the unconscious processes that are supposed to occur during 'incubation,' the imagery employed in creative thinking and its significance for the effectiveness of the thinking, and, above all, the phenomenon of 'illumination.' "[24] They go on to state,

If we are willing to regard all human complex problem-solving as creative, then . . . successful [computer] programs for problem-solving already exist, and a number of their general characteristics are known. If we reserve the term "creative" for activities like discovery of the special theory of relativity or the composition of Beethoven's Seventh Symphony, then no example of a creative mechanism exists at the present time.[25]

In this sense, creative thinking is very much like judgment or intuition. The authors go on to state,

Problem-solving is called creative to the extent that one or more of the following conditions are satisfied:
1. The product of the thinking has novelty or value (either for the thinker or his culture).
2. The thinking is unconventional, in the sense that it requires modification or rejection of previously accepted ideas.
3. The thinking requires high motivation and persistence, taking place either over a considerable span of time (continuously or intermittently) or at high intensity.
4. The problem as initially posed was vague or ill-defined, so that part of the task was to formulate the problem itself.[26]

The late Prof. John E. Arnold is reported to have pointed out that the pressures of mass education and group activities tend to cause people to conform more or less to established patterns of thought and behavior, thus stultifying the natural creativeness with which people are born.[27] Inhibitions are developed that block creative thinking. Some of these blocks are "perceptual blocks, cultural blocks, and emotional blocks."[28]

Perceptual blocks prevent the thinker from getting at appropriate information about the problem situation being analyzed. The analyst tends to see in the situation only that which he wants or expects to see. Cultural blocks are social inhibitions that cause the thinker to conform to an accepted pattern, for instance, to put too much faith in reason and logic. Emotional blocks include fear of making a mistake or making a fool of oneself. Presumably the way to overcome these blocks is to be

---

[24] *Ibid.*, p. 63.

[25] *Ibid.*, p. 65.

[26] *Ibid.*, p. 65.

[27] Reported by Jere W. Clark, "Can Creativeness Be Taught?" *Management Review*, Vol. 54, No. 6 (June, 1965), pp. 51–54.

[28] *Ibid.*, p. 51.

constantly aware of them and alert to opportunities for overcoming them during the analysis phase of decision making.[29] A skeptical, questioning attitude seems to help in this process. So-called brainstorming sessions—unrestricted, free-thinking, idea-generating group discussions, in which one novel idea tends to generate others from the group—are an increasingly popular method of overcoming these blocks to creative thinking.

Most importantly, an appropriate organizational climate for the stimulation of creativity is a paramount problem of the manager. Faced with the demands of the marketplace and all the resulting time constraints on production, together with the pressure to reduce costs, the development of an appropriate atmosphere for creative thinking is not easily done in practice.[30]

Formal Analysis

The most effective analysis in decision making most certainly would include large doses of judgment and creative thinking. However, systematic reasoning that is guided by a logical process tends to preclude making large errors, particularly errors of omission. At the start of this chapter John Dewey's steps in problem solving were listed as: (1) What is the problem? (2) What are the alternatives? (3) Which alternative is best? Such a process may be called "formal analysis." While the act of following prescribed steps in a formal process might tend to preclude the use of judgment, intuition, and creative thinking, it need not, as there are ample opportunities in each step to exercise these types of thinking if one is alert to them.

There are almost as many versions of the steps in a logical formal process of decision making as there are writers. An attempt to examine all of them would require several chapters. Therefore, the following is offered, without defense, as a useful one:

1. Identification and definition of the problem, including the establishment of an appropriate objective or criterion by which alternative solutions may be judged (called "the criterion for decision making," "the objective function," or "the measure of effectiveness").

2. Identification of alternative courses of action (solutions).

3. Assessment of all factors entering into each course of action leading to evaluation of each course against the criterion for decision making.

---

[29] For an enlightening paper on the characteristics of the creative individual, see William E. Scott, "The Creative Individual," *Journal of the Academy of Management*, Vol. 8, No. 3 (September, 1965).

[30] The major aspects of this problem are explored in a paper by Larry L. Cummings, "Organizational Climates for Creativity," *Journal of the Academy of Management*, Vol. 8, No. 3 (September, 1965), pp. 220–27.

4. Choosing one of the alternatives based upon the evaluation in step 3, giving effect to final judgments in the matter.

DECISION STEPS BY TYPES OF PROBLEMS

Perhaps the most meaningful way to examine each step in the process suggested above is to do so in the light of the various generalized types of problems arising in production, as elsewhere. For this purpose we choose the following classifications: well- versus ill-structured problems, and problems with few versus numerous alternative courses of action. Since these classifications are associated principally with steps 2 and 3 in the decision process listed above, we shall now treat step 1, then return to problem classification.

Problem Identification

Much managerial effort and time can be wasted by working on the wrong problem or on something that is not really a problem in the light of some broader aspect of operations. Common sense dictates that before scarce managerial time is expended in analytical work, the question, "Do we have a problem here and is it really this or something else?" ought to be carefully investigated at least up through the next higher level of management. As indicated in the section of this chapter on hierarchy of objectives, the task of establishing an appropriate objective or criterion for decision making, one that is consistent with higher level objectives, tends to focus attention on whether or not a problem really exists and its true nature.

Step 1 also tends to focus attention on the hierarchy of subproblems within larger problems and thereby helps to answer the question, "Should we be working on this problem now, or a higher level subproblem which, when solved, will cause this problem to disappear?"[31] In short, *problem identification should focus in great part on the sequential nature of complex problems* as described earlier in the chapter. Management decision systems are developed in part for the purpose of ensuring that sequential decision making is properly designed. This is so important in the totality of managerial decision making that we devote all of Chapter 5 to this subject. Now we return to a treatment of the various

---

[31] Not all complex problems are solved optimally by proceeding from the "larger" to the "smaller" subproblem. In some types of problems an appropriate sequential decision process is just the opposite: from the smaller to the larger. In most cases, as in the case of financial planning discussed in Chapter 5, the sequential process is a dual one in which analysis proceeds from the smaller to the larger, and simultaneously from the larger to the smaller subproblem. Then the resulting discrepancies are resolved, largely through judgment.

types of problems before examining steps 2 and 3 in the generalized decision process stated earlier.

Problem Structure

In actual management practice, problems run the gamut from precisely structured to highly ill-structured types. With the well-structured type at one end of a continuum and the ill-structured at the other end, the degree of ill structure rises from zero at the first end to, theoretically, infinity at the second end of the continuum.

Well-structured problems are, of course, the relatively simple types, often but not always involving relatively few alternative courses of action. In addition, step 3 in the generalized decision process—evaluating the alternatives—is relatively simple, often characterized by arithmetic techniques.

Ill-structured problems, on the other hand, are those in which the alternative courses of action are not clear and tend to branch and multiply as the analysis proceeds. Often this type of problem is characterized by risk and uncertainty, while the well-structured types are not so characterized. In highly ill-structured problems, the analyst often does not really know how to proceed. Accordingly, he resorts to trial and error, probing until he makes a discovery or discerns a clue that points the way to the next trial. Discoveries and clues are remembered, stored in memory to combine with each other, and, through the mysterious processes of creative thinking such as incubation and illumination, the analyst discerns the ultimate meaningful alternatives.

More likely, the analyst's trial and error approach involves simultaneous use of steps 2 and 3 in the generalized decision process. That is, alternative courses of action are discerned and evaluated simultaneously. *The process is also iterative, as "trial and error" suggests, often with backtracking to prior decision points in the branching process.* Analysis of this type is often called "heuristic."[32]

Heuristics and Decision Trees. John F. Magee uses the simple case of deciding the location of a cocktail party to explain the branching involved in heuristics that is often called a "decision tree."[33] Figure 3–4 reproduces his example.

The alternatives in the cocktail party location problem are only two: indoors or outdoors. The implicit objective in the problem is, of course, a successful cocktail party in which all the guests are happy, comfortable,

---

[32] See Paul J. Gordon, "Heuristic Problem Solving, You Can Do It," *Business Horizons*, Vol. 5, No. 1 (Spring, 1962), pp. 43–63. This article offers a complex problem to be solved first by the reader, then examines the heuristic process used by the reader.

[33] John F. Magee, "Decision Trees for Decision Making," *Harvard Business Review*, Vol. 42, No. 4 (July–August, 1964), pp. 126–38. He then goes on to apply the decision tree concept to several complex problems that typically arise in business.

and would want to come back again, or invite the host to their parties later. The host must deal with the risk of rain. He will try to choose a party date during a five-day forecast of fine weather.

The decision tree as depicted in Figure 3–4 lays out the problem situation and helps in its analysis by showing the alternatives and their consequences. By assigning probabilities to the event "rain or no rain," arrived at perhaps by gathering facts from the local weather forecast bureau, the analyst can evaluate the alternatives against his objective.

In complex problems involving heuristics, the discerning or discovery of appropriate clues at branch points in the decision tree is not always

FIGURE 3–4

Decision Tree for Cocktail Party

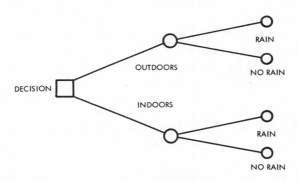

SOURCE: *Harvard Business Review*, Vol. 42, No. 4 (July–August, 1964), p. 127.

easily done. Creative scientists and engineers often resort to the journal literature for the purpose of reading articles on subjects relevant to their problem, hopefully to provide clues when they are "stumped" at a branch point. Another method of bringing to light appropriate clues is group analysis, much like that described earlier as "brainstorming."

Problems with Few Alternatives

Managerial problems take such form as to result in alternative courses of action ranging from none, in which case there is only one action open to the decision maker and he has no choice, to numerous—literally hundreds of alternatives. Inasmuch as there are usually many constraints that cannot be removed in most problems, many problems are of the type having relatively few alternatives.

Often the number of alternatives can be reduced quickly by inspection. Here the manager's judgment or intuition tells him that certain alternatives are clearly inferior to others. He has, in effect, quickly moved to step 3 of the total decision process—evaluation of alternative courses

of action. The desire to reduce the number of alternative courses of
action is understandable in view of the time and cost involved in analysis
of complex problems. However, this desire should not be allowed to deter
creative thinking for the purpose of discerning novel and otherwise
untried alternatives.

Problems with Numerous Alternatives

Consider the problem of the correct quantity of an item to purchase
for resale. There are certain costs involved that vary *directly* with order
size. There are other costs that vary *inversely* with order size. How would
one go about deciding the optimum quantity to order? Obviously there
are innumerable alternatives in such a problem. The alternatives range
from an order size of one unit all the way up to as many units as can be
resold during the planning period ahead. It would be time-consuming,
costly, and in fact, impossible in some cases to calculate the total cost of
each alternative for the purpose of finding the order size resulting in the
lowest total cost. There are many problems of this type in operations,
particularly in the *economics* of operations, where one is usually concerned with "how much." In such problems, *an appropriate decision
process ought to point directly to the one best solution so that each of
the many alternatives need not be evaluated.* Further, it is desirable that
the decision process result in a formula that becomes a rule to follow
every time the same problem recurs. In the literature of management
science, such formulas are appropriately termed "decision rules." A
process that fits these requirements (but is not confined solely to such
problems) is called the scientific method.

EVALUATING COURSES OF ACTION

Before examining the scientific method of analysis, let us first examine
briefly step 3 in the generalized decision process offered earlier—evaluating alternative courses of action. Obviously, evaluating implies "weighing," and weighing must be done against some sort of standard. The
standard is, of course, the objective established in the first step of the
decision process. Also, weighing implies some sort of quantification,
either cardinal or ordinal. Cardinal quantification involves our standard
numbering system . . . 1, 2, 3, etc. Ordinal quantification may be used
where cardinal numbers are not easily arrived at or are not applicable.
For instance, in the decision tree shown in Figure 3–4 three alternatives
might be recognized: rain, no rain, humid. These are three ordinal values
of dryness.

One can sometimes find or develop cardinal numbers by which to
make ordinal values manipulatable by mathematics. For instance, relative humidity measurements may be used to cardinally quantify "dry-

ness." One might designate "no rain" as anything less than 30 percent relative humidity, "rain" as 100 percent relative humidity, and "humid" as anything short of rain but over 70 percent relative humidity, all as measured by wet-bulb thermometer.

In operations problems one frequently encounters in the process of evaluating courses of action a number of factors that can be measured only ordinally. Absolute cardinal values cannot be obtained. In such cases the task of weighing alternatives against the objective will often involve the establishment of indexes to express ordinal values numerically, as in the rain, no rain, humid example above. Many of the values used in expressing various aspects of our national economic conditions, such as the Federal Reserve Board Index of Industrial Production, are really ordinal values expressed numerically. Such values can, with proper handling, be used in the quantitative analysis involved in weighing alternatives against an objective. The development and use of such indexes often requires a good deal of creative thinking. Examples of this type are presented in later books in this series.

THE SCIENTIFIC METHOD OF ANALYSIS

Let us now turn to an examination of the scientific method of analysis, particularly as it applies to problems with numerous alternatives. There are a number of descriptions of the scientific method, but they all come down to the same thing.[34] One version, the one we shall use hereafter, prescribes the following steps:

1. Observe the problem situation, establishing an objective for decision making.

2. Build a hypothesis that explains the relationship of all relevant factors in the problem to each other and to the objective.

3. Test and revise the hypothesis until it serves as an appropriate model of the problem situation.

4. Develop the decision rule.

5. Apply the decision rule.

The scientific method is perhaps so named because of the fact that early scientists, particularly those in the physical sciences, first employed it. Many of the formulas of physics are decision rules developed from a hypothesis that has been tested in the laboratory and found to be true. The method of the physical scientist has been adopted by virtually all successful researchers in the relatively new sciences, for example, the social sciences, and more lately by the so-called operations researcher and management scientist in business.

---

[34] For an extensive and rigorous discussion of the scientific method see Russell L. Ackoff, *Scientific Management* (New York: John Wiley & Sons, Inc., 1962).

The scientific method is actually a special case of the generalized decision process offered earlier. In problems where there are numerous alternatives, making it undesirable if not impossible to examine them all, *the appropriate approach is to establish and prove the validity of a hypothesis that describes the relationships between the variables in the problem as they would exist in the best alternative.* Hence, steps 2, 3, and 4 of the scientific method are actually the equivalent of steps 2 and 3 of the generalized decision process presented earlier.

The various comments made earlier in connection with implementing the steps in the generalized decision process apply in implementing the steps in the scientific method. However, there are some special considerations involved. Most of them derive from the fact that, in implementing the scientific method, the analyst usually is *particularly concerned with quantification of all factors involved in the problem. The method isolates all nonquantifiable factors,* leaving these to be brought into the solution in step 5, applying the decision rule.

Observation

In the observation stage an appropriate measurable objective or criterion for decision making must be established. This is necessary if one is to accomplish the task of identifying the factors (variables) that influence the objective, and also to make at least a preliminary determination of the functional relationships between the variables and the objective.

Building the Hypothesis or Model

The second step in the scientific method is concerned with developing an explanation of the functional relationships between the variables and the chosen objective. If the first stage, observation, has been done effectively, the decision maker will be able to relate the variables to each other and to the chosen objective in a manner that meaningfully explains the problem situation. This explanation is, at this point, merely a hypothesis. Until the hypothesis is tested, it is a dangerous vehicle for making decisions.

How does one go about building a hypothesis that represents a *useful,* if not perfect, explanation of the problem situation? First, the observation stage must be thoroughly exhausted. One can hardly build a satisfactory explanation of the relationships among factors in a problem that he isn't thoroughly acquainted with.

A necessary process in building the hypothesis is that of *abstracting,* a word used frequently up to this point. In fact, throughout all of the materials presented in this text, the process of abstracting takes place. Theorists, businessmen, even housewives use it to develop satisfactory explanations of events. In an attempt to explain a complex situation, we do not include every little jot and detail involved. *We assume away factors that we believe have little influence in the situation. We abstract from the real situation only those factors we think important.* By developing a set of reasonable assumptions, we reduce a highly complex situation to a manageable one. *In short, we convert the actual problem into an idealized problem through the process of abstracting.* Of course, one should keep careful track of the assumptions made in the abstracting process, for two reasons: (1) to preclude a situation in which the problem has been assumed away, (2) to be able later to refer back to the assumptions in order to adjust the final decision through judgment in step 5 of the process.

Having abstracted from the actual complex situation under study and arrived at a plausible explanation of the situation, we have, in the language of the scientist, a *model.* A model is anything that usefully represents the real thing in relatively simple form. There are various types of models that are useful in decision making. Rather than examine them at this point, we shall defer their treatment to Chapter 4. For now, let us continue our examination of the steps in the scientific method.

Testing the Model

The hypothesis, or tentative model, is a plausible representation of the problem situation. It explains in a useful if not perfectly accurate manner "what's involved in the problem" as it relates to the chosen objective. However, one should not proceed to make a decision based on an untested model. To do so in important problems could result in grave errors. Sometimes an appropriate test cannot be found or carried out, and we are forced to make a decision directly from an untested model. Wherever practicable, however, the model should be tested.

In general there are two types of tests. One is a test of explanation and the other is a test of prediction. The latter is the more positive and desirable test. *A test of prediction refers to one in which an experiment is undertaken to determine whether the model can successfully predict events.* This is the technique of the physical scientist. For instance, to test the hypothesis that all freely falling objects accelerate at a certain rate, he predicts from his hypothesis how fast two different objects dropped from a certain height should be traveling after so many seconds. He then sets up an experiment to test this. If the measured speed conforms to his prediction, his model has passed a test of prediction and is considered a useful explanation of the phenomenon of freely falling objects.

Texts of prediction are very often difficult, dangerous, or even impossible to make in business. For instance, an actual test of a hypothesis concerning the effect on sales volume of certain changes in price and advertising could conceivably wreck the business if the hypothesis proved invalid. A going business can be a dangerous laboratory in which to test hypotheses!

Where a practical test of prediction cannot be devised, the second type of test is often relied upon: the test of explanation. In such a test, past data of the company are appropriately inserted in the model to determine whether the model satisfactorily explains past events in the company. If it does, this is taken as sufficient reason for believing it can satisfactorily predict future events *of the same nature.*

Developing the Decision Rule

When the model has been tested favorably, it can then be used for decision making. However, to enhance its use it should be converted, whenever possible, into a so-called decision rule. A decision rule merely restates the model in a form that is directly related to the objective. To effect this restatement, the model must be manipulated mathematically into a form in which the "variable of interest," or the objective function, is clearly shown in its proper relationship to other variables in the problem. In this condition it often takes on the characteristics of a formula, for example: minimum $x = a + b$, where minimum x is the variable of interest, or the objective, and a and b are the other variables in the problem, preferably variables controllable by management.

Applying the Decision Rule

To use the decision rule one merely has to establish the values of the variables. However this does not give the final answer. It merely gets the final decision maker on the target, not the bull's-eye, and in this sense is *only an aid to decision making.* The final answer involves adjusting the solution from the decision rule upward or downward to give effect to judgments involved in the problem. Certain imponderable (nonquantifiable) factors may have been assumed away in the abstracting process of building the model. The final decision maker must introduce into the solution the effect of these imponderables through judgment. This is step 5 of the method.

Furthermore, steps must be taken whereby the analyst may test each new situation in which the same problem seems to arise before applying a previously developed decision rule. Ideally, this involves setting up control devices that automatically indicate when the situation has changed sufficiently to render the old decision rule inappropriate. At this point, the problem must be reanalyzed and a new decision rule developed.

Problems that are solvable by the development of a mathematical model are of the type previously termed well-structured. The mathematical techniques used to solve well-structured problems are often referred to as algorithms. Ill-structured problems by definition are not solvable by algorithmic methods. Heuristic processes are usually required. Both types of problem occur in operations management, and examples are treated fully in subsequent texts in this series.

OPERATIONS RESEARCH AND MANAGEMENT SCIENCE

The practice of operations research grew out of World War II. Prior to the entry of the United States in the war, the British armed forces established a special group of scientists to solve some of the more perplexing problems in the use of scarce resources. For instance, aircraft and destroyers were in very short supply and faced a difficult task in protecting convoys from submarine attacks. The British group was known as "operational research." The American Armed Forces followed suit and their work was known as "operations research." The scientists, working as a team, reformulated old military problems and attacked new problems, principally with the scientific method of analysis explained above.

The work of the scientists proved that many complex problems that were previously solved principally through the informal judgment of military men could be solved better by formal scientific analysis. After the war the practice of operations research spread to industrial problem solving and lately to the work of other governmental agencies. However, many early operations researchers in industry apparently were not very well read in industrial engineering. Neither were many of the writers who extolled the virtues of the "new" practice of operations research. A well-known operations researcher was asked by the writer in 1955, "What's the difference between operations research and industrial engineering?" The answer was, "Very little, or none, if you are referring to the practice of top industrial engineers."

Undoubtedly the work of the operations researchers showed that highly formal analysis, and particularly the use of advanced mathematical techniques, could be applied profitably to perplexing industrial problems. The advent of linear programming techniques and the upsurge of mathematical statistics immediately after World War II undoubtedly gave impetus to industrial operations research. It is noteworthy that many of the early operations researchers were professional mathematicians, or scientists with heavy mathematical backgrounds.

As the practitioners broadened their field of interest to include nearly all of the problems of management, particularly those termed "econometrics," a number of them named their practice "management science," forming The Institute of Management Science in 1954. The journals of these two groups, many of whose members are common to both groups, regularly publish articles explaining the application of complex mathematical analysis to problems of operations that have confounded managers for many years. The authors in this series draw from a number of these journal articles in later texts.

Industrial engineers, operations researchers, and management scientists are constantly striving to develop formal methods of analysis for problems further and further along the continuum in the direction of ill-structured problems. Their early work was centered in the well-structured end of the continuum. And to their credit, they showed that many problems that were once considered so ill-structured as to defy solution via formal mathematical analysis could be converted into problems well-structured enough to be solved in this manner. More powerful mathematical techniques were gradually employed in the process.[35] Their techniques are increasingly employed in organizations of all types, and to remain competitive no business firm can safely ignore them.[36] A number of these techniques are employed in the other texts in this series.

Computerized Decision Making

World War II also gave birth to the modern digital electronic computer capable of making extremely high-speed computations, storing large quantities of information in its "memory," which can be retrieved selectively on signal, to be used in complex mathematical operations. Starting in about 1955 managers recognized the usefulness of the electronic computer for problem solving and its rate of use has grown tremendously.[37] The computer has advanced the science of decision making greatly. It has permitted the use of extremely complex mathematical formulations that would have been impractical and uneconomical by "hand" methods. Accordingly, it has often been the key ingredient in reducing more and more hitherto ill-structured problems to well-structured problems.

Until now the luxury of large-scale electronic computation has been confined to large organizations that had enough computer work to warrant this high-cost specialized equipment. However, with enough small companies sharing the time of a large-scale computer, the cost is brought down to a level that the small organization can afford. The first such

---

[35] For a survey of some of these techniques, see James E. Mulligan, "Basic Optimization Techniques—A Brief Survey," *Journal of Industrial Engineering*, Vol. XVI, No. 3 (May–June, 1965), pp. 192–97.

[36] For a treatment of the usefulness, limits, and myths of operations research from a manager's viewpoint, see Harvey M. Wagner, "Practical Slants on Operations Research," *Harvard Business Review*, Vol. 41, No. 3 (May–June, 1963), pp. 61–71. The author explains why and where O.R. must be used to remain competitive.

[37] For a text on the history of the development of computers and their use by management see John A. Postley, *Computers and People* (New York: McGraw-Hill Book Co., Inc., 1960).

"computer utility" was reported in operation in Boston, Mass.[38] Users send their problems directly to the computer by teletype or other desk-sized access devices. The computer is designed so that it can handle many problems simultaneously. It can also handle assigned priorities, holding up work on one problem to handle a higher priority item, then returning to the original problem to finish it. As a result of this development, *the pressure of competition can now be expected to force more and more small organizations into the use of sophisticated analytical methods heretofore reserved to large organizations.*

Systems Analysis and Computer Simulation

The concept of a "system" is an old one—for instance, we speak of our solar system, our economic system, a production control system. Generally, the term is used to *denote a phenomenon that is complex and has many interrelated aspects.* Interrelationships are the key attribute of a system. Managerial problem solving is certainly characterized by many interrelationships. In fact, one can hardly find a management problem of any consequence that is not somehow interrelated with one or more other management problems. An appropriate solution for one problem in such a system of problems must take explicit account of the interrelationships within the entire system. Sequential decision making, examined earlier in the chapter, is greatly aided by a systems approach, explicitly taking account of the problem interrelationships within the sequence.

When the analyst has diagnosed a problem situation, recognizing its complex of subproblems and their interrelationships, he is in a position to build a model of the system. *This model may be called a decision system.* It may be composed partly of mathematical equations and partly of decision trees as employed in heuristics. The analyst may then *simulate* the decision system by programming an electronic computer to carry out the various interrelated steps comprising the system. The analysis of many complex decision systems found in business today would not be possible without the use of the electronic computer. The "systems concept" and "system simulation" is developed more fully in the next chapter.

DECISION THEORY AND ORGANIZATIONAL DESIGN

In Chapter 2 the organizing function of management was defined as "establishing the relationships between work, workplace, and people." The word "relationships" is quite general and includes all such matters as division of labor, both nonmanagerial and managerial, authority-responsibility relationships, and at lower levels the establishment of work

---

[38] *Business Week* (August 7, 1965), pp. 61–63.

procedures. We also learned that *managerial authority is the requirement to make decisions* for others to carry out. Thus *decision making is directly related to organizational design.*

A decision-making approach to the study of management is thus useful in highlighting the objectives, the alternatives, and the choices involved in the organization and throwing light on its appropriate design.[39] In particular, a *decision systems* approach to the study of management focuses on the "relationships" aspect of organizing mentioned in the definition above. Those who contend that decision making should occupy a considerable portion of the manager's time will find no counterargument here. In fact, we would argue that *decision systems design is a central aspect of the entire management process.*

Modern decision theory tells us much about the operation of an organization. However, it has yet to shed much light on two important aspects of managerial decision making: how long to stave off making certain decisions, and when not to make one at all. This is particularly true in matters of organization structure. The traditionalists tell us that organization structure should be flexible—readily changeable with changes in objectives and plans. They also tell us that organization structure should be stable, not changing frequently for the common sense reason of giving people time to learn their jobs and how to coordinate with one another. Accordingly, the manager must steer an optimal course between organization stability on the one hand and flexibility on the other. In a dynamically competitive situation the optimal *rate* of organizational *change* is difficult to determine. Piling change on change before the prior changes are assimilated has been disastrous in a number of cases. Here is a subject in which the behaviorists could make a fine contribution to management theory via decision theory: an appropriate formal decision process for deciding at what *rate* to make certain types of organizational changes. As of now, managers rely strictly on judgment to solve this problem.

REVIEW QUESTIONS

1. What are the phases of Professor Simon's decision process?
2. What is the first step of a total decision process? How does this step manifest itself down through the levels of management?
3. What is meant by sequential decision making? Why does one employ sequential decision making?
4. Explain the relationship between levels of managerial decision and planning periods.

---

[39] For an extended analysis of the decision-making role of the manager, see William R. Dill, *Decision Making*, Reprint No. 158 (Pittsburgh: Graduate School of Industrial Administration, Carnegie Institute of Technology, 1964).

5. Explain the relationship between the cost of decision making and the number of iterations of the sequential decision process.

6. Explain objective and subjective probabilities and their role in decision making.

7. Under what conditions is problem solving considered creative?

8. What steps might be taken to overcome the perceptual blocks to creative thinking?

9. What are the steps in a logical formal process of decision making?

10. How can the decision tree concept help effective decision making? Explain the relation between heuristics and sequential iterative analysis.

11. What steps are involved in the decision process for problems with few alternatives?

12. What is the difference between cardinal and ordinal quantification in evaluating courses of action?

13. Explain the scientific method of analysis. For what types of business problems is it most useful?

14. Explain the building of a hypothesis that represents a useful explanation of a phenomenon under study.

15. What is the difference between a test of prediction and a test of explanation?

16. What is a decision rule?

17. What is the main contribution of operations researchers to industrial management? What are their main tools?

18. What is the main contribution of the computer to decision making?

19. Why is a decision-making approach to the study of management useful?

SUGGESTIONS FOR FURTHER STUDY

BENNION, EDWARD G. "Econometrics for Management," *Harvard Business Review*, Vol. 39, No. 2 (March–April, 1961), pp. 100–112.
Article stresses how mathematics aids in communications and understanding. Presents reasons why newer techniques are slow in adoption.

BOOT, JOHN C. G.; KLOEK, TEUN; AND THEIL, HENRI. *Operations Research and Quantitative Economics.* New York: McGraw-Hill Book Co., Inc., 1965.
This book discusses the questions with which quantitative economics and operations research are concerned. It integrates econometrics and operations research, thus forming a new combination. Written primarily for the nonspecialist with only a high school background in algebra.

BURGESS, A. R. "A Strategy for Checking Sequential Errors," *Industrial Engineering*, Vol. XIV, No. 4 (July–August, 1963), pp. 181–85.
Presents analytical approach to determining how a sequence of operations can be broken down into subgroups so that checking work will be reduced to a minimum.

COLLENS, G. H.; AND KARASH, J. I. "Four Steps to Answers for Plant Operating Problems," *Factory*, Vol. 122, No. 6 (June, 1964), pp. 81–83.
Provides general statement of problem solving with objectives, abstrac-

tions, alternatives, and solution. Discusses application at Reliance Electric Co. to production problems.

CYERT, RICHARD M., AND MARCH, JAMES G. *A Behavioral Theory of the Firm.* Englewood Cliffs, N.J.: Prentice-Hall, Inc., 1963.
    Discusses the business firm and the way it makes economic decisions. Provides detailed observations of techniques now used by firms to produce models that may predict actual decisions.

DRUCKER, PETER F. "The Big Power of Little Ideas," *Harvard Business Review*, Vol. 42, No. 8 (May–June, 1964), pp. 6–19.
    All great accomplishments start with small ideas. Article discusses the need to take risks with ideas.

————. "Managing for Business Effectiveness," *Harvard Business Review*, Vol. 41, No. 3 (May–June, 1963), pp. 53–60.
    General treatment of management analysis, allocation, and decisions.

FEIGENBAUM, EDWARD A., AND FELDMAN, JULIAN (eds.). *Computers and Thought.* New York: McGraw-Hill Book Co., Inc., 1963.
    Twenty research reports and discussions of outstanding accomplishments in the use of computers in the simulation of human thought process.

HOOPES, TOWNSEND. "Creativity: Key to Organizational Renewal," *Business Horizons*, Vol. 6, No. 4 (Winter, 1963), pp. 35–42.
    Author discusses the need and uses of creative people and ideas in a company's management structure.

KAVANAGH, T. F. "Decision Structure Tables—A Technique for Business Decision Making," *The Journal of Industrial Engineering*, Vol. XIV, No. 5 (September–October, 1963), pp. 249–58.
    Describes decision structure tables and an associated systems-oriented language, TABSOL. Presents various approaches to automatic computer solution of tables.

PORTER, DONALD E. "Two Experiments on Group Decision Making: Are N Heads Better than One," *The Journal of Industrial Engineering*, Vol. XIV, No. 2 (March–April, 1963), pp. 67–72.
    Discusses two experiments that show group size has an effect on the ability of a committee to solve a problem when all members are fully informed but little effect when each member is informed only in unique parts of the problem.

Proceedings of a Symposium on Decision Theory. Athens, Ohio: Division of Research, College of Business Administration, Ohio University, 1963.
    Herbert A. Simon represents the behavioral sciences and William J. Baumol provides an insight into linear and integer programming in discussing recent developments in decision theory.

SASS, MARGO A., AND WILKINSON, WILLIAM D. *Computer Augmentation of Human Reasoning.* Washington, D. C.: Spartan Books, Inc., 1965.
    Contains reports presented at a symposium called to stimulate interest in the synthesis of the capabilities of man and computer.

SHELLY, MAYNARD W., AND BRYAN, GLENN L. (eds.). *Human Judgments and Optimality.* New York: John Wiley & Sons, Inc., 1964.
    Series of readings on relation of judgment to decisions, judgmental

differences between individuals, learning and optimal judgments, the role of judgment processes, and application of judgments to decision making.

WOODSON, WILLIAM S. "Creative Techniques—A Comparative Analysis," *The Journal of Industrial Engineering*, Vol. XV, No. 2 (March–April, 1964), pp. 60–66.

Shows contemporary creative techniques more similar than dissimilar to historical techniques. Any technique works if applied correctly. Stresses proper environment must be established.

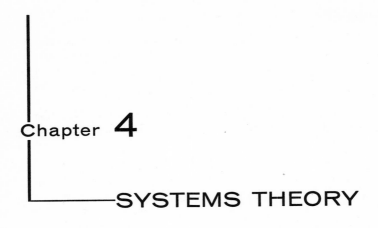

Chapter 4

SYSTEMS THEORY

INTRODUCTION

AT THE END of the previous chapter the concept of a system and how it is related to decision making was introduced. This chapter explores the systems concept more fully, as it plays an important role in the task of solving the more complex problems of operations management. Because of this, one might view *systems theory as a logical extension of decision theory,* which in turn is a logical extension of the traditional "management process," as explained in Chapter 3.

The word "system" is a very old one. It has been used for many years in everyday language and by specialists. It has come to the fore in recent years perhaps because modern technology as employed in "weapon systems" and in large-scale production organizations has accentuated the task of solving complex phenomena composed of parts that are extremely interrelated. Apparently "systems analysis" as a distinct discipline has come of age as evidenced by the announcement by Secretary of Defense Robert McNamara that Dr. Alain Enthoven would fill the newly created post of Assistant Secretary for Systems Analysis.[1]

Many large companies have in recent years created a specialized department named variously systems, systems analysis, or systems engineering. These departments are often established to provide a specialized analytical service for the entire organization, and thus they report to top management. Their members include systems engineers, mathematicians, operations researchers, industrial engineers, management scientists, and electronic computer specialists such as programmers.

Definition of a System

When we try to establish an operational definition of "system" by observing how the word is currently used, we find the task very difficult.

---

[1] *Business Week,* July 17, 1965, p. 41.

At the outset we find that the concept of a system containing interrelated parts called "subsystems," and all the rest of the related terminology, is now widely used. One writer relates hearing on television a minister extolling the superior values of "the systems approach to salvation," identifying each of the values of the good life and "elaborating on their complex interrelationships."[2]

In the systems literature there are various definitions, a few of which are related here for the purpose of settling upon one for our use. Warren E. Alberts stated in answer to the question, "What is a system?": "As you can probably guess, a system is anything you want it to be."[3] He went on to say that they decided not to spend too much time on this question. Perhaps this decision reflects the recognition that almost every intelligent person understands the meaning of "system" and recognizes that it is an old concept. Allan Harvey states that advocates of the *systems approach* exaggerate its newness and further states, ". . . the principles on which it is based are actually time-honored. They are in fact the principles on which many of our great businesses have been built." He goes on to identify a number of business leaders and states that they "had the ability to view the business as an *integrated whole*, that is as a system."[4]

Another author states, "The basic notion of a system is simply that it is a set of interrelated parts." He goes on to say that implicit in this concept is "a degree of wholeness, which makes the whole something different from, and more than, the individual parts considered separately."[5] This aspect of the whole being greater than the sum of its parts, termed the synergistic effect,[6] is of course, not a new one. You learned in basic economics that this is an attribute of an economic system, caused principally by the so-called multiplier effect, a phenomenon that causes the gross national product to increase by an amount greater than an increase in one of its components, say personal consumption expenditures. Not all systems display a synergistic effect, however.

Another writer offers this definition: "The idea of a system is addressed, not to an individual phenomenon, but to the total pattern of phenomena that create an environment and a state of being for a given process."[7] Optner uses "systems analysis" and "problem solving" almost synonymously. This is evident in his statement,

---

[2] Allan Harvey, "Systems Can Too Be Practical," *Business Horizons*, Vol. 7, No. 2 (Summer, 1964), p. 59.

[3] *Report of System Simulation Symposium* (New York: American Institute of Industrial Engineers, May 16, 17, 1957), p. 3.

[4] Harvey, *op cit.*, p. 63. Italics are mine.

[5] Seymour Tilles, "The Manager's Job—A Systems Approach," *Harvard Business Review*, Vol. 41, No. 1 (January–February, 1963), p. 74.

[6] See John F. Mee, "The Synergistic Effect," *Business Horizons*, Vol. 8, No. 2, (Summer, 1965), pp. 56–58.

[7] Stanford L. Optner, *Systems Analysis for Business and Industrial Problem Solving* (Englewood Cliffs, N.J.: Prentice-Hall, Inc., 1965), p. 9.

There is a second reason to employ a system methodology. Solutions in the business environment tend to be *final outcome oriented* . . . pointed at end results without respect to intermediate outcomes and alternatives. The *process orientation* conceives the problem as intrinsically complex, irrespective of its apparent simplicity . . . [requiring] that a problem be divided into its component, serially-related parts . . . broken into manageable segments to be formally restructured for solution.[8]

This statement closely parallels the meaning of the terms *decision process* and *sequential decision making* as explained in Chapter 3.

Finally, we read, "The systems concept is primarily a way of thinking about the job of managing. It provides a framework for visualizing internal and external environmental factors as an integrated whole."[9] We could go on examining many diverse statements about the systems concept, but will probably learn more about it by getting into the subject, which we shall do after offering the following definition: A system is a set of elements so *interrelated and integrated* that the whole displays unique attributes. This definition implies that to understand the *cause* of the attributes of a system one must understand the interrelationships of the elements, called *subsystems*, and how they are *integrated*. If one were to cause a change in the interrelationships of the elements and thereby bring about a different integration, one would expect the system to display different attributes.

TYPES OF SYSTEMS

We are entirely surrounded by, live within, and we ourselves are systems. All of us are familiar with the universe, which is, we think, the all-inclusive system, containing all possible subsystems. That is why it is named "universe." Within this system are all sorts of interrelated subsystems classifiable broadly as natural and man-made.

Natural Systems

The natural subsystems include the galaxies, of which our solar system is a part or subsystem, which in turn includes various planetary subsystems such as the earth-moon set. All these subsystems are explicitly interrelated, as explained in great part by Einstein's theory of relativity. The science of astronomy is concerned with these interrelationships.

Other natural systems include the biological systems such as man with his skeletal, organic, nerve, and muscle subsystems, all highly interrelated to form an integrated whole.

---

[8] *Ibid.*, p. 8.

[9] Richard A. Johnson, Fremont E. Kast, and James E. Rosenzweig, *The Theory and Management of Systems* (New York: McGraw-Hill Book Co., Inc., 1963), p. 3.

Man-made Systems

A social system is, perhaps, the highest-order man-made system on earth. We probably understand less about this system than any other, perhaps because it "grew" rather than was planned and because it is an "open-ended" system, constantly changing on its own (perhaps through synergistic effects) and constantly being changed by man, hopefully to improve it.

Our economic system is man-made, but it too "grew" and was largely unplanned. All of our efforts to improve it, while generally successful to a degree, disclose that, while we know a lot about it, we do not yet fully understand all the complex interrelationships ("structure," as the economist would say) of a high-level dynamic economy.

Hierarchy of Systems

From the above, one can quickly discern that there are systems within systems, within systems . . . man, muscles, nerves, organs, skeleton, for example. Each is a subsystem and is a part of a higher order subsystem, on up through a hierarchy of subsystems to the final system—the universe. Each subsystem has its own interrelated elements that themselves may be subsystems, for example protons, neutrons, mesons and other sub-atomic particles definitely interrelated to form atoms. These in turn are subsystems that are definitely interrelated to form molecules. Remember in your study of chemistry the complex chemical equations that expressed these interrelationships!

Obviously there is a hierarchy of systems, just as, for instance, there may be a hierarchy of management in business, and there is most certainly a hierarchy of problems in management practice. Each system in the hierarchy is a subsystem of a higher order system that includes other subsystems that are interrelated. Just when one is dealing with a subsystem or a system depends upon the point of view and, more particularly, the purpose behind the inquiry. The contractor producing the capsule for an orbital space flight views the capsule as a system composed of many subsystems (life support, guidance, and so on). The project manager in charge of the entire space flight project views the same capsule as a subsystem of the larger system including the booster, launch pad, ground control equipment, and the astronaut. The administrator of the National Aeronautics and Space Administration views the project as a subsystem of a larger system of effort, say space exploration. In any case one can readily discern that, as in the case of the hierarchy of objectives explained in Chapter 2, appropriate subsystem design (man-made systems) calls for subsystem design criteria that tend to support, not conflict with, higher level system design criteria (which of course are really a form of objective).

ORGANIZATIONS AS SYSTEMS[10]

The term systems has been used for many years in business organizations, particularly to denote interrelated procedures. Highly successful executives, as indicated in the Harvey reference given earlier,[11] have always viewed the business firm as an integrated set of subsystems even if they didn't use the jargon of systems analysis.

The successful top manager also recognizes that his organization is a subsystem within the larger environmental system that includes competitive organizations as interrelated subsystems. Sometimes the business manager tries to integrate too closely with competitors and gets into trouble with the Department of Justice Antitrust Division (a part of the firm's environment that can be viewed as a governmental or legal subsystem). In any case he knows that he and his competitors are closely interrelated with the market segment, the needs and desires of which they are trying to fill with their products. This market segment is an environmental subsystem interrelating with all other market segments to form larger market systems. One measure of interrelatedness of market subsystems is the economist's "cross-elasticity of demand."

The successful manager knows that it is useful to treat his organization as a system composed of three subsystems: a social, an economic, and a technological subsystem. We can generalize and say that almost every internal operations problem of any consequence has in some degree these three subsystem aspects interrelated in varying degrees of complexity.

The organization is also usefully viewed as a system composed of interrelated *functional subsystems* variously termed operations, distribution, finance, research, and so on, in whatever manner the top manager finds it most useful to organize his total system as a set of interrelated functional subsystems. Figure 4–1 depicts some of the major functional subsystems interrelated with major environmental subsystems of a business organization. Feedback loops between functions are indicated by dashed lines. Only a few are shown so as not to clutter up the diagram.

Another useful system view of an organization is in terms of "macro" versus "micro" or "coarse" versus "fine" systems.[12] For instance, the general ledger system of accounting for the business firm's finances, including the balance sheet and the profit and loss statement, would be a macro, or coarse, system while the cost accounting system would be a micro, or fine, system that is explicitly integrated with the general ledger system to form the total financial control system. We shall build heavily

---

[10] Gerald Nadler stresses this concept in his *Work Systems Design: The Ideals Concept* (Irwin Series in Operations Management [Homewood, Ill.: Richard D. Irwin, Inc., 1967]).

[11] Harvey, *op. cit.*, p. 63.

[12] Optner, *op. cit.*, p. 31.

FIGURE 4-1
A General Business System Model

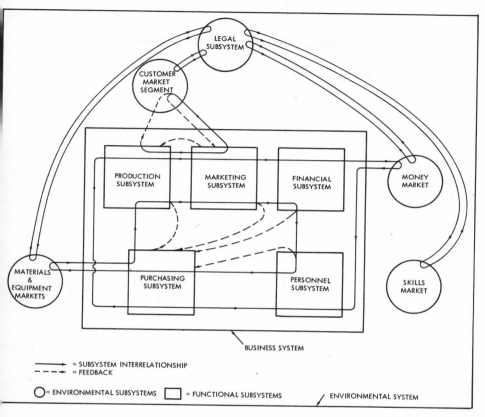

LEGAL SUBSYSTEM

CUSTOMER MARKET SEGMENT

PRODUCTION SUBSYSTEM

MARKETING SUBSYSTEM

FINANCIAL SUBSYSTEM

MONEY MARKET

MATERIALS & EQUIPMENT MARKETS

PURCHASING SUBSYSTEM

PERSONNEL SUBSYSTEM

SKILLS MARKET

BUSINESS SYSTEM

⟶ = SUBSYSTEM INTERRELATIONSHIP
---→ = FEEDBACK

◯ = ENVIRONMENTAL SUBSYSTEMS   ☐ = FUNCTIONAL SUBSYSTEMS   ╱ ENVIRONMENTAL SYSTEM

on this concept in developing *decision systems* for operations in the next chapter.

Production Subsystems

Man-machine configurations in production processes have long been recognized as systems that include interrelated subsystems. The industrial engineering profession, including its educators, has long recognized this in its approach to professional practice. Early texts in the field recognized the importance of a hierarchy of systems when they taught: before attempting a motion and time study of a man-machine (or man only) operation, conduct a careful study of the process of which the operation is a part (the higher level system of which the man-machine system is a subsystem). A number of man-machine systems problems are examined in other books in this series, particularly in Nadler's, *Work Systems Designs: The IDEALS Concept.*

Information Systems

Perhaps the earliest consistent use of the term "systems" was in connection with the transmission of information within the organization as well as to and from its environment. The term "office systems" is an old one, referring originally to the procedures by which documents containing information (data, instructions, orders, acknowledgments, correspondence, and so on) were transferred from sources to points of use in the organization.

Figure 4–2 depicts an information system used in a relatively small manufacturing firm managed by the author in the period 1946–49. The diagram shows the flow of information in the production (volume) planning and control function. Each box in the diagram represents an organization unit. Those in dashed-line boxes were not within the authority-responsibility framework of the production manager in this particular organization. The diagram indicates how the information subsystem for volume of conversion processes in the shop was *explicitly integrated* with the information subsystems for purchasing, product engineering, methods engineering, inventory control, quality control, cost control, payroll, cost accounting, suppliers, tool engineering, shipping, sales, the customer, and the shop worker. Of course these other information subsystems are not fully depicted in Figure 4–2. They are indicated only at the "interfaces" (points where they are integrated) with the volume control system. Each of these subsystems was equally as complicated as the one for volume control. Furthermore, there was a separate, properly integrated, information subsystem for the continuous production work done in this firm. It is not shown in Figure 4–2 in order to simplify the presentation.

It is obvious from Figure 4–2 that the design of information subsystems that are properly integrated with each other is no simple task. The designer must know what information is needed at each decision point and action point in the organization, where this information is generated, and in what form it is needed by the user, among other things. In short, the information system designer must have intimate first-hand knowledge about the work, both managerial and nonmanagerial, for which he is designing the system. He must also know a good deal about the work of *related functional subsystems* in order to properly integrate the information subsystems. Accordingly, the typical information system designer is one who has actually worked in many of the key organization units of the firm, knows first-hand the types of decision making done in each unit, and thereby knows their information needs.

One can easily appreciate, by extrapolation from the subsystem shown in Figure 4–2, which was for a relatively small company, the extreme complexity of systems required for information flow in modern large-

FIGURE 4-2

Information System for Intermittent Production Control, Massey-Harris, Goble Division

COMMUNICATIONS IN INTERMITTENT PRODUCTION

SOURCE: Howard L. Timms, *Production Management* (Bloomington, Ind.: Indiana University, Bureau of Business Research, 1958), p. 43.

scale organizations. The task has magnified in complexity to the point where the electronic data processing machine is almost a necessity for further profitable growth. Thus lately the term "information systems" refers increasingly to sophisticated subsystems designed around the computer as a key subsystem. The computer's ability to process vast amounts of information accurately and rapidly is the key to modern large-scale systems design. The economics involved in systems design of this kind is complex and represents a significant body of thought in its own right.[13]

Total Systems

Over the past few years there has been considerable fanfare in the journal literature in support of "total systems" which sounds very much like an extrapolation from preceding fanfare for "integrated data processing" (IDP). Presumably the organization should develop a *total* information system composed of integrated information subsystems, all centrally computerized, rather than slowly spread the introduction of computerized information subsystems within the organization, as has been done in most cases. For instance, most companies first computerize the payroll subsystem, then parts of the accounting subsystem, say accounts payable and customer billing. These subsystems involve relatively simple hierarchal decision processes and thus the information input and processing problem is relatively simple, even if expensive.

The "total system" proponents rightly observe that, having achieved operational efficiency in the first computerized subsystem installed, one finds that it must be redesigned somewhat in order to integrate properly with the next subsystem installed. Recognizing that serially installed subsystems thereby incur a great deal of redesign, and resulting disruption of operations, they press for *simultaneous* design and installation of the "total system" of integrated subsystems.

The task of designing and installing a total information system is a formidable one even in a relatively small manufacturing firm, as can be appreciated by recognizing that Figure 4–2 represents only one subsystem among many in use in the company. In a large dynamically changing company, with relatively frequent changes in products, processes, procedures, organization structure, personnel, and so on, the total system designer can barely keep up to the changes, let alone successfully incorporate them into his evolving total system design. He has a desperate

―――――――
[13] For a short presentation see John F. Mee, "Information Economics," *Business Horizons*, Vol. 6, No. 4 (Winter, 1963), pp. 61–62. For a full-text treatment, see Adrian M. McDonough, *Information Economics and Management Systems* (New York: McGraw-Hill Book Co., Inc., 1963). For texts that focus on the computer subsystems, see E. Wain Martin, *Electronic Data Processing* (Homewood, Ill.: Richard D. Irwin, Inc., 1965), and Claude McMillan and Richard F. Gonzalez, *Systems Analysis: A Computer Approach to Decision Models* (Homewood, Ill.: Richard D. Irwin, Inc., 1965).

desire to ask top management to hold things constant for a while ("stop the world!") so he can get ahead of the problem. Of course this cannot be done in the typical competitive situation.

To cope with the vast, constantly changing problem situation, the total system designer resorts to what he believes are plausible abstractions. For instance, he will choose to ignore certain subsystems that he believes have a minor influence on the total system. Too often (*always* to the author's knowledge) he is wrong and learns sadly that the exclusion of the "minor" subsystems causes his total system to fail.[14] Accordingly, most people who have had wide experience with the various information subsystems required in even moderate-sized organizations, and who have grappled with the "interface" problems involved, caution the total systems designer to take a less ambitious approach. As one author puts it, "The present quest for 'total systems' should be recognized as a hazardous quest for the ideal. If the use of 'total systems' leads to the impression that it is simple to integrate systems—or if it is only a merchandising slogan—then the term should be discarded."[15]

SYSTEMS AND PROBLEM SOLVING

The concept of an "abstract system" is an important one, particularly for our development of the content of Chapter 5, "Decision Systems." As one author puts it, "Concepts, plans, hypotheses, and ideas under investigation may be described as abstract systems."[16] Whereas physical systems involve things, objects, tangible items as in the case of weapon systems, *abstract systems deal with thoughts.* Thus a rational decision process involving complex interrelated alternatives, with complex variables and constraints, becomes, when properly designed, a *decision system.* Symbolic language is usually used to express the thinking implicit in a decision system. Various diagrams such as flow charts and decision trees, together with mathematical expressions, constitute the expression of a complex decision system.

There are, of course, many systems that are composed primarily of physical elements. Their *design* however, is primarily a thought process—a problem-solving task that involves conceptualizing and then executing a decision process. This is the essence of engineering analysis—complex decision making in respect to physical systems.

---

[14] For one version of a compromise between serially designed and installed systems versus the total system, see John Deardon, "How to Organize Information Systems," *Harvard Business Review,* Vol. 43, No. 2 (March–April 1965), pp. 65–72. At the end of this article there is listed a set of eight articles on information systems available as a composite series of reprints.

[15] Adrian M. McDonough and Leonard J. Garrett, *Management Systems: Working Concepts and Practices* (Homewood, Ill.: Richard D. Irwin, Inc., 1965), pp. 7–8.

[16] Optner, *op. cit.,* p. 28.

Systems Engineering

An examination of the typical approach to the design of a physical system, which may be called "systems engineering," and the analytical part of the task, called "systems analysis," is useful in discerning the essential unity of scientific problem-solving techniques, whether the problem be one in engineering, economics, or any other discipline involving complex matters.

In a paper on the design of physical systems J. K. O'Keefe, Senior Research Engineer, Lockheed Missiles and Space Company, offers a framework "that will *optimize the system functions* in accordance with *system requirements* derived from the design, management, and economic objectives."[17] He stresses that "it is important that the system be properly defined before quantitative analysis is begun. To accomplish this, systems analysis is separated into two parts—qualitative and quantitative."[18] Qualitative analysis is concerned with determining the external (to the system) requirements and transforming them into specifications to be used in the design process. This brings to mind the *product general specifications* (equivalent of "requirements") and *product technical specifications* (design) previously shown in our Figure 1–2. Qualitative analysis identifies the external and internal interfaces of the system, describing the interrelations between the subsystems. "The objective is to establish a conceptual model relating the external requirements to specifications."[19]

The conceptual model developed by qualitative analysis provides the basis for quantitative analysis. The latter is directed toward optimizing the system relative to its environmental requirements. Optimization results from "defining the external and internal characteristics of the system under the constraint of design feasibility. This quantitative analysis, involving all of the technical disciplines applied in the design process, is approached using the applied mathematical concepts common to operations research."[20]

The first part of qualitative systems analysis is a step-by-step organization of the effort. This is essential "because of the iterative process by which complex problems are solved."[21] The steps suggested appear in Figure 4–3.

As indicated in this diagram, the analysis begins with a careful appraisal to "identify the boundaries of the problem," for the purpose of making "a careful statement of the problem."[22] The second step—analyze

---

17 J. K. O'Keefe, "An Introduction to Systems Analysis," *The Journal of Industrial Engineering*, Vol. XV, No. 4 (July–August, 1964), pp. 163–67. Italics are mine.

18 *Ibid.*, p. 163.

19 *Ibid.*, p. 164.

20 *Ibid.*, p. 164.

21 *Ibid.*, p. 164.

22 *Ibid.*, p. 164.

FIGURE 4–3

Organization of the
Qualitative Systems Analysis Process

SOURCE: J. K. O'Keefe, "An Introduction to Systems Analysis," *The Journal of Industrial Engineering* (official publication of the American Institute of Industrial Engineers, Inc., New York), July–August, 1964, p. 164.

problem—is directed toward fully understanding the problem in terms of the problem statement, for the purpose of building a conceptual model of the system. The arrow shown in Figure 4–3 after this step, going back to the start of the previous step, indicates the iterative nature of the task. The model is developed by successive reanalyses of the problem and usually, in physical systems, will be a set of simultaneous equations defining the interrelationships of subsystems and their elements.

The fourth step—test the model—usually will result in backtracking several times, to reconceptualize the model of the system, reformulating the equations that represent the simultaneous interactions of subsystem variables. This iterative process finally results in the proposal of a new model that the analyst believes plausibly represents an appropriate system in terms of fulfilling the requirements, given the design constraints.

In the last step of the sequence the model is used in *quantitative* systems analysis, utilizing the appropriate mathematical techniques. As indicated in Figure 4–3, *the result of this step may cause another iteration resulting in the proposal of a revised model.* Finally, the result of the last step may disclose design specifications that are so questionable as to cause the analyst to iterate the entire process, starting with a complete reanalysis of the problem as indicated by the dashed arrow.

This example of the analysis involved in the design of a physical system is essentially the same process identified as the scientific method of analysis in Chapter 3. The last step shown in Figure 4–3 is equivalent to the step described in Chapter 3 as "developing the decision rule." In the case of physical systems this is concerned with design specifications—key dimensions, forces, voltages, and other relevant physical factors. In economic analysis this step is concerned with relevant costs, revenues, amounts (number of items), and so on.

This technique of iterating a sequence of steps in a decision process is a pervasive one in complex problem solving of almost all kinds, *in all disciplines,* including managerial problem solving. Is it any wonder that all those in the nonhard sciences, even criminal investigators, claim that they employ "scientific analysis" in their work? In many of the specific problem situations presented in subsequent texts in this series, this iterative, sequential, problem-solving approach is applied.

General Systems Theory

The pervasiveness of the scientific method, by whatever name it may be designated in specialized fields, leads one to believe that at some happy date in the future there may evolve a *general systems theory*[23] that will relate the empirical findings in all disciplines to one another. This general systems theory will provide a general framework and, most importantly, a common scientific language, whereby analysts in all disciplines may be able to conduct their research and report their findings in a manner that is understandable to analysts in all other disciplines.

Those who have had an opportunity to read across the literature of a number of disciplines are convinced that research is being replicated many times over, simply because the researchers are not aware that the work has already been done in other disciplines. Even in situations where the researcher believes this to be the case, he cannot be sure he understands the findings in the other disciplines because they are reported in a specialized jargon that is unfamiliar to him.

Also, one senses from the increasing number of journal articles with the words "new" and "breakthrough" in their titles that authors and editors alike are more interested in promotion (both types!) than in

---

23 Johnson, Kast and Rosenzweig, *op. cit.,* p. 6, attribute the origin of this term to Ludwig Von Bertalanffy, "General System Theory: A New Approach to Unity of Science," *Human Biology,* December, 1951, pp. 303–61. Another reference they offer is Kenneth Boulding, "General Systems Theory: The Skeleton of Science," *Management Science,* April, 1956, pp. 197–208.

contributing to the unity of science. In fact, the effort appears to be precisely in the opposite direction—differentiating their "product" with contrived superficiality, often accomplished by creating new jargon for commonplace ideas. This trend has gone so far that practicing managers are increasingly wary of "breakthroughs" offered as panaceas, then after they have been exposed as something quite short of this, characterized meekly as "a new way of thinking." To the oft-bitten manager, these new ways of thinking often turn out to be the scientific method expressed in new terms.

MODELS AND SYSTEMS

The word "model" has been used quite freely so far in this text. It was defined earlier in Chapter 1 as any representation—a scaled-down replica, a verbal framework, a diagram, a mathematical expression (or set of them), which usefully represents an actual situation or condition. We referred in Chapter 3 to the hypothesis or model in an examination of the steps in the scientific method. The model was employed in systems engineering, examined in the previous section of this chapter. Several of the quotations offered earlier from the systems literature employed the word "model." Perhaps we should now examine the various types of models.

The Verbal Model[24]

Everyone is familiar with the verbal model. Any statement in words that describes an actual situation by abstracting only the important aspects is a model of that situation. Businessmen continually use verbal models in their daily discussion of problems. The physicist may frame a verbal model explaining the phenomenon of the energy in a moving object as follows: The energy contained in a moving object (kinetic energy) is a function of its weight, its speed, and the acceleration of gravity.

The verbal model is useful, and in many cases almost indispensable in the early stages of analysis using the scientific method. However, its weaknesses make it useless as a final hypothesis or model from which a decision rule can be developed. In particular, the verbal hypothesis is imprecise and does not lend itself directly to testing. Fnally, in many complex problems a verbal hypothesis cannot be developed at all. Our language does not lend itself to the ready explanation of many complex problems. Only by resorting to the precise language of the mathematician can really complex problems be explained through a model.

---

[24] For a distinctly different method of classifying models see C. West Churchman, Russell L. Ackoff, and E. Leonard Arnoff, *Introduction to Operations Research* (New York: John Wiley & Sons, Inc., 1957), pp. 157–62.

The Mathematical Model

All of the weaknesses of the verbal model are overcome to a great degree by the mathematical model. It is extremely precise. It lends itself more readily to testing. It can be manipulated into the form of an explicit decision rule. The language of mathematics lends itself more readily to the explanation of complex phenomena.

For example, let us convert the physicist's verbal hypothesis or model, cited earlier, to matthematical form. It can take the form $E = f\,(w,\,v,\,g)$ in which E represents kinetic energy, f represents a mathematical function, w represents the weight of the moving object, v represents its speed, and g represents the acceleration of gravity. Through testing the relationships between variables and their effect on the variable of interest, E, the physicist has determined the mathematical function to be as follows: $E = wv^2/2g$. This serves as a precise model and at the same time is in the form of a useful decision rule.

Physical Models

In addition to the verbal and the mathematical model, there are other types of models. Not all of them permit prediction. Nevertheless they are useful aids to decision making. Almost everyone is acquainted with the physical models used by scientists and engineers. By gathering test data on a small physical model of a ship's propeller operating in a tank of water, the engineer can, by applying the mathematical technique known as dimensional analysis, predict how the full-scale propeller will perform. The product engineer finds a physical model, called a *mock-up*, useful in solving design problems too complex to solve completely through the abstractions of layout drafting. Also, he uses the mock-up to test conclusions of his theoretical layout. Problems of fit between product components that assume complex spatial relationships are amenable to solution through use of the mock-up. The design layout, which is itself a schematic model, often does not readily lend itself to positive testing of fits, whereas the mock-up does.

Schematic Models

All forms of diagrams, drawing, organization charts, and graphs are models which, as a class, are sometimes called *schematic models*.[25] They are models in the sense that they represent and explain something. A graphical representation of a certain phenomenon is a model because it

---

25 See Edward Bowman and Robert Fetter, *Analysis for Production and Operations Management* (3d ed.; Homewood, Ill.: Richard D. Irwin, Inc., 1967), chap. ii.

describes how the phenomenon "works." The industrial engineer's material flow chart is a model because, while not being the actual thing, it plausibly represents the actual flow of material from work station to work station. All the figures presented in this text are schematic models.

Process charts, activity charts, PERT networks, man-machine charts, Gantt charts, design flow charts, systems diagrams, assembly diagrams— all these devices and others used by the industrial engineer and others are abstractions of actual complex situations and are models thereof. Many of them do not permit prediction, but nevertheless they aid decision making, and are highly rational techniques of analysis. While they cannot always produce maximizing or minimizing solutions, they aid in doing so. In many problem situations the cost of developing a more elegant model would not be repaid by greater savings.

The schematic model is often useful in deriving a model permitting prediction, for example, the mathematical model. Schematic models are often useful in the observation stage and in the next stage of the scientific method—building the hypothesis. At many points throughout this series the use of schematic models is demonstrated in solving the problems of operations management.

System Models

Because systems can take many different forms: physical, functional conceptual, and so on, as explained earlier in the chapter, *models of systems can take many forms*. One may develop a verbal model of a system, perhaps, then improve it by converting it to a schematic model, then improve that model by converting it to a mathematical model. The model of a decision system may be composed of several types of models. For instance it may be represented by a set of simultaneous equations interlocked with single equations via a decision tree. A model of a system may be composed of a heuristic process expressed by a decision tree, with its decision points expressed as decision rules which themselves were developed from models, as explained in Chapter 3. The characteristics of such a decision system may then be studied by computer simulation of the system, using the model as a basis for programming the computer.

Two broad classifications of models are termed "deterministic" and "probabilistic." The former class is employed where uncertainty and the attending risk, or uncertainty caused by variability, is not a central factor in the problem situation. *Where uncertainty constitutes the central feature of the problem, models employing probability theory and mathematical statistics are the appropriate type.* Decision processes employing such models are often called stochastic processes. Since such processes are often difficult and costly to construct, and often involve the use of subjective (judgmental) measures of probability, the manager will go to great lengths to minimize their need in his business.

Another approach taken to minimize the use of unwieldy probabilistic models is to choose a planning period (for which the decision is being made) short enough that the uncertainty and risk involved are small enough to warrant ignoring them. For instance, rather than planning aggregate production to meet expected demand for a year ahead, the latter part of which is difficult to forecast, the manager may plan only by quarter-years ahead, believing from experience that he can forecast demand during a future three-month period with little risk of error. One does not get something for nothing in these matters, however. In the very least, such a procedure will incur the cost of decision making four times during the year instead of once.

AUTOMATIC CONTROL SYSTEMS

A central feature of man-made systems of all types is the effort in their design to effect control of the interrelationships of system elements so as to *regulate the final output of the system.* For instance, to regulate the temperature in a room, a heating system is designed with a regulating device that *senses and compares* the room temperature with a *requirement,* for instance 75 degrees. This device, called a thermostat, sends appropriate signals to the furnace causing it to turn on and off, thus regulating the temperature of the room within limits close to 75 degrees. The thermostat "feeds back" to the furnace appropriate signals to effect control of room temperature. Accordingly the terms "feedback" and "feedback control" are applied to this regulating aspect of systems.

Feedback Control

A system may be designed as an "open-loop control" system or "closed-loop control" system. Figure 4–4 shows diagrammatically the difference between the two. An open-loop control system does not provide the close control provided by a closed-loop control system. For instance, a street lighting system may be controlled by a clock mechanism which causes the lights to come on at 7:00 P.M. and go off at 5:00 A.M. This is an open-loop system in which the requirement of the environment to be controlled, darkness in this case, is *not sensed directly and compared to a standard for control, nor is the result of this function fed back to affect the input and/or the processor.*

A closed-loop system, on the other hand, does all these things. In the case of the street lighting system, a device (probably a photometer) would sense the degree of actual darkness, compare its finding to a standard which was established as an appropriate requirement of the environment, and affect the electrical input of the system accordingly. The lights would be turned on and off within rather close tolerances of a given degree of darkness set up as the requirement. Thus finer control can be achieved by the closed-loop or feedback control system.

Figure 1–1, the first offered in this text, depicted the firm as a closed-loop system called a *servosystem*. This term is a general one denoting all types of *systems that include one or more feedback control subsystems*. The history of the development of control systems, from "regulator" to "servomechanism," "feedback control," and "servosystem" is given by Chestnut and Mayer.[26] They trace the contributions to modern mathematical "servo theory" from that done in connection with automatically controlled ship steering in 1922 to relatively recent work in the design of automated production equipment with electronic computers built into the feedback subsystem. Throughout the texts in this series, schematic

FIGURE 4–4
Open- and Closed-Loop Control Systems

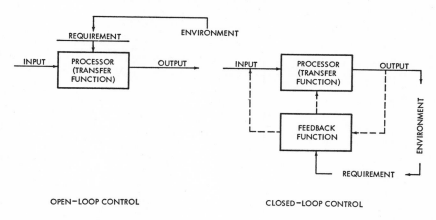

OPEN–LOOP CONTROL   CLOSED–LOOP CONTROL

models of feedback control systems are presented in connection with the design of *decision systems* that take account of appropriately *interrelated decision processes* in operations management.

Stability of Systems

As indicated earlier, feedback control associated with the closed-loop system provides finer control. Offsetting this is the tendency of the feedback to cause the system to become unstable and inaccurate. One may compare stable operation of a feedback control system to the case of a system manually controlled by a well-trained and conscientious opera-

---

[26] Harold Chestnut and Robert W. Mayer, *Servomechanisms and Regulating System Design* (New York: John Wiley & Sons, Inc., 1959), pp. 13–19.

tor. Unstable system operation would be what one would expect from a system manually controlled by an untrained and negligent operator.

Where the feedback subsystem incurs significant delay and amplification in its response to changes in the environment being controlled, the result can be erratic and/or sustained oscillations in system performance. Ordinarily, finer (more accurate) control can be effected by amplifying the feedback signal. This in turn requires a shorter time duration for the signal to effect the required corrective action. If the feedback signal is prolonged beyond this required duration, the system output will tend to overshoot the desired level. Those who remember their physics will

FIGURE 4–5

Amplification of System Output Caused by Lagging Feedback

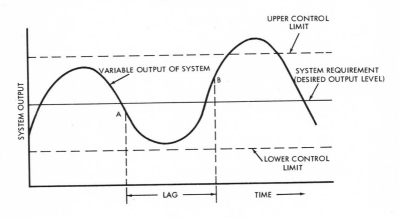

A = Point in time when direction of output is noted.
B = Point in time when corrective feedback signal is applied.

recognize as a parallel phenomenon the *hysteresis effect* when magnetizing iron. Also, those who remember their economics will recognize the *acceleration principle* as an equivalent phenomenon.

If the timing of the feedback signal is erroneously applied in the operation of a system, erroneous response and sustained oscillations can be expected. Figure 4–5 illustrates a situation in which a poorly timed (lagging) response to a sensed change in the output of a system causes an undesirable amplification of system output.

Appropriate feedback subsystem design calls for providing an adequate margin of stability and includes features that cause the system output to recover quickly from ill-timed corrective signals as well as the shocks of irregular inputs. All of these matters are treated in the subject of "servo theory" which is concerned with the mathematics of feedback control design. It is quite complex, involving the application of higher mathematics, and inappropriate to examine fully in this basic text.[27] Nevertheless, the features of feedback control explained above provide a firm basis for the development, in subsequent texts in this series, of production decision systems involving feedback.

Automation

Del Harder of the Ford Motor Company is reputed to have coined the term "automation" in 1946. At that time the term described highly automatic conversion process equipment in which the functions normally performed by several standard machine tools, with separate material handling operations between them, were telescoped into a specially designed machine called a "transfer machine." Within this machine, the piece being machined was automatically transferred from station to station, each station containing certain cutting tools that would automatically perform their task, then back out of the way while the workpiece was automatically moved to the next station. The transfer and positioning of the workpiece, together with the movement of the cutting tools, were all "programmed" and carried out by electromechanical devices—servomechanisms of various types.

Many of these machines were fully automated in the sense that they operated as part of a production line without human intervention. For instance, in 1946 Selas Corporation of America developed for Inland Steel Company a heating apparatus that processed a continuous strip of electrolytically plated steel. This unit included a servosystem in which the temperature of the strip was sensed by a pyrometer which in turn activated a selsyn unit that in turn activated the heat source to continuously correct for slight variations in the temperature of the rapidly moving steel strip. A computer was not required for fully automatic feedback control in this apparatus. A number of similar fully automatic production processes were developed in the period immediately following World War II.

With progress in the development of the electronic computer, particularly in its reliability and miniaturization, more complex production processes were fully automated. The computer permitted the use of multiple feedback systems that could not have been synchronized by ordinary electromechanical servomechanisms. Thus cutting tools could be adjusted automatically for tool wear. Desired production quality as

[27] Those wishing to pursue this subject further should see Chapter 6, "Methods for Determining Systems Stability," in Chestnut and Mayer, *ibid*. Other texts containing a treatment of this subject are: Gordon S. Brown and Donald P. Campbell, *Principles of Servomechanisms* (New York: John Wiley & Sons, Inc., 1953); John G. Truxal, *Automatic Feedback Control System Synthesis* (New York: McGraw-Hill Book Co., Inc., 1955); Arnold Tustin, *The Mechanism of Economic Systems* (London: William Heinemann, Ltd., 1953).

well as quantity could be achieved without direct human intervention in the process. Thus we have automation in production processes as well as automation in the office—automatic data processing, and, more generally, information systems. Automated production processes are physical systems, with multifarious feedback subsystems, within which the computer is a subsystem.

SYSTEM SIMULATION

If we *know enough* about an actual system, whether it be a physical, functional, information, or decision system, we can develop a model of the actual system. We can then use this model in various ways, hopefully *to learn more about the operation of the system as a whole than we knew when we constructed the model.* We can, for instance, manipulate the parameters, variables, constraints, and alternatives comprising the model, and thus, hopefully, the system itself. In short, we can *simulate* a variety of ways in which the actual system might be caused to operate by manipulating its model. This simulation may disclose aspects of the system that either were not known at all or, if we were aware of them, we had no idea of their true nature, magnitude, or variability.

Simulation and Problem Solving

The operation of a system may be simulated "by hand" or by computer, depending upon the complexity of the model and its manipulation. For instance, in designing a facility such as a plant, one must develop a layout (arrangement) of the equipment such as machine tools in a factory or storage bins in a warehouse, deciding their optimal locations relative to one another and to the plant environment (receiving and shipping docks, ingress and egress points for workers, for instance). There are often numerous *alternative relative locations* of the equipment, and therefore of the *flow of goods* and the *travel of workers* in the plant. If the number of alternatives is not excessive, one can use a physical model of the plant, including its floor space and templates of the equipment, all at reduced scale, to evaluate alternative locations. One can *experiment* with alternative locations, using a heuristic decision process, to arrive at an optimal arrangement of equipment, thus solving the layout problem. This problem is explained fully by Reed in his book in this series.[28]

On the other hand, if the number of alternatives involved in such a layout problem is quite large, and particularly if multiple criteria are involved in evaluating alternatives (often the case in respect to working

---

[28] Ruddell Reed, Jr., *Plant Location, Layout, and Maintenance* (Irwin Series in Operations Management [Homewood, Ill.: Richard D. Irwin, Inc., 1967]).

conditions), and further, if all possible alternatives cannot be clearly recognized, the manipulation required for meaningful experimentation is often so complex and time-consuming that use of the computer is appropriate if not mandatory. The analyst will develop appropriate decision trees, together with appropriate decision rules for each decision point in the tree. This is essentially a schematic model of the layout decision process. The schematic model will then be reproduced as a *computer program,* using "appropriate computer language." This is known as a *computer model.* Sometimes the inherent limitations of the computer force the analyst to further simplify his model of the decision process. This, of course, may result in a solution that is less than optimal. In the extreme, this condition can result in a downright foolish solution. Thus the analyst must always apply judgment to the computer solution, and perhaps iterate the decision process over again.

The above is a description of experimentation with a model to simulate the operation of a system, and thus experiment with the system "on paper" rather than "in the flesh." The system is a *dynamic* one in that flow of goods and travel of workers is involved. In this type of simulation, the analyst is interested in finding the best state of *dynamic equilibrium* of the system. This example is also one of the many *simulations for decision making* that have been employed for many years "by hand," and more recently by computer. A great number of physical problems, such as those in engineering, and especially those involving dynamic equilibrium, have been solved for many years by product designers and by industrial engineers using hand methods of simulation and, more recently, computer methods.[29]

The layout problem described above is one normally decided at the middle management level in a large firm (by the chief industrial engineer, for instance), or by top management in a small firm, with perhaps, only two management levels. Not all management decision processes that involve creative thinking, judgment, and heuristic thinking are top management problems, by any means. Some writers are prone to divide management decision making into two classes: ill-structured problems that are more or less the province of top management, and well-structured problems that are more or less the province of lower management. This is a dangerously misleading classification for at least two reasons: (1) it does not apply in the case of small firms whose problems, in operations at least, are essentially the same as those of the large firm— and such a firm often has only one level of management, (2) a study of the decision making required in the problems these writers would consider lower level problems reveals a large number of ill-structured problems. The major ones are examined in detail in other books in this series.

---

[29] See, for instance, Roy E. Lave, Jr., and Handy A. Taha, "A Program for Simulating the Operation of an Overhead Crane," *Journal of Industrial Engineering,* Vol. XVI, No. 2 (March–April, 1965), pp. 87–93.

Perhaps those who associate ill-structured problems primarily with top management have in mind the problems of *policymaking*. This type of decision making usually is the province of top management in an organization of any size. In the context of the concepts developed in this text, *policymaking is problem solving, usually of the ill-structured type, but is not the only ill-structured type.*

Simulation and Policymaking

Some researchers assert that simulation occurs whenever a model of any sort is used in analysis.[30] The model is itself a simulation of the actual problem situation. This view coincides closely with the concepts developed in this text. According to this view, simulation is useful in decision making at all management levels, not just the policymaking level, and has been in use for many years.

In the past decade, however, research has been increasingly directed toward the improvement of decision making of the *policy formulation* type. Policy problems for the organization as a whole should evolve from the operation of the organization as a system, with feedback subsystems integrating the organization with its environment. Additionally the organization's proper operation should have its functional subsystems explicitly integrated with each other by feedback subsystems. Increasing acceptance of this systems concept of the organization, and especially the feedback feature, together with the ability of the computer to handle many complex numerical and branching (yes-no) manipulations, has led to greater use of computer simulation for policymaking. Some examples that give promise of being helpful to top management in policymaking are explained in the next section.

LARGE-SCALE MICRO MODELS

A number of models have been constructed for aiding in decision making in *large-scale microsystems—large portions of the organization's work.* A few of the large-scale micro systems that have been reported in the literature are described below. It is not always clear from the articles whether these decision systems are in actual operation or whether they are still under test. Several that your author has investigated have been dropped. They were used as a research tool—to provide better insights into operating problems, rather than as a continuing decision-making tool. After wringing out all the insights possible, the model (and the "running" of it as a computer simulation) has been discontinued. At the most, it improved the judgment of the decision makers. At the least,

---

[30] W. K. Holstein and William R. Soukup, *Monte Carlo Simulation,* Institute Paper No. 23 (Institute for Quantitative Research and Economics and Management, Graduate School of Industrial Administration, Purdue University), p. 1.

it compressed a good deal of synthetic but valuable experience into a short period of time.

Waiting Line Simulations

Perhaps the most widespread large-scale decision systems that have been modeled and run as computer simulations are those involving queuing or waiting line situations. These situations are ubiquitous in operations. Several were mentioned in previous sections of the chapter, and others are explained fully in subsequent books in this series.

Warren E. Alberts of United Airlines described a simulation begun in 1954 of the "operation of the entire maintenance situation at one of United Airlines' major stations."[31] The irregular arrivals of maintenance tasks at the station could not be expressed as a mathematical model. Accordingly, they were simulated by the technique called "Monte Carlo." This is a method, using random number tables, of devising a model in which there occurs the same long-run frequency of artificial events as the actual events the analyst is studying. In this problem of aircraft maintenance, the events are arrivals of aircraft for maintenance at the station, forming a waiting line. The Monte Carlo technique is useful in analyzing many waiting line problems. It is explained fully by Ruddell Reed, Jr., in his series text.[32]

Having developed a model of the maintenance task arrivals at the station and a computer program for it, the United Airlines people could experiment on paper rather than "in the flesh" with the operation of the maintenance station. Using a computer to run the system model of the station, they could test various changes in alternative combinations of system inputs—"the number of men on each shift, the facilities required, the schedule pattern [production schedules] and our maintenance philosophy [set of policies]. As output, we get reports such as one would actually get in actual operation."[33] The computer model yielded reports on 100 days of station operation in 12 minutes.

The schematic model of the problem situation, including the role of the computer in the operation of the system, is indicated in Figure 4–6. Various alternative combinations of system inputs as indicated in the schematic model were tested for the purpose of learning more about the system's synergistic effects, if any, and thus aiding in the design of a total decision system for actual operation of the station. Thereafter, as input conditions shifted materially, the system could be remodeled and retested

---

[31] Warren E. Alberts, "Report to the Eighth AIIE National Convention of the System Simulation Symposium," *Report of System Simulation Symposium* (New York: American Institute of Industrial Engineers, Inc., 1958), pp. 1–5.

[32] Reed, *op. cit.*

[33] Alberts, *op. cit.*, p. 3.

FIGURE 4–6

Schematic Model of the Operation of a United Airlines Maintenance Station

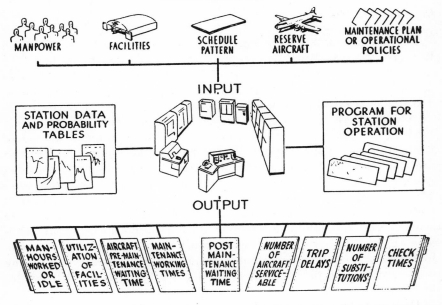

SOURCE: *Report of System Simulation Symposium* (held in conjunction with the 8th National Convention of the American Institute of Industrial Engineers, May 16, 17, 1957), p. 1.

to determine whether or not the total decision system should be revised and in what ways.

Other early waiting line problem simulations were briefly described in the 1958 symposium referenced above. R. R. O'Neill reported on research being done on a simulation of a cargo-handling problem.[34] In this problem, various types of incoming cargo to be loaded on a ship form a line awaiting the availability of loading equipment. The problem is one of optimizing the amount of and use of the loading equipment. Mr. O'Neill presents the mathematics of the exponential distribution of the waiting line events.[35] Similar mathematical presentations are given in other texts in this series.

Norman H. Jennings reported on a simulation used by the Port of New York Authority to study the effect of using various sizes of passenger platforms at the Mid-Manhattan Bus Terminal.[36] Approximately 17,000 commuters required approximately 370 suburban bus departures during the 5:00 to 6:00 P.M. rush hour. Lines of commuters and of buses at the loading platforms presented a problem in depot design, layout, and

---

[34] R. R. O'Neill, "Simulation of Cargo Handling," *ibid.*, pp. 24–27.

[35] *Ibid.*, pp. 24–25.

[36] Norman H. Jennings, "Computer Simulation of Peak Hour Bus Operation," *ibid.*, pp. 28–31.

operation. Computer simulation of the problem situation permitted a useful study of various combinations of alternatives.

Other researchers reported in the 1958 symposium on the use of simulation in inventory control problems. An inventory is a stock that is reduced as orders are filled from it. The orders may be random in size and in time of arrival. A waiting line of orders builds up. The problem can take the form of optimal inventory (quantity) required to service an incoming flow of orders. Robert G. Brown of the consulting firm of Arthur D. Little, Inc., reported on a "General-Purpose Inventory Control Simulation" for this purpose.[37] Jack K. Weinstock of The Ramo-Wooldridge Corporation reported on the use of simulation in an inventory study made for one of the largest suppliers of automotive replacement parts. "The problem they faced was whether or not the present inventory dollars were being used most effectively. That is, could the total inventory be redistributed among commodities and branch warehouses in such a way as to reduce the percentage of lost sales?"[38] The company's policy was to maintain the total inventory as low as possible while maintaining the percentage of lost sales (because of an "outage" of a given item) to demand at about 10 percent. The simulation permitted testing on paper various alternative methods of achieving low inventory while conforming to this policy and, conversely, testing other policies for achieving a higher return on inventory investment. This problem is treated in another book in this series.[39]

Finally, Allan J. Rowe of General Electric Company reported on the use of simulation in the production scheduling problem in what is perhaps the most difficult type of production from the scheduling point of view—slow-moving items or "job shop" production.[40]

The problem arises because, with low volume of the various processes, the shop machines, or more generally, work stations, cannot be specialized in their use. For instance, a stamping press must be used for a number of different stamping operations on a number of different product components, on a drill must be used to perform drilling operations on a number of different product components. There is insufficient volume of a given operation to warrant specializing a particular machine in that operation as in the case of a so-called production line. Accordingly, there arise waiting lines of work orders ahead of the various work stations used in a sequence to perform the total conversion processes.

This job shop scheduling problem has many facets: in process planning and plant layout, it is a problem of optimal investment in work

---

[37] *Ibid.*, pp. 6–16.

[38] Jack K. Weinstock, "An Inventory Control Solution by Simulation," *ibid.*, pp. 65–71.

[39] James H. Greene, *Operations Planning and Control* (Irwin Series in Operations Management. [Homewood, Ill.: Richard D. Irwin, Inc., 1967]).

[40] Allen J. Rowe, "Computer Simulation Applied to Job Shop Scheduling," in Alberts, *op. cit.*, pp. 59–64.

stations (install one, two, or three punch presses, for instance). In the case of the plant in being, the problem becomes one of optimally scheduling the work orders across the various existing work stations. This problem is explained fully by Greene.[41]

DYNAMIC MACRO MODELS

Earlier in the chapter a distinction was made between "micro" and "macro" models. These are relative terms depending upon the point of view. From the point of view used in this text, a dynamic macro model of the production function would include all the functional subsystems described in previous chapters, together with all the integrated decision subsystems that cause the functions to be performed on an ongoing (dynamic) basis, and all the information subsystems that provide inputs to decision systems and outputs from decision systems to functional subsystems. This concept of a "total system" was decribed earlier in the chapter. There are to date no known cases of such dynamic macro models in use. There are some models under study, however, that approach this definition and give promise of pointing the way to future development of true dynamic macro models of operations. Two such simulation models are explained below.

Industrial Dynamics

This term is the name given to research being done by Prof. Jay W. Forrester and his associates at the Massachusetts Institute of Technology. Forrester defines industrial dynamics as "A method of systems analysis for management. It deals with the time-varying interactions between the parts of the management system.[42] These "parts" are identified as "flows of information, orders, materials, money, personnel, and capital equipment."[43] Forrester continues, "Industrial Dynamics is the study of all the information feedback characteristics of industrial activity to show how organization structure, amplification (in policies) and time delays (in decisions and actions) *interact* to influence the success of the enterprise."[44] The "interactions" are accomplished in Forrester's computer model by employing feedback routines that express the structure, delays, and amplifications of the system, as explained in general terms earlier in this chapter.

Forrester explains, "The structure of a system tells how the parts are related to one another. Delays always exist in the availability of infor-

---

[41] Greene, *op. cit.*

[42] Jay W. Forrester, *Industrial Dynamics* (Cambridge, Mass.: The Massachusetts Institute of Technology, 1961), p. 9.

[43] *Ibid.*, p. 8.

[44] *Ibid.*, p. 13. Italics are mine.

Response of Production-Distribution System to Sudden 10 Percent Increase in Retail Sales

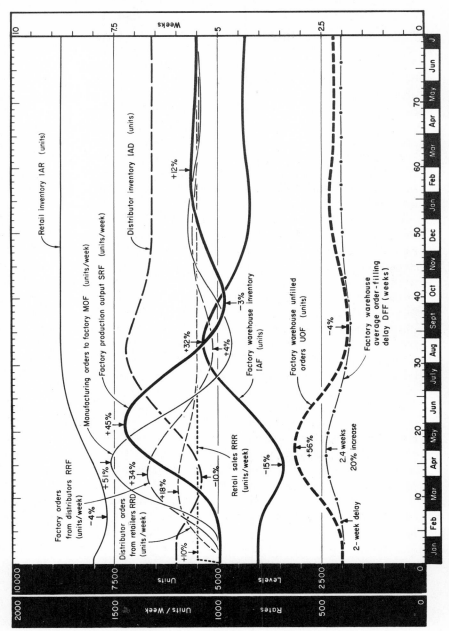

Reprinted from *Industrial Dynamics* by Jay W. Forrester by permission of The M.I.T. Press. (Cambridge, Mass.: Massachusetts Institute of Technology, 1961), p. 24.

mation, in making decisions based upon information, and in taking action based upon the decision. Amplification usually exists throughout such systems, especially in the decision policies of our industrial and social systems.[45]

Amplification in the flow of materials has been known to economists as "the acceleration principle." A simple example is as follows: "A firm has been selling 1,000 units a month. *Policy is to carry 2-months stock*, or 2,000 units. Management forecasts a drop in sales next month of 10%, down to 900 units. Thus, next month's stock should, with the *policy unchanged*, stand at 1,800 units. Purchases should now cover 900 units to replace the expected sales, less 200 units to lower the month-end stock to 1,800 units. *Thus purchases drop 30%, down from 1,000 to 700 units in a month, to accommodate an expected drop of only 10% in sales*. Multiply this back through the chain of processors to the extractor of raw materials and the cumulative effect is impressive."[46]

Forrester's studies have generally emphasized relationships *between institutions* in the chain of producer-sellers of goods as shown back in Figure 1–3, *rather than between functions and stages within the firm.* Accordingly, his simulations are not "total" in the sense of dealing with problems at all levels within the firm. His studies of decision making have been directed toward *policy decisions* rather than the decision processes required to implement policy. He would be concerned, for instance, in the example cited above, with the policy of carrying two months' sales in inventory. The amplification effect resulting from this policy (30 percent versus 10 percent) gives a clue that such a policy may be a poor one in certain market situations. Accordingly, a computer simulation of the flow of materials between institutions in a long chain of producer-sellers may be useful in studying the effect of revising certain policies when faced with changing conditions. The outputs of Forrester's computer simulations are expressed as time series which, when plotted, express graphically the dynamic response of the various "flows" to changes in the marketplace, given certain policy decisions, Figure 4–7 is an example of one of his graphs.

For the reasons given above, Forrester's model cannot properly be called a model of the total decision system for production. Nevertheless, his research represents a forward move in the task of applying the scientific method (and simulation) to the management of operations.

Intrafirm Models

Whereas the researchers in industrial dynamics stress relations *between* institutions—for example, the flow of orders and goods between

---

[45] *Ibid.*, p. 15.

[46] Howard L. Timms, *Inventory Management of Purchased Materials* (New York: National Association of Purchasing Agents, 1958), p. 9.

factory, field warehouse, dealer, and ultimate customer—other dynamic macro models have been developed for studying the interrelations between subsystems *within* the firm. Perhaps the first model of this type was developed by Charles P. Bonini.[47] His model combines macro features, that is, consideration of the firm as a whole, and some micro features, that is, considerations of the effect of changing decision rules in various subsystems of the firm. His model is quite realistic in at least two respects: (1) it deals with control within the firm by using the accounting system (budgets)—a refreshingly realistic approach; (2) it takes account of behavioral patterns that are quite realistic in general, if not in particular organizations at particular times.

Bonini's model relates behavioral patterns to accounting control via budgets through the concepts of *organizational slack* and *pressure*. Slack is likely to occur in the organization when cost budgets and sales budgets, and thus profit goals, have been achieved for some time. Members of the organization tend to "ease off," and inefficiency creeps into operations.[48] Conversely, when budgets are not being met, pressure builds up within the organization to achieve better performance. By the use of an Index of Felt Pressure devised for each decision maker in his model firm, Bonini is able to *interrelate* accounting control and human behavioral patterns and thus take account of system effects in his simulation.

The Bonini model, employing as it does both accounting control and interrelated behavioral patterns, is quite realistic. Where it lacks realism is in the area of decision processes leading to decision rules. Most of the decision rules in his simulation appear to be the product of rather unsophisticated decision processes, very much like those one would expect to find in a small firm whose volume of business (and/or quality of management) does not permit having specialized analysts in the organization.

Aside from this, the Bonini model, like the industrial dynamics model, is essentially static in that it does not take account of the adding and dropping of products, the improvement of processes through changes in technology that affect processes directly or indirectly through changes in product specifications, and resulting opportunities for better plant layout, and so on.

It is important to recognize that models such as Forrester's and Bonini's are not yet operationally useful to the manager in carrying out his task. This is true if only because to date the computer models have been limited to second order, linear, and single feedback systems. The order of a decision system relates to the number of integrations involved.

---

[47] Charles P. Bonini, *Simulation of Information and Decision Systems in the Firm* (Englewood Cliffs, N.J.: Prentice-Hall, Inc., 1963).

[48] This concept is explained more fully in R. M. Cyert and J. G. March, "Organizational Factors in the Theory of Oligopoly," *Quarterly Journal of Economics*, Vol. 70 (February, 1956), pp. 52–58.

Closely related to the order of the system is the multiplicity of feedback loops. Most operations problems involve many orders of integration and many feedback loops, as other texts in this series will show. Finally, the interactions of the multiple feedback systems normally produce non-linear effects in actual operations. As Professor Forrester puts it, "Only the simplest of feedback systems have been explored."[49] Nevertheless, every operations manager should keep abreast of research such as Forrester's and Bonini's, if he is to be ready for possible future opportunities to improve his operations.

SYSTEMS AND MANAGING

The concept of a *management system* logically follows from the definition of "system" offered earlier in the chapter. Also, it logically follows from the "traditional" approach to management thought—the so-called *management process* described in Chapter 2.

The Management Process as a System

The management process was described in Chapter 2 as (1) establishing objectives, (2) planning work (mental as well as physical) so as to achieve the objectives in an optimal fashion, (3) organizing the planned work (assignment of *authority—the making of decisions*, and responsibility), (4) motivating workers to carry out planned work as organized, and (5) controlling the performance of work. We can convert this *verbal model* of managing into a *schematic model* as shown in Figure 4–8.

The traditionalists never described the management process as a static step-by-step process. They described it as a system, but did not use the word. They recognized that having established objectives, the successful manager did not then plan, without ever going back, perhaps, and altering the objectives, or without taking into account the organizational aspects of the total task, nor the controlling aspects. In fact, they recognized that the "functions of management" constituted an *iterative process* in which the functions were highly *interrelated* when performed by a capable manager. In this sense, the functions of management are equivalent to the elements of a system, with feedback between the elements or subsystems, as indicated by the dashed lines in Figure 4–8.[50]

Further, the traditionalists recognized that the management process is

---

49 For a fuller explanation of the limitations of the present state of the art of employing feedback in business simulation, see Jay W. Forrester, "The Structure Underlying Management Processes," *Evolving Concepts in Management* (Proceedings of the 24th Annual Meeting, Academy of Management, Chicago, Ill., December 28–30, 1964), pp. 59–61.

50 For another figure indicating equivalence between the management process and the systems concept, see McDonough and Garrett, *op. cit.*, p. 10.

FIGURE 4–8
Systems Model of the Management Process

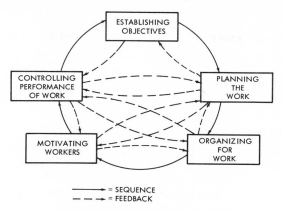

———▶ = SEQUENCE
— — —▶ = FEEDBACK

a dynamic one (the manager's work is never done!). As changes occurred in the environment (subsystems) of the firm, these changes were noted by the management,[51] were fed back into the continuously performed management process, resulting in revised objectives, and so on. In practice, capable managers attempt, usually in the face of a dynamically changing competitive environment, to achieve a state of dynamic equilibrium in the execution of the management process. However, equilibrium is rarely achieved because of the changing environment. Accordingly, the management process is also dynamic on a time scale. This point was made back in Figure 3–3, *Continuous Cycles in Decision Making*.

Feedback and Management Control

Just as the feedback loop is a subsystem of the system it controls, feedback is a subsystem of the control function of management. The traditionalists cited "management by exception" as a "principle" in the control function. All engineers know that it is next to impossible to design a physical feedback system that can control the system output, say the torque of a rotating shaft under varying load, to be absolutely constant. Rather, they approach the task by deciding the system requirement in respect to varying torque—the variation in torque that can be tolerated. Then they design the system so as to maintain the variation in torque within these prescribed limits. When the actual torque exceeds certain "control limits," the feedback system signals the processor to take certain corrective action. As long as the torque is within the control limits, the processor takes no corrective action.

---

[51] Herbert A. Simon's "Intelligence" function—see footnote reference 2, Chapter 3.

The same is true in the control function of the management process. Corrective action is exerted on an "exception basis." Control limits are established, formally where possible and informally otherwise. When performance of work, either physical or mental, or both combined, exceeds control limits, corrective managerial action is taken. As long as performance is within control limits, no corrective action is taken.[52]

Systems Analysis and Organizational Design

Chapter 3 closed with a section on "Decision Theory and Organizational Design." We stressed the fact that decision making is the heart of the functions comprising the management process. It logically follows that a *decision systems* approach to management should be useful.

The organizing function of the management process, as explained in Chapter 2, is concerned with *structure* at the top management level, and *procedures* at the lower management levels. (In the single-manager firm there is no problem of management structure, just procedures.) The organizing function is also concerned with dividing and grouping non-managerial as well as managerial work. In short, the capable manager will organize his firm as a set of *procedural or functional subsystems*, interrelated by means of a set of interrelated *information systems*, which in turn feed a set of interrelated *decision systems*, which in turn operate the functional subsystems.

Thus the task of designing the total organization is essentially one of designing three interrelated internal subsystems: functional, information, and decision. These in turn must be interrelated with environmental subsystems as indicated back in Figure 4–1. In turn each of these is composed of interrelated subsystems. Feedback characterizes the entire system. Figure 4–9 indicates the three-dimensional nature of the total internal system.

In designing each of the three systems, the designer must take into account the other two. A functional system designed without regard for the decisions necessary to cause it to operate properly is not a well-designed system. In turn, an information system designed without regard for the decision system required to make the functional system work successfully is also poorly designed. When the total system is designed and operating, the functional system feeds its data outputs into the information system, which in turn feeds its output into the decision system, which in turn feeds its outputs back to the functional system. Thus, the whole is a closed-loop system. In this series the *decision system* element of the total system design task is emphasized.

---

[52] Statistical methods for establishing control limits are explained in Robert B. Fetter, *The Quality Control System* (Irwin Series in Operations Management [Homewood, Ill.: Richard D. Irwin, Inc., 1967]).

UNIFIED MANAGEMENT THEORY

We have tried in Chapters 2 through 4 to unify in some degree management theory, decision theory, and systems theory, all for the purpose of proceeding in a knowledgeable way with a study of managing the operations function. We have not *proven* that there *is* a "unified theory of management." To do so, if it is possible at all with the present state of knowledge about managing, would require a full-length text. Undoubtedly we are witnessing the evolution of a theory of management,

FIGURE 4–9
Total System Elements

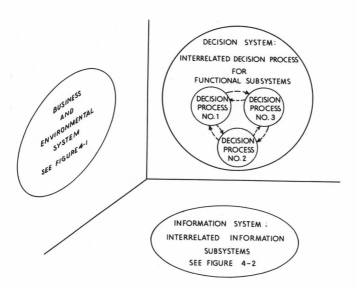

starting with the writings of the "traditionalists" and proceeding along a continuum of development with occasional relatively small forward spurts contributed by various disciplines.

When one looks back 35 or more years to the days of the "master mechanic" reporting to the "works manager" and reflects on how his job has expanded through the years into methods engineering, industrial engineering, statistical quality control, statistical cost control, operations research, management science, decision theory, and systems analysis, one might very well discern in retrospect only a long continuum of persistent application of the scientific method to the increasingly complex problems of management.

On the other hand, someone in the not-too-distant future may articulate a "General Theory of Management" that nicely fits all the pieces together in a manner that is much more useful to the manager than today's fragmented and often contradictory "schools of thought" about managing. What will this general theory be called—General Organization Theory? General Decision Theory? General Systems Theory? General Theory of Management? Which school's pet name will win out? Perhaps the great synthesizer who in the future articulates the general theory acceptable to all schools of thought will necessarily have to coin an entirely new name for it!

REVIEW QUESTIONS

1. What definition of a system best serves the purposes of this book?
2. What are several examples of: (*a*) natural systems and (*b*) man-made systems?
3. What must a systems designer know to properly design an information subsystem?
4. What is the advantage of developing a total information system in an organization? What problems are encountered when designing and installing a total system?
5. Explain O'Keefe's model for qualitative analysis of a physical system. How is it related to operations research techniques?
6. Why is there a need for a general systems theory?
7. Explain the unique aspects of: (*a*) verbal models, (*b*) mathematical models, (*c*) physical models, (*d*) schematic models.
8. When would one use a deterministic model? a probabilistic model?
9. What might be done to avoid the use of complex probabilistic models?
10. What is the difference between "closed-loop control" and "open-loop control" systems?
11. What can be done to help reduce delays, amplifications, and oscillations in system response triggered by feedback?
12. What might we learn by manipulating a model that simulates an actual system?
13. What is meant by a dynamic system?
14. What are several of the dangers involved in simulating a system with a computer model?
15. Explain briefly Forrester's "Industrial Dynamics."
16. Briefly explain Bonini's simulation. How does it differ from Forrester's?
17. Did the traditionalists think of the management process in terms of a system? Discuss.
18. Describe the concept of "control limits" when using feedback in management control.
19. Explain the relationship between the concepts "decision making," "system," and "organizational design."

SUGGESTIONS FOR FURTHER STUDY

BASIL, DOUGLAS C.; CONE, PAUL ROGER; AND FLEMING, JOHN E. *Executive Decision-Making through Simulation.* Columbus, Ohio: Charles E. Merrill Books, Inc., 1964.

A case study and simulation of corporate strategy in the rubber industry. Provides simulation (management game) suitable for teaching.

EMERY, JAMES C. "The Impact of Information Technology on Organization," *Evolving Concepts in Management.* Chicago, Ill.: Proceedings of the 24th Annual Meeting, Academy of Management, 1965, pp. 69–78.

Author discusses his belief that information technology will affect organization structure through its influence on the planning process.

EVANS, M. K. "Impact of Information Technology on Organization (Discussion)," *Evolving Concepts in Management,* Chicago, Ill.: Proceedings of the 24th Annual Meeting, Academy of Management, 1965, pp. 79–81.

Discusses changes in organization structure in cases where routine information handling activities are taken away from functional department managers and transferred to centralized information centers built around the computer.

HERTZ, DAVID BENDEL. "Simulation for Problem Solving," *Report of the Second System Simulation Symposium,* American Institute of Industrial Engineers, 1960, pp. 26–29.

D. B. Hertz of Arthur Anderson & Co., management consultants, briefly introduces simulation as a problem-solving tool.

LEDGERWOOD, B. K. "The New World of Industrial Control," *Mechanical Engineering,* Vol. 86, No. 7 (July, 1964), pp. 37–49.

Article discusses the radically changed industrial control field with industry survey of the newest in control. Discusses the need for greater economic gain as systems grow more complex and carry greater responsibility for successful process operation.

LIPSTREU, OTIS, AND REED, KENNETH A. "A New Look at the Organizational Implications of Automation," *Academy of Management Journal,* Vol. 8, No. 1 (March, 1965), pp. 24–31.

Authors tested empirically certain organizational hypotheses related to the introduction of automation. Article reports the changes in organization in the partially automated plant.

MALCOLM, D. G. "The Use of Simulation in Management Analysis," *Report of the Second System Simulation Symposium,* American Institute of Industrial Engineers, 1960, pp. 1–26.

D. G. Malcolm of System Development Corporation reviews briefly what has been done and why in the realm of computer simulation as applied to management analyses and training. Article discusses categories, purposes, types, industrial uses, problems, and future of simulation.

NEUSCHEL, R. E. *Management by System.* 2d ed. New York: McGraw-Hill Book Co., Inc., 1960.

The role, payoff, elements, and techniques of systems and procedures analysis are fully explained in this book.

OLDENBURGER, RUFUS. "Automatic Control," *Mechanical Engineering*, Vol. 87, No. 4 (April, 1965) pp. 39–45.
State-of-the-art report tracing development of automatic control from Watt's fly-ball governor, to the servomechanism, to electronic computers.

"Plant of 1970 Is Here in '64," *Factory*, Vol. 122, No. 2 (February, 1964), pp. 62–65.
Detailed description of Kitchens of Sara Lee's new total control system. System directs entire manufacturing operation from the receiving dock to the shipping platform. This system is one of the most advanced to date.

SCHULTZ, GREGORY V. "You Need Systems Engineering," *Factory*, Vol. 122, No. 4 (April, 1964), pp. 80–85.
Describes systems engineering as the process of selecting and construct-into a unified pattern the devices, mechanisms and equipment necessary for optimum operation and control of a complex manufacturing, processing, or service system. Discusses benefits, costs, tools and techniques, skills and staff, training and installation problems.

SIMON, HERBERT A. "Experiments with a Heuristic Compiler," *Journal of the Association for Computing Machinery*, Vol. 10, No. 4 (October, 1963), pp. 493–506.
Report discusses some experiments in constructing a compiler that makes use of heuristic problem-solving techniques. Report analyzes several of the problem-solving processes involved in writing computer programs.

YOUNG, STANLEY. "Designing the Management System," *Academy of Management Journal*, Vol. 7, No. 2 (June, 1964), pp. 137–48.
Case study of the establishment of a planned management system in a general hospital.

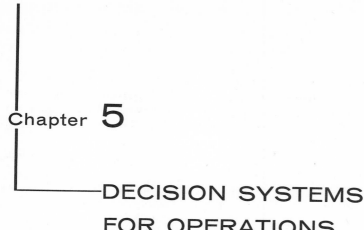

Chapter 5

DECISION SYSTEMS FOR OPERATIONS MANAGEMENT

INTRODUCTION

IN THE PREVIOUS FOUR CHAPTERS we have examined in some depth the meaning and import of each of the key words in the title of this chapter. With this background we are now in a position to survey the spectrum of problems arising in production. The main purpose of this survey is to show how production problems are interrelated with each other and with problems in other subfunctions of the firm. This survey will occupy the bulk of the chapter. In the remainder we will quickly survey what has been done in business toward implementing the decision systems approach and simulation in production, winding up with a model of actual practice that has not yet been simulated.

THE TOTAL DECISION SYSTEM

Back in Chapter 1 the generalized subfunctions of operations were depicted in Figure 1–2. The problems arising in the production function were introduced. These problems can now be stated more specifically as deciding the optimal:

1. Output level.
2. Product technical specifications.
3. Production processes.
4. Plant layout, location, and maintenance policies.
5. Production schedules.
6. Purchased items.
7. Product cost.

The above problems constitute a hierarchy of problems that are *interrelated*. Therefore their appropriate decision processes must be *integrated, and executed as a system*. The set of problems 1 through 7 are interrelated in that an appropriate solution to the last one (7) requires a prior solution of problems 6 back up through 1. In turn, an appropriate solution to problem 6 requires a prior solution of problems 5 back up through 1. Finally, problem 1 cannot be solved until one has a solution to problem 7!

The apparent dilemma expressed in the above paragraph is much like the proverbial problem, "Which comes first, the chicken or the egg?" Unlike that problem, however, this set of problems *must* be solved by the manager. Ideally, he *should solve all seven problems in the set simultaneously*. He should express each of the seven problems as mathematical models—equations explicitly stating the relationships between all parameters, variables, limits (constraints), and the objective functions, that are common to all the problems in the set, and those that are not. He would then have a *total decision system*, composed of seven integrated decision subsystems. Then, by converting the total decision system into a computer model, he could feed relevant quantitative data into the computer and crank out a simultaneous, and thus optimal, solution for each of the seven problems in the set.

THE TOTAL PRODUCTION SYSTEM

If an operational (as opposed to a conceptual) total *decision* system could be established, and proved as a model by favorable testing on the computer, the decision maker would be at the threshold, at least, of managing operations (if not the entire business) in a highly scientific manner. If the total decision system were in turn supported by a *total information system*, including proper data collection, computer storage, and retrieval subsystems, then, if these combined systems could be made to cause the information retrieval subsystem to insert the proper data into the total decision system (integrate the two systems), decisions could be made very quickly, accurately, and even cheaply.

With the capability of making *all* production decisions very quickly and cheaply the manager could choose short planning periods, thereby reducing uncertainty to negligible proportion. If, also, he could find a way to reduce variability of the data generated by the *total business functional system* to negligible levels, all the simultaneous equations of the total decision system could be *deterministic* rather than *probabilistic*. Then operating decisions could be arrived at even more cheaply. The solutions generated would also be more accurate.

Suppose, further, that the state of technology were such that one could automate the acquisition and conversion functions of production. One could then integrate the total decision system with the total automated functional system and have decision data feed directly out of the former into the latter. At this point the manager would be well on his way to having a fully automated *total production system.* Unfortunately, however, the present state of the art affecting all the "ifs" in the previous paragraphs is not so far advanced as to permit all this.

An examination of what is involved in each of the seven problems comprising the total decision system, even in a general manner, as we shall do in the next section of the chapter, should disclose a number of major reasons why one cannot yet develop a total system for most production situations. If we fail in this disclosure, fuller treatment in depth of each of these problems in the other texts in this series should be convincing. These texts show why many of the problems are highly ill-structured and cannot be stated mathematically. They also show that the list of seven problems is itself an abstraction. That is to say, there are hierarchal subproblems *within* the seven listed, thereby compounding the difficulty of building a simultaneous mathematical model for the set. These subproblems were omitted from the list in order to simplify the presentation.

ITERATED SEQUENTIAL PRODUCTION DECISIONS

How does the manager solve the set of seven hierarchal problems listed earlier, if he cannot set them up as simultaneous equations? He does so by an iterative *process of successive approximations.* Figure 5–1 depicts the nature of this process. It is essentially the same procedure used by the systems engineer in designing a physical system as depicted back in Figure 4–3.

New Organization versus Organization in Being

Before examining the meaning of Figure 5–1, we should say something about this total decision process in the two extreme cases of *starting a new organization* versus *operating an existing organization. The total decision process applies in both cases.* There are some significant differences arising in the execution of the process, however. In the case of a new plant, for instance, the analyst starts with a clean slate. He is not encumbered with an existing set of physical and operating conditions. Therefore, fewer constraints are imposed on the decision process. He has a relatively free hand. In this sense the decision process is easier to execute. Also, he does not have to cope with the task of making decisions that are operationally implementable in a dynamically changing, ongoing plant. In this sense, the analyst has an easier job. He can make the complete set of decisions depicted in Figure 5–1 without being concerned about the existing production system changing in the meantime. Offsetting these advantages is the fact that there usually are far more iterations necessary than in the case of the plant in being.

One can conceive of two production decision systems rather than a single one as in Figure 5–1: (1) *design* of the integrated physical systems —product, process, plant; and (2) *operation* of these systems. This is a dangerous concept if it leads one to believe that system 1 can be designed optimally without reference to system 2. Anyone who has ever designed a new plant, and especially anyone who has had to manage it after installation, knows that the *total* set of problems, down through production schedules and product cost, *must* be decided if optimal product, process, and plant design is to be achieved. This is why, for instance, engineers who don't know anything about *operating* a plant are likely to design poor products, processes and plants.

In the case of an *existing business or plant*, the hierarchy of problems

FIGURE 5–1

Iterated Sequential Production Decisions

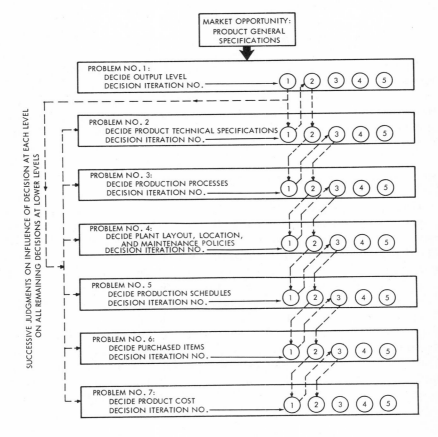

exists principally because of the dynamic nature of the firm's environment. All of the environmental subsystems depicted back in Figure 4–1 are constantly changing. The intelligence system of the firm is evaluating these changes and making top management decisions for change in the firm's functional subsystems. In production these changes often cause reanalysis of the entire hierarchy of problems depicted in Figure 5–1. For instance, a proposed change in product general specifications cannot be finally decided optimally without going down through the entire hierarchy to product cost, thence back up to the output level decision, and back down again—through several iterations.

On the other hand, because of the constraints imposed by the existing physical and functional systems, the analyst is usually confronted with far fewer alternatives than in the case of the new plant. This usually results in considerably fewer iterations in the total decision process. In many cases, it may be intuitively evident (judgment) that a proposed change at one level or stage in the hierarchy may cause no change in all or most of the successive levels. The total decision process is thus truncated as far as formal analysis is concerned. We now return to our examination of the decisions depicted in Figure 5–1.

Deciding the Output Level

Figure 5–1 states that, first, all production decision making starts with assessing conditions in the product marketplace for the purpose of making *decisions on the expected volume of sales* for a product of proposed general specifications as explained in Chapter 1. The general specifications cover such matters as *performance* and *appearance* of the product as well as *services* that go with the product. These specifications, together with the *quality level* specifications and the *price* specifications, permit a decision on expected volume of sales during an appropriate planning period ahead.

Not until one has decided (first iteration) the expected volume of sales for the product can one make rational decisions in the remaining subproblems in the hierarchy.[1] The degree of standardization and specialization appropriate in optimal decisions on product technical specifications and process specifications, together with process inputs, depends heavily on the "extent of the market."[2] This is true also in all

---

[1] The product research and development people may object to this statement, asserting that the total decision process starts with the decisions on what research projects to undertake. These in turn lead to preliminary product designs that are then tested against the conditions in the marketplace. This is not so, as Lewis N. Goslin explains in *The Product Planning System* (Irwin Series in Opertations Management [Homewood, Ill.: Richard D. Irwin, Inc., 1957]).

[2] George Stigler, "The Division of Labor Is Limited by the Extent of the Market," *Journal of Political Economy*, Vol. LIX, No. 3 (June, 1951).

other functional subsystems of the firm, as well as in production. This is true in the entire hierarchy of decisions in finance, personnel, marketing, and all other subfunctions of the firm. They too have a hierarchy of interrelated problems similar to and interrelated with those depicted in Figure 5–1.

The Price-Volume Decision. Economic theory tells us that the firm should choose that volume of output at which the marginal revenue derived from the sale of output equals the marginal cost of operating the firm, as indicated in Figure 5–2. The output level "at the margin" brings

FIGURE 5–2
Price-Volume Chart

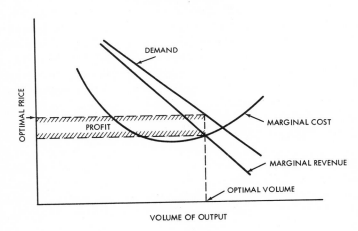

maximum profit. One unit more or one unit less output will decrease total profit. We have shown in Figure 5–2 the marginal revenue derived from the product demand curve of the typical firm operating in a market characterized by "imperfect" competition, for instance the highly prevalent "differentiated" (product) competition. For our purposes it is unnecessary to go into this matter for special cases of competition such as monopoly, duopoly, and oligopoly. Such an inquiry is more germane to a basic marketing course (concerned with the demand side of the business).

If management *could* determine meaningful equations for marginal revenue and marginal cost, the latter could be subtracted from the former, giving an equation for profit. In a situation like that shown in Figure 5–2, the profit curve would be concave downward. That is, profit would rise with increase in volume of output to a maximum (the point of "diminishing returns to scale"), then decline. By applying differential calculus to the profit equation, that is, differentiating the equation with respect to the variable of interest to management—output level—one would obtain a formula or decision rule that states the *simultaneous relation between product price and output level, or volume, for maximum profit*—the objective.

The above price-volume construct is a correct and useful *conception*, but in the vast majority of cases in business it is not *operational*. That is, the manager can and should understand this concept, but he cannot use it *directly* for either price or volume decision making. There are many reasons for this. However, we shall examine only the prime reason. Figure 5–2 is essentially a static model. It states, "*Given* the firm's marketing effort (advertising, promotion, selling, choice of distribution channels, etc.), and *given* the production function—the specifications for the product and the conversion processes and their inputs, and *given* all the effects of the efforts of all other functions of the firm on the cost and revenue curves, together with *given* reactions of competitors to all these moves and *given* states of all the other environmental subsystems affecting the firm's operation, *there exists, during the period for which all these "givens" hold, a set of curves as shown in Figure 5–2.* We can put all this more succinctly by using the economist's phrase, "given the state of the art of producing and selling outputs," there exists a condition such as that shown in Figure 5–2.

Actually, *the state of the art is constantly changing.* Competitive firms in a dynamic economy are constantly reacting to and influencing (feeding back) this dynamism by changing various combinations of the "givens" cited above. Accordingly, the firm's cost and revenue curves don't hold their levels and shapes very long. The set of curves "dances" through time from one level and shape to another, with the tempo of the dance now rising, now falling, spurting, and slowing. Under such conditions management never really knows when a set of segments of aggregate revenue and cost curves generated from past operating data are meaningful for decision making for the future.

In this predicament, *management directs its attention to making favorable changes in all the "givens"* mentioned above. Rather than take the economists' black box approach as depicted in Figure 5–2, top management directs its attention to the task of interpreting the effect of environmental system factors in the past and the present on all the givens cited above. From this position, it tries to forecast environmental factors in the future, and make decisions for rational changes in all the givens for an appropriate planning period ahead. These decisions are directed primarily toward achieving upward *shifts* in revenue curves and downward *shifts* in cost curves. Attention and resources are only secondarily directed toward finding *the optimal point* of operation along the curves. Perhaps this is why the typical economist (of the past at least), steeped in his "given the state of the art" approach, berates the businessman for irrationally operating at other than the optimal point along his demand and cost curves. This type of economist tends to deprecate the business manager's decision-making ability.

Engineers and managers, on the other hand, intuitively know that a policy of spending more on *shifting* cost and revenue curves, rather than on finding *optimal points along curves,* is likely to be more productive. Engineers, whose prime interest lies in developing and applying new technology for the purpose of designing new and improved products, processes, and plants, are almost wholly interested in *shifting* these curves favorably. So are managers, who almost instinctively back away from the use of highly involved and sophisticated decision processes for finding optimal points of operation along curves. When they are faced with this situation, they say, in effect, "We must certainly be approaching a point

FIGURE 5–3
Break-Even Chart

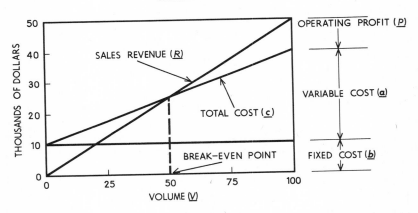

of diminishing returns to funds spent in this manner. Rather than spend more to develop more highly sophisticated decision processes for this purpose, let's spend the money in a manner that will tend to *shift the curves favorably."*

Actually, both approaches are appropriate, of course. Also, one can often compare the likely effects of the one versus the other in *specific* problem situations, as explained in other texts in this series. However, the task of formally deciding how much to spend on one approach versus the other *in the aggregate for the firm as whole* is, in most cases, impossible. We shall learn why this is so and how managers cope with this problem in the last section of this chapter.

The Break-Even Chart. Another model for determining optimal output level (volume) is known as the break-even chart. A simplified example is shown in Figure 5–3. A break-even chart may be made for the firm's overall operations, or for only a portion of the firm's operations, such as a division, a department, or even a single operation within a department, provided the revenue earned by the unit may be determined.

The total cost of any operation or departmental activity, or the operations of the entire company, is composed of elements of fixed cost and of variable cost. Some cost elements are called semivariable, but these actually have both a fixed and a variable element that usually can be separated using statistical techniques.

The total cost (c) = fixed cost (b) + variable cost (a). Fixed cost is, by definition, fixed regardless of volume of output. Hence, if the firm produced and sold nothing (zero volume in Figure 5–3), it would incur a loss equal to (b) dollars, the fixed cost. However, as volume increases, both sales revenue and total cost increase, as shown in Figure 5–3. Eventually the sales revenue increases to a point where it just covers fixed cost. At this point, the loss incurred is the variable cost (a). As volume continues to increase, *sales revenue eventually just covers fixed plus variable cost, that is, total cost. This is the break-even point:* at this point, loss is zero and profit is zero. As volume increases beyond the break-even point, profit increases. Management obviously should plan an output level above the break-even point. If management cannot reasonably expect this volume of sales, the only alternative, if profit is to be made, is to *shfit the fixed and/or variable cost curves downward* through appropriate changes in operations.

The break-even chart (and the equivalent mathematical model) has certain weaknesses that limit its use as a decision-making tool. First, like the price-volume (P-V) chart treated earlier, it is a macro model and does not often lend itself to micro problem analysis. One cannot often determine, for instance, that portion of the firm's total revenue earned by a particular division, department, or operation.

Secondly, the firm's revenue and cost functions are normally curvilinear as shown in the P-V chart, rather than linear as indicated in the break-even chart. Actually, this is not always as great a weakness as is often believed. The firm normally *operates in a relatively narrow range of volume* during the previous, current, and next planning periods combined. Across this range, the firm's revenue and cost curves closely approach straight lines—often close enough for practical decision-making purposes. Of course, the manager should check this point as it pertains to his particular firm.

More importantly, the great weakness of the break-even chart developed from data generated in past operating periods, say fiscal years, is its *static nature.* Like the P-V chart, it is true for a given set of operating conditions and is valid only for a period over which these givens hold. In a well-managed firm in a dynamic environment, this is usually a short period indeed. All the remarks offered earlier about the P-V chart concerning the *shifting of curves versus finding optimal points of operation along them* apply to the break-even chart.

This is as far as we will carry our examination of the output level, or volume, decision at this point. We shall come back to it again in the last section of this chapter, and of course, a full study of the problem involves getting much deeper into the firm's marketing function than we wish to here. This problem lies precisely at the interface of the production and marketing subsystems. Its proper solution constitutes appropriate *integration* of marketing and production decision processes.

Nonbusiness organizations such as government units theoretically do not, or should not, compete. For instance, they are usually established because there is no market competition in providing the product that the legistature believes the public needs or wants. Accordingly, the P-V chart depicted in Figure 5–2 does not apply to these organizations. They are funded directly or indirectly through tax revenues and are interested in providing their product efficiently. Thus, their objective is, or should be, to maximize their benefit/cost ratio, or for a specific project, its effectiveness/cost ratio, rather than profit.

Deciding Product Technical Specifications

Referring back to Figure 5–1, we see that the next problem in the hierarchy of interrelated production problems is that of designing the product. With the first iteration decision on output level and product general specifications (including quality level and price) in hand, the product designers have a basis for proceeding with their first iteration in deciding technical specifications. They may have already conceptualized the technical specifications in a general way, and even developed certain critical detailed specifications through laboratory tests and drafting layout work. This may have been done to help the marketing people focus more easily and quickly on certain product *general* specifications.

One can hardly generalize about the matter of where and when the iterative process of deciding product general specifications and then technical specifications begins. This is an "academic" question in most cases. The important point to note is that the two sets of specifications are specifically *related* through an iterative approach that *integrates* all the considerations involved.

The task of developing product specifications is explained more fully in other texts in this series.[3] Our purpose in this section is merely to *stress the feedback* required in the decision process for establishing product general and product technical specifications. Each alternative in the one influences those in the other. There are often so many permutations and combinations involved that the analyst is not able even to recognize all of them at once. They are "discovered" through a heuristic process as the

---

[3] See Goslin, *op. cit.*, and Robert B. Fetter, *The Quality Control System* (Irwin Series in Operations Management [Homewood, Ill., Richard D. Irwin, Inc., 1967]).

iterations proceed. The iterative analytical process will, finally, tend to disclose and resolve the major alternatives.

After the first set of preliminary product technical specifications is established, their influence on market volume via the compromises made in the general specifications (perhaps price and/or quality level) will be assessed. This is shown in Figure 5–1 with the dashed arrow back up to iteration No. 2 in problem No. 1.

The Role of Judgment. We should now examine the meaning of the dashed arrows along the left side of Figure 5–1. They mean simply that *one cannot make a decision in any iteration at any level in the hierarchy without making a tentative judgment concerning the influence on product cost at the bottom of the hierarchy.* This is indicated by the dashed arrow going leftward at the top just below iteration No. 1 of problem No. 1 (all the other arrows like this below each problem are omitted from the figure to simplify it). This is true because of the *simultaneous relationship between cost, price, and output level* as shown in the P-V chart, Figure 5–2. While the analyst cannot directly use the P-V chart, for reasons given earlier, he cannot ignore it, as also indicated earlier. *He must judge the final effect of each iteration on product cost,* which means making a judgment on the *itervening levels* of problems shown in Figure 5–1.

Thus the role of judgment in the total decision process is enormous and even critical. At one extreme the analyst may, after an iteration of a higher level problem, judge the ultimate effect on product cost, and thus profit, as being so adverse (low profit) as to discontinue consideration of the project. If his judgment is erroneous, the firm may very well have given up a fine profit opportunity. At the other extreme, poor judgment may permit the costly iterative process to proceed when in fact it should have long since been terminated and the project dropped.

One might well ask, "Why the judgment? Just work down through the entire hierarchy using formal analysis in each and every iteration till one comes to the final cost/price/volume/profit result." The answer to this is simple. First, the subproblems composing each of the problems shown in Figure 5–1 are not so well-structured as to permit formal analysis without a good deal of judgment. The other texts in this series will bear this out. More important, however, is the fact that analysis is time-consuming and costly.

Perhaps the time factor is more important. For instance, top management will establish what it believes to be a propitious date in the future for putting the product on the market. In many projects involving a new or revised product, advertising and sales promotion activity must get underway considerably in advance of this date. Also, new or revised channels of distribution may have to be arranged. All this takes time. The entire project will be planned on a time scale, starting with the final event—product available in the market place—and working backward in the calendar, setting target dates for each key event in the total project, with appropriate lead times between events. Invariably, if all the analytical work in the entire project were allowed to proceed at the relatively slow pace of formal analysis, the total project time would be quite lengthy. Conversely, it can be shortened appreciably by displacing some of the formal analysis with judgment and intuition. Since firms compete on how rapidly they can enter a new market opportunity (and many have been hurt badly by being at the tail end), there is usually tremendous pressure to shorten the total project time. One way to do this is to substitute judgment and intuition for time-consuming formal analysis. This is one reason firms pay more for seasoned experience than unseasoned brilliance!

Deciding Production Processes

Having established a second iteration decision on product technical specifications, the next step in the hierarchy of decisions is *a first iteration decision on process specifications* indicated as problem No. 3 in Figure 5–1. Here the analyst is knowledgeable in the capabilities and the economics of various types of process equipment, together with the various other inputs required in their use, such as tooling (jigs, dies, fixtures, etc., for machine tools in manufacturing). He will solve a number of subproblems at this level The more important of these problems are explained in another series text.[4] Here it is sufficient to generalize about his decision process. He is after an *optimal combination of technologically feasible process inputs*—optimal in the sense that they will contribute most to profit maximization.

Process Inputs. We have learned from economic theory that the least-cost combination of inputs comprising a production process is that combination in which the marginal physical product of each input is equal.[5] This is true when the unit costs of inputs are equal. At this point (the margin) if the combination of inputs is changed in any way, the physical output of the process will decrease. Where the unit cost of the various inputs is different, *the least-cost combination is where the ratios of the marginal physical products and their input costs are equal.* In other words:

---

[4] Gerald Nadler, *Work Systems Design: The Ideals Concept* (Irwin Series in Operations Management [Homewood, Ill.: Richard D. Irwin, Inc., 1967]).

[5] The student who does not recall the basic economic theory of production may refresh his memory by referring to Paul A. Samuelson, *Economics, An Introductory Analysis* (6th ed.; New York: McGraw-Hill Book Co., Inc., 1964), chap. 25. The student may also wish to review the Appendix, "Graphical Depiction of Production Theory," pp. 528–35. More advanced students, particularly those with background in higher mathematics, may review parts of the small book by Sune Carlson, *Pure Theory of Production* (New York: Kelley & Millman, Inc., 1956).

$$\frac{\text{Marginal physical product of } A}{\text{Cost of input } A} = \frac{\text{Marginal physical product of } B}{\text{Cost of input } B} =$$

$$\frac{\text{Marginal physical product of } C}{\text{Cost of Input } C}$$

However, the least-cost combination of inputs determined in such a manner—that is, from physical products (outputs)—does not take account of the dollar revenue earned by the physical product, and hence does not take account of profit. Since the economic objective of the firm is to maximize profit, we must take account of the revenues earned by physical products. We learned back in Figure 5–2 that the firm will earn maximum profit when it operates at a level of output at which marginal revenue is equal to marginal cost. Thus, we are concerned with marginal revenue product, which is price multiplied by marginal physical product.

Process planners will substitute cheaper process inputs for more expensive inputs until no further gain in total profit can be realized. If unit costs of the various inputs are different, as they usually are, the combination of inputs chosen is *that combination in which the ratios of marginal revenue product and unit cost of each input are equal.* In other words:

$$\frac{\text{Marginal revenue product of } A}{\text{Unit cost of input } A} = \frac{\text{Marginal revenue product of } B}{\text{Unit cost of input } B} =$$

$$\frac{\text{Marginal revenue product of } C}{\text{Unit cost of input } C}$$

Therefore, since output level (volume) influences marginal revenue product, *the appropriate choice of process inputs depends upon the level of output as well as the unit cost of inputs.*

The layman apparently does not believe that managers implement the foregoing economic concepts in their decision making. They say that managers merely use common sense in deciding operations or processes. Actually, the forgoing economic concepts constitute common sense. It is obvious from the common sense viewpoint that one should substitute cheaper inputs for more expensive inputs to attain outputs.[6]

However, the concept explained above is a static one (as was the P-V chart examined earlier). To take account of the dynamics of the usual situation, we should state the rule as follows: *Management should so plan its production processes that the discounted stream of their future marginal revenue is equal to the discounted stream of their future marginal cost. To achieve the latter at its lowest level, every process*

---

[6] For a forceful demonstration that businessmen in general understand and implement these concepts, see the article demonstrating how our nation's manufacturers substituted equipment for relatively more expensive plant (buildings), and the methods by which this was done during the period 1935–58: "Business in Brief," bimonthly letter No. 28, Economic Research Department, The Chase Manhattan Bank, New York. September–October, 1959.

should employ inputs up to the point where the ratios of the marginal revenue product of each input to the unit cost of the input are equal. Again, while successful managers understand these concepts and use them intuitively in their decision making, it is often very difficult to apply them explicitly and formally. Appropriate decision processes for dealing with discounted future revenues and costs are explained in another book in this series.[7]

For now, it is sufficient to learn from the pure theory stated above that *process specifications cannot be determined rationally without taking into account the relative cost of inputs simultaneously with the relative revenues earned by alternative processes.* This is shown in Figure 5–1 by dashed arrows which indicate that the analyst must check the influence of his first choice of process inputs back up through the hierarchy of problems to determine the effect on the price/volume situation, while using judgment to determine the effect down through the hierarchy on product cost. Putting the two together, he has determined the effect on profit. In choosing the inputs that comprise an optimal process, certain changes are likely to be required in the preliminary product technical specifications, which in turn may call for revisions in general specifications that in turn affect the prior price/volume decision. Based upon what he learns from this first iteration he then makes a second iteration, to further improve the process specifications.

Deciding Plant Layout, Location, and Maintenance Policies

Having achieved a set of process specifications that are optimal at least through their second iteration, the analyst is in a position to think about the plant that will service and house the processes. By "plant" we mean the building and grounds, together with all the physical subsystems that service the conversion processes: heat, light, water, sewage, and so on. Like the equipment used in most conversion processes, the plant is normally long-lived. As a result, the analyst must think in terms of discounted future revenues and costs. The decision processes examined by Morris apply to plant as well as process equipment.[8]

The plant planning problem (No. 4 in Figure 5–1) includes the location, layout, and maintenance policy subproblems. When the preliminary process plans are made (problem No. 3), the analyst is in a position to specify the required service systems. He is then in a position to arrange the equipment in appropriate relative locations, which is known as the "Plant Layout Problem." This problem is solved through simulation, as explained briefly in the previous chapter and more fully in another series

---

[7] William T. Morris, *The Capacity Decision System* (Irwin Series in Operations Management [Homewood, Ill.: Richard D. Irwin, Inc., 1967]).

[8] *Ibid.*

book.[9] With a preliminary layout in hand, the designer is in a position to specify the plant building requirements (or building changes as required by layout changes in the case of the plant in being).

At this point—knowing what sort of production facility is required—the analyst must face the question of plant location which includes, in the case of an existing firm, whether or not it should stay where it is. The introduction of new products and major revisions in existing ones are events that call for review of the location question. The analysis involved is explained fully by Reed.[10]

A plant is not completely designed until the matter of maintenance policy is settled. Problems that arise in the maintenance of facilities affect the design of the facilities themselves. In short, process design, service systems design, layout, and building design are all interrelated with maintenance policy. To ignore the latter until all the other decisions are irrevocably made is to invite serious difficulty. Maintenance is a sufficiently large element of product cost to require its inclusion in the hierarchy. Reed explores this subject fully.[11]

When the analyst has taken his work through the second iteration (down, up, and back down the hierarchy of Figure 5–1), he is then in a position to analyze formally the production scheduling problem (No. 5 in the hierarchy shown in Figure 5–1). He will have been taking it into account, of course, in prior iterations of the total decision system, and many of the decisions already made in the hierarchy of problems will have already eliminated a number of alternatives in this problem. The production scheduling task is central to the succes of the business. It is fully explained in another series book.[12] However, the task is previewed in general terms in the next section of this chapter to demonstrate how it interrelates with, and thus must be taken into account in, the higher level problems indicated in Figure 5–1, as well as in the lower level problems.

Deciding Production Schedules

As indicated in Chapter 1, the total production function requires decisions with respect to time. There is an old saying that time is money. Thus the time dimension of input-output situations is an economic factor. Finally, while the economist separates time and place utilities in his abstractions from total human satisfaction, the two are very closely related as explained in Chapter 1. A simple illustration will refresh your memory.

---

[9] Ruddell Reed, Jr., *Plant Location, Layout, and Maintenance* (Irwin Series in Operations Management [Homewood, Ill.: Richard D. Irwin, Inc., 1967]).

[10] *Ibid.*

[11] *Ibid.*

[12] James H. Greene, *Operations Planning and Control* (Irwin Series in Operations Management [Homewood, Ill.: Richard D. Irwin, Inc., 1967]).

If the storeroom of a manufacturing firm is out of a particular product component (a stockout), assembly operations cannot proceed. The component may be in process (supply to the storeroom) back in the welding department. Poor scheduling has failed to supply the weldment at the right *time* and *place*. If the welding department is in a plant located a mile from the assembly department, the scheduling has been done more poorly than if the welding department were next door to assembly. This is true because it will take more *time* to get the finished weldment to the right *place*, the assembly department. Or, conversely, it will take longer for the assembly department to acquire this input.

Thus, *time and place utilities are very closely related.* From here on this abstraction of the economist is not used in our analysis of managerial decision processes. It has served its purpose in the transition from economic theory to operations management. Rather, we shall introduce another abstraction to take its place, one which we believe is more useful for our purpose. This is the concept that *scheduling decisions have two dimensions: time and quantity.*

The Time and Quantity Dimensions of Scheduling. If a firm wishes to provide a given amount of a good or a service to a customer at a certain time and place, it must acquire the necessary inputs sufficiently in advance of this time to carry out the conversion function completely. This includes transporting the good or service to the customer, even though this operation may be done by the customer (pick up his order). The function must be done regardless of the institution doing it. The *time taken to acquire the necessary inputs plus the conversion time is known as lead time.*

The Time Dimension of Scheduling. The lead time of the production function of a *firm* is the total time required to acquire all necessary inputs and convert them into the final output of the firm. The lead time of a process within the total production function of a firm is the total time required to acquire the inputs to this process, which may include the outputs of previous processes, plus the time for conversion of these inputs in the process. For instance, in a manufacturing firm the lead time required to produce a product is the total time required to acquire all the inputs to the processes constituting the total conversion process, plus the times required for performing these processes, plus any time lost between them. The product may be produced through a series of processes such as machining, welding, and painting. It takes a specific amount of time to acquire the inputs to each process and convert them into the output. This time may be termed the *process lead time. The sum of the process lead times plus delays that may occur between processes is total production lead time of the firm.*

In order to compete effectively, as well as efficiently, management strives to reduce the total production lead time. In this way, the firm competes not only on a price basis through greater efficiency, but also by more effectively providing the time and place characteristics desired by the customer. Reduction of total lead time not only promotes effectiveness in meeting customer needs and desires, it also promotes efficiency. The reason for this is that there is a time dimension to the cost of acquiring and converting inputs. *Both ownership and rental costs of inputs increase with time. The faster the inputs are acquired and converted to outputs (higher turnover), the lower are these costs.* Hence, reduction of total production lead time tends to enhance both effectiveness and efficiency of production.

Total production lead time may be reduced without departing from the optimum output level or volume of production. This can be done by *reducing the component lead times* of the conversion and acquisition functions. Reduction of lead time in this fashion may be done in several ways. The conversion function is examined first, followed by the acquisition function.

Reducing Conversion Lead Time. Total conversion lead time may be reduced by (1) simultaneous performance of processes and (2) reducing the component work station times. For instance, sets of processes producing outputs which are components of an assembly, such as an automobile engine, may be performed simultaneously. By so doing, the total lead time of producing engines is reduced by the extent to which sets of processes can be overlapped in time. This applies also to individual work stations. One man can be assembling the generator on an automobile engine while another is assembling the carburetor.

The second method of reducing total conversion lead time is obvious: Reduce the time required to perform the work at each work station. The time required for assembling the carburetor to an engine, receiving savings at the bank teller's window, unpacking goods in a retail storeroom, or auditing a file of receivables in a public accounting firm can be *reduced by simplifying the content of the work itself.*

The analytical processes for accomplishing reduction of production lead time by overlapping processes, and sets of processes, and by reducing operation times at work stations, by simplification of content, are both technological and economic. Overlapping and simplification have technological limitations, and there are alternatives within these limitations.

Reducing Acquisition Lead Time. Total production lead time can also be reduced by *reducing the lead time of the acquisition subfunction.* By reducing the time required to marshal the inputs to a production function, its lead time is reduced. In Chapter 1 it was explained how the time required to obtain the various types of inputs can be reduced. For instance, "inventories" of physical facilities, raw materials, and human skills can be carried. Some are owned, some are leased or rented, and some are obtained by mere transfer from the customer.

In all cases where an inventory is used, whether it be human skills, physical facilities, or raw materials, there is the unique problem of waiting lines. For instance, workers waiting for raw materials at the storeroom window because of a lack of storekeeper skills available in the storeroom represent a cost to the firm. Adding storekeepers to reduce the waiting line also costs money. Deciding the correct number (inventory) of storekeepers involves the analysis of all such cost elements.

The same is true of physical facilities. An inventory of five milling machines (as compared to an inventory of, say, three) may add to total costs less than the resulting costs saved by other necessary inputs being idle waiting for a milling machine to be available (waiting line). An increase in the inventory of dock space in a warehousing firm may represent an increase in ownership cost which is less than the decrease in cost that the additional dock space makes possible by reducing the number of idle trucks and their drivers waiting for dock space (waiting line). The analysis of waiting line problems such as these is treated in other texts in this series.

The Quantity Dimension of Scheduling

It is obvious that the conversion function of production will require more time if the quantity of the goods produced, or the amount of the service rendered, is increased. For instance, an order for 1,000 cartons of canned peaches will take more time for the wholesaler to fill than will an order for 100 cartons. It will take more time to convert the inputs to a welding operation for an order of 1,000 automobile chassis than for an order of 100. *Hence, the quantity dimension influences the time dimension in the conversion function.* It may also influence the time dimension in the acquisition function of production. For instance, even if the source of an input can deliver an order of 1,000 units at the same time as an order of 100 units, say from stock, succeeding internal operations making this input available at the proper time and place with the other necessary inputs to a process often will take longer. Hence, the quantity dimension influences the time dimension of the total production function.

It was explained earlier that total cost will vary with volume of output, and that the firm should operate at an output level where marginal cost is equal to marginal revenue. *This is also true of production processes within the total production function of the firm.* Hence, there is an *optimum* level of output, or quantity of production, for the firm *and* for individual production processes *within* the firm. At this level, total profit is at a maximum. Putting the above two concepts together, that is, an optimum quantity plus the fact that the quantity dimension influences the time dimension, it follows that *there must be an optimum production lead time*, which is not necessarily minimum lead time. Thus, the firm trades some of its ability to compete in respect to providing time and place characteristics in the product with cost in producing the product. This permits the firm to compete more effectively on a combined delivery and price basis. In short, the two bases of competition are interrelated.

There is a good deal more to the task of deciding optimal production schedules. However, it should be evident from this short general treatment that the *scheduling decisions are related to all problems above and below them* in the hierarchy of problems in Figure 5–1.

Deciding Purchased Items

Many references were made to the purchasing decision in previous sections of the chapter. Consequently, it is clear that problems in this area are interrelated with those in the remainder of the hierarchy shown in Figure 5–1. A few additional remarks may make the point a little clearer. Obviously, another company that specializes in producing certain items, or services, that are part of your product, processes, or even maintenance, may enjoy an output level sufficiently greater than yours to warrant their employing more specialized inputs, and thus they will have a lower cost curve than yours for the same item. Accordingly, you may be able to purchase the item more cheaply than making it. Another point—if you buy rather than make an item, your acquisition lead time is reduced, other things being equal, with all the benefits accuring from shorter production lead time, as described above. All such questions are examined more fully in another book in this series.[13]

Deciding Product Cost

All of the considerations involved in the hierarchy of problems shown in Figure 5–1 are profit oriented—the economic objective of the firm. Thus product cost shown at the bottom of the hierarchy is coequal in importance with the revenue decision implicit in the output level decision indicated at the top of the hierarchy. This is the message of Figure 5–2, the P-V chart, that *cost and revenue are interrelated.* All the intervening level problems shown in Figure 5–1 have cost and revenue aspects that are interrelated. For instance, in process planning, the analysis may come down to a choice between two alternatives that are equal in all respects except that one alternative may be capable of producing an output of higher quality level than the other, thus perhaps contributing to a higher revenue. Problems of defining and controlling quality level should be well understood by the product designer and the process designer, as all three problem areas are interrelated. These problems are examined in Fetter's series book.[14]

---

[13] Wilbur B. England, *The Purchasing System* (Irwin Series in Operations Management [Homewood, Ill.: Richard D. Irwin, Inc., 1967]).

[14] Fetter, *op. cit.*

Traditionally, product costs are identified and recorded in a manner dictated by the conventions of accounting. While economic cost elements and conventional accounting cost elements are not always the same thing, it is true that *a production function that is planned and controlled rationally on the basis of economic costs will show an appropriate level of accounting cost*—appropriate in the sense that return on investment or benefit/cost ratio is maximized in the long run. Thus, properly established economic cost elements such as *incremental costs* and *opportunity costs* should be reflected in traditional accounting cost terms to serve as budgeted costs. Effective planning and control can then be exercised by the production manager using these budgeted accounting costs as standards. Problems arising in the cost control function are examined in another book in this series.[15]

Output Time Standards. Wherever production processes include a significant amount of the input of human skill, the planning and control of output volume and cost may be quite complex. On the other hand, where almost completely automatic processes prevail, planning and controlling output volume and cost are considerably less difficult. As long as an automatic process is operating effectively (product specifications are being met at planned quality levels), the output volume and cost can be predicted quite accurately with relative ease from the design characteristics of the process. On the other hand, *a process that includes a considerable amount of human labor normally is susceptible to greater variation in output volume and thus unit cost of output*. Therefore, the establishment of time standards is necessary in such cases for the control of output costs and for the scheduling and controlling of output volume as well as maintaining planned process lead time. Thus production cost control and production volume control (scheduling and follow-up of the flow of work)—two problems in the hierarchy shown in Figure 5–1 —are very much interrelated. The problems of establishing performance time standards for cost and volume control are treated fully by Nadler.[16]

Obviously the iterative decision process depicted in Figure 5–1 can be carried on and on, as long as there is a single alternative of any consequence remaining to be examined at any level in the hierarchy. Just where is it cut off and the design "frozen"? Obviously, as in any other effort, there is a point of diminishing returns to analytical effort, beyond which the cost of further effort is not recovered in increased profit or benefit. Just when this point is reached is never very clear. To date, decision theory tells us nothing on this point beyond the generality stated above. Accordingly, the question is settled via judgment or intuition. More often, the analysts race the clock and squeeze in as many iterations

---

[15] Robert N. Anthony and James S. Hekimian, *Operations Cost Control* (Irwin Series in Operations Management [Homewood, Ill.: Richard D. Irwin, Inc., 1967]).

[16] Nadler, *op. cit.*

as possible in the time allotted to the project. Too often they plan too long, leaving the operating manager insufficient time to get the project underway and outputs into the marketplace at the right time to take full advantage of the advertising and sales promotion campaigns. In an effort to squeeze out another dollar of profit through more iterations in the total decision process, they miss the market and lose a great deal of profit.

It is much better to be on time in the marketplace with a product, process, plant, and all the rest that are something short of perfectly planned rather than to get into the market late with a better planned product. After all, the analysts will still be on the payroll and available to tidy things up by continuing the iterations after the design is frozen. The resulting decisions give rise to product, process, plant, scheduling, and purchasing *improvements* after the product is on the market. This contributes to improved product cost and also keeps the analysts busy till the next new project is undertaken.

A COMBINED DYNAMIC MACRO AND MICRO DECISION SYSTEM

A realistic model of the typical total decision system in the industrial firm has not yet been developed for simulation purposes. The conceptual model presented back in Figure 5–1 is, of course, for the production subsystem, not the entire firm and its total environment. The best we can do in the present state of affairs is to describe the best practice of well-managed companies. Figure 5–4 is a conceptual model of this practice.

We shall now examine briefly each of the elements of Figure 5–4. We cannot treat them fully here, first because this is a text on operations and our purpose here is to show only how decisions in operations are interrelated with decisions in other subsystems such as distribution and finance, secondly, a full treatment of all the elements of Figure 5–4 in one text would result in a very long text indeed!

Long-Range Planning and Control

The further ahead one can plan meaningfully, the better basis he has for short-range decisions. It might truthfully be said that one who does no long-range planning is a complete opportunist. There are those who claim that most managers do no long-range planning. Others say, "Why do it when you know full well you will not follow the plans? You will undoubtedly change them drastically a few years from now." These reservations notwithstanding, the fact is that managers are indulging in long-range planning when they approve research and development projects that they know will require five years or more to complete—and hopefully bring new products into the line at the time. Secondly, when management decides to purchase an asset, say a machine tool, that will

FIGURE 5–4

Combined Dynamic Macro and Micro Decision System

Decisions	Main Type of Analysis	Subsystems Involved
1. Long-range planning & control	Informal/Intuitive/ Creative	All, macro level only
A. Products: Strategic/Competitive		
2. Intermediate-range planning & control	Incremental/Heuristic	Financial/Macro /Micro
A. Fixed asset planning		
1. Capital budgeting		
3. Fiscal planning & control	Incremental/Formal	All functional subsystems
A. Demand forecast		
1. Prices/Costs		
2. Selling expense		
3. Terms of sale		
B. Adjusted demand		
1. Inventory shift		
C. Production plan	Incremental/Formal	Production/Personnel/Financial/ Purchasing
1. Product mix		
a) Aggregate direct materials budget		
b) Aggregate direct labor budget		
2. Smooth production		
a) Optimal manning and inventories		
b) Final direct labor budgets during year		
4. Factory overhead budget	Incremental/Informal	Production/Financial
A. Profit		
B. Profit margin		
5. Administrative expense	Incremental/Informal	Administrative
6. Cash budgeting	Incremental/Exploded from programs	All
A. Flow of funds		

be productive for 10 or 20 years, management is doing in the very least some implicit long-range planning.

Finally, plans do not enslave the firm. They are not supposed to be rigid or inviolate. They should be reviewed as time passes and the view of the future unfolds. Long-range plans should be flexible so as to put the company in the best strategic position. Strategy considerations relative to future market opportunities and products to fill them are central to effective long-range planning. Having made general, as opposed to detailed, decisions concerning the expected future market and product opportunities, *general* plans can be made for processes, plants, their location, etc.—the problems shown back in Figure 5–1.

Long-range decision making is informal, intuitive, and at its best involves a great deal of creative thinking. Here is where the big-idea man is more productive. A big idea for the present or the near future often is not practical, as there are usually too many constraints in the current and near future situation, for instance the plant and work force in being, to permit successful implementation in the short run. Accordingly, the big idea is logically part of the long-range plan in most cases.

Planning is not to be confused with forecasting. The latter is concerned with factors over which management has no, or very little, control—especially environmental factors. Plans, on the other hand, are concerned with matters in which management can take action to cause events in the future to occur as they wish. Also, management planning in great part *causes* the future business environment to be what it is. In this sense managers have some control over the environment of the future.[17]

For instance, it has been said that the so-called standard forecast of future economic conditions, made by a group of business economists, turns out to be a very good forecast because so many businessmen base their planning decisions and actions on this forecast. Thus the net result of all their action tends to come out like the forecast. To this extent they have controlled future economic conditions. It is surprising how much top managers can do to influence the future environment. A bold, decisive set of plans, carried out vigorously, can cause the future to turn out very much like top management forecasts it. The most successful managers do not lie back, passively accepting a future that is claimed to be unforecastable. They aggressively influence it.

Intermediate-Range Planning and Control

The set of long-range plans which, incidentally, embraces all the subfunctions of the firm and its environment *provides a basis for more detailed intermediate-range planning*, say for five years ahead—year by year. A most important contribution to economic stability in the period since World War II (no severe depressions as in the 1930's) is said to be the propensity of businessmen to plan further ahead and hold to these plans, rather than permit short cyclical recessions to "bluff" them out of their confidence in their long-run expectation. Annual surveys of company plans for expenditures on plant and equipment reveal that a large percent of businessmen make these plans for as far ahead as five years. *Because rational investment in long-lived assets such as plant and process equipment calls for predicting the future stream of income and costs associated with the investment*, management increasingly establishes financial plans for as far ahead as its long-range plans permit. In turn, this need induces management to do more explicit long-range planning.

Model for Dynamic Planning. While long-range planning cannot be done in explicit quantitative terms, successful managers give effect to their long-range plans in intermediate-range financial planning. *A posi-*

---

[17] For a brief article discussing causative thinking as a means for making events happen instead of adapting to an unforeseen future, see John F. Mee, "Causative Thinking," *Business Horizons*, Vol. 6, No. 2 (Summer, 1963), pp. 45–46.

tive attempt is made to link short-run decision making, for the next fiscal year, for instance, to long-range plans through formal financial planning for the intermediate range ahead. This calls for establishing a dollar value for all the items in the profit and loss statement and the balance sheet in such a manner as to *reflect the expected influence of long-range* plans for as far ahead as five years or more. On a time scale, the entire decision system may be depicted as in Figure 5–5, which is an extension of Figure 5–4, omitting the breakdown of problems shown under (3) fiscal planning. These are treated in a subsequent figure.

FIGURE 5–5
Dynamic Decision System for Operations

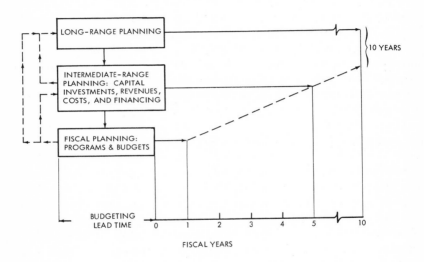

The solid arrows downward depict a *sequential decision process* through three problem levels. The dashed upward arrows depict *feedback from one decision level to prior levels* and thus imply an *iterative decision* process. The act of making these related decisions is shown taking place during a "budgeting lead time," often a three-month period prior to the start of the next fiscal year (the last quarter of the current year). The shorter this lead time, the better, because the decision process calls for predicting the situation at the start of the next fiscal year (time 0 in Figure 5–5). But analysis takes time, and in a complex business a full quarter is often necessary to complete all the problem solving involved.

The dashed arrow angling upward to the right indicates the planning horizon for each of the decision levels: 1 year for fiscal planning, 5 years for intermediate-range planning, and upwards of 10 years for long-range planning.

The *entire* decision system is *repeated during the budgeting lead time* each year for the next year. Top management reviews and revises the long-range plans set last year, adding a year to maintain the 10-year character of the plan. The financial committe reviews and revises projected profit and loss statement and balance sheet amounts for each of the five years of the intermediate plan, adding a year to maintain its five-year character. Finally, the fiscal plan is established for next year in the light of prior decisions. Perhaps four or five iterations of the total decision system will be required to attain a set of plans that are "judged" to be optimal.

The more iterations of the decision system, the closer to true optimality are the plans, of course. However, as indicated earlier, a point of diminishing returns to further analysis finally is reached (discerned by judgment), and the plan is "frozen." This is not to say that no further decisions or action will be taken to improve operations as the fiscal year unfolds, of course. But the *emphasis shifts from planning to control.* When the plans for the fiscal year are embarked upon, control is emphasized so as to *realize the plan as closely as possible and to learn from the actual operations all that is of value for the planning process for the subsequent year.*

Thus *the total decision process is a dynamic one.* It takes account of the past and the expected future conditions. The fiscal plan for next year is the result of five reviews, one when it first became the fifth year in an intermediate financial plan, second when it occupied the fourth year position, and so on down to when it is finally firmed up as next year's fiscal plan. The process of *successive refinement generally results in a fiscal plan that is both operational* (because it is an extension of past operations) *and forward looking* in that it puts the firm in a financial posture that is appropriate for subsequent years' plans.

Model for Financial Planning—Macro Level. Figure 5–6 shows a model for the financial planning that is central to intermediate-range planning.[18] This is a *macro model* in the sense that it covers the financial affairs of the *entire firm* and is in "gross" measures common to all activities of the firm, that is, dollars.

Figure 5–6 depicts in the lower branch (moving to the right from profit margin) the typical profit and loss statement of an industrial firm. This branch ends at the right with the components of production cost as typically expressed: direct material cost plus direct labor cost plus factory overhead. Adjusting the sum of these three elements by the changes in the value of inventory from the beginning to the end of the fiscal year

---

[18] This model is an adaptation of the "DuPont Formula," so named because an early explanation was provided by the treasurer of E. I. DuPont Co. See R. T. Davis, *How the DuPont Organization Appraises Its Performance,* Financial Management Series No. 94 (New York: American Management Association, 1950), pp. 3–23.

gives *cost of goods sold* (sometimes called "cost of sales"). The latter added to selling expense, administrative expense (S & A, as accountants say), and income taxes gives total cost.

The middle branch of Figure 5–6 beginning at the left with long-term capital depicts the typical balance sheet. Total assets are shown composed of current assets and fixed assets, which in turn are broken down into their typical components. Sales divided by long-term capital gives investment turnover. The latter multiplied by profit margin gives the measure of the ultimate *dynamic* economic objective: *rate of return on investment.* The numbers shown next to the boxes in Figure 5–6 are for purposes explained in the last section of the chapter.

The only items in Figure 5–6 not measured in dollars are: the figure for sales volume, which is in units of product; and the four boxes starting with money market conditions and moving leftward. These factors are not quantified in the model, nor do they show mathematical relationships between them. The three boxes covering respectively cost, availability, and manageability of short-term versus long-term capital are a condensed statement of the task of predicting and evaluating future money market conditions for the purpose of deciding the use of long- and short-term capital to finance total assets. In short, *problems of capital structure, of which capital budgeting is a logical part, interrelate with money market conditions.* In turn, these considerations interrelate with total assets required to produce the sales volume and sales revenue at the total cost shown in the plan. We will not get into decision making in matters of capital structure and capital budgeting in this text.[19] Our purpose here is to show that in the total decision system for the firm *production problems (Figure 5–1) are interrelated with financing problems.*

Decision Process for Financial Planning. In establishing the values for the factors in the financial planning model, Figure 5–6, management will not depart very far from past ratios between these factors if, of course, these ratios have resulted in a favorable return on investment in the past. When return on investment has not been favorable in the past, the contributing ratios, for example, investment turnover and profit margin, will be established at more and more favorable levels for each year in the intermmediate-range planning period, *reflecting the rapidity with which management believes it can effect corrective action.*

In general, *where favorable ratios have existed in the past, management will depart from them very little in its intermediate-range financial planning.* If a favorable return on investment of 30 percent has been achieved in the past with a profit margin of 15 percent and an investment turnover of 2.0, management tends to cling to the 15 percent and 2.0 figures. This is done because with the present state of the art of decision

_____

19 The next book in this series picks up the line of thought established here and goes on to explain capital budgeting as it is concerned with investment in capital equipment. William T. Morris, *op. cit.*

FIGURE 5–6
Model for Financial Planning and Control

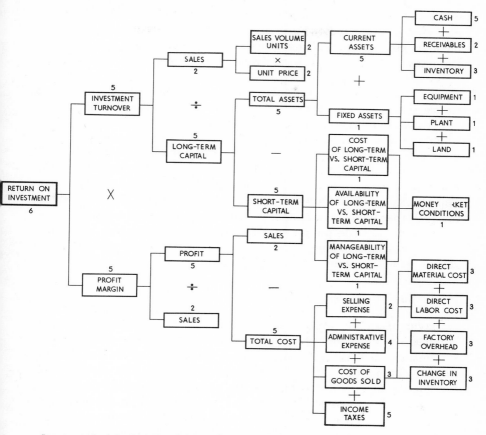

Investment is defined as long-term capital.
Long-term capital is defined as equity capital + long-term debt.

making, there is *no way of evaluating all of the combinations and permutations represented by the various ways in which a 30 percent return could be achieved.* In the absence of a formal decision process for this purpose, management sensibly takes a "don't rock the boat" attitude. Accordingly, *past financial ratios are changed only incrementally* in establishing each year's figures in the five-year intermediate-range plan. One economist likened this process to the action of a thermostat that allows the room temperature to depart only incrementally from a known comfortable temperature—in other words, an automatic control system.[20]

---

[20] See Kenneth E. Boulding, "Implications for General Economics of More Realistic Theories of the Firm," *American Economic Review*, Vol. XLII, No. 2 (May, 1952), pp. 35–44.

Capacity Decisions and Capital Structure. In the ongoing production decision process depicted back in Figure 5–1, process and plant planning decisions are being made for future implementation. The installed cost of various new process equipment and plants (buildings, service systems, and grounds), together with planned replacement of obsolescent equipment, is estimated from engineering studies including quotations from suppliers. The nature of these decision processes is explained in the next series text.[21]

With these estimates of installed cost in hand, management decides the future date, keeping in mind the market opportunity, for making the various capacity investments. These decisions affect the values appearing in the boxes marked 1 in Figure 5–6. Incremental changes in these values are made, giving effect to the desired capacity changes year-by-year over the five-year plan. Compromises must often be made so *as not to impair the capital structure of the business.* Sometimes a promising market opportunity must be forgone because expected money market conditions are such that the cost, availability, and manageability of long- and short-term capital are not appropriate. This is an example of how an environmental subsystem—money markets—as shown back in Figure 4–1 inter-relates with operating decision processes.

Production Micro Decision System

Having made the dollar decisions for future capacity, year-by-year, and adjusted the dollar values accordingly in the boxes marked 1 in Figure 5–6, management is now in a position to make the micro level decisions for production. This task is one of final refinement of the fiscal plan by *developing an operating program and associated budgets for the next fiscal year.* This calls for refining next year's preliminary financial plan only through relatively small incremental changes in the amounts shown in the boxes of Figure 5–6. The process of deciding these incremental changes results from solving the simultaneous set of problems indicated in Figure 5–4 as number 3, A, B, C, 4, 5, and 6, together with their subproblems. This is the micro part of the combined macro/micro decision system.

Demand Forecast. The first step in the micro decision process, which is, incidentally, a sequential and iterative process of successive approximations, is to establish the expected demand for the firm's products next year. Here we get into the marketing man's field of responsibility, so we will do no more than cite the fact that the forecasters will be concerned with the three-dimensional problem listed as 3, A, 1, 2, 3 in Figure 5–4. Armed with the preliminary production cost figures from the financial plan, and the preliminary profit margin figure, the forecasters decide how

---

[21] Morris, *op. cit.*

much of each product can be sold (a probability distribution), given the unit price of each product (required to produce the preliminary sales revenue and profit figures in the financial plan), together with two programs: the best mix of advertising, sales promotion, and personal selling that adds up to the preliminary selling expense figure in the plan, and the terms of sale (discounts of various types) that relate properly to the preliminary average receivables balance shown in the financial plan. The result of this process is to decide for next year the incremental changes to all the items marked 2 in the preliminary financial plan, Figure 5–6.

Adjusted Demand. The next step in the sequential decision process is 3, B in Figure 5–4—adjusting the product demand determined in the prior step *for a planned shift, if any, in the ending inventory for next year.* This year's ending inventory can be projected quite accurately for the remainder of the year from current inventory figures and the current backlog of orders. Top management may expect a rising price level that would warrant some hedging by building inventory, or the opposite, next year. This process results in an incremental change in two of the items marked 3 in Figure 5–6—change in inventory and average inventory balance (a current asset).

Production Plan. Keeping in mind that the items marked 1 in the financial plan (Figure 5–6) have been decided in a preliminary fashion as part of capital budgeting, as explained earlier, management is now ready to decide the incremental changes in the remaining items marked 3 in Figure 5–6.

The adjusted product demand figures are now adjusted again to attain an optimal product mix, which is an *allocation of the planned productive physical capacity* (resulting in the items marked 1 in Figure 5–6) *to production of the various products in the line.* Linear programming can often be used to solve this problem *because the profit curve is generally very close to linear over the short range for which this incremental change is being decided.*

The measure of optimality used in the product mix problem is *maximum contribution to total overhead and profit.* That is, at planned product prices (the prior demand forecast step), the optimal product mix to produce and sell within the adjusted demand schedule is a mix that results in the *largest difference between the sales revenue and the total direct cost of producing and selling the products in the mix. This difference is the total contribution to overhead and profit* (TCO & P).

Having thus decided TCO & P, planned profit is subtracted from TCO & P, leaving TCO. This figure provides a basis for making an incremental change in factory overhead. Next, the direct material and direct labor costs may be "exploded" from the product mix solution. This is done by using the planned standard cost data developed in the process planning decisions shown back in Figure 5–1, which in turn were used in the prior planning of physical capacity (items marked 1 in Figure 5–6), as explained earlier. These same data, incidentally, are used in the linear programming solution to the product mix problem. Hence, one can now see how all these decisions are explictly interrelated, as required by a systems approach.

While top management has arrived at aggregate factory overhead, as described above, supervisors of factory departments and all other overhead centers such as the product research and development department, industrial engineering department, and so on, have been developing their overhead budgets *based upon the preliminary product mix figure.* Their individual budgets are then aggregated and the total is reconciled with the aggregate factory overhead figure in the financial plan. This reconciliation process is one of making incremental changes in the aggregate factory overhead figure of the financial plan with incremental changes in each of the departmental overhead budgets.

This is a rational approach in the sense that the figure in the financial plan is the *result of top management's view of the firm's environment—* product and money markets, as explained above. They normally do not or cannot take time to understand all the details of lower level departmental operation. On the other hand, supervisors of these departments have this *detailed knowledge that top management lacks,* but do not have the understanding of the firm's environment that top management has. They are "inside" men and cannot be expected to have this understanding of the environment of the firm. The process described above—one of overhead budgeting "from the top down" and simultaneously "from the bottom up," then reconciling the aggregate difference with incremental changes in all the figures, represents a reasonably rational approach to *integrating the two equally important views of what constitutes an appropriate overhead figure.*

Smoothing Production. We now come to the leveling or smoothing problem in the micro plan for production, indicated in Figure 5–4, as 3, C, 2. The aggregate product mix determined in a prior decision usually does not sell at a level rate *during* the fiscal year. Most people tend to think that seasonal markets are confined to products like clothing (spring and fall) and farm equipment (spring). On the contrary, it is difficult to find a product that does not have a seasonal demand in some degree. Accordingly, the aggregate output should be smoothed or leveled by manning the plant to build inventory in advance of the season sales peaks. This also tends to level the manning of the plant, reducing layoffs and rehires, and the cost associated with this practice. Offsetting these cost decreases is the cost increase incurred by owning inventory (carrying costs) in advance of when it finally sells. Offsetting this is a likely reduction in sales lost by not having products available when demanded by customers (stockouts). Through a decision process that reconciles these costs, a plan for manning the plant optimally (minimum total cost) is developed. *From this smoothed production plan comes the data on direct labor budgets by payroll periods and by months, as well as month-end inventory figures.*

We have now established the incremental changes in all the items marked 3 in the financial plan. With this knowledge, top management now has a basis for establishing administrative cost—4 in Figure 5–6. For instance, the personnel department knows the planned layoffs and rehires under the smoothed production plan and can plan its own work and costs from this base.

Having established administrative cost, total cost before taxes is calculated. This figure subtracted from sales gives profit before taxes. The income tax calculation is then made, resulting in an incremental change in the profit figure (5) in the financial plan. Profit margin is then easily calculated using the sales revenue figure from the prior optimal product mix solution, which was reconciled with the earlier figure for sales revenue by an incremental change in both figures.

Top management is now in a position to make the incremental changes in the items marked 5 in the financial plan. The cash budget is drawn up, which, together with the statement of flow of funds (from the direct labor, direct materials, factory overhead and administrative budgets, sales revenue, long-term capital employed, and so on), will result in an incremental change in short-term capital employed. From all this it can be determined whether or not long-term capital employed can be shifted downward by accelerating amortization of loans. In the well-managed firm with a good capital structure, it is usually unnecessary at this late date (relative to next year's operations) to increase the long-term capital employed.

At this point in the decision process, investment turnover can be calculated and a final (in this iteration) calculation of return on investment (item 6 in Figure 5–6) is made. This figure should differ only incrementally (upward) from the original figure in the financial plan for next year. Additional iterations of the entire integrated decision process as described above may be made before a final sales and production program, with associated budgets, is settled upon for the next fiscal year. However, with the complexity of the total task, *not many iterations can be made before a point of diminishing returns to analysis is reached. At this point, by definition, management has a plan for maximizing the return on investment next year.*

We have now completed an examination of the integrated macro and micro decision processes that form the total decision system for the firm. It has its roots in past operations but focuses on the future—both long-range and intermediate-range. It is a dynamic decision system in that it is iterated annually, with a good deal of observation, thought, and discussion taking place via the control function during the year. It is operationally practicable. It is a reasonable approach to implementing the theory of the price-volume chart of the economist, Figure 5–2. It takes account of new technology via the decision making indicated in Figure 5–1.

We are now in a position to examine *in depth* the decision processes for production indicated back in Figure 5–1, as well as all the subproblems involved. This is accomplished in the other books in this series. But keep in mind as you read these books that *these decisions are made within the constraints of the total set of macro/micro decisions described above*. They are not "open-ended" decisions.

REVIEW QUESTIONS

1. Explain the set of conditions required for a fully automated total production system.
2. Explain the set of production decisions involved in the total production system, stressing why the problems are interrelated.
3. How does the role of judgment enter into the concept of a hierarchy of production decisions?
4. What differences are involved in applying the total production decision system in the case of a new plant versus the case of a plant in being?
5. Why is the determination of the output level the starting point for all production decisions? Explain in terms of the economist's P-V chart.
6. Why is the economist's price-volume concept useful but not often operationally applicable?
7. What emphasis do managers and engineers stress in using the economist's price-volume concept?
8. What weaknesses are found in the use of the break-even chart as a decision-making tool?
9. Why must the analyst have a set of preliminary process specifications before he can attempt an analysis of the layout, location, and maintenance policy problems?
10. What types of considerations are central to production scheduling decisions?
11. What are (*a*) lead time and (*b*) total production lead time?
12. Discuss the advantages of a short production lead time.
13. How can conversion lead time be reduced?
14. How can the acquisition lead time be reduced?
15. Discuss the tradeoffs a firm must make to compete effectively on a combined delivery and price basis.
16. Under what conditions might the firm buy an item rather than produce it?
17. Is there any way of knowing when the iterative decision process of Figure 5–1 has been carried far enough? What is the usual limitation?
18. Explain the distinction between planning and forecasting.
19. How is intermediate-range planning linked to long-range planning? To fiscal planning? To next year's program and overall budget?

20. How is dynamism achieved in managerial planning?
21. Why is the total financial plan called a macro plan?
22. Explain the "DuPont Formula" in terms of the firm's balance sheet and profit and loss statement.
23. Explain the use of historical ratios in financial planning. How are they used to effect corrective action in the operation of a firm?
24. Explain how capacity decisions are related to the money market subsystem.
25. What are the major elements of the production micro decision system?
26. Can the direct labor budget be exploded from the optimal product mix solution? If not, why not?
27. Explain the cost elements involved in the production smoothing problem.
28. How do the decisions in the production macro/micro decision system relate to the concept of the "closed loop"?

SUGGESTIONS FOR FURTHER STUDY

ANDERSON, THEODORE A. "Coordinating Strategic and Operational Planning," *Business Horizons*, Vol. 8, No. 2 (Summer, 1965), pp. 49–58.
   Discusses some of the major problems involved in achieving effcient interrelationships between strategic and operational planning.

ARNSTEIN, WILLIAM E., AND MACK, EDGAR A. "A New Approach to the Break-even Chart," *Management Services*, Vol. 1, No. 1 (March–April, 1964), pp. 60–62.
   Suggests a break-even chart based on markup on variable costs as a useful tool for decision making in a dynamic situation.

BUFFA, ELWOOD S. *Models for Production and Operations Management*, chap. xix. New York: John Wiley & Sons, Inc., 1963.
   Chapter xix discusses large-scale system simulation. Examples of models are presented.

EWING, DAVID W. (ed). *Long Range Planning for Management*. Rev. ed. New York: Harper & Row, 1964.
   Series of articles presenting the best current thinking on long-range planning, analyzing the pertinent problems, suggesting ways to handle, and stimulating fresh thinking on the subject.

GREENWOOD, FRANK. "Effective Long Range Planning Requires Action," *Academy of Management Journal*, Vol. 7, No. 3 (September, 1964), pp. 224–28.
   Discusses what corporate planners can do to help management implement long-range plans.

IJIRI, Y.; LEVY, F. K.; AND LYON, R. C. *A Linear Programming Model for Budgeting and Financial Planning*. Reprint 149. Pittsburgh, Pa.: Graduate School of Industrial Administration, Carnegie Institute of Technology, 1963.
   Reports on an experiment in using modern mathematical methods (linear programming and double entry accounting are joined) to solve management problems in budgeting and financial planning.

LEONTIEF, WASSILY W. "Proposal for Better Business Forecasting," *Harvard*

Business Review, Vol. 42, No. 6 (November–December, 1964), pp. 166–82.
Discusses the U.S. Commerce Department national input-output tables as aids in business forecasting.

MILLER, DAVID W., AND STARR, MARTIN K. *Executive Decision and Operations Research*, chap. x. Englewood Cliffs, N.J.: Prentice-Hall, Inc., 1960.
Chapter x covers the typical set of problems arising in the production function.

Planned Profits, Iron Age
A reprint of four articles: "Ratio Systems Give Management the Tools for Big Decisions" (July 14, 1960), "Ratio Analysis: A System That Controls Production Profits" (July 21, 1960), "Ratio Systems Appraise Sales" (July 29, 1960), and "Living Ratios Produce Formulas to Gage Capital Evaluation" (August 4, 1960)—combine to provide tools for evaluation and control of production, sales, and capital to achieve planned profit.

RAVENSCROFT, EDWARD A. "Return on Investment: Fit the Method to Your Need," *Harvard Business Review*, Vol. XXXVIII, No. 2 (March–April, 1960).
The author develops "a consistent approach to the return on investment concept which can be applied to three types of return: operating, cash, and equity. Each type has its own particular usefulness as an evaluation tool."

REISMAN, ARNOLD, AND BUFFA, ELWOOD S. "A General Model for Production and Operations Systems," *Management Science*, Vol. 11, No. 1 (September, 1964), pp. 64–79.
Article presents a structural and a mathematical framework for the analysis of the many variables in the operation of any dynamic production system.

ROBERTS, EDWARD B. "New Directions in Industrial Dynamics," *Industrial Management Review*, Vol. 6, No. 1 (Fall, 1964), pp. 5–14.
Article reviews the foundations of and growth of industrial dynamics and attempts to forsee its future.

RUMBAUGH, G. N., JR. "Profitability Analysis," *Mechanical Engineering*, Vol. 86, No. 8 (August, 1964), pp. 43–45.
Discusses an economic model of a capital project that aids proper communication between management and engineering.

SCOTT, BRIAN W. *Long-Range Planning in American Industry*. New York: American Management Association, 1965.
Discusses the planning techniques used by major U.S. companies to stay on top. Explains how to assess the future and to recognize environmental, social, political and industrial factors that will affect the future.

TARPEY, LAWRENCE X. "Advertising Theory and Capital Budgeting Model," *Business Horizons*, Vol. 8, No. 2 (Summer, 1965), pp. 87–93.
Discusses the idea of placing certain types of advertising expenses in the capital budget.

TILLES, SEYMOUR, "How to Evaluate Corporate Strategy," *Harvard Business Review*, Vol. 41, No. 4 (July–August, 1963) pp. 111–21.
Article discusses what business strategy is, how strategy is evaluated, and how properly evaluated strategy can lead to a successful future.

AUTHOR INDEX

*Not including authors of annotated supplementary readings
listed alphabetically at the end of each chapter.*

SUBJECT INDEX

155

This book has been set in 10 and 9 point Cale-
donia, leaded 2 points. Chapter numbers are in
14 point Venus Medium Extended; chapter
titles are in 16 point Venus Medium Extended.
The size of the type page is 27 by 46½ picas.